MW01012545

LIKE A METEOR BLAZING BRIGHTLY

The Short but Controversial Life
of Colonel Ulric Dahlgren

To Bill —

with very best wishes,

[signature]

Colonel Ulric Dahlgren
HARPER'S WEEKLY

LIKE A METEOR BLAZING BRIGHTLY

The Short but Controversial Life
of Colonel Ulric Dahlgren

ERIC J. WITTENBERG

EDINBOROUGH PRESS

2009

Edinborough Press
P. O. Box 13790
Roseville, Minnesota 55113-2293
1-888-251-6336
www.edinborough.com

The book is set in Adobe Jenson.

LIBRARY OF CONGRESS CATALOGING-IN-PUBLICATION DATA
Wittenberg, Eric J., 1961-

Like a meteor blazing brightly : the short but controversial life of Colonel
Ulric Dahlgren / Eric J. Wittenberg.

p. cm.

Includes bibliographical references and index.
ISBN 978-1-889020-33-4 (casebound : alk. paper)
ISBN 978-1-889020-34-1 (softbound : alk. paper)

1. Dahlgren, Ulric, 1842-1864. 2. Soldiers—United States—Biography.
3. United States. Army—Officers—Biography. 4. United States—
History—Civil War, 1861-1865—Campaigns. 5. Kilpatrick-Dahlgren Raid,
Va., 1864. 6. Gettysburg Campaign, 1863. I. Title.
E467.1.D135 W58 2009
973.7'3—dc22

2009020036

Contents

Maps

This book is respectfully dedicated to the memory of every American cavalryman who has answered the call, "Boots and saddles." It is also dedicated to the memory of Ulric Dahlgren, who died defending a cause he believed in most fervently.

Foreword

"ULRIC DAHLGREN was born to be a soldier," writes Eric Wittenberg, and in this first-ever biography of the young Yankee colonel he makes a very convincing case. An expert artillerist, a bold cavalryman, a recklessly daring scout—Dahlgren played all of these roles, and more, in his brief, incandescent Civil War career. His final role, in the notorious Kilpatrick-Dahlgren raid on Richmond in 1864, has until now defined him in history's judgment. By unearthing new sources and re-examining old ones, biographer Wittenberg offers a new and clearer definition of this complex character.

Even though Dahlgren was killed in action just short of his twenty-second birthday, he left an invaluable paper trail—letters and diaries and other documents—that unlock mysteries of his short and violent military career. Here for the first time, too, is an in-depth examination of his formative years. The dominant figure in this all-too-brief life was his father, Rear Admiral John A. Dahlgren, a close friend of President Lincoln's and a man whose own ambitions fed Ulric's soldierly ambitions. Of equal importance, there is much newly discovered source material here to clarify and give a defining focus to the Kilpatrick-Dahlgren raid.

Ulric Dahlgren could not wait to go to war, and once in it, could not wait for the next mission, the next battle, the next test. A reviewer of John Hersey's powerful World War II novel *The War Lover* described it as "A subtle demonstration of what lies coiled on the floor of the minds of those who really like war." That could as easily describe young Colonel Dahlgren. He was a type, of course; others of the sort that come to mind are J.E.B. Stuart and George Armstrong Custer. War lovers all, and, incidentally, all cavalrymen. What lay coiled on the floor of the mind of Ulric Dahlgren as he rode off toward Richmond on February 28, 1864, can be glimpsed in *Like a Meteor Blazing Brightly*.

Stephen W. Sears
Norwalk, Connecticut

Muss at Camp

LIBRARY OF CONGRESS

Author's Preface

FOR MOST OF MY ADULT LIFE, I have studied the exploits of Civil War cavalrymen. Every once in a while, a fascinating character flashes across the heavens like a brightly blazing meteor and then fades away just as quickly, triggering my keen interest and causing me to speculate about what might have been. One such character is Col. Ulric Dahlgren. Although he had absolutely no formal military training, he served as the chief of artillery for an entire corps of infantry at the tender age of twenty. A full colonel at twenty-one and dead in combat before he turned twenty-two, Dahlgren's life was an unfinished work. At once brilliant, reckless, daring, scheming, boundlessly ambitious, heroic, and inspirational, this young man clearly had what author Tom Wolfe has called "the right stuff." Dahlgren might have achieved greatness as a cavalryman had he lived.

What makes his death in March 1864 all the more interesting is that it was shrouded in mystery and controversy, and the truth of it probably will never be known. The mysterious circumstances of his death have overshadowed his many contributions to the Union victory in the Civil War. Because of the pall cast over his untimely demise, history has largely forgotten Ulric Dahlgren. If he is remembered at all, it is either as a villain, or as a footnote to a failed cavalry raid that bears his name. Completely forgotten are his many daring exploits as a scout and his fine work as an artillerist.

He was born into a life of privilege, the favored son of a brilliant naval officer who became a very close friend and confidant of the President of the United States. No other twenty-one-year-old Army captain enjoyed more or better access to President Abraham Lincoln as did Ully Dahlgren, and perhaps no other twenty-one-year-old unrelated junior officer in history has enjoyed such unfettered access to the Chief Executive than did Dahlgren. He became the youngest full colonel in either army and demonstrated real courage and ability on the field of battle. He parlayed that access to Lincoln's administration into a daring scheme that has forever tainted his name and legacy with unsavory controversy. Sadly, that unsavory controversy means that his good traits—courage, inspirational leadership, prodigious talent for artillery tactics, and a real gift for leading scouting expeditions—have been largely overlooked. Likewise overlooked is the important role he played during the Battle of Gettysburg and during the forgotten Second Bull Run Campaign.

I hope I have painted an accurate portrait of this fascinating young man by placing him squarely in the context of his times. I show how he used his father's political connections to achieve inordinately high rank at a precocious age, and how the pursuit of his unbridled ambition ultimately cost him his life. By contrast, I demonstrate that he was a brilliant young man, possessed of a keen mind, a charming, charismatic personality, with boundless courage, and the ability to inspire and lead men in battle. I explore the controversy surrounding his death, and conclude by analyzing the young man's legacy and assessing him as a soldier. An appendix addresses the question of the validity of the so-called "Dahlgren Papers."

All interpretations and conclusions set forth herein are strictly my own, and I take full responsibility for them as such.

As with every project of this nature, there are many people to thank. First and foremost, I owe a debt of gratitude to Prof. Herschel Gower, of Dallas, Texas, who has spent years studying the Dahlgren clan. Professor Gower kindly shared the fruits of his labor, enabling me to put much more meat on the bones of this project. Likewise, Bryce A. Suderow of Washington, D. C., and Steve L. Zerbe of Cherry Hill, New Jersey, my trusted research assistants, uncovered a great deal of useful primary source information for me that helped to round out this story. Ted Alexander, the National Park Service historian at Antietam, who is a life-long resident of Greencastle, Pennsylvania (where Ully Dahlgren made his greatest contributions to the Union victory in the Civil War), showed me important sites related to Dahlgren, and shared his encyclopedic knowledge of the Civil War in Franklin County. The eminent Civil War historian Stephen W. Sears read my manuscript, gave me some extremely useful feedback that made this a better book, and wrote the excellent foreword. I am indebted to Steve for his guidance and his willingness to help.

Paula Gidjunis made a special trip to try to locate Admiral Dahlgren's former home in Warwick Township, Bucks County, Pennsylvania for me (sadly, it's been demolished). Lawrence Clemens, a librarian at the United States Naval Academy in Annapolis, Maryland, provided invaluable assistance in tracking down information on the elusive Acting Master Charles H. Daniels. Jennifer Goellnitz of Cleveland, Ohio was very helpful in tracking down manuscript materials by Maj. Gen. Franz Sigel at the Western Reserve Historical Society, as well as an extremely hard-to-find volume of the proceedings of Philadelphia's

Franklin Institute from 1861. Thanks to Jenny's help, two large holes in the narrative were plugged.

J. David Petruzzi, of Brockway, Pennsylvania, provided me with data on life in Washington, D. C. in the 1850s, and also read and commented on this manuscript, as did Michael F. Nugent of Wells, Maine, Robert F. O'Neill, Jr. of Eureka, Montana, and Horace Mewborn of New Bern, North Carolina. Horace also suggested that I turn my fascination with Ulric Dahlgren into a book-length treatment, and Bob O'Neill provided useful information on Dahlgren's role in November 1862. Tonia J. Smith, of Pinehurst, North Carolina, assisted with the research and read this manuscript for me. Rob Wick provided me with very useful information about Everton J. Conger, and told me where I could find a war-time photograph of Conger. Col. Peter G. Tsouras (Ret.) provided useful information on the connection between Ulric Dahlgren and the Bureau of Military Information and caught a couple of factual errors I made. Scott C. Patchan gave his time to review this manuscript for me, and I value his expertise on the Second Bull Run Campaign of 1862. My friend and mentor, the late Brian C. Pohanka, inspired me to write this book and to uncover the true story of Ulric Dahlgren's life. Like Dahlgren himself, Brian was cut down too soon, and I miss his steady hand and sound advice.

I would be remiss if I did not thank my wonderful, loving and infinitely patient wife, Susan Skilken Wittenberg, for her endless support and unfailing understanding of my need to tell the stories of Civil War cavalrymen. I could not accomplish the things that I do without her help and support.

Eric J. Wittenberg
Columbus, Ohio

LIKE A METEOR BLAZING BRIGHTLY

*The Short but Controversial Life
of Colonel Ulric Dahlgren*

"Studying the Art of War": Dahlgren with fellow officers. Photogragh by Alexander Gardner

Introduction

DARKNESS CAME EARLY during the first days of March 1864 in Virginia. As it did every year, spring struggled to shove winter out of the way, but at the beginning of the month, winter still regularly won the ongoing battle. Even though it was still winter, a large force of Union cavalry departed the Army of the Potomac's comfortable encampment in Culpeper County, Virginia on February 28, headed straight for the Confederate capital of Richmond. A dashing, one-legged twenty-one-year-old colonel commanded one portion of the raid column, leading 500 veteran troopers. It was cold. So cold, it crept into the marrow of the blue clad horse soldiers. And wet. So frigidly soggy, in fact, that their bodies had all but forgotten the sun and forgotten the warmth of the roaring campfires they left behind as they headed south across the Virginia countryside.

On March 2, the colonel and his men reached the outskirts of Richmond and, after clashing with Confederate troops, were repulsed from the capital's outer ring of defenses with fairly heavy losses. Along with about 100 men of his command, the one-legged Union colonel was cut off from his main body and then fell back into King and Queen County. Shortly before midnight, the colonel unexpectedly encountered enemy resistance. He rode forward and challenged the men in his front, drawing his pistol and demanding their surrender. However, a volley dropped him from the saddle. His body riddled with bullets, the handsome young colonel toppled onto the road, killed instantly. The rest of his command scattered, leaving his body behind. They were either captured or surrendered the next day.

Later that night, a thirteen-year-old local boy named William Littlepage came forward to examine the body. After searching the colonel's pockets, he found some documents hidden inside a cigar case in the colonel's inside breast pocket. These documents included dispatches that looked like they might provide important military intelligence, and several specific documents that would be of interest to the highest levels of the Confederate government. Littlepage gave them to his teacher, a man named Edward W. Halbach, who read them carefully. Realizing that these documents needed to get into the hands of the authorities, the next afternoon, Halbach sought out Lt. James Pollard of the 9th Virginia Cavalry, commander of the detachment that had helped set the ambush for the Union cavalrymen.

Until that moment, Pollard had known nothing of these documents. Halbach told the lieutenant the nature of their contents, and then, at Pollard's request, permitted him to read the papers. Stunned by what he read, Pollard asked for permission to take them to the Confederate authorities in Richmond. At first Halbach refused, thinking that simply mailing them to Richmond would suffice. However, Halbach's friends prevailed upon him to surrender the papers to Lieutenant Pollard since they would reach Richmond much more quickly through his efforts than through a semi-weekly mail. Halbach consented, and Pollard took them directly to the Confederate authorities, who were appalled by the contents of the documents.

The documents suggested that a primary purpose of the Union cavalry raid was the kidnapping and assassination of Confederate President Jefferson Davis and his cabinet, as well as the ransacking and burning of most of Richmond. The Confederate authorities were understandably shocked by documents that appeared to be orders to the Federal horse soldiers to engage in atrocities. Such things were unknown in the early months of 1864, and the suggestion that the Federal government had sanctioned such conduct raised a hue and cry at every level of Confederate society. Within days, the Richmond newspapers published the contents of the documents verbatim, and an outraged public responded so virulently that the Confederate authorities ordered that the dead Union colonel be buried in an unmarked grave in a Richmond cemetery late at night in order to avoid its mutilation.

That Col. Ulric Dahlgren, son of Admiral John A. Dahlgren, commander of the Union naval forces investing Charleston, South Carolina, and a close confidant and advisor of Abraham Lincoln, was the officer carrying these documents made it all the more incredible. He was considered to be an officer of great promise and of great ability, and nobody expected such a horrific thing from him.

That Ulric Dahlgren was killed in an ambush is beyond dispute. However, that is about all about this episode that is not deeply immersed in controversy. In the months after his son's death, Admiral Dahlgren penned a letter vehemently denying that the documents were authentic. The documents may have been forgeries. Or they may have been real. No matter whether they were forgeries or were authentic, the United States government officially disavowed Ulric Dahlgren and triggered a controversy that still rages today among students and scholars of the Civil War.

How did this handsome, charismatic, brilliant, and fearless young man, who had such a bright future, end up as a villain—an outlaw disavowed by his own army and government? This is the story of Ulric Dahlgren's short but controversial life.

John Dahlgren
LIBRARY OF CONGRESS

CHAPTER ONE

A Boy's Proud Family Legacy

THE DAHLGREN FAMILY'S ANCIENT ROOTS stretch back to Sweden. The paterfamilias of the family was Borje Ericsson, or Ersson, who was born in Dahlen, Sweden in 1593. In 1615, he assumed the name Dahlgren, which was derived from the name of, Dahlen, the ward of the town Norrköping, where he lived, and grén, which means "branch" or "bough," suggesting that he was an offshoot or branch of his hometown. Consequently, the name "Eric" appears frequently in the extended Dahlgren family genealogy.[1]

The Dahlgren family has a long history of devoted and distinguished public service, accruing great wealth and enjoying the favor of the Swedish Crown. Several members also dedicated their lives to the advancement of medicine and science. Many of them served in the military, loyally sacrificing wealth and stature for the common good."His paternal ancestry stretching back through a long, honorable and cultured lineage of Sweden, gave to him a noble blood and high examples of the virtues which he reviewed and emulated as a true and favored son of that great Scandinavian race, which has so long stamped its resistless impress on the historic fortunes of Europe," observed Ulric Dahlgren's eulogist in 1864.[2] Ully proudly carried on his family's name and military tradition.

Johan Adolf Dahlgren was the son of Bernard Ebbe Dahlgren and Anna M. Neuhauser. Born in 1744 in Norrköping, a town on the Baltic coast to the southwest of Stockholm, he was educated by private tutors and then studied chemistry and pharmacy with the Admiralty chemist in Stockholm. He enrolled at the University of Uppsala on November 2, 1764, became a protégé of the famous naturalist Carolus Linnaeus, and graduated as a medical doctor in 1775. This extended course of study prepared him for the rigors of medicine, and the faculty soon held Doctor Dahlgren in great esteem. On October 14, 1789, Dahlgren was appointed Chief Physician and Assessor of the Province of Finland, where he lived out the rest of his life. Johan Adolph married Maria Rådde, the daughter of a fabric dyer Stockholm.[3] He died on May 14, 1797 at the relatively young age of fifty-three, "much respected by the authorities, and beloved by the poor, who in a large body followed his remains to the grave,—a civic funeral having decreed him by the town Uleåborg, where he had resided."[4]

His son Carl Adolph followed him into the field of medicine. Carl Adolph was appointed as a sub-physician in the Royal Navy in 1797 and served for three years. With the coming of war in 1808, he offered his services to the Crown and assumed a position as staff surgeon in the Finnish army, where he served out the war. He then re-entered the Navy, and was appointed Court Physician in 1809. In 1813, he was named Field Surgeon to the army operating in Norway. In 1838, he became Field Surgeon in Chief to the Elfsborg Regiment and was given an order by the King of Sweden, probably the Order of the Sword (Svärdsorden) in recognition of his long years of service. Sir Carl Adolph died in Stockholm in 1844.[5]

Carl Adolph's son Johan Adolph was born in 1813, and represents the last member of the Dahlgren family to achieve prominence in their native Sweden. Sir Johan Adolph authored various treatises on chemistry and medicinal botany, and was also an inventor and chemist. In 1871, his health poor, Sir Johan Adolph resigned the Directorship of the Royal Military Hospital in Stockholm, and enjoyed a quiet retirement. He died at sixty-three on June 7, 1876.[6]

Bernhard Ulrick Dahlgren, the father of Admiral John A. Dahlgren, was born on May 12, 1784, and was a son of the first Johan Adolph Dahlgren. He stood more than six feet, four inches tall, and possessed majestic Nordic proportions and features. He graduated from Uppsala and became an adventurous traveler at an early age, making frequent expeditions to various locations around the globe. However, unlike his father, Bernhard did not loyally serve the Swedish monarchy. In 1804, he was caught passing out literature that advocated republican principles, an act akin to treason against the Crown. As a result, he fled Sweden, and King Gustavus confiscated his property. After a lengthy and hazardous journey of nearly three years, he sold his guns and most of his possessions to raise $80.00 for passage. He embarked for New York from Spain, landing there on December 4, 1806, after "a boisterous passage." Although fluent in Swedish and French, Bernhard knew little English and took any menial job that he could find in order to survive. He promptly applied for naturalization and soon became a U. S. citizen.[7]

In 1807, he went to Haiti as a cashier for Thomas Lewis and Co. at a salary of $800 per year, but the Swede never grew accustomed to the heat and humidity of the Caribbean. He returned to the United States, settling in Philadelphia this time. The City of Brotherly Love was a logical choice for Bernhard. Swedish settlers had arrived in Pennsylvania as early as 1638, well before the earliest English settlers arrived. These sturdy Swedes established a settlement on the site of present-day Philadelphia called Wicaco. The eastern part of what we know today as Pennsylvania, most of New Jersey, and all of Delaware were part of a region commonly known as New Sweden.[8] Although the Dutch who governed New York eventually conquered New Sweden in 1654, the area continued to draw Swedish and Finnish immigrants.[9] The oldest church in Philadelphia, called Gloria Dei Church, is known as Old Swedes' Church, and was a major hub of Swedish culture in North America. Its pastor, Rev. Nicholas Collin, was a noted Swedish scientist and student of medicine as well as a noted theologian, and he would have been acquainted with Johann Adolph Dahlgren's scientific work in Sweden.[10] Also, Philadelphia's status as a major trading port drew Dahlgren's attention.

Despite being a U. S. citizen, Bernhard Dahlgren remained loyal to the Swedish Crown even though he had lost all of his worldly possessions to it. "My father refused to desert his King Gustavus to the interest of Napoleon, who placed Bernadotte on the throne, and was driven from Sweden and his property seized," inaccurately recalled Bernhard's son Charles, "but afterward triumphed in the return of his possessions when Sweden became hostile to Napoleon." As a reward for his fealty to his country, Bernhard received clemency from the Swedish Crown, and an appointment as Swedish and Norwegian Consul at Philadelphia, a position that he held until his death in 1824.[11]

Bernhard was a skilled and successful merchant and a man of integrity. He engaged in the lucrative slave trade, owned part of a banking company, and speculated in real estate. When the state capital was moved from Philadelphia to Harrisburg, Bernhard signed a petition for permission to build a bridge across the wide Susquehanna River, looking to capitalize on the increased traffic that would inevitably result from the establishment of the state capital on the banks of the river.[12]

A prominent New York lawyer named Daniel Lord once described Bernhard as "The Man of Ross," alluding to his reputation for strict probity, and noted that he regularly decided disputed matters in order to avoid litigation. "So great was the confidence reposed in his impartial and clear judgment, that his arbitration was accepted as conclusive," observed Admiral Dahlgren's second wife Madeleine in 1882. He conducted himself by the motto "Candor and Fidelity," and earned the respect of the community.[13] Fellow Philadelphians considered him "a man of strong mind," "highly respectable," and "unquestionably one of our most respectable and worthy citizens." Bernhard, possessed of strong republican sentiments, actively participated in Thomas Jefferson's Democratic-Republican Party, became a respected officer in Philadelphia's influential Masonic organizations, and enjoyed the theater.[14]

Bernhard married twenty-two-year-old Martha Rowan, daughter of James

Rowan, on November 19, 1808. Like Bernhard, James Rowan lost his estate in Ireland as punishment for his republican activities, and settled in Philadelphia. During the Revolutionary War, Rowan took up arms and served as assistant commissary to General James Lacey's brigade of the Pennsylvania Line. He fought in the battles of Brandywine, Germantown, and Princeton.[15] He "lived to see his principles triumph at the peace of 1783," recalled his grandson Charles Dahlgren.[16] Rowan was a lineal descendant of an influential northern Irish family, and claimed collateral lineage of the De Rohan family of Brittany.[17] He married Jane McConnell and had several children, including Martha. Rowan had advanced his own funds to pay for supplies for the army, and either was never reimbursed for those advances, or was paid in worthless Continental money, leaving him largely destitute. However, he was a strong patriot and a walking paradox—Rowan was a member of the Society of Friends, also known as the Quakers, a pacifist sect that did not participate in war. He was excommunicated from the Society for taking up arms in the Revolutionary War. James Rowan was also a respected soldier, and he passed his military bearing, strong sense of duty, and patriotism on to his daughter and grandsons.[18]

Martha Rowan Dahlgren was "a lady richly endowed with the best qualities of head and heart, the memory of which has remained with her son during a long and varied career," fondly remembered her oldest son, Admiral Dahlgren, in 1868. She had a special talent for inventiveness and designing, a trait that she passed on to her son John.[19] The family settled in a comfortable house at the corner of Walnut and Third Streets in Center City Philadelphia. Their first child, John Adolphus Dahlgren, was born on November 13, 1809. Charles Gustavus Ulric followed in 1811, as did George Washington, who died in infancy; Martha Matilde, who was known to her family as Patty, arrived in 1818; and William Theodore was born in 1820. William Theodore later shunned the Dahlgren name and heritage and instead assumed the moniker William de Rohan. By all accounts, it was a happy household.

Respecting his family's rich educational tradition, Bernhard laid out a rigorous course of study for his sons, which included Latin, Spanish, and mathematics. He spared no expense in the education of his boys, and occasionally attended school with them in order to make certain that they received the sort of academic challenge he desired. John later described his youth as being spent as "a hard student" under his father's watchful gaze.[20]

However, Bernhard's sudden death at the age of forty on July 19, 1824 shattered the family's happiness. His friend Dr. Collin officiated over his funeral, and he was buried in the Gloria Dei Church cemetery in downtown Philadelphia.[21]

Martha followed him there fourteen years later. Bernhard's unexpected death left John Dahlgren the head of the household at the tender age of 15.[22] "Had [Bernhard] lived a few years longer [he] would have left his family in excellent circumstances had his talents and industry continued to yield what was in the receipt of at the time he died," said a family friend. "As it is the children must as early as possible free themselves from dependence on the Mother."[23]

John received a good education at the nearby Quaker schoolhouse, and possessed a gift for languages and mathematics. Always interested in ships and sailing, and fascinated by the naval vessels being built and repaired at the Philadelphia Navy Yard, he often visited there. However, Bernhard's passing left the family in poor financial condition, and to continue his education, John had to find a way to pay for it. He soon found the means—pursuing his lifelong interest in ships and the sea, he looked to join the United States Navy.

In 1825, at the age of sixteen, John applied for a midshipman's warrant but was rejected because there were already too many young men from Philadelphia in the service.[24] Undaunted, John registered as a seaman on a merchant brig, and continued his campaign for a warrant. Finally, on February 1, 1826, Secretary of the Navy Samuel L. Southard appointed him a midshipman in the United States Navy, beginning a long and successful career that brought him fame and glory.[25]

He served as a midshipman and learned the sailor's trade the hard way, on the job. Passing his midshipman's examination in 1832, he joined the United States Coast Survey two years later. The Navy's archaic system for promotions prevented him from advancing his career in any meaningful fashion until he finally received a promotion to lieutenant on March 8, 1836, ten years after joining the service. Dahlgren vented his frustration—and jeopardized his career— by publishing a series of articles critical of the Navy under the pseudonym "Blue Jacket." Had the true identity of the writer been determined, Dahlgren's Naval career undoubtedly would have ended ignominiously. Fortunately, the Naval hierarchy never learned the true identity of "Blue Jacket", and Dahlgren's career continued to lurch forward in fits and starts.[26]

John Dahlgren remained very proud of his Swedish heritage. On April 1, 1844, while on a cruise through Europe, he visited a Swedish warship in Toulon harbor in France. "As I stood on the deck and gazed on the Northern race around me, fair as women, stalwart seamen as they were, it was not forgotten that these were the countrymen of my good father," he wrote in his diary. "Amid all the thoughts that crossed his mind, could he ever have imagined that his son would some day stand in the relation of a foreign officer to Swedish men? I asked an officer who stood near me if he had ever met with any of my name. His eyes glistened and his face lit up at the very mention. 'Oh, yes,' said he, 'it is a real Swedish name.'"[27] Partly as a result of his strong pride in his heritage, Dahlgren gave his third child the traditional Swedish name Ulric. He also made certain that his sons knew well their illustrious Swedish heritage.

When thrust into the role of family leader upon Bernhard's death in 1824, John Dahlgren developed a strong sense of self-discipline and rigorous principles to implement that strong sense of self-discipline. Those rigorous principles led him to engage in at least one duel, and almost triggered another during a European cruise from 1843-1845. "What indeed can be so degraded as a man without courage," he wrote in 1845, "unless it be a woman without virtue."[28]

An eye injury incurred in the line of duty that nearly cost him his sight kept him from seagoing duty for several years. However, because of the nature of the wound, he collected his full salary while recuperating. He purchased an 86.5-acre farm "with a comfortable dwelling-house upon it" near Hartsville, Bucks County, Pennsylvania, not far from the banks of tranquil Neshaminy Creek, where he clearly savored being a gentleman farmer.[29] Hartsville was a pleasant community settled near the beginning of the eighteenth century that served as George Washington's headquarters during the Revolutionary War.[30] Dahlgren's handsome 1790 farmhouse had three bedrooms. It sat half a mile east of Hartsville on the old Bristol Road, and was a "substantial but unpretentious plastered stone house."[31]

While recuperating from his optical problems, John Dahlgren married his sweetheart, Mary Clement Bunker, on January 8, 1839. Born in 1817, Mary was eight years younger than John. She was "beautiful in person—lovely in disposition and noble in character," as her sister-in-law Patty Dahlgren Read recalled. "All who ever met her not only admired but loved her, and her dear children were as dear to me as they could have been if they had been my own."[32] In 1855, Dahlgren described his wife in loving terms:

> One does not often meet with a person as intelligent, refined, and accustomed to intercourse with people of the highest social position, yet so perfectly natural and unsophisticated. Her bright, joyous soul associated itself instantly with poor or rich, high and low, and sympathized freely with every sorrow. Most unselfish, she gave freely of all she had, and retained so little for her own use, that she seemed to possess nothing more, absolutely, than just what the moment required. All the finery and trinkets in her drawers would not have satisfied the merest girl. The little jewelry she had, was

made of two or three memorials of her parents or my own . . . Her figure was rather tall, her face beautiful, and the dress, whatever it was, seemed to be just what it should be. Her raven tresses and brilliant black eyes more than equaled any ornament she could wear. In company, her manner was fascinating to a charm, and she commanded the attention of those who did not know her, and the affectionate greetings of those who did; for to the least glance was evident the most lovely creature,—one kind, elegant, and as unsuspicious of harm as an infant.[33]

John also fondly recalled, "She was one who, to every charm of rare beauty and a lovely presence, added the attractive graces of refined social life, and a Christian piety that never failed to win the admiration of her friends and the affectionate attachment of her family."[34]

Fortunately for John Dahlgren, Mary also came from a good family. Her father, Nathan Bunker, was a prominent Philadelphia merchant who enjoyed power, influence and connections that could only help his new son-in-law's career. Mary's two sisters both married well, to wealthy merchants, James W. Paul of Philadelphia and S. Abbott Lawrence of Boston.[35] Knowing the importance and benefits of having friends in high places, Dahlgren did not hesitate to take advantage of these connections in his quest to advance his career.

Although John's naval duty often took him away from Mary once his eyes were well enough to permit him to return to sea in 1842, they had a happy marriage. "Three months have elapsed since I left you, and they have weighed on me like years," he wrote while away on duty. "All my pleasure has been centered in one, and now that I am exiled from this, how different does all else seem to me."[36]

In the meantime, John happily worked his farm while waiting for his vision to improve, and watched his family grow. His first child, Charles Bunker Dahlgren, was born on the farm in 1839, and was followed by Elizabeth in 1840.[37] Their third child, Ulric, was born on April 3, 1842, and was baptized by Rev. J. P. Wilson, the Presbyterian minister who later presided over the boy's funeral.[38] "His very name was a presage of his character, derived as it was from the mighty Alaric, king of the Visigoths, and conqueror of Rome," observed Ulric Dahlgren's eulogist in 1864.[39] Two other children, Elizabeth and Lawrence, both died in infancy; John never even saw Elizabeth, who was born and died while he was at sea. "My child—my child—what have I done that you should be taken from me thus," he mourned in a letter to Mary. "Have not afflictions sufficient enough been heaped on me already but that death must strike down one of my little flock—and make desolate a stricken heart—Spare them, oh spare them, they are the treasure of a lone & sorrowful soul—in mercy let me be called first."[40] The birth of another daughter named Eva and a son named Paul in 1846 somewhat assuaged Dahlgren's grief.

John Dahlgren loved his children deeply, and doted on them. He made sure to include passages in his letters for Mary to read to the children. "Kiss all the babies for Papa and bid them be good and do as Mama tells them," he wrote. "I have no separate remembrance for either, they are all alike—Charley is Papa's boy—Sissy is the one little duck—Ully is bandy and Mister 4—has a black noodle—Good and sufficient reasons I am sure why Papa should be very fond of them." He loved carrying them up and down the stairs piggyback style, and wanted them to grow up in the country, far from the evils of the city.[41]

When Ully, as the family called him, was just over a year old, Lieutenant Dahlgren went to sea for an extended European training cruise, prompting the family to move from the farm to Wilmington, Delaware. There, Ully "passed five years of happy childhood under the eye of a lovely and affectionate mother," wrote his father, "upon whom the sole charge not unfrequently rested during the absence of her husband in the discharge of professional duties."[42] The laughing, sprightly, mischievous lad brimmed with health, intelligence, and high spirits. "His maternal patronage springing from a family of beautiful and accomplished women, endowed him with whatever is delicate and refined, gentle and endearing, trustful and true in the highest attributes of manhood," noted an observer.[43] His father doted on him, and the boy quickly became the apple of his father's eye.

Little Ully wanted for nothing. "Every accessory to the fullest indulgence of his juvenile activity might be found in the snug, cosy home, which was just fitted for the high place and holiday of children; their happiness unmarred by the fear of spoiling carpets or furniture," remembered the Admiral. "And there, at any time in the day, might be seen and heard little Ully, with his rosy, laughing face,—chirping and galloping around, whip in hand, making terrible commotion among imaginary horses and wagons in the shape of stools and chairs; while near by sat a fond mother, glancing now and then from needle and work towards her boy thus engaged; or, perhaps, when sorely worsted by the sport, demurely poring over his slate, with pencil in hand, limning uncouth but violently active figures, which, to his eye, took the shape of living animals of every description."[44]

John returned from his cruise on November 12, 1845, and walked into his house to find Mary and the children at the dinner table. The children had grown so much that John barely recognized them. Almost nine months to the day later, their fifth child, Paul, arrived. He enjoyed spending time with his family while he waited for his next assignment, which did not come until January 1847, when he was ordered to ordnance duty at the Department of the Navy's headquarters in Washington, D.C. He also served as Professor of Gunnery at the United States Naval Academy in Annapolis, Maryland. This duty quickly proved arduous and exhausting. "One year since I left home for Washington on Ordnance duty," Dahlgren wrote in his diary on January 8, 1848. "Since that time I have returned home on leave four times. Besides the regular duty at Washington, I have been on duty twice to New York in the spring, once to Philadelphia in July, once to Richmond in December, and six times to Annapolis, while doing the duty of Professor of Gunnery at the School—about nineteen hundred and ten miles in all, of travel."[45]

Two months later, the Secretary of the Navy took pity on Dahlgren, whose ordnance work had proved indispensable. The Secretary arranged for Dahlgren to receive an annual allowance of $500.00 for rent, in order to enable him to move his family to Washington. In May 1848, John Dahlgren rented a home in downtown Washington. He then went to Wilmington, gathered his family, and moved them all to the national capital, where he settled into his new job.[46] "And thus little Ully was transplanted to the national capital, where the remainder of his short but glorious life was to be passed, and to receive its future form and direction," noted John in 1872.[47]

Even from a very early age, Ulric Dahlgren felt at home in Washington, where he learned important lessons about power, influence, politics, and intrigue. He learned those lessons well. In particular, he learned first-hand how important political influence and ready access to the halls of power could be beneficial to the advancement of an ambitious young man's career. These lessons served him well during the course of his short but controversial life.

Charles Bunker Dahlgren
LIBRARY OF CONGRESS

Paul Dahlgren
LIBRARY OF CONGRESS

CHAPTER TWO

Growing Up in the Nation's Capital

JOHN DAHLGREN discovered his true calling during his tenure at the Washington Navy Yard. While there, he found himself in an important role as a designer and developer of naval ordnance. He had a real genius for designing powerful naval weapons, and his inventions are his greatest legacy to the United States Navy, earning him the proud title, "The Father of Modern Naval Ordnance." His most important contribution was the development of the so-called "Dahlgren gun," a heavy cast-iron, muzzle-loading smoothbore shell gun for use on ships. The nine thousand pound, bottle-shaped gun fired a 9-inch shell, and modernized naval gunnery.[1] "Commander Dahlgren is the best Ordnance officer in the country," declared Commodore Joseph Smith in March 1855, "and the Navy is under the greatest obligation to him for improvements introduced."[2]

On his fortieth birthday, November 13, 1849, he was nearly killed when one of his guns exploded a few feet away from him, killing the unfortunate gunner manning it, and affording Dahlgren a very narrow escape. A court of inquiry ultimately cleared Dahlgren of any wrongdoing and determined that the incident was neither foreseeable nor preventable.[3] The Navy eventually adopted this gun as its main ordnance for ships of the line. In March 1851, as a reward for his innovation and fine service, Congress passed a new Naval Appropriation Bill that included a rider granting Lieutenant Dahlgren the pay of a commander at sea, the princely sum of $2,750.00 per year.[4] On October 11, 1855, he finally received a long overdue promotion to commander. He had spent more than nineteen years as a lieutenant.[5]

Washington, D.C. was an interesting place to raise a child in the 1850s. The city was poised between East and West, as well as between North and South, and was often described as being the "southern element in the great compromise." Indeed, it had a very Southern atmosphere—slavery was legal, and the town had a real tidewater feel about it. It numbered nearly 45,000 residents in 1855, and was one of the largest cities in the United States.[6] "Washington was nothing but a place in which Congress could meet and politicians carry on their games at high stakes for power and place," noted one observer of the antebellum District of Columbia.[7]

Opportunities abounded for an ambitious, politically astute officer, and John

Dahlgren quickly found his niche in this rarefied atmosphere. The rough sailor had to learn to fit into the complex social scene of the seat of power. "Washington society life is principally official; or rather, society here is composed, in so great a degree, of official personages who represent the mechanism of the State, that the social obligations and customs have become about as complex as the constitutional laws upon which the official are based, and yet we have no constitution, or defined code, which makes our social laws as clear as our political."[8] His son Ulric enjoyed the fruits of his father's extensive political connections.

Six years old at the time of the move, Ully spent another couple of years enjoying childhood before his formal education began. The inquisitive, quick-minded boy loved horses. His father took him to the White House to meet President Zachary Taylor, prompting the youngster to inquire, "Where is Whitey?" asking Taylor about the horse that had carried the old general into battle during the Mexican War. Taylor granted permission for Ully to visit the famous warhorse, thrilling the boy. Even at a precocious age, the boy had access to the seat of power in the White House. He grew up being familiar with its halls, and often visited it.[9]

Religion played an important part in the family's life. The Dahlgrens joined Washington's First Presbyterian Church not long after the family settled there. Ulric remained active in the congregation for the rest of his life. John Dahlgren noted that the church was "but a stone throw from my house," and that Rev. Byron Sunderland, the pastor, passed by his door every day on the way to and from work. The Admiral also noted that Reverend Sunderland saw his son Ulric "almost daily as he played or sat near his home, saw him regularly at the Church & Sunday School for years," and that the Reverend came to know the boy very well.[10]

"He was, from the age of six till he left the city in his seventeenth year, an exemplary and constant attendant in this church, upon the instructions of the Sabbath School and the public services of Divine Worship," recalled Reverend Sunderland in 1864. "Here he learned those lessons of God and the great salvation of Christ and the Atonement, of the blood remission and justification by faith, of repentance and the foregiveness of sin, of the Holy Ghost and the regeneration of the human heart, of obedience and the acceptance of the Gospel, of Death, Resurrection and Immortality."[11] The teachings of the Presbyterian Church molded the boy's character and became an integral part of his moral fiber.

All of these influences helped to form the man Ulric Dahlgren eventually became. "At home, there was regularity and comfort, without ostentation," recalled John Dahlgren, "at school, steady, firm, conscientious instruction; while at both home and school, all due regard was paid to the religious training." He spent many happy hours with his father at the Washington Navy Yard, observing John's efforts and disciplined approach to innovation. The constant hum of activity in the Navy Yard captured the boy's attention. "At the battery, he gazed with deep interest on the hardy seamen, as they whirled onward the light howitzers with well-trained arms, or manned the ponderous cannon; then the stunning blast, the whir of the missile, and its quick flash as it burst far away, aimed at the distant mark," fondly recalled his father. "Around him was every contribution that invention or labor could give to the subject,—he heard discussed and saw tried every species of cannon and small arms, shot, shell, fuses, etc. that disciplined thought or wild fancy could devise; while his keen eye and sober thought were noting all and working out their own conclusions, so that, when afterwards launched upon the field of action, his judgment and experience in artillery were perceived and duly estimated by his superior officers."[12]

Ulric was eight years old when the Crisis of 1850 occurred. In 1849, a party of Texas slave owners traveled to California intending to make the new state a slave state. Before long, a violent and destructive debate over whether new states entering the Union would be free or slaves states erupted, prompting inflammatory rhetoric and the shedding of fraternal blood. Ill will quickly spread across a country that threatened to tear itself apart at the seams. Southern politicians, such as Robert Toombs of Georgia, spoke openly of secession if the North prevented Southerners from bringing slaves into new territories such as California and New Mexico. Obviously, the issue of slavery would have to be resolved one way or another if the country had a chance to survive. On July 9, 1850, Whig President Zachary Taylor died after only sixteen months in office. His Vice President, Millard Fillmore, a New Yorker who was determined to find a compromise that would hold the Union together, succeeded Taylor.

Stephen Douglas of Illinois and Henry Clay of Kentucky led the search for compromise in the Senate. Eventually, they crafted a temporary solution to the problem that, in reality, only delayed the inevitable showdown that was sure to come. The compromise admitted California as a free state. It also permitted the legislatures of New Mexico and Utah to settle the question of slavery for themselves, enacted a stringent Federal law mandating the return of runaway slaves, abolished the slave trade in the District of Columbia, and gave Texas $10 million to give up its claims to territory in New Mexico east of the Rio Grande.[13]

The great national paroxysm fascinated the Dahlgren boys. "Sorely puzzled were the boy and his brothers to comprehend how professed friends to the country could approach its destruction so nearly," recalled their father, "for the wild declamation of disloyal men, and an unreasoning portion of the press, were inflaming the common mind to madness, and it was no easy task for the mast-spirits to rule the tempest."[14]

These tempestuous times molded young Ulric's political views, as the threat of civil war threatened to eviscerate the young American republic. Although his brother Charles Bunker leaned toward the Democratic Party's philosophy, Ully embraced the central principles of the Whig Party, which promoted internal improvements such as roads, canals, railroads, the deepening of rivers, and other improvements to the national infrastructure that would help the country become an economic superpower. Many Westerners, including a rising Illinois lawyer named Abraham Lincoln, embraced the Whig philosophy. Ully and Charley often engaged in vigorous debates about politics. "On one occasion, having exhausted their arguments and their breath, appeal was made to the father, who told them that both creeds were designed for the common good, dissimilar as they seemed," recalled the Admiral with a chuckle, "but, as disunion was now openly proposed as the only possible remedy, they were earnestly cautioned to beware of any political dogmas that tolerated such an idea, and to withdraw from all who countenanced it." Thus, even at an early age, young Dahlgren shared the basic political worldview of Abraham Lincoln.[15]

Writing in August 1864, John Dahlgren described his son. "Ulric Dahlgren was to the type of an American in its best form—He had all the fervor & religious bent of the Puritan, with none of his sternness—on the contrary he was all gentleness."[16] However, one overarching trait emerged during Ulric Dahlgren's youth, a trait that carried him to glory and to an early grave. As his father put it, "a very striking characteristic was the intense earnestness with which he pursued an object when once engaged in it; if he studied, it was not so much with the abstraction of a student as with the resolution to accomplish a set purpose,—while mixing in boyish sports he was just as intent,—nor was he less steadfast in adhering to a friend."[17]

Writing in 1872, John Dahlgren summed up his son's most prominent personality trait in a single sentence: "It seemed as if he obeyed by instinct the scriptural injunction, 'Whatever thy hand findeth to do, do it with all thy might.'" This single-minded pursuit of an objective made him a great soldier, but it also cost him his life.[18] John Dahlgren added, "It was plain that the bent and scope of the lad's nature found their end in ACTION. Where others thought, he seemed to think and act concurrently."[19]

Ully understood his restless nature and his constant need for activity. He once wrote his father, "When I have nothing to occupy my mind, I always feel dissatisfied until I find myself busy again." In another letter, he expressed a desire to "return to the hard work again which he prefers to all the rest."[20]

In June 1855, when Ully was thirteen years old, another event occurred that helped mold his character. Mary Bunker Dahlgren's health had been declining for several years. In the fall of 1854, she suffered the first attack of what John described as a "stricture of the bowels." Each episode sapped her strength. On March 27, 1855, the final episode began. For nearly three months, her condition ebbed and waned, sometimes giving her family hope, and other times, causing them to sink into the depths of despair. On May 21, 1855, she realized that she was going to die, and her interest in eating and in her surroundings dropped dramatically. It was obvious to her, her doctors, and to John that it was now just a matter of time.[21]

Early on the morning of June 6, she called to John to help turn her in bed, which he did. Her condition deteriorated rapidly, her breathing grew thin and shallow, and she became incoherent. She recognized John and her daughter Eva until the end, but as afternoon fell, she closed her eyes, clasped her hands across her chest, and "slipt out of life so quietly that I could not say when the breathing ceased," noted John in his diary.[22] Devoted to his beloved mother, Ulric now became especially attached to his surviving parent.

"On this sad occasion, it was observed that he never left his father, who chose constantly to continue near the remains of one so cherished," recalled the Admiral in 1872. "There sat the dear boy, bowed in silent grief, utterly regardless of all passing objects. He felt there was good reason for sorrow, for he had lost a devoted mother, who had been faithful to every want,—in sickness or trouble her own hand ministering to his necessities, while by her precept and example the child knew what it was to pray, and to fail not in Sunday-school or in church. Her parting words deepened those impressions, and her last bequest to him was a Bible."[23]

The next morning, young Ully and his father again sat with Mary's body until it was time to go to the funeral parlor. There, an Episcopal minister read a service to comfort the grieving family. The following morning, John, his children, his sister Pattie, and a few other family members boarded a train that carried Mary's coffin to Philadelphia. She was buried in Laurel Hill Cemetery, overlooking the placid waters of the Schuylkill River. John stayed in his hometown for the weekend, taking Charley and Ully on a nostalgic tour, showing them the house where his mother had lived in 1832, the house where he was born, and his youthful stomping grounds. It was a bittersweet visit.[24]

A letter written by Ulric a few months later gives great insight into the boy's psyche. Now motherless and being raised by a procession of aunts while his father's naval duties took him away from the family, thirteen-year-old Ulric wrote to his other's sister Salllie and her husband, Abbott, demonstrating impeccable penmanship and excellent grammar and spelling. Even at that young age, he was restless. "I want to see you so much that I have a great mind to come and see you," he declared in his beautiful handwriting. He then echoed a theme that surfaced often in the boy's short life. "I am going to save up my money and buy a quarter of a section of land out West to live on when I am a man." Until Ulric became a soldier, he often entertained the prospect of living and working in the great American west. His letter concluded by betraying his youth. "Will you please bring me a little monkey for a pet when you come home?" he asked. "I like them because they are so amusing."[25]

Young Ulric was a fine student. His first academic experiences were at a private school run by two sisters named Koons, where he studied natural sciences, mathematics, and the classics. In 1850, nine year-old Ully entered the Rittenhouse Academy in Washington, "an institution for the instruction of boys, of long established reputation for its high moral and thorough intellectual training—for many years under the superintendence of Mr. Otis C. Wight, its present, capable, efficient, and honored Principal."[26] Some of Washington's most prominent young men attended this school, and a diploma from the Rittenhouse Academy was prestigious. The 1858 circular for the school stated, "The course of instruction is comprehensive, and it is the constant aim to make it more thorough and practical; introducing from time to time such improvements as experience or careful attention to the progress of the cause of education may suggest." It continued, "Attention to the morals and manners of the pupils will, at all times, be made a matter of primary importance, and no effort will be spared in endeavoring to render the general influence of the school conducive to the highest mental and moral culture of those connected with it." All students had to demonstrate good character as a condition of admission, and Mr. Wight enforced strict discipline at all times. He maintained a record of offenses—demerits—with different numbers of demerits assigned for the severity of the offense. If any student accumulated 500 demerits within a single quarter, 750 within two, 900 within three, or 1,000 within four quarters, he was expelled from the school.[27]

Ulric attended Rittenhouse Academy for eight years, completing its rigorous curriculum early and commencing college level studies while still enrolled there. The curriculum emphasized the classics: mathematics, including trigonometry and geometry; languages such as Greek, Latin, and French; history; chemistry; biology; rhetoric; logic; philosophy; and political economy, as the study of economics was then known. There were weekly exercises, and regular examinations. Tuition was $15.00 per quarter. In 1858, Ulric's last year at Rittenhouse Academy, ninety-one students of all ages attended the Academy, and were taught by three full-time faculty members, including Principal Wight.[28]

Ulric's preceptor recalled, "He was a good boy, an excellent scholar, highly esteemed by his teachers and schoolmates, prompt to every duty, earnest and self-reliant, making attainments rarely reached in an academic course, and exciting high expectations of future success."[29] Reverend Byron Sunderland left this very detailed description of the schoolboy Ulric Dahlgren:

> The traits of character which have recently burst forth like a halo in his conduct were thus gaining depth and distinctness during this passage of his school-boy days. Nothing mean or narrow, nothing contentious or insubordinate in his relation with his companions and instructors marred the growing strength and beauty of his life. Sportive yet studious, affable yet spirited, kind yet resolute, thoughtful at times even to sadness yet singularly intrepid, he scorned an unworthy motive, disdained the company of the vicious, and held himself entirely aloof from those frivolous habits of school-time annoyances to which so many youths are unfortunately addicted. He set a striking example of respect for order, submission to law, and fidelity to the claims of duty. As he grew older among his fellows, he became at length the favorite and confidant of them all. To him, as by one consent, they deferred the trusts and honors with which school-boy life—the miniature of after life—is charged. And he, faithful and modest in all, wore on his way towards the hour of his graduation. Meantime he was in full communion with his books. He conned the lore of physical science, and saw outspread before him the geography of the world and the manifold wonders of its varied elements and living tribes. He diligently threaded the mazes of history, and poured over the annals of the past to find that he belonged to a country and a people than whom no other have ever had a more stupendous and glorious mission to accomplish.[30]

When he reached the Academy's equivalent of high school, called the Senior Class, Dahlgren grappled with complex mathematics problems, learning with delight the importance of precision and attention to detail. He also honed his imagination by studying poetry and oratory. He became fluent in Latin, reading

Tacitus, Virgil, the Commentaries of Caesar, and the orations of Cicero.[31] These lessons—well-learned by Dahlgren—prepared the youth for the rigors that awaited him in the outside world.

Had he not left early, one of Ulric's classmates at Rittenhouse Academy would have been another young man born in 1842, David "Davey" Herold. Davey grew up in a large brick house just outside the main gate of the Washington Navy Yard. His father was the chief clerk at the Navy Store at the Washington Navy Yard for more than twenty years and the family was well off financially. Like young Dahlgren, Davey was bright, religious, and handled himself well with the younger boys, and he enjoyed hunting and being in the outdoors. Ulric and Herold grew up in very close proximity, had a great deal in common, and may well have played together as children. Had Ulric completed the full course of study at the Academy, they would have been classmates for their final year; Herold transferred to the Rittenhouse Academy after studying at Georgetown University from October 1855 to April 1858, when he transferred to the Academy. Their probable acquaintance had significance—and a great deal of irony—years later.[32]

Though an accomplished student and skilled draftsman, Ully's restless nature had already kicked in. His father preferred that he remain in school but, "such unmistakable symptoms of distaste to further confinement to scholastic pursuits, and such eagerness to put in practice results already acquired." John Dahlgren acquiesced to his son's wishes and allowed him to end his time at Rittenhouse Academy to begin learning a trade. After careful evaluation, Ulric selected civil engineering and the law. He walked out of Rittenhouse Academy for the last time on December 17, 1858, a cold, wintry day, when "he bade farewell to his friends in the Academy, and never did there go forth from its walls a truer heart or a nobler genius than when his shadow faded from the threshold," observed Reverend Sunderland in 1864.[33]

School provided good exercise for his mind. But the constantly restless Ully Dahlgren craved regular physical activity. When he accompanied his father to the Navy Yard, he spent many happy hours swimming and rowing under the instruction of veteran ordnance seamen. Under their diligent eyes, he soon became an expert swimmer and boatman. Tall, graceful, and athletic, the youth cut a striking figure with his blonde hair and flashing blue eyes.[34]

In November 1857, John Dahlgren returned from a trip to England. Ully was eager to see his father and to be the first to salute him. He persuaded some of the old ordnance salts to take him out in a longboat to meet his father's ship. He and the sailors rowed down the Potomac River to Alexandria, where, getting a tow from a schooner, the boat came alongside his father's ship just opposite Mount Vernon. Ully greeted his surprised father with a snappy salute. The next year, when his father went to sea again, he did just the opposite—he rowed out as far as he could, waved his last farewell from his skiff, and then returned to the Navy Yard, glowing with satisfaction.[35]

Dahlgren also demonstrated an early fascination with politics and the workings of the halls of power in the nation's capital. He often visited Congress, watching the goings-on with fascination, admiring the eloquence and oratory brilliance of the likes of such political giants as Daniel Webster and Henry Clay. His father's prominent position as the master of naval ordnance also meant that the boy enjoyed frequent visits to the White House, where he became acquainted with more than one President of the United States, a remarkable thing for one so young.

Although his duties often took John away from the family for extended periods of time, Ulric and his father maintained a voluminous and regular correspondence.[36] He was the dutiful son, doing all his father asked of him, and John doted on his special favorite. It soon became clear that the young man bore the burden of all of John's hopes and dreams, and that his father expected him to accomplish great things.

In 1856, he and his brother Charley accompanied their father on a trip on the *Merrimack*, the first of a new class of steam-powered frigates to be completed, and which later became famous as a Confederate ironclad. The ship carried the Dahlgren gun, and Commander Dahlgren went on its shakedown cruise in order to witness the first firing of its battery of guns. The ship's crew welcomed the two boys, capturing their imaginations. Not long after, Charley followed in his father's footsteps and joined the Navy. Perhaps this cruise was the deciding factor.[37]

Tragedy haunted the family. In 1844, Ully's infant brother John died. In 1851, death took his brother Lawrence, and in 1858, his sister Lizzie passed away at the age of seventeen. She was tall, slender, strikingly beautiful, and Ully adored her. Her death cast a shadow upon the Dahlgren household and upon the sixteen-year-old boy that lasted for the rest of his life. He wore a ring of hers on his right hand for the rest of his life.

Losing his beloved wife was a real blow for John Dahlgren, and losing his beautiful daughter nearly destroyed him. In June 1858, he poured out his despair to his sister Patty. After informing her that he would be home from sea soon, he said, "it will hardly be a pleasure to return to a home where so much sorrow has fallen on me and I almost desire that Providence may destine it otherwise, for I am without a hope in the future." His suffered from deep and unrelenting melancholy. "It is no use to write more in this strain so I close, wishing you all that happiness and freedom from misery that has been denied me and clouds my middle life with the gloom of the grave," he lamented, "there indeed, my heart was with my unfortunate child in her untimely tomb. Lightly may the sods of earth cover the poor dear girl."[38]

Still grieving his sister's death in 1858, and with his time at Rittenhouse Academy over, Ully spent the rest of the year evaluating previous field surveys, mastering the techniques of the trade, and receiving instructions from his father in the use of the tools of the trade. With a view toward getting some experience performing surveying in the field, he accepted an invitation to visit his uncle Charles Dahlgren at his handsome plantation in Natchez, Mississippi. The visit lasted for nearly a year.[39]

Charles, John's younger brother, began his career in banking in their hometown of Philadelphia. As a young man, he went to Natchez as the representative of the powerful financier Nicholas Biddle, the president of the Second Bank of the United States. In 1836, when President Andrew Jackson successfully fended off the renewal of the Second Bank's charter, Charles took a job with a local bank in Natchez. By 1849, he was an affluent planter, captain of a company of militia cavalry, and had a family of his own. In his own right, Charles became every bit as prominent as his brother John.[40]

Ulric's eighteen-year-old first cousin, Charles Routh Dahlgren, finally persuaded his father to invite Ulric to come to Natchez for an extended visit. Charles Routh and his younger brother Bernard, twelve, were active boys who enjoyed hunting, fishing, camping, fencing boating, horseracing, and other vigorous outdoors activities. The restless, fun-loving Ully fit right in with them. He readily joined his cousins in their adventures, gleefully engaging in any sport they chose, including wrestling and shooting. They also made a trip to Washington.[41]

Dahlgren and his cousins set out from Commander Dahlgren's Washington home in January 1859. They arrived in Richmond, Virginia, a few days later, settling into the Exchange Hotel. Ulric penned a letter to his father describing what he saw as he walked around the town. "Little did the brave boy dream, as he traversed the streets of the Virginia capital, that a few short years would see him reappear on the scene, bringing with his charging squadrons hope to imprisoned comrades and terror to rebel councils,—then his own lifeless body would be borne along, perchance just where he trod, with every mark of indignity that panic-stricken traitors could offer, and destined by them to be forgiven in some nameless spot." A few days later, the merry little band finished its journey and arrived at Charles Dahlgren's house in Mississippi.[42]

Ully's letters to his father indicate that he thoroughly enjoyed his time in Natchez. He and his cousin Charlie enjoyed hunting expeditions.[43] "Very busy surveying . . . Went hunting . . . Knocked over a splendid buck . . . Have a bay colt . . . just broken . . . gaiting him . . . am on horseback the whole time . . . I carry the compass on horseback at full speed and jump a large ditch with ease . . . the alligators plenty . . . bellow like bulls."[44] Knowing that his father disapproved of such activities, he hoped to pull a fast one on his old salt father, adding, "I am going to swim the lake when it is warm enough, where there are dozens of alligators. They won't touch white men, but eat negroes whenever they catch them."[45] He spent a delightful summer learning to speak French and mastering fencing.[46]

At one point, he reported that his uncle was keeping him busy surveying, and that he "would rather survey than eat."[47] He proved to be a quick and eager study and quickly demonstrated a knack for surveying work. He rode horseback from Natchez to Marydale, Mississippi on a weekly basis, inspecting work on levees there, leaving Natchez at 5:00 a.m. and arriving at the plantation at 3:00 p.m., covering a distance of forty-eight miles. On one of these expeditions, his luck almost ran out. "I would have been drowned today if I had not learned. My horse gave out swimming a bayou," he reported to his younger brother Paul. "I tried to cross the bayou two hours ago on Charlie's horse 'Derrick' and when I had got half way over he sank right down from under me, so I had to strike out and swim to shore, and directly I saw him rise and come across, but he is such a rascal that I could not catch him, being wet I could not run fast so I had to swim back to get home."[48]

These experiences served Ulric Dahlgren well. He often ventured out into the bayous accompanied only by his horse and a rifle, and he learned to fend for himself. He learned the trials and tribulations of caring for horses, and he also learned how to survive in the deep woods. He took to it like a duck takes to water, and he mastered skills that he would need in the coming conflict. "His sinews were toughened to an almost incredible endurance of physical hardship and fatigue," observed Reverend Sunderland, "while his taste for the sturdy sports of the field, and his love of the art equestrian were fully gratified." The utterly fearless young man was a splendid horseman.[49] Now almost eighteen years old, the boy stood five feet ten and a half inches tall, but weighed a mere 136 pounds of lean muscle. He was tall and whippet thin, with piercing blue eyes and short-cropped blonde hair.[50]

In the meantime, Commander Dahlgren was involved in a fight for his professional life. A great debate raged over whether the Navy should use rifled or smoothbore guns, and although he eventually prevailed and got authorization to develop a rifled naval gun, the episode and the debate wore heavily on him. Ulric wanted to join his father and work by his side, as they had often done during his boyhood. "I do not wish you to be in the battle with me," he informed Ully in February 1860. "It will be savage, and one of a family at a time is enough— you have done enough, for the time." Commander Dahlgren wanted Ully to continue his education instead of joining him at the Ordnance Bureau.[51]

The son, however, had other ideas. After that year in Natchez, Ully informed his father that he felt ready to try to make his way in the world. He was an experienced surveyor, and recognized that the more western states and territories, such as Texas, Kansas, and Arizona, offered the best opportunity for a new surveyor. The South, on the other hand, was "too civilized," and there was "no room to move ahead in these wealthy cotton states" unless a man owned a large plantation and a number of slaves. "The whole of it is, I want to earn my living, which I am doing now, but in a very indefinite way," he told his father. At the same time, the young man realized that his older, worldlier father had more life experiences to draw upon and that Commander Dahlgren might have different ideas. John Dahlgren summoned his son to come home to Washington, so that they could discuss such an important decision. Ully responded, "As you know what is best for me, dear father, I will cheerfully and willingly follow your advice." With $450 of his uncle's money to pay for the trip, he set out for home on March 30, arriving in Washington in April 1860.[52]

After a lengthy and far-ranging discussion, Ully made his case and Commander Dahlgren agreed that his son should continue his surveying work. Ulric returned to Natchez in May at his uncle Charles' invitation "to study law and be admitted in 18 months." While reading law and serving his apprenticeship, he could earn a salary of $25.00 per month for services such as "writing, fixing papers." With his father's approval, young Ulric accepted his uncle's offer.[53] Anticipating his return to Natchez, Ulric wrote to his cousin Frank to make the necessary arrangements. "It is very doubtful whether I will go by way of N. York as it is time for the yellow fever in New Orleans & Havanna & there would be some risk in going that way, if I do not I miss the opportunity of seeing you all. I wish you would come on here," he wrote.[54] He made the trip uneventfully and arrived in Natchez safely. On June 18, Ully completed a painting of his uncle's new house and presented it to the family, where it occupied a place of honor.[55]

A few days before he departed for Natchez, Ulric paid a visit to Matthew Brady's photographic studio in Washington, and had his photograph taken.[56] That photograph survives today. It shows the tall, gangly young man, seated uncomfortably with his legs crossed, one hand in his lap, intently and earnestly staring straight ahead at the camera's lens. His face is clean-shaven and he looks much younger than his eighteen years. His hair is cut short, and he wears a white shirt, vest, waistcoat, and bow tie. He is all angles, long legs, and eager earnestness. The photograph perfectly captures the youth's restless nature, and gives a glimpse of the man he became.[57]

Events of great national importance were brewing, and the young man's life changed forever as a consequence. A former Congressman from Illinois named Abraham Lincoln had gained the presidential nomination of the Republican Party, and he espoused limiting the expansion of slavery. Lincoln's candidacy stirred up emotions in the South, and tensions increased dramatically as a consequence. Sen. Stephen Douglas of Illinois won the Democratic nomination, and Vice President John C. Breckinridge of Kentucky ran as a third party candidate. Breckinridge and Douglas split the vote of those opposed to Lincoln. On November 26, John Dahlgren wrote his son, "Mr. Lincoln is conservative, but cannot express himself before the [electoral] ballots are cast, which will be in ten days. The North too has to say whether it will compromise with the South or not, after the latter offers its alternative."[58] When the Electoral College elected Abraham Lincoln president of the United States, the Rubicon was crossed.

Charles Dahlgren was a prosperous Southern planter, slave owner, and an ardent supporter of states' rights. Therefore, it came as no surprise when he became an ardent secessionist. His brother John, on the other hand, was a political moderate who wanted to do whatever it took to preserve the Union. Ully shared his father's proclivities. Although he was close to his Uncle Charles, the increasingly intense debate caused a great deal of stress and tension in the relationship. "As the period of the election drew near, the symptoms of trouble became more portentious," recalled John Dahlgren, "and Ulric was recalled to his home; for his father was unwilling that one so much loved should be separated from the hearth-stone of the family at such a crisis."[59]

At the same time, Ulric did not make a favorable impression on everyone he met that pleasant summer. His uncle Charles owned a mountain retreat in Beersheba Springs, Tennessee, and the family spent a final idyllic summer there. A family friend named Lucy Virginia French, a prominent poet and novelist, met Ulric that summer. As years passed, she remembered him clearly, but not

Ulric Dahlgren
LIBRARY OF CONGRESS

Charles G. Dahlgren
LIBRARY OF CONGRESS

for a good reason. She once overheard Ully making unfavorable comments about a local mountain girl named Darl, and those comments rankled her. "He had said to me one morning as she [Darl] passed us on the plank walk, 'Heavens! What magnificent eyes! What ten thousand pities they should be wasted on a mountaineer! I know many a belle who would give thousands of her dollars and some years of her life for such a set of living diamonds!'" Mrs. French never forgave Ulric's comments, which she viewed as rude. She remembered him as an arrogant young man with patronizing ways toward the people in the local mountain community of Beersheba Springs.[60]

On August 31, 1860, with Ully's departure for Washington looming, the family memorialized the event in an appropriate fashion. He and his cousin Charles Routh found a small rounded boulder in the pine thicket near the family cottage at Beersheba Springs. The boys took a hammer and chisel and carved their initials on the top and sides of the boulder, engraving a total of twelve sets of initials on the rock. They also carved the date on the rock. Although his aunt, uncle, and cousins had no way of knowing it, they would never see Ulric Dahlgren alive again.[61]

Arriving in Washington during the latter part of September 1860, Ully visited with his siblings for a couple of days, and then traveled on to Philadelphia, where he found a room in a boarding house and apprenticed himself to his maternal uncle, James W. Paul, a prominent and well-respected lawyer. A few days later, his aunt invited him to reside with her, but Ully declined, preferring to pay his own way. Instead, he moved to more comfortable quarters in October.[62]

Characteristically, Ulric applied himself to his studies with his usual earnestness and diligence. "And thus the destiny of the youth reverted to the association where it truly belonged," observed his father. "It was a sore struggle to forsake a mode of life so well suited to his instincts,—the free, fresh air of the forest for the confined atmosphere of a large city, the wild excitement of the chase for the quiet avocation of the office, the untrammeled freedom of rural life for the guarded conventionalities of an exalted nature." Always the dutiful son, he did so at the behest of his father.[63]

Commander Dahlgren continually reminded Ully to stick to his studies. "My son you are the architect of your own fortunes and the work is fairly and fully before you," he encouraged on December 18, "habit is everything and there is nothing like sticking to your purpose, swerving neither for pleasure nor from difficulty."[64]

His legal studies imprinted new ideas on his active mind. "He acquired a new knowledge of the fundamental doctrines of individual and public welfare;

he derived a new sense of the value to mankind of the institutions of free Government; he was filled with a stronger conviction of the importance of preserving the Republic in its purity and integrity, while he drew as it were from the fountains of Sacred, Roman, English, and American jurisprudence, a fresh inspiration of the proud fealty of patriotism and a soul-thrilling allegiance to all rightful authority," remembered Reverend Sunderland.[65]

Ully spent the balance of 1860 diligently studying the law and exercising at a local gymnasium, followed in the evening by attendance at the Franklin Institute, a science museum named in honor of Benjamin Franklin. His day began at 7:00 a.m., and he arrived at the office at 8:00. He worked until 1:00, when he took an hour for lunch, and then resumed working at 2:00. The workday ended at 4:30, when he went to the gymnasium for an hour and a half of hard exercise. At 6:00, he ate his supper, followed by a visit to the Franklin Institute, where he remained until his bedtime between 9:00 and 10:00. Occasionally, he visited with old school chums and his brother Charley. Characteristically, on October 19, he reported to his father that he had been quite busy as of late, "which he likes amazingly."[66] He even enjoyed himself at his landlady's quilting party in early November, dancing until morning.[67] Although storm clouds were gathering over the country, Ully diligently studied the law and continued making good progress toward admission to the bar.[68]

Always interested in politics, the astute young man realized that Lincoln's election would bring the crisis to a head. Southern firebrands, led by Edmund Ruffin of South Carolina, loudly called for the Southern states to secede from the Union, and it appeared that an armed clash loomed. On December 18, Commander Dahlgren spelled out his position in a letter to Ulric, and gave his son clear instructions. "In the North there is no personal servitude, but there is the Slavery of the classes, so well understood that when a man does rise from it, so much is made of it, as when copper approaches the White level," he declared. "But however this may be, what right has the Northern man to infringe on the admitted duty to the White man in order to discharge a factitious & gratuitous duty to the Negro? Let him see the starving laborers in Kansas and elsewhere at hand. The mischiefs of this unconstitutional interference are not far from wrecking this Union. At this very time it is about to cost our Constellation one of its stars, and more will drop out if the evil is not staid by patriotic hands."[69] Thus, according to Commander Dahlgren, a true patriot would take up arms to preserve and protect the Union. John Dahlgren had already sworn an oath to do just that. He had now made it clear that he expected his son to do likewise if South Carolina actually seceded from the Union.

South Carolina passed an Ordinance of Secession on December 20, 1860. John Dahlgren wrote his son, "It may do for old fogies to argue the abstract right of secession but practical men will deal with facts, and when the danger is imminent must see how it is to avoided peaceably. No American with the feelings of a man can fail to regard the present crisis with the deepest solicitude."[70] Four days later, on Christmas Eve, he continued. "I have a good opportunity of noting the current of feeling as well as of events. Most of the prominent men I know intimately. One evening I pass with a Northern Senator and hear the Republican view—no trepidation—no misgiving, but he & his friends behold the coming tempest with firm hearts. Some[times] I spend the evening with a Southern extremist;—[Robert] Toombs and & Jeff Davis &c. are there—as I am perhaps the only outsider [to whom] they speak freely—the question in all its bearing is treated without the least temper or disrespect to the other side. But so decidedly that all hope seems to vanish."[71]

Ully took ill that holiday season. On Christmas Eve, his father wrote, "I am sorry to hear of your indisposition. It seems to be a biliary derangement, contracted no doubt by the Southern residence and developed by the present life and climate. The young branch does not seem as hardy as the old trunk." John told Ully that if he was going to be sick, he had better come home and be treated by the family doctor in Washington. However, not even illness calmed the boy's restless soul.[72]

As the storm clouds of war gathered, it became obvious to all who knew Ulric Dahlgren that the law, which had only a tenuous hold on his heart and soul, had lost its sway with him, even though the young man diligently continued his studies in compliance with his father's wishes. However, he just went through the motions. He felt that another vocation was calling him: the profession of arms. "Throughout this interval he appeared restless and ill at ease," noted one observer. "His fervid nature awoke in all its energy."[73]

Writing to his father at Christmas, he said, "I have been waiting anxiously to see something done by some party, and at last it has come in the shape of Fort Moultrie [located on Sullivan's Island, just outside of Charleston, South Carolina] being abandoned, which will, no doubt, precipitate Southern action."[74] President James Buchanan, the lame duck Democrat, announced that he had no power or right to coerce the Southern states to remain in the Union, and the long-feared crisis had finally arrived. That crisis molded and shaped Ulric Dahlgren's few remaining yeas.

CHAPTER THREE

The Gathering Storm

"THERE IS MUCH EXCITEMENT here in regard to [Major Robert] Anderson's movements. I hope they will take some definite action," Ully declared to his father on New Year's Day, 1861.[1] Several days later, he added, "Everything seems worked up to the highest pitch of excitement on account of political affairs generally."[2] The drums of war began beating loudly, and young Ulric heard them. "I would like much to belong to a military company," he said a few weeks later. He waited for his father to give his blessing. However, as long as hostilities had not actually broken out, Commander Dahlgren remained adamant that Ully should continue his studies. Knowing this, Ully noted in the same letter, "I am getting on very well with my studies and like it very much."[3]

Ulric moved to a different boarding house, located at 7th and Chestnut in Center City Philadelphia. "I have a nice room with gas, fire, carpet and plenty of furniture & good eating," all for the sum of $3.50 per week. Three other boarders shared the house, including one of his schoolmates.[4] However, by the end of January, he was complaining. "I don't visit much (once in six weeks) for the people are so curious here," he reported to his father, "if you don't appear in dress suit in the evening, they think themselves insulted & if you call to see them, an invitation follows & you <u>must</u> go; so I have concluded they & society with them are humbugs." He concluded his letter with a stirring patriotic declaration: "Equality within the Union or Independence out of it."[5] Ulric Dahlgren's patience, which was limited even in the best of circumstances, was rapidly running out. He desperately wanted to be where the action was.

Ully had to learn to get by on a student's budget, and he regularly provided his father with a detailed accounting of his expenditures. Money was always tight, and his family knew it. By February, Ully's Aunt Pattie had offered him money on a number of occasions, but "I never accept, and so we came to an exact understanding beforehand about places of amusement," he reported to his father. "She says she has no one to take her, and that when I go with her, she is to pay, as it is for her amusement, and that I only go with her to escort her. This I agree to as it is nothing but justice, and beyond this I want nothing from any of them." He was learning an important lesson that all men must learn sooner: that women can be difficult for the male psyche to understand. "I notice a little inclination among womenfolk to bring to notice things that they have done years back, so I want to let them view everything in the right light without offense to anyone," he concluded wisely.[6]

The secession crisis splintered the Dahlgren family. John Dahlgren remained staunchly committed to the Union and to the oath he swore to defend the Constitution. His brother Charles, transplanted to Mississippi, where he enjoyed the genteel lifestyle of a wealthy planter, rabidly supported secession. When Mississippi seceded, Charles declared his allegiance to his state and the newly-formed Confederacy, and began organizing and raising a regiment of infantry. He accepted a commission as a brigadier general of Mississippi troops. His son, Charles Rauth Dahlgren, enlisted in a cavalry company that later became part of the Jeff Davis Legion.[7] Thus, the Dahlgrens embodied the family schisms that made this conflict so tragic.

In March 1861, Ulric wrote a lengthy letter to his father wherein he clearly spelled out his views on the secession crisis:

> My political status has not changed in the least. I base all my views on the same foundation, but when I have been under a wrong impression in the details—for truth is the great foundation of everything—I think is only just to correct it; now Southern interests lie in a different manner than other parts of the Union and I hold that they are proper and right and should not be interfered with by the South, and not that Northern rights should be made subservient to the South. In whole I am for the Union with the motto "Equality within or Independence without." [Former Virginia governor John] Floyd is a rascal laying politics aside and [General David] Twiggs a traitor & coward. Anderson is a Southern man yet he remains true to his duty both to God and man.

While this letter demonstrated that the young man entered the conflict with a practical and realistic view of the political situation that emphasized moderation, his views changed dramatically as time passed and he became radicalized.[8]

As the crisis deepened, Ully maintained the illusion of normalcy, spending his days and evenings studying intently.[9] "I am progressing with the law, if study will do it and yet find the time rolling swiftly by," he reported to his father on February 26. "I am studying Geology in the evening along with coal and iron as far as regards their source—at the same time keeping an eye on Mathematics, the base of all knowledge."[10] However, his heart was not in the books—this young man craved action and desperately wanted to be in the thick of the inevitable fray. That month, Jefferson Davis was elected president of the new Confederacy, and it became obvious that the issue could only be resolved by a contest of arms. Military officers, who had proudly served the United States of America, resigned their commissions to serve not their country but their home states, and the fabric of American society unraveled quickly.

The situation at Charleston erupted into a full-blown crisis in early 1861. When South Carolina passed its Ordinance of Secession in December 1860, the question of who would control the Federal forts around Charleston—Forts Moultrie and Sumter—became the focus of that crisis. Fort Sumter, located in the very mouth of Charleston's harbor, was in an unfinished state and without a garrison. On the night of December 26, 1860, Maj. Robert Anderson, a native Southerner, dismantled Fort Moultrie and removed his command to Fort Sumter by boats. When ordered by South Carolina militia to return his garrison to Fort Moultrie, Anderson replied, "Make my compliments to the governor, and say to him that I decline to accede to his request; I cannot and will not go back." With that, Anderson raised the American flag over Fort Sumter, and prepared to defend the post.[11]

Anderson's treatment by the South Carolinians caused outrage in the North. "The American flag should never have been insulted," declared an indignant Ulric Dahlgren, "there was no necessity for it. Anderson is a Southern man, yet he remains true to his duty, both to God and man."[12] When the War Department tried to reinforce and re-supply Anderson's garrison by dispatching a supply ship to Charleston in January, the South Carolina batteries opened on the ship, which immediately beat a hasty retreat. Anderson prudently held his fire, briefly averting the crisis. However, when Lincoln took office that spring, events spiraled out of control. Lincoln did not recognize the legality of the secession of South Carolina, and resolved to preserve the Union by arms if necessary.

However, on April 11, the Confederates again demanded that Anderson evacuate and surrender Fort Sumter. Anderson refused, and the next day, the South Carolina batteries opened fire on the beleaguered garrison. Left with no choice after Southern gunners pulverized the masonry fort, Anderson surrendered on April 15, marching his garrison out with their colors and arms. The day so long dreaded had finally arrived—war had come. Now, there would be no turning back.[13]

Droves of young men, both North and South, flocked to enlist. When Lincoln called for 75,000 volunteers to enlist to put down the rebellion, the upper tier of southern states, Arkansas, Virginia, North Carolina and Tennessee, which had maintained a "wait and see" attitude, also left the Union. Before long, eleven Southern states had seceded. Parts of Maryland, particularly in the Baltimore area, had strong secessionist leanings. Baltimore was the key, as northern troops would have to pass through the city on their way to Washington, D.C. Force became necessary to keep this vital corridor open. Trapped between these two bastions of secessionism, the fate of the nation's capital hung in the balance.

John Dahlgren met the new president for the first time on April 3 in a meeting that lasted thirty minutes.[14] However, a few days after the surrender of Fort Sumter, Lincoln demonstrated his confidence in Dahlgren by placing command of the critical Washington Navy Yard in the commander's competent hands. "For quickly, upon the secession of the border states [Virginia, Arkansas, Tennessee, and North Carolina], the officers of the Washington Navy Yard, who happened to belong to them, abandoned their duty, to join the standards of what they considered their paramount allegiance," he wrote a few years after the end of the war, "and the command of the most important position thereby devolved upon [me], who alone remained faithful to his trust."[15] The Navy Yard took on new significance—it had vast stores of ordnance and ammunition, and was also the key to the city's defenses on the left, controlling the bridge and the approaches by water from the eastern shore. Fortunately, John Dahlgren proved to be the right man for the heavy task at hand.

At first, Dahlgren had only 150 men with which to defend the Navy Yard. However, on April 25, Union troops from the north began arriving in the city, easing the strain. During this period, Dahlgren forged a close and warm relationship with his commander-in-chief. When a secessionist innkeeper in Alexandria, Virginia killed Lincoln's friend, Col. Elmer Ellsworth, on May 24, 1861, Dahlgren brought the fallen hero's body back to the Navy Yard. Lincoln frequently visited the Navy Yard, and the commander and the president enjoyed spending time together. The President, always fascinated with gadgets and technology, found a kindred spirit in John Dahlgren. "The President often comes to see the Yard," noted Dahlgren in his diary on June 9, 1861, "and treats me without reserve."[16]

Before long, John Dahlgren served as the President's unofficial naval aide. Lincoln often sought Dahlgren's steady counsel and came to rely upon him increasingly. When more senior officers objected to Dahlgren's having command of the Navy Yard due to his relatively junior rank, Lincoln rebuffed them. "The Yard shall not be taken from [Dahlgren]," he declared. "He held it when no one else would, and now he shall keep it as long as he pleases." In August,

Congress enacted legislation to permit Dahlgren to hold the position as a mere commander. By November, he had finally received the long-desired promotion to captain, and found himself a political insider who had Lincoln's ear. Before long, so did his son Ulric.[17]

In June, Commander Dahlgren oversaw the movement of the many new regiments arriving in Washington from the Navy Yard to Virginia, prompting Confederate troops, who had seized the Federal armory there in April, to withdraw from Harpers Ferry. "The armies are gathering up as the Regiments arrive," Commander Dahlgren reported on June 16, "and though it is easy to guess the limit within which the Generals will move, yet no one can indicate with any precision how or when a blow may be struck."[18] Hearing this news, Ully itched to be in the midst of the excitement. Pulsing with energy, he longed to join his father, and in late June, the invitation to come home to Washington finally arrived. On July 1, he reached the Navy Yard, stunned by the buzzing hive of activity that Washington had become. Gone was the sleepy Washington of his childhood. To him, the city seemed like a vast armed camp, and each arriving train brought more soldiers from the North. These new regiments had to find accommodations, meaning that the public buildings and grounds crawled with soldiers. "The avenues were thronged with columns of infantry and artillery, gaily moving to the crash of numerous bands, while the townspeople looked on with wonder." The Navy Yard was just as busy and chaotic, and Ully drank in the sights and sounds, fueling his desire to be part of the action.[19]

On July 16, the great army that had been assembled marched, determined to go "on to Richmond," the new capital of the Confederacy, which lay about 100 miles south of Washington. Five days later, the armies clashed on the banks of Bull Run, near Manassas, and the Confederates routed the Federals at the end of a long, hard day of fighting. The broken Northern army streamed back toward Washington in a panic, prompting Lincoln to visit Commander Dahlgren at the Navy Yard to make certain that steps had been taken to ensure that the Potomac River approaches to the city were protected. On July 24, Dahlgren received orders to remove three of his heavy guns from the Navy Yard and move them to the front. With his father's permission, Ully joined this expedition as an aide to the commanding officer, Lieutenant Foxhall A. Parker, Jr., who normally served as his father's executive officer. "And thus began that career in the service of his country which, for a short season only, was to be distinguished by the most unselfish devotion," as his father later put it.[20] Lieutenant Parker, with one hundred ten sailors and some Marines, left with three 9-inch Dahlgren guns and five howitzers.[21]

The guns were to be placed on a range of hills to the southwest of Washington, by a bend in the Potomac River at Long Bridge, and extending from Alexandria to above Georgetown. The works overlooking Alexandria were incomplete, and there was a gap in the defenses through which an enemy force could pass and seize the town. Lieutenant Parker's naval guns would fill that gap. Parker's expedition marched on July 24, and Ully maintained a diary of his experiences on the mission.

Parker transported the guns to Fort Ellsworth in Alexandria via boat. By the next day, the guns were in place, platforms and breastworks constructed, and the men ready. Commander Dahlgren visited and approved the disposition of the battery. Before long, soldiers from nearby camps began coming by to see the famed Dahlgren guns, expressing surprise at how quickly the battery had been constructed. On July 26, the United States flag fluttered over the installation to the cheers of the men, and Parker named the place Fort Dahlgren. Two days later, Generals Irvin McDowell and George B. McClellan, newly appointed to command the Army of the Potomac, inspected the battery. In attendance were Commander Dahlgren and several prominent politicians. The men went about their duties with professional precision, impressing young Ully and fueling his already burning urge to become a soldier.[22]

Ully spent his spare time exploring the nearby camps of the volunteer infantry regiments, watching the new soldiers drilling, and soaking up everything his nimble mind could absorb. He watched as the volunteer regiments became proficient at drill and began operating as brigades and divisions. McClellan was melding an army to save the Republic, fascinating Ulric Dahlgren, who renewed old acquaintances and made new friends.[23]

Before long, his curiosity got the best of him. Even though he was still a civilian, some of his new friends invited him out on Federal skirmish lines thrown out to annoy the nearby Confederate forces. One of these tempting enemy outposts occupied Munson's Hill, a prominent elevation plainly visible from the Navy Yard. A Confederate flag floated defiantly atop the hill, offering a tempting target for marksmen stationed at the Yard. On September 5, Ully reported to his father, "I am in the midst of very exciting and interesting events. Last Friday and Saturday I was in two skirmishes near Munson's Hill, in which we lost several killed and wounded, and they lost some also." A good marksman from his time in Mississippi, Ully became proficient with the Maynard rifle. "It is regular Indian-fighting that we do every day near here, and I have a Maynard rifle, with which *I send a telegram* south occasionally. At present, my knees are so sore from crawling in the bushes, and fighting them in their own style, that I can hardly walk."[24]

During the first part of August, Prince Napoléon Joseph Charles Paul Bonaparte, a great nephew of the Emperor Napoleon, visited the Navy Yard. Ulric also got to meet the Prince de Joinville and his two nephews, the Comte de Paris—pretender to the French throne—and his brother, the Duc de Chartres. Francois d' Orleans de Joinville and his nephews staunchly supported the Union, and the Comte de Paris served as a staff officer at the headquarters of the Army of the Potomac. As the war progressed, Ully Dahlgren and the Comte de Paris came to know each other well.[25]

However, in the wake of the debacle at Bull Run and the realization that the gathering Union armies would need extensive training before they could take the field again, it became obvious that the war would not end quickly and that McClellan needed time to coalesce his disorganized units into an army. Thus, there probably would not be any real activity until spring. Consequently, Commander Dahlgren ordered Ully to return to Philadelphia and resume his studies. Ever the obedient son, he complied. "The remarkable facility with which he yielded his own wishes to those of his father was never more strikingly exemplified than in this instance," wrote Commander Dahlgren. "Putting aside his rifle, and all the 'pride, pomp, and circumstance of glorious war,' he departed for Philadelphia, and again took his place at the desk, as cheerfully as if his earnest nature had never been absorbed in the great events of the passing struggle, not burned with intense desire to bear any part, however humble, in the cause of his country."[26]

Ully had extracted a promise from his father, however. In exchange for his agreement to return to his studies, his father agreed that once the time came for the Army of the Potomac to take the field, Ully could return to share in the first opportunity for service that might arise. With that promise in mind, Ully diligently applied himself to his studies, counting the days until he could experience the excitement of combat again. "The city is so dull that scarcely any of them are doing much," he complained to his father on September 19.[27]

That same day, Ulric attended the monthly meeting of Franklin Institute. Founded in 1824, and named for Benjamin Franklin, the most famous citizen of Philadelphia, The Franklin Institute was established as the first professional organization of mechanical engineers and professional draftsmen in the United States. Given Ulric's tendencies toward his father's inventions and engineering feats, the Institute was a natural draw for the restless young man. That night, Ulric exhibited and explained a number of photographs to the assembled members, including photographs of a Chinese fort captured by the French and British in 1860, views of the naval battery he and Parker had set up, views of the country between Washington and Alexandria, the position where a naval officer named Capt. James Ward was killed in June 1861, the officers of the 71st New York Infantry taken just before they departed for the Battle of Bull Run, and examples of Confederate ordnance, including an Infernal Machine. The photographs were "viewed with much satisfaction by the members." That Ulric was permitted to make such an important presentation at the tender age of 19 speaks volumes for the esteem in which he was held and the nature of his inquiring mind.[28]

Commander Dahlgren also entrusted his son with an important task that kept Ully busy for weeks to come. His father had written a detailed drill manual for the operation of the Dahlgren gun, and the Commander gave Ully the task of supervising the printing of the manual. Ulric visited printers, screened out unsuitable candidates, obtained price quotes, and consulted with his father regularly. "I don't think this man will suit you. He don't seem to be very bright," he reported regarding the printer on September 19. "His business is principally religious works."[29] Once they chose an appropriate printer, Ully supervised the process, ensuring that the manual was successfully and properly printed. The manual was later circulated throughout the Navy.[30]

Young Dahlgren also found another pastime. A number of patriotic young gentlemen of means in Philadelphia decided to form a militia company of light artillery, and Ully eagerly joined them. With his usual zeal, he pitched into his new duties enthusiastically. Having spent his childhood sighting and firing large-bore naval guns, he knew artillery and artillery tactics well. As a result, he soon became a lieutenant in the company of home guard artillery. They faced one major problem, though. An artillery company, of course, requires guns in order to be effective, and they had none. Ully's earnest pleas to his father led to the Commander arranging for four Navy howitzers to be lent to the company for its use. On November 2, John Dahlgren informed his son, "I am ready to forward two howitzers to the City of Philadelphia on loan for the present, but some formal application is necessary for our records from the City authorities."[31] When the guns finally arrived, the unit was named the Dahlgren Howitzer Battery to honor the unit's patron.[32]

"I have gotten command of the two, & it will form a section of a battery," Ulric proudly reported a few days later. "I was very busy yesterday putting the guns in their places & will finish today."[33] By the beginning of February, the rookie gunners had become proficient. "I have trained the men until they can go through the motions of loading and firing 8 times per minute & will try to reach higher," Ulric proudly told his father.[34] Brig. Gen. Augustus Pleasonton, commander of the Philadelphia Home Guard troops, later submitted an application for an additional two howitzers, which Ulric forwarded to his father.[35] The Dahlgren Howitzer Battery soon numbered six guns provided by John Dahlgren. The young men drilled and practiced their gunnery, anxiously waiting for the day when they could put their new skills to use.[36]

Ully whiled away the rest of the fall and the winter, still earnestly pursuing his legal studies. He attended law school, listened to lectures by legal scholars, and passed a final examination on February 24, 1862. "Never sacrifice a principle," entreated his father in January.[37] Steadfastly obeying his father's instructions, the boy diligently studied the law even though his heart was not in it.[38]

As winter broke, McClellan's huge army—now more than 100,000 men strong—was ready to take the field. The coming of spring once again stoked Ully's need for action. "He could brook inactivity no longer, nor fix his thoughts on the quiet pursuits of the law-office when the din of arms resounded throughout the land, and every loyal heart was bent on the coming struggle, which again it was fondly hoped would crush the rebellion at a blow," noted his father. Ully gently but persistently made his wishes known, and his father, realizing that he had to honor his promise to the boy, grudgingly gave his consent. "And so, not hastily, but carefully, and almost reverentially, the youth laid down the reasonings of the great expounders of the law, that he might take his place in the ranks," Commander Dahlgren admitted, "for he felt that the argument had been closed forever in the great council of the nation, and that the decision lay with the sword."[39]

As spring came, Commander Dahlgren received a new assignment. With fears over the development of a fleet of Confederate ironclad ships growing, the Navy wanted Dahlgren to develop a new 15-inch naval gun to deal with the threat. The Confederate ironclad C.S.S. *Virginia*, constructed from the wreck of the sunken *U.S.S. Merrimack*, had fought an epic battle with the new Union ironclad, the *U.S.S. Monitor*, in Hampton Roads in March 1862, dawning the age of ironclad fighting ships. "It was a serious business," wrote Commander Dahlgren in a letter to Ulric. John Dahlgren optimistically assumed that the combination of the *Monitor's* victory and Maj. Gen. Ulysses S. Grant's capture of Fort Donelson on February 16 signaled the beginning of the end of the rebellion. "After the capture of Fort Donelson I allowed 60 days for the final dénouement—things move rapidly now."[40] Dahlgren was obviously wrong. In May, the Confederates abandoned Norfolk. With no home base to return to, her crew scuttled the *Virginia* and the crisis passed. However, Commander Dahlgren wanted his son by his side while he worked on designing a new gun. The new generation of turreted Union navy ships built along the lines of the *Monitor* carried a new rifle designed by him.[41]

In mid-April 1862, Ully put away the law books for the last time, packed up his belongings, and went to Washington to begin his military career in earnest. By mid-month, he was in Washington. On April 19, he accompanied his father on a visit to the *U.S.S. Miami*, a revenue cutter lying at anchor at the Navy Yard. President Lincoln, Secretary of War Edwin M. Stanton, Secretary of the Treasury Salmon P. Chase, and several other dignitaries were aboard. They spent several pleasant hours there, with Lincoln "in his usual way, and telling many a joke."[42] Once again, Ully rubbed elbows with the most powerful men in the country, fitting in comfortably among them. By late April, he joined his father's inner circle as a member of the Ordnance Department staff at the Navy Yard. "On Saturday Ully began his career as my assistant," noted Commander Dahlgren in his diary on April 26, "of which he had the choice."[43] Finally, Ulric Dahlgren was going to enter the fray, this time with his father's blessing. "Thus, he drew nigh to the work which Providence had assigned him," recalled Reverend Sunderland in 1864.[44]

Ulric Dahlgren was just twenty years old. His skin bronzed by the sun from his time spent in Mississippi, he stood nearly six feet tall. He was long and very lean, weighing only about 140 pounds. He regularly worked out at the gymnasium, enjoying perfect health and the resilience of youth. He would need that resilience. Great challenges lay ahad for him.[45]

CHAPTER FOUR

Ulric Dahlgren Makes His Mark

The Harpers Ferry Expedition of May 1862

FINALLY FREED from the tedium of his legal studies, Ulric Dahlgren settled into his new role as his father's unofficial military aide, devoting his considerable energies to helping his father. "In former days it had been a pastime, now it was to be a duty as well as a pleasure," recalled his father, "and in the discharge of that duty he felt himself to be no privileged incumbent." He immersed himself in his duties, arriving at his Navy Yard office early and leaving late, "industriously occupied with such writing, or drafting, or other duty, as might be assigned him."[1] Before long, Ulric had gained his father's complete and unflinching confidence, and had demonstrated that his legal studies had taught him to pay attention to details. These skills served him well.

He spent his days in the stately but quaint old mansion inhabited by his father as commandant of the Navy Yard. The old house had long galleries, where Ulric "might be seen, seated in thoughtful repose near the door, his eye wandering over the singularly contrasted view of green trees and shrubbery, from which rose here and there the tall chimneys of busy forges and glowing furnaces. Or in the quiet dining-room, father and son might be found over the daily meal, in happy companionship."[2] In fact, working side-by-side, father and son grew even closer than ever. Before long, Commander Dahlgren invested all of his hopes and dreams in his oldest son.

Ully bided his time, waiting for an opportunity to test his mettle in the field again. Secession caused massive resignations from the Army, as Southern officers stayed loyal to their home states and joined the Confederate service. This meant that experienced officers were in short supply, and that shortage created lots of opportunities for ambitious young men like Ulric Dahlgren. He made the most of that opportunity when it finally arose.

In the interim, John A. Dahlgren itched for a promotion to chief of artillery for the U. S. Navy. However, the Secretary of the Navy resisted the promotion on the grounds that Dahlgren was too junior an officer to hold such a high rank, frustrating Commander Dahlgren to no end. Looking to mollify his friend, Lincoln penned a quick letter to Stanton. "I need not tell you how much I would like to oblige Capt. [sic] Dahlgren," he wrote. "I now learn, not from him, that he would be gratified for his son Ulric Dahlgren, to be appointed a lieutenant in the Army. Please find a place for him."[3] With this sort of influence being brought to bear on his behalf, there was little doubt that a commission for Ulric would ensue as soon as the opportunity presented itself.

In the meantime, he enjoyed the perquisites that flowed from his father's relationship with Abraham Lincoln. One afternoon in late May, he received an invitation to board his father's steamer, the *U.S.S. Miami*, for a presidential cruise down the Potomac River to Aquia, above Fredericksburg. The Secretaries of War and the Treasury also came along for an inspection of forces under command of Maj. Gen. Irvin McDowell, who boarded the yacht to pay his respects to the President. Ulric listened intently to McDowell's report, and in particular, to McDowell's recounting of the exploits of Col. George D. Bayard's cavalrymen. He watched Secretary Stanton pencil down Bayard's name for promotion to brigadier general.

Lincoln came ashore to get a closer look and to inspect the troops. He rode to Chatham, a handsome mansion overlooking the town of Fredericksburg from the north side of the Rappahannock River. There, Lincoln reviewed his troops. Ulric accompanied Lincoln, and sat by his side during the review. Few twenty-year-old volunteer aides have ever enjoyed unfettered access to the Secretary of War and the President of the United States. Ulric made the best of this opportunity, and both Stanton and Lincoln grew fond of the bright, personable young man.[4]

The Confederate high command had sent Maj. Gen. Thomas J. "Stonewall" Jackson to create chaos in the Shenandoah Valley in the hope that his operations there would prevent McDowell's large corps of infantry from marching to Richmond and joining McClellan's army. After largely having his way with the Union forces in the Valley for weeks, Jackson unexpectedly found himself in a pinch. In late May, Federal armies operating in the Shenandoah Valley converged upon Jackson's small army. The end of May found Federal pincers converging on his rear. Maj. Gen. John C. Frémont's army approached Strasburg from the west. McDowell, with two divisions, including one under command of Brig. Gen. James Shields, headed for Front Royal from the east.[5]

The Confederate high command therefore decided that Jackson should press the enemy at Harpers Ferry, threaten an invasion of Maryland and an assault on Washington, D. C., and thus create such chaos that additional troops would to be pulled away from McClellan's army on the Peninsula to meet the threat.[6] The news that Jackson's army, 20,000 strong, was making a beeline for them jolted the defenders of Harpers Ferry. On May 31, Lieutenant James Gillette,

Rufus Saxton
LIBRARY OF CONGRESS

C. H. Daniels
AUTHOR'S COLLECTION

3rd Maryland (U.S.) Infantry, wrote, "The men are utterly exhausted with want of sleep and food. If not heavily reinforced or better organized soon—they will be almost demoralized."[7]

Well before daybreak on Saturday, May 24, the *Miami* docked at Washington Navy Yard. As President Lincoln disembarked, an aide handed him a telegram. He read it, put it in his pocket, got into his carriage and rode off. The telegram startled him—it informed the President that Jackson's army had eluded Frémont's force, pounced upon and defeated the army of Maj. Gen. Nathaniel P. Banks, severed his lines of communication and supply from Harpers Ferry, and was then marching straight for the critical Federal armory and supply dump there. Banks barely escaped with his army intact, pulling back across the Potomac River at Williamsport while Jackson marched on Harpers Ferry. This turn of events raised the level of alarm in Washington, because Harpers Ferry was not prepared to meet such a looming crisis.

Reacting quickly, the War Department sent reinforcements and supplies scrambling toward Harpers Ferry. The Navy also contributed, sending 38 cannons—consisting of heavy Dahlgren guns, and naval howitzers—and a body of 300 select seamen, including the entire complement of sailors from the steamer *Satellite*, and a detachment of Marines to man those guns. These men were to report to the commanding officer, Brig. Gen. Rufus Saxton, at Harpers Ferry.[8] At the order of Assistant Secretary of the Navy Gustavus Fox, Acting Master Charles H. Daniels and Ulric Dahlgren commanded this naval contingent.[9] Although Ulric possessed no formal military training and had only his Fort Ellsworth experience to draw upon, he was a natural choice for this assignment. The boy grew up around artillery, knew it well, and had fired cannons on his father's ordnance range since childhood. He knew those guns as well as any Regular officer, and his knowledge of them proved invaluable during this assignment. This expedition gave Ully his first opportunity to make his mark on the war effort, and he made the best of it. His life was never the same afterward.[10]

Acting Master Daniels was not much older than Ully. Born in Troy, New York in 1839, Daniels entered the U. S. Naval Academy's class of 1863 as a midshipman. He resigned from the Naval Academy in March 1861 in the middle of his third-class year. The reasons for his resignation are not known, but on April 26, 1861, he enlisted and served as a clerk to the commanding officer of the *U.S.S. Pawnee*, Commander Stephen Clegg Rowan. On September 2, he was promoted and assigned to the *U.S.S. Hetzel* with the rank of Acting Master, where he participated in Maj. Gen. Ambrose E. Burnside's North Carolina expedition. Daniels received a severe wound to his left wrist during the New Bern expedition when a Dahlgren gun barrel exploded and shrapnel gouged his hand. His assignment to the *Hetzel* had just ended on May 2 with his re-assignment to the Washington Navy Yard.[11] Daniels was chosen to lead this expedition because he had prior experience commanding howitzers.[12] When he assumed command of the Naval Battery and led it to Harpers Ferry, Daniels was only twenty-three years old, and did not possess much more experience than did Ulric Dahlgren.[13]

When he arrived at the Navy Yard, Ulric reported to Brig. Gen. Rufus Saxton, a thirty-eight-year-old graduate of West Point who had temporarily assumed command of the defenses of Harpers Ferry. Saxton, born in Massachusetts, graduated from West Point in 1849. He spent most of his pre-war service in the artillery, both on active duty and as an instructor of artillery tactics at West Point. He was appointed a brigadier general of volunteers on April 15, 1862, and served in the defenses of Washington, D.C. He had only been assigned to assume command of the defenses of Harpers Ferry on May 24.[14] The veteran artillerist was a good choice to command such a large contingent of heavy guns. He arrived at Harpers Ferry on May 26.[15] "From the well-known military abilities of General Saxton it was confidently expected that he would be able to resist the advance of the rebels," a newspaper correspondent optimistically predicted.[16]

Dahlgren and Daniels were to place the guns atop Maryland Heights. This high ground commanded the town, the confluence of the Shenandoah and Potomac Rivers, and for miles beyond.[17] The sailors loaded the guns on railroad cars and took them upriver, arriving at Harpers Ferry on May 27th along with several regiments of infantry sent to reinforce the garrison. When the expedition arrived at Harpers Ferry, Ulric and Acting Master Daniels reconnoitered to find the best possible location for the deployment of the huge nine-inch Dahlgren guns, which had to be dragged up the Heights by hand. Ulric strained alongside the rugged sailors to drag the guns into place.[18]

"I have arrived and reported in obedience to orders," Daniels reported on May 27th. "The nine (9) inch gun is stationed on the heights opposite Harpers Ferry and over two thousand (2000) feet above the level of the sea. The howitzer battery has not as yet been assigned to any place but expect it to move with the army."[19] Lugging the big Dahlgren gun up Maryland Heights had been an ordeal, but it was now there, in place and ready to meet any threat the enemy might pose.

Jackson wisely elected not to attack. Nearly 40,000 Union troops rushed to meet the threat posed by his 15,000-man army (which was reduced by casualties), and Saxton held a very strong position at Harpers Ferry. "He moved to Harpers Ferry on the 28th of May, and spent the 29th in making demonstrations against the force that had been rapidly gathered there, but which was too strong posted to be attacked in front," noted one of Jackson's staff officers. "Time did not allow a crossing of the river and an investment of the place." If Jackson remained in place, the converging Federal armies would trap his army against the river, so he wisely began a strategic withdrawal on the morning of May 30, ordering all of his troops, except a single brigade of infantry and his cavalry, to fall back to Winchester. Brig. Gen. Samuel Winder's infantry brigade and his horsemen covered his rear and continued demonstrating in front of Harpers Ferry.[20]

After resting fitfully, the men got up again early the next morning and completed the construction of a platform for the big guns. In the meantime, Saxton sent out scouting parties in an effort to locate the enemy infantry. "Lieutenants Daniels and Dahlgren have their battery in position on the heights, commanding all the points in this vicinity," reported Saxton that afternoon, "and had some splendid practice with the larger Dahlgren, shelling the woods and heights across the Shenandoah, where our scouting party was killed."[21] The Union soldiers did everything possible to prepare for an enemy assault. "Every preparation was made for heavy fighting as everything showed indications of an attack from there," noted Ulric in his diary on May 28. "Spies were captured in town. Signals were seen all around and nothing which we saw indicated anything but a fierce onset." The men stayed up all night, lobbing shells at the Confederates. "Our skirmishers fell back and everything done to receive them well. The night passed over and we saw nothing further than during the day previous," he concluded.[22]

On May 29, with the naval battery now in position, Dahlgren returned to Washington to request more men, ammunition, and wheels to make moving the guns easier. He arrived at 7:00 in the evening, and reported to his father. "Ully came down for supplies for the guns, bringing some information as to the state of affairs," recalled his father, "which was not very promising as to the resistance that could be made at Harpers Ferry."[23] After hearing Ulric's report, Commander Dahlgren and his son went straight to War Department, where they met with Lincoln, Stanton, Assistant Secretary of the Navy Gustavus V. Fox, and other assorted staff officers. Given the importance of the armory and the psychological effect of losing Harpers Ferry, the Union high command was anxious for news from the front, and they welcomed Ulric's report. Lincoln,

Stanton, and Fox interrogated young Dahlgren at length, milking as much intelligence from him as they could. "Ully said what he had to say," recalled his father.[24] The grilling lasted for nearly two hours, with the Union high command hanging on Ulric's every word late into the night.[25]

Apparently, the thoroughness of Ulric's briefing on the military situation at Harpers Ferry impressed Secretary Stanton, who remembered Lincoln's request that he find a commission for Ully. Stanton offered the young man a captain's commission and an assignment on Saxton's staff. Dahlgren readily accepted the unexpected favor. Despite the late hour, Adjutant General Lorenzo Thomas was still at his desk, and Thomas made out the necessary documents immediately. Stanton swore the delighted Ulric into the United States Army and he left the War Department that night with a captain's commission in hand.[26] "The Secretary of War made [Ully] Captain on the Staff so that when we left the War Department Ully was a Captain, not having had the most remote idea of it when he entered," proudly recorded John Dahlgren in his diary that night.[27]

"I immediately made my preparations and left the next morning at 7:40," recalled Ulric, who departed wearing his brand new uniform, captain's bars adorning each shoulder.[28] Thus, "with his wonted celerity, he was on his way back under his new commission, having passed, as in a moment, from the civilian to the soldier, and urging forward, he joined Saxton at Harpers Ferry on the 31st of May, in 1862," remembered Reverend Sunderland two years later.[29] He arrived at Harpers Ferry at noon and reported to Saxton immediately. Saxton was preparing to go out to inspect his positions, so Ulric joined him. "The enemy were now so near as they could be without a general fight," he recalled. They assigned another gun and some sharpshooters to take position on Bolivar Heights on the other side of the river to answer enemy skirmishers, who were advancing on the town, and "which were in a short distance of us." Saxton and Dahlgren rode their lines, carefully reconnoitering Jackson's positions.

Saxton had anticipated an attempt to outflank his position. Knowing that his small force could not defend both sides of the Potomac River, he withdrew his command, including his pickets, onto Bolivar Heights and concentrated it there under the protection of the heavy guns atop Maryland Heights.[30] Ully, who was out riding the picket lines gathering up wayward skirmishers, drew enemy artillery fire. Several shells burst quite near him without so much as disturbing his composure. Instead, he coolly rode on, fulfilling his mission. The young man survived his baptism of fire.[31]

As darkness fell, the tired Union soldiers lay down to rest. A wild thunderstorm set in, with the crashing thunder shaking the very mountains and the vivid flashes of lighting illuminating the night sky. General Saxton described these events in colorful detail: "The scene at this time was very impressive. The night was intensely dark; the hills around were alive with the signal-lights of the enemy; the rain descended in torrents; vivid flashes of lightning illumined at intervals the grand and magnificent scenery, while the crash of thunder, echoing among the mountains, drowned into comparative insignificance the roar of our artillery."[32] None of the Federals expected another attack that night under such terrible conditions.

The Confederates, however, did not try and other attack with the raging tempest to cover their approach. The blueclad defenders responded to the threat quickly. The Dahlgren guns opened up, announcing that the Federals were ready to receive the assault. The surprised Southerners fell back after enduring an hour's solid shelling.[33] "A shell thrown at night from our batteries passed over the mountain and exploded directly in their camp," a bemused General Saxton reported to Washington.[34] "They kept up a heavy skirmish all night with both musketry & artillery, killing 1 & wounding several," noted Ulric in his diary.[35] After the defenders repulsed an assault by some Louisiana and Mississippi infantry, the enemy disappeared and withdrew out of range of the guns. They had accomplished their main purpose of compelling Maj. Gen. Irvin McDowell to abandon his advance toward Richmond and to divert to Front Royal instead, so there was no longer any reason for them to stay.

The next morning, June 1, the Union garrison awoke. "Everyone fully expected a battle, and they were drawn up for it within ½ mile of our pickets," Ulric reported in a letter to his father. All were surprised to find the enemy gone.[36] "A scouting party advanced several miles, discovering the main enemy force, "and our fun was all stopped at once," as Ulric recalled. "So we were once more quiet."[37] The Southern artillery opened on the scouts, prompting a response from the naval battery atop Maryland Heights. The extremely accurate fire of the naval battery wreaked havoc on the enemy positions below. "Our shell burst (after the second fire) right in their midst scattering them in every direction," Ulric proudly informed his father. "They it is reported breaking & running. But for this they would certainly have made the attack."[38] The Confederate infantry, under command of Brig. Gen. Charles S. Winder, pulled back all the way to Charles Town, with Union scouts following cautiously, watching their movements.

Confederate deserters informed the Federals that they could not stand the shelling laid down by the big naval guns, "which had played mischief with them." Perhaps they had. However, Brig. Gen. John D. Imboden, a Confederate cavalry commander and a native of the Shenandoah Valley, claimed that the attack was just a ruse to cover the removal of Jackson's booty. "General Saxton, with some 7000 men, held Harper's Ferry, 32 miles from Winchester," he claimed. "Jackson paid his respects to this fortified post, by marching a large part of his forces close to it, threatening an assault, long enough to allow all the captured property at Winchester to be sent away toward Staunton, and then returned to Winchester."[39]

Another of Jackson's officers claimed, "Jackson had no time at his disposal for crossing the Potomac and investing the enemy on all sides. He had already carried out his instructions, to threaten an invasion of Maryland and a movement upon Washington, to the extreme point consistent with safety." Having fulfilled his mission, Jackson broke off and withdrew, much to Saxton's great relief.[40]

General Saxton praised his gunners lavishly. "I cannot speak too highly of the services of Lieutenant Daniels, U. S. Volunteers, and his splendid rifled 9-inch Dahlgren," he reported to Secretary Stanton late that afternoon. "Both he and they did their work well."[41] Ulric echoed a similar note in a letter to his father. "We are now relieved of their attack, much to the regret of those interested in the Naval Battery which has saved Harpers Ferry and much more with it," he declared.[42]

It fortunate for Saxton that Jackson had not pressed the attack that day. Saxton had only 7,000 "effective men, being completely worn-out by fatigue and exposure," while he correctly estimated that Jackson had between 25,000 and 30,000 men and more than fifty pieces of artillery. As a result, Saxton "deemed it not prudent to advance."[43] Instead, the Union troops withdrew to the defenses around Harpers Ferry. With the crisis over, local residents began returning to their homes, thanks, in no small part, to Saxton's cool and steady leadership. "The operations here on Thursday and Friday reflect credit on General Saxton," noted a correspondent on June 2. "But for his efforts, Jackson's forces would have pushed over the railroad bridge toward Baltimore."[44]

"Everything quiet," noted Ulric in his diary on Sunday, June 1. "A secessionist horse was brought in by a citizen who rode him off as the Rebel officer went into a house to see someone."[45] He formally assumed command on Monday, relieving Saxton, whose assignment at Harpers Ferry was temporary and solely for the purpose of quelling the emergency posed by Jackson's advance. The young man's short tenure as his aide-de-camp impressed Saxton, who singled Ulric out for praise when he penned his official report of the action a few days later.[46] In fact, Saxton apparently recommended Ulric to become chief of artillery of the Harpers Ferry garrison, but a Regular army captain outranked him and assumed the position by virtue of seniority, even though Saxton preferred Dahlgren.[47]

With the crisis now past, Ulric now faced a different challenge. He had been riding a captured horse, but turned that horse in to the quartermaster, who assigned the animal to pull a wagon. Now he had to obtain his own mount. "My pay is $150 (and a little more) per month including everything, but we are required to get our own horses," he informed his father, "the U.S. feeding them & paying if they are lost." "I am in the saddle all day & have been notified that I am required to have a horse, so I have to have money to buy a horse here & there is none to buy here if I had." The only horse he could find would cost nearly a month's pay, $120.00. Ully sent his father an urgent request for money to pay for a horse and accouterments.[48]

Young Dahlgren also had to learn the intrigues of army politics. "There is a great rivalry among the staff officers to distinguish themselves & with a little assistance, I think I can make myself useful." He continued, "Genl. Saxton told Actg. Master Daniels that he would mention him to the Dept. for important services rendered in hurrying on the battery—so much for representing a command." Having learned the importance of politics from his father, Ulric was always conscious of his own place in the hierarchy. His tone made it sound as if he felt slighted by Saxton in favor of Daniels.[49]

Nevertheless, Dahlgren did quite well in his first role as an Army officer. He had made the transition easily and seamlessly, finally falling into the long-coveted role for which he had always been inclined. "And so, suddenly and without warning, Ulric passed from civil life to the field, and rejoiced in all that belonged to his new calling. He was once more, as he loved to be, in the free air of heaven, his frame invigorated and his spirit buoyant with its freshness," recalled his father. With Saxton gone, Dahlgren now began serving on the staff of the new commander, Maj. Gen. Franz Sigel.[50]

Sigel played a major role in the next phase of Ulric's development as a soldier. Born on November 18, 1824, at Sinsheim in the Grand Duchy of Baden, Germany, Sigel graduated from the military academy at Karlsruhe, and served in the army of Grand Duke Leopold. When insurrection broke out in 1848, Sigel served as minister of war for the revolutionary forces, which were defeated by the Prussians. Forced to flee, Sigel went first to Switzerland, then to England, and finally to New York, arriving in 1852. He taught school in New York and St. Louis, and held a major's commission in the 5th New York Militia. By 1861, he served as director of schools in St. Louis, a city with a very large German

Franz Sigel
LIBRARY OF CONGRESS

immigrant population. The new Lincoln Administration wanted to woo the German immigrants to the Union cause and made Sigel a brigadier general on August 7, 1861. He received a promotion to major general in March 1862, and rallied countless German immigrants round the flag of the Union. "I fights mit Sigel" became their proud war cry.

"He brought a splendid military reputation with him," observed Maj. Gen. Carl Schurz, another refugee of the Baden revolution. "He had bravely fought for liberty in Germany, and conducted there the last operations of the revolutionary army in 1849. He had been one of the foremost to organize and lead that force of armed men, mostly Germans, that seemed suddenly to spring out of the pavements of St. Louis, and whose prompt action saved that city and the State of Missouri to the Union."[51] All expected Sigel to be one of the leading lights of the Union cause.

Unfortunately, Franz Sigel's military skills did not match his political stature. He did well in St. Louis during the early days of the war under command of Brig. Gen. Nathaniel Lyon. His military career reached its zenith at the Battle of Pea Ridge in March 1862, when he contributed greatly to a critical Union victory. However, Sigel became ill shortly after the battle and took medical leave. From there, it was all down hill. Schurz believed that Sigel never should have come east, as doing so exposed him to political intrigues. Sigel was not a West Pointer, and he was not an easterner. "When a volunteer general, and a 'foreigner,' too, was transferred from the West to the East as a man of superior qualities and military competency, who might perhaps teach them something, it went much against their grain, and that man was often looked upon as a pretentious intruder and obliged to encounter very watchful and sometimes even rancorous criticism," commented Schurz. "Moreover, General Sigel was not well fitted to meet the difficulties of such a situation. He possessed in a small degree that affability of humor which will disarm ill-will and make for friendly comradeship. His conversation lacked the sympathetic element. There was something reserved, even morose, in his mien, which, if it did not discourage cheerful approach, certainly did not invite it."[52]

When he recovered sufficiently to resume his duties, he was summoned to Washington. On June 1, 1862, Sigel reported to the War Department, where Secretary Stanton ordered him to go to Harpers Ferry and take command of the troops stationed there. He arrived at Harpers Ferry late that afternoon and immediately took up the task of organizing the troops under his command, which were part of Maj. Gen. Nathaniel P. Banks' corps, detached from McClellan's Army of the Potomac.[53] "I find the troops here in a very inefficient condition," Sigel reported on June 2. "General Saxton insists on being relieved. The number of troops here are about 8,000. Of these, 1,200 are useless, and all the balance are undrilled and undisciplined."[54]

Sigel had his work cut out for him. "The defense of the Shenandoah Valley and the co-operation with Frémont is regarded by the President as one of the most important duties now before the Government, and much reliance is placed upon your military genius and skill, so I hope you will not deem your present duty inferior to any other," Secretary Stanton implored a few days later.[55] This would be a heavy task, to be accomplished with an undisciplined and unreliable force, and Sigel was expected to co-operate with Frémont, an egomaniacal general of questionable competence.[56]

However, his presence did wonders for the morale of the Harpers Ferry garrison. "General Sigel arrived here this morning in company with his staff," reported a Philadelphia newspaper on June 2. "It is presumed he will immediately assume command. This idea seems to inspire this column with great confidence."[57] Whether Sigel would earn that great confidence remained an open question.

On June 1, while Sigel was en route to Harpers Ferry, Ulric and another staff officer rode to Charles Town to reconnoiter Jackson's positions, and were surprised to find the Confederates gone. They then returned to Harpers Ferry that afternoon. "On arriving back I found Gen. Sigel (who had relieved Gen. Saxton that morning) was preparing to advance," Ulric told his father. "So I saw Saxton and asked him if he wished me to accompany him to Washington & if not I would like to go with Sigel. He told me I was right & gave me an introduction & mentioned my case which was kindly granted." Upon reporting to Sigel, the new commander asked Dahlgren, "Have you a horse?"

"No, sir, but I will find one before you start," replied Ulric. Dahlgren secured a spare cavalry mare from another staff officer, and then "had to leave baggage &c. & everything behind, for I only had 5 minutes to prepare." Mounting up, he put spurs to his mare and galloped off after Sigel in the heavy rain, catching up with him on Bolivar Heights. "I have been drenched through all the time—with nothing to eat or sleep on," he groused a few days later.[58]

Sigel knew that he had no time to spare if he had any chance to catch Jackson's army. The German kept his men marching constantly, "nearly killing man & beast," as Ully noted on June 4. "You never saw such a march, & I have had my share of it. It would take a fine horse to do my riding."[59] The columns slogged through the thick mud, were soaked to the skin, and deprived of food and rest. "Sigel seems disposed to let no grass grow under his feet," as one newspaper correspondent observed.[60]

Ulric seemed to thrive in spite of the exhaustion and hardship. "He is in his element, and begins as he will end, ahead with his troopers,—now searching Smithfield for a rebel flag, and then, with willing spirits ready for any adventure in quest of some rebel officers," observed Admiral Dahlgren. "But pursuit has its termination as well as battle, and when Winchester is reached, Sigel's corps, reduced in number and in ill condition, must pause and act as a reserve."[61]

On June 4, Sigel reported, "I sent scouting parties to Strasburg and Front Royal to ascertain the position of our own and of the enemy's troops."[62] Dahlgren led one of these scouting parties and spent the day at Bunker Hill, near Front Royal, waiting to meet General Banks and his command. After meeting up with Banks and delivering dispatches from Sigel, Dahlgren then galloped to Smithfield, and arrived at 5:00. He found headquarters, dried off, found new shoes and socks to replace the soggy ones he had been wearing for three days, and scribbled a quick letter to his father. "I am very comfortable now," he declared, his relief palpable. "Jackson is thought to be in the neighborhood," he continued. "We expect a big fight unless Jackson gets past Frémont, or use the Shenandoah." General Sigel also passed a message on to John Dahlgren. "Sigel told me to tell you that if he had more men or if these mere were better disciplined he would give Jackson the mischief but he says he is ordered to attack him and will do it."

The German general quickly became a mentor to Ulric. "Sigel is a genius,"

Ulric proclaimed in a June 4 letter to his father, "quick is not the word for him. He executes as quickly as he thinks, pouncing like an eagle. He speaks broken English, but is a trump. He told me he would like to have me on his staff—he is entitled to 3 Aids & has only two. I want active service & would like to be transferred to his staff. In the meantime I will continue on as a volunteer aid. I think this is as sure as anything I know of," he concluded.[63]

By June 6, Frémont's army was at Harrisonburg, and on June 8, caught up to Jackson's rear guard at Cross Keys, handling the weary Confederates roughly. The next day, General Shields, anxious to join the fray, attacked Jackson's retreating army at Port Republic, but he did so with insufficient force. When Jackson concentrated his entire force and brought his numeric advantage to bear in a hard fight, Shields' men broke and ran, suffering heavy losses in the process.[64] By June 12, both Frémont and Shields had retreated into the northern Shenandoah Valley, leaving Jackson's army to operate almost unmolested.[65]

All of the time spent in the saddle took its toll on Ulric. "I have been so unfortunate as to have a large boil just where the saddle presses most," he told his father on June 10, "and have not been in the saddle for 4 days, but have been assisting & acting as Assist[ant] Adj[utant] Gen[eral]." A twenty-mile reconnaissance mission inflamed the boil badly, but Ulric successfully completed the trip anyway, reporting his findings to Sigel. Although he had had the boil lanced and it was finally healing, the army was getting ready to move again, and the boil would soon be inflamed all over again. Sigel was concerned; Dahlgren was already an important part of his staff. On the night of June 9, "the general came into my room . . . after I had gone to bed & told me privately that he wanted me to try and get it well because he would move soon & did not want to leave me behind by any means."[66]

In fact, Ulric had so impressed Sigel with his knowledge of artillery that the German general told him that as soon as he was recovered from the uncomfortable boil and the rest of his staff reported for duty, Ulric would become the chief ordnance officer for Sigel's division. In that role, Ulric asked his father where he might obtain a supply of better infantry weapons for Sigel's command, which carried a hodgepodge of obsolete and ineffective weapons such as much-maligned and unreliable rifles of Austrian manufacture. "Sigel has a miserable army," Ulric declared to his father, "half equipped &c., but is going to make them first rate, not leaving a stone unturned to affect it. I want to stay with him because he is a man that will effect something wherever he is—of most untiring nature, working day & night."[67]

Ully remained keenly conscious of rank. "I want an opportunity to have my appointment [as captain] confirmed [by Congress] & made permanent and in the artillery," he wrote. "Saxton mentioned Daniels very favorably. I wished I had commanded that party instead of being second, for I did nearly all the work while there & the men said they would wish a bit for Daniels if I had not been there. But still he represented them & Saxton was so glad to be saved the big guns that he mentioned every one he could think of." Ulric had learned the importance of politics well from his father, who played the game expertly.[68]

The next day, Dahlgren informed his father that Sigel's command had run terribly short on artillery, mounting only nine guns for 10,000 men. Thinking creatively, Ulric obtained permission to organize the naval howitzers from Harpers Ferry into a battery and for that battery to join the command in the field. "This battery I think if properly organized & backed can be of immense service and will you ask Sec. Stanton to give me the authority to organize it and if possible send a Company of Artillerists from some of the forts to man it." The artillery would have to come from Commander Dahlgren's supply at the Washington Navy Yard, and would have to be carried to the army by train and wagon. He asked his father to move on this request expeditiously. "Genl Sigel says he cannot do much with these raw troops without artillery," stated Ulric.[69]

Unfortunately, this was not possible. "The howitzers that were at Harpers Ferry have been brought back to Washington by order of the Navy Department and there is no way to get them again except by a Requisition of Genl Sigel, who is very welcome to anything I have here that can assist his operations," responded his father the next day. Always conscious of politics and inter-service rivalries, Commander Dahlgren cautioned his son. "It is a matter of great delicacy for an officer of the Navy to interfere in the arrangements of the Army and the Ordnance Bureau would growl terribly," he wrote. "The Navy Howitzers have been used by the Army in all their sea-coast operations, particularly with Burnside [in coastal North Carolina]." Ully did not see the execution of his plan to augment Sigel's meager artillery detachment.[70]

By June 12, Frémont had advanced as far as Mount Jackson, but by then, Jackson's army was too far out of reach. On June 18, Jackson and his Army of the Valley marched off to join Robert E. Lee's Army of Northern Virginia in the defenses of Richmond. Jackson's departure left Col. Thomas T. Munford's cavalry as the only significant force of Confederates still operating in the Shenandoah Valley. Without Jackson's marauding army to harass them any more, the Union forces concentrated at Winchester, where Sigel began training and drilling his raw troops, getting them ready for action in the field. "Sigel keeps us busy as bees," Dahlgren noted in a letter to his father on June 15. "Sigel is blunt and requires great promise and energy—very quick in battle." Ulric spent his days inspecting the artillery, drilling the gunners, and working on improving the accuracy of their fire.[71]

However, Sigel believed that he needed more heavy guns to strengthen his divisional artillery's limited punch. Ully agreed. On June 21, Ulric informed his father. "A requisition will be forwarded to the War Department by Genl Sigel with Genl Banks' authority for three (3) nine (9) inch guns & one (1) large rifled. Can they be obtained, ammunition included?"[72] His father responded immediately. "Three (3) nine inch guns can be had here and several rifled fifty-pdrs. and can be sent if authorized," wrote Captain Dahlgren. He concluded on a more personal note. "Your horse was sent from here to Winchester several days since."[73]

By June 23, Sigel's command had moved about thirty-four miles from Winchester to Middletown, by way of Front Royal. On arriving there, Ulric finally received the horse purchased for him by his father. The young horse required a great deal of training before it would be reliable in the field. While picking out a position for a battery, Ulric and horse tried to jump a fence, but failed miserably, the animal dumping its rider and falling hard. Ulric suffered a bruised leg and foot, and was out of commission for a while. The horse suffered only a scratch on its side and a few bruises. It could have been much worse.[74]

An accomplished and tireless rider, Dahlgren feared that he required more than one horse. "Ulric was a graceful and skilled rider, and had a perfect passion for horses from his early childhood," recalled Admiral Dahlgren. The young man had a real gift for training and managing horses, with "a quiet way of bringing himself in contact with the animal by passing his hand kindly and softly about the head and shoulders, and carefully avoiding whatever was sensitive; so that the horse seemed to recognize the friendly touch, and the most restive found him mounted before there was a chance for rebelling."[75]

Ulric Dahlgren regularly carried orders back and forth to and from Dumfries to Falmouth, a distance of more than twenty miles each way, a ride he typically accomplished in about two hours. He returned the next morning, having covered nearly fifty miles in a short period of time. He never seemed to grow weary from his travails.[76] "From that hour forward, he seems never to have paused or rested," noted Reverend Sunderland in 1864. "He was ever in the van, not rashly but piously daring and devoutly doing for the love and fealty he bore to his native land."[77] His seeming immunity to fatigue served him well, earning him the trusted position of Sigel's most daring and most dependable scout.

By now, he was deeply immersed in his duties with Sigel's division. "I am looking out for the artillery," Ulric told his father on June 23. "Genl Sigel always sends me to superintend the firing but I cannot be any official Chief of Arty because I am appointed as Aid & through some red tape cannot be such—but when the big guns can I'll do it any how." By the end of June, Sigel depended upon Ulric heavily in a number of different capacities, and the young man—not yet twenty years old—served as Sigel's *de facto* chief of artillery. Considering that he had no formal military training, this was quite remarkable indeed. The years spent at his father's side, studying the physics and tactics of artillery now paid dividends.[78]

Constantly worrying about adding to the firepower of Sigel's contingent of artillery, Ulric kept trying to find more guns. Knowing this, Captain Dahlgren gladly did all he could to assist his son's efforts. "If the guns mentioned in your telegram of yesterday just received, should be ordered from this yard the wheels may be sent with them," wrote Captain Dahlgren on June 24. "I send you today a package by [Addams] Express."[79]

On June 26, McClellan's Army of the Potomac suffered defeat in the first of the Seven Days Battles around Richmond. The previously independent commands of Frémont, Banks, and McDowell, including Sigel's division, were consolidated under Maj. Gen. John Pope, who had been brought east by Lincoln and Stanton to assume command of the newly-formed Army of Virginia. Pope was to do three things: "attack and overcome the rebel forces under Jackson and [Maj. Gen. Richard S.] Ewell, threaten the enemy in the direction of Charlottesville, and render the most effective aid to relieve General McClellan and capture Richmond."[80] With a new commander came new opportunities. Ully Dahlgren did some of his best service in Pope's ill-fated army.

CHAPTER FIVE

Ulric Dahlgren Finds His Niche

The Second Bull Run Campaign

ORTY-YEAR-OLD Maj. Gen. John Pope had a distinguished pedigree. He was a collateral descendant of George Washington, his father was territorial secretary and delegate from the Illinois Territory and later served as a Federal judge, and his uncle was a United States Senator from Kentucky. Most importantly, he was related by marriage to the family of Mary Todd Lincoln, and his father-in-law was a powerful Congressman from Ohio named Valentine B. Horton. He was a member of West Point's distinguished class of 1842, which produced seventeen general officers of the Civil War. Pope was brevetted twice for gallantry during the Mexican War. He was appointed brigadier general of volunteers on June 14, 1861, and performed extremely well in the early campaigns of the Western Theater. He executed a brilliant campaign to capture Madrid and Island No. 10 in the Mississippi River in March and April 1862, and received a promotion to major general of volunteers on March 22 in recognition of those excellent campaigns.

During the Union advance on Corinth in May, he commanded a wing of Maj. Gen. Henry W. Halleck's massive army, and was at the height of his military career when he was summoned to Virginia in June. Pope assumed command of all Union forces in the East except for McClellan's Army of the Potomac, which was then slugging it out with the Confederates on the Peninsula. Lincoln and Stanton hand-picked Pope, and they expected great things of him. If his performance in the West was any predictor of how he would do in the East, all signs pointed to great success. Unfortunately, the signs were wrong. Pope's service in the East was brief and unhappy.[1]

Further, Pope had no interest in serving in the east. "I was most reluctant to leave an Army Corps which I had myself organized and successfully commanded up to that time and to which I was greatly attached," Pope wrote in his post-war memoirs, "and I especially disliked the idea of service in an army of which I knew nothing beyond the personnel of its chief commanders, some of whom I neither admired nor trusted. The Secretary of War, however, was imperative, and I was compelled to undertake a duty hopeless of successful performance, except under the most favorable circumstances and the most genuine and zealous cooperation, both of which were conspicuously absent, as I strongly suggested would be the case at the time."[2]

Designated the Army of Virginia, Pope's new command was tasked with defending Washington, D.C. and operating along the line of the Orange & Alexandria Railroad in the hope of easing some of the pressure on McClellan, who faced stout resistance to each step on the way to Richmond. Pope recognized that he faced a difficult task in trying to meld an army out of the troops assigned to his command. McDowell's, Banks', and Frémont's formerly independent commands, as well as Brig. Gen. Samuel Sturgis' troops from the defenses of Washington, joined to form the 45,000 man-strong Army of Virginia. "The officers most directly affected by this action of the President were Generals Frémont, Banks, and McDowell, who commanded respectively the three army corps which were consolidated into the Army of Virginia," recalled Pope years after the war. "All of these generals were my seniors in date of commission and McDowell had always been my senior. Naturally they were not pleased with an arrangement which deprived them of independent commands and which subordinated them to their junior in rank."[3]

Pope's analysis was absolutely correct. When a miffed Frémont, who had been Pope's senior in Missouri, refused to serve under Pope, he was immediately relieved of command. "Frémont took this in high dudgeon and threw up his commission and retired from the service of his country," sniffed a Chicago newspaper. "His friends will regret this hasty and huffy conduct."[4] Sigel then assumed command of the 12,000 men in Fremont's First Corps, which he described as being "in a very bad condition in regard to discipline, organization, construction of divisions and brigades, equipments, and to a great extent demoralized."[5] With Sigel's promotion, Ulric Dahlgren found himself an aide-de-camp to a corps commander facing a daunting task.

Pope, a frothy braggart, set the tone for his army's short and unhappy existence with his very first address to his troops. "Let us understand each other. I have come to you from the West, where we have always seen the backs of our enemies; from an army whose business it has been to seek the adversary and to beat him when he was found; whose policy has been attack and not defense," he began, with characteristic bluster. "I am sorry to find so much in vogue amongst you . . . certain phrases [like] . . . 'lines of retreat,' and 'bases of supplies'. . . . Let us study the probable lines of retreat of our opponents, and leave our own to take care of themselves. Let us look before us and not behind. Success and glory are in the advance, disaster and shame lurk in the rear."[6] This sort of bombast did not sit well with either the men or the generals who would have to carry out Pope's orders. Pope's tenure in command did not begin auspiciously.

In addition, this new army was an army in name only. Since none of its component units had ever served together it lacked infrastructure and unit cohesiveness. His veterans, run ragged by Jackson's vaunted "foot cavalry", lacked confidence in themselves and their officers. Morale sagged, and their verbose leader had yet to prove himself against the Confederate veterans in Virginia.

McDowell and Banks were both used to independent command. In addition, Pope and Sigel did not like each other. Sigel found the army commander offensive, arrogant, pompous, and believed that he "did not [manage] from sound course or judgment but from mere fancy and desperation. . . . [He] was ignorant of distance and topography of country . . . [and would often] throw his wrath against subordinate officers . . . [after talking] behind their backs." Like the departed Frémont, Pope's elevation over him peeved Sigel because Sigel believed he was entitled to command of the new army and not Pope.[7]

For his part, Pope had a similarly unfavorable impression of the German. They had served together in Missouri early in the war, where Pope formed the opinion that Sigel was worse than miserably inept. He called Sigel "the God damnedest coward he ever knew." Pope swore to his staff that he would "arrest Sigel the moment he showed any signs of cowardice."[8] Although it was hard to imagine, Pope preferred Frémont to Sigel, and did not care who knew it, causing constant tension between the two officers.

This sort of chaotic situation was fraught with peril for an ambitious young officer's career, but Ulric Dahlgren made the best of it. As chief of Sigel's nine batteries of artillery, which consisted of nearly sixty guns of various sizes and bores, he did some of his finest work in Pope's short lived Army of Virginia. He found his real niche during this time.[9]

Little happened during July, Pope's first month of command, which was just as well. Pope needed the time to get his army into condition for active campaigning in the field. "Remained at Middletown without doing much," noted Ulric in his diary on July 3.[10] As long as McClellan's Army of the Potomac kept Robert E. Lee's Army of Northern Virginia pinned before Richmond, the Confederates largely left Pope alone to concentrate and reorganize his new army.

Likewise, Sigel had to organize his troops into workable brigades and divisions and get them ready to take the field, a process that took time.[11] On July 12, Pope ordered Sigel to move his corps to Warrenton, which would serve as his supply depot. The corps arrived there that same afternoon.[12]

Ulric made one trip to Washington to obtain ammunition for Sigel's corps on July 17, surprising his father in the process. "In the morning Ully came in unexpectedly, just from Sigel's camp," he noted in his diary. "He looks hearty, and brown as a berry." Ully stayed for a couple of days, and related his adventures to his father, who observed that service in the field suited his son's restless nature. They celebrated John's long-awaited promotion to captain, which finally came through the day before.[13] As John Dahlgren later noted, Ulric "was now in fine health and spirits; for the life he led was well adapted to the development of both,—ever active, sleeping and eating whenever the night found him, and invigorated by the bracing mountain air."[14]

Lee drove McClellan from the gates of Richmond after seven days of hard fighting. McClellan fell back to the protection of his gunboats, establishing a base of operations at Harrison's Landing on the James River. By the end of July, it was obvious that his campaign to take Richmond from the east had failed, and that the Army of the Potomac would have to withdraw from the Peninsula. On August 3, Halleck ordered McClellan to pull his army out, and the withdrawal began.[15] The removal of McClellan's army from the Peninsula freed Lee to focus his attentions on John Pope, whom he viewed as a "miscreant." Pope's General Orders 11 allowed his soldiers to round up any man they considered disloyal, hold them as prisoners, and hang them if necessary. These orders produced an immediate and outraged reaction from the usually taciturn Lee. Acting on behalf of President Davis, Lee sent a letter to General Halleck that essentially said that by his actions, Pope and such subordinates that enforced G.O. 11 had surrendered their right to be treated as prisoners of war if captured. Instead they would be "held in close confinement" and not be eligible for parole under the terms of the Dix-Hill cartel.[16]

On July 13, Lee again detached Jackson's corps and ordered it to march to Gordonsville, the important junction of the Orange & Alexandria and Virginia Central Railroads about seventy miles west of Richmond. Given Jackson's recent successes in the Shenandoah Valley, he seemed the right man for the job. The Confederate infantry arrived at Gordonsville on July 19, just in time to block a foray by Union cavalry intended to wreck the Virginia Central. Pope's cavalry commander, Brig. Gen. John P. Hatch, chose not to advance when he learned that Maj. Gen. Richard S. Ewell's Confederate infantry division had reached Gordonsville. Disgusted with the cavalryman but undaunted, Pope ordered another foray against the railroad, to be led this time by Col. Judson Kilpatrick of the Second New York Cavalry. Kilpatrick's Empire Staters caused minimal damage but their success encouraged the Union commander to act against the Virginia Central one more time. When Hatch's second foray failed on July 24, Pope relieved him of command. The commander himself had not even accompanied his army into the field—he had remained in Washington, waiting to meet with Halleck to plan out the coming campaign.[17]

Stonewall Jackson carefully watched Pope's movements, sizing up his enemy and patiently waiting for an opportunity to strike. However, with only 13,000 men to oppose Pope's force of 45,000, he would need reinforcements if he had any real hope of doing more than simply annoying Pope. On July 27, Lee decided to reinforce Jackson with Maj. Gen. A. P. Hill's division and a brigade of Louisianans. Jackson's reinforced army was now strong enough to strike a blow against Pope. Hill's division arrived at Gordonsville on July 29, and Jackson began planning in earnest.

Coincidentally, Pope left Washington on July 29 and took command of his army that afternoon. His troops were "in the best of spirits, and an enthusiastic feeling prevailed at the prospect of future 'business,'" recounted a newspaper correspondent attached to Pope's headquarters.[18] On August 3, Pope promised General-in-Chief Maj. Gen. Henry W. Halleck, "Unless [Jackson] is heavily reinforced from Richmond I shall be in possession of Gordonsville and Charlottesville within ten days." On August 6, he ordered his army to concentrate at Culpeper, where he planned to move against Jackson's left in the hope of driving the Confederates back and cutting the Virginia Central between Gordonsville and Charlottesville.[19]

With McClellan's army being pulled from the Peninsula, Halleck instructed Pope to maintain a line along the Rapidan and Rappahannock Rivers. Halleck also ordered Pope to maintain his left near Fredericksburg in order to remain in contact with Maj. Gen. Jesse Reno's division of Maj. Gen. Ambrose E. Burnside's Ninth Corps infantry, which was coming to reinforce Pope from coastal North Carolina. Pope began moving toward Culpeper, a move that Jackson watched carefully, all the while searching for a chance to strike. "Nearly the whole Army of Virginia is now on the move forward in the direction of the enemy," reported a correspondent of the *New York Times* that day.[20] The Army of Virginia was finally in motion, and there would be no turning back.

On August 7, Jackson learned of Pope's move, and also learned that Banks' corps was isolated near Culpeper while Sigel's corps stopped at Sperryville. Jackson got his command moving, looking to defeat Banks in detail. However, his vaunted "foot cavalry," known for covering incredible distances in a single day of marching, covered only ten miles that day, and lost its opportunity to catch Banks by surprise. On August 8, Pope ordered Sigel to march to Culpeper with alacrity, reporting the advance of the enemy. Sigel marched within the hour, but his command did not reach Culpeper until late in the day on August 9, but it was already too late.[21] That morning, Jackson attacked Banks at Cedar Mountain, eight miles south of Culpeper. A day-long, bitter, see-saw fight ensued that inflicted heavy losses on both sides. However, at the end of the day, Jackson held the field. Cedar Mountain marked the beginning of the end for Pope.[22]

Characteristically, Ully rode ahead of Sigel's corps, arriving while the battle still raged.[23] Sigel and the rest of his staff arrived later that day, and took up a position where they could see an advanced Confederate battery about thirteen hundred yards or so away. Dahlgren immediately asked permission to advance a battery to a point where it could enfilade the enemy guns from a distance of 700-800 yards. Ully personally positioned the guns, "and then sighted each gun myself, and gave the order to fire by section; which being done, the rebel battery ceased firing and retreated through the woods, leaving the captain, a lieutenant, and fourteen horses dead on the hill." The next morning, he rode out to examine the ground and determined that the artillery fire that had inflicted such severe damage came from the direction of the battery placed by Dahlgren, which drove the enemy off. General Sigel publicly commended Ulric on the battlefield the next day.[24] Once again, Dahlgren had demonstrated his coolness under fire. He was rapidly making himself indispensable to Sigel.

By August 10, Pope's entire army had concentrated at Culpeper. Realizing he risked his entire command if he stayed where he was, Jackson ordered his army to withdraw across the Rapidan on the evening of August 11. While Jackson gained little tactically from his slugging brutal match with Banks, the fight at Cedar Mountain shook John Pope, who suddenly turned passive and went on the defensive, abandoning the initiative to Jackson.[25] On August 13, Pope ordered Sigel to make a reconnaissance in force in the direction of Slaughter Mountain. Sigel soon encountered enemy infantry and cavalry, prompting Ulric Dahlgren to deploy his artillery in response. A spirited artillery duel broke out, and the Federals discovered that Jackson had withdrawn. With that, the reconnaissance in force ended and Sigel returned to his camps.[26]

Jackson's army pulled back into Orange County, returning to its old camps around Gordonsville. With the help of his trusted map-maker, Jedediah Hotchkiss, Jackson began planning his next move. Solid intelligence verifying McClellan's withdrawal from the Peninsula allowed R. E. Lee to reinforce Jackson. On August 13, per Lee's orders, ten brigades of Maj. Gen. James Longstreet's First Corps, Army of Northern Virginia, boarded the Virginia Central railroad bound for Gordonsville to join Jackson. Their arrival eradicated Pope's manpower advantage.[27] "Everybody feels satisfied that [Stonewall Jackson] is in the right place, and will pounce upon Pope when and where he least expects an attack," prophetically declared a Confederate soldier.[28]

While Lee made his bold move, Pope remained inactive, his confidence shaken. His army camped on the Rapidan with his left, under Maj. Gen. Jesse Reno, at Raccoon Ford, the center, under McDowell, occupying both flanks of Cedar Mountain, and his right, under Sigel, extending to Robertson's Run. He soon learned that Lee was sending massive reinforcements to Jackson from Richmond, which further weakened his resolve. His army was ripe for the picking; if Longstreet could link up with Jackson before Pope moved, they would trap Pope's army in the triangle of land between the Rapidan and Rappahannock Rivers. Robert E. Lee himself set off to join Jackson on August 15.

By August 16, Sigel was in position along the banks of the Rapidan River. That day, an enemy force feinted a crossing of the river but met stout resistance from Sigel's corps, which drove the sortie across. "All is quiet," reported a correspondent of the *New York Times* in the wake of the repulse of the Confederates foray.[29] Even though Pope had little respect for Sigel's abilities, he nevertheless gave the German's troops the most difficult and most important assignments, and they continued to perform well under difficult conditions.

On August 18, as Longstreet's corps embarked to join Jackson, Maj. Gen. J.E.B. Stuart's cavalry camped around Verdiersville, a small settlement on the Orange Plank Road. Stuart intended to meet Brig. Gen. Fitzhugh Lee there, and sent his adjutant general, Maj. Norman FitzHugh, ahead to find him and bring Lee to the cavalry chief's headquarters. While his adjutant searched for the missing Lee, Stuart and his staff retired for the evening. Instead of finding Lee, FitzHugh found 1,000 Yankee horse soldiers, commanded by Col. Thornton Brodhead of the 1st Michigan Cavalry, on a raid far from the bulk of Pope's army. The blue-clad troopers captured FitzHugh and came within a whisker of capturing Stuart himself at the Rhodes house. Stuart escaped by jumping his horse over a fence, losing his trademark plumed hat and his silk-lined cape among the booty taken from the Rhodes house by Brodhead's men. But it was Major FitzHugh who proved to be the real bonanza for the Federal riders. The hapless young man happened to be carrying important dispatches, including an order from Lee to Stuart which laid out the Confederate plan for destroying Pope's army before reinforcements from McClellan's army could reach him.[30]

As a result, Pope discovered just what a precarious position he occupied, and hastily retreated from his exposed location. "Everything from Gen. Pope's army indicates preparation for a desperate struggle," observed a newspaper correspondent on August 18.[31] He pulled all the way back to the Rappahannock River, concentrating his army from Rappahannock Station to Kelly's Ford, several miles to the south. However, morale remained high. "This army is not running away, nor is Gen. Pope outgeneraled yet by Stonewall Jackson," recounted an officer assigned to Army of Virginia headquarters. "Threatened on the left flank, threatened by an army that counts its hundreds of thousands of miserable and desperate troops, the Army of Virginia retreats indeed, but it retreats to fight by daylight. The battles of this war are about to begin."[32] Sigel's corps held the right, extending north almost all the way to Beverly's Ford. Reinforcements from McClellan's army—in the form of Maj. Gen. Fitz-John Porter's Fifth Corps and Maj. Gen. William B. Franklin's Sixth Corps—would be sent to Pope's aid. The first of these men did not reach Pope's army until August 22.

Pope had two options—he could either fall back behind Cedar Run, find a strong defensive position and wait for the rest of McClellan's army to get there, or he could take a more aggressive posture by crossing the Rappahannock, pivoting northward, and then attacking the enemy's flank and rear. Pope preferred the more aggressive option, and when he asked Halleck's opinion, the general-in-chief agreed that the latter option was the better one. Pope wanted to re-take the lost initiative.[33]

However, before he could move, heavy rains set in, and the level of the Rappahannock rose too high for Pope's army to ford. The floodwater washed away a temporary bridge constructed by his engineers the day before. He abandoned his aggressive plan, and instead held his position along the banks of the river. Consequently, the Confederates continued to hold the initiative for the entire campaign. Jackson made the best of that opportunity.

Lee learned of Pope's retreat at mid-day on August 19. He now had Pope just where he wanted him, and he intended to pounce on his army before Porter's men could arrive. The Army of Northern Virginia reached the Rappahannock on August 21, and artillery skirmishing broke out along the opposing lines. Confederate cavalry, probing the strength of Pope's flank, pushed across the Rappahannock and advanced on Sigel's position near Beverly's Ford. Ully Dahlgren, who was now acting as Sigel's *de facto* chief of artillery, "went out looking around with a few cavalry," and discovered the Confederate advance. With enemy cavalry chasing him, Dahlgren galloped back to Pope's headquarters and breathlessly announced that the enemy was "trying to outflank us." The response surprised him. "Pope ridiculed us, but told Sigel to keep his eye on the place."[34]

Fortunately, Sigel did much more than that. He sent a brigade forward to reinforce his flank and to drive back the aggressive Confederate cavalry. He succeeded, discouraging Jackson from attempting a crossing in force at Beverly's Ford. When the Confederates tried to push across the river, supported by artillery, one of Dahlgren's batteries replied. "In a little while our fire slackened, and then ceased, having apparently been silenced or withdrawn," noted a reporter. Three rebel regiments rushed across the ford, with no resistance. "No sooner had they crossed than Sigel opened his battery," continued the reporter, and the accurate artillery fire, combined with "a deadly fire of musketry assailed the rebels in front. Their retreat was cut off, no hope being left. A few shots from our battery, a charge, and they are ours. Not one man escaped."[35] Through diligence and effective and accurate intelligence gathering, Dahlgren prevented the enemy from outflanking Pope's army. "On Thursday morning, five regiments of the enemy, cavalry and infantry, crossed the river on a pontoon bridge, which they had built during the previous night, almost walking into the masked batteries of Gen. Sigel, which opened upon them with canister and grape, mowing them down by the scores."[36]

The next day, August 22, seeing that Stuart had withdrawn his cavalry from his front, Sigel pushed a regiment of infantry and a regiment of cavalry across the Rapidan at Freeman's Ford. "There was evidently no strong force of the enemy on this side of the river," Sigel reported early that afternoon.[37] The going was slow; Sigel's wagons constantly bogged down in the thick Virginia mud. After advancing about two miles in the direction of Sulphur Springs, a heavy skirmish broke out, with enemy artillery fire taking a heavy toll on the advancing Federals. "The shells fell around us as thick as hail," noted one South Carolinian. "The air above our heads was fairly rent with the shrieks of the cannon balls and shells bursting. It was truly dreadful."[38] Ulric noted, "We fought all day—used up nearly all our artillery ammunition."[39] Among the casualties was Union Brig. Gen. Henry Bohlen, killed in the day's fighting. Sigel brought up reinforcements.

Sigel put Dahlgren in charge of three regiments of infantry and three pieces of artillery, with directions to harass the enemy's left and also to outflank it if possible. After a rapid and hard march, Dahlgren found the enemy's flank and deployed his guns near a stand of woods held by men of Confederate Brig. Gen. Jubal A. Early's Virginia infantry brigade. However, his men could see little through the darkness and dense woods, and their first artillery volley did little damage. The Union infantry gave three cheers as it prepared to charge the woods, but no attack came. Instead, Early brought up a couple of his own guns and opened on Dahlgren's pieces. "This fire was so well directed," Early reported, "that the enemy was thrown into confusion and driven back, as was manifest from the cries and groans of his men, which were plainly heard by ours."[40] Another Confederate said "but for the river, [we] would have carried their battery."[41] Under the cover of night, and worried about having a raging torrent at their backs, the Confederates withdrew. Although his task force had not accomplished much other than to make a lot of smoke and noise, Dahlgren had "executed to the full satisfaction" of Sigel his orders, prompting the German to write, "Captain Dahlgren's services, generally, on the line of the Rappahannock, where he was continuously engaged in meeting the enemy's batteries with our own, to facilitate thereby the march of our troops and trains alongside of the river, were most valuable."[42]

Pope's army reached Warrenton on the morning of August 24 and prepared to move on Sulphur Springs in force. When Pope learned that Early had pulled back, he ordered Sigel to advance as far as Waterloo Bridge, about four miles above Sulphur Springs. Neither army had the advantage; the best they could do was to trade volleys of artillery fire across the river. On August 25, Sigel faced a large force of enemy infantry and artillery at Waterloo Bridge. Pope ordered Sigel to "hold my position at Waterloo Bridge under all circumstances and to meet the enemy if he should try to force the passage of the river." By mid-day, Sigel believed that the enemy intended to attack and asked Reno and Banks for reinforcements. Sigel was astonished to learn that Reno and Banks had already marched south, leaving his corps alone and unsupported at the bridge. When conflicting orders arrived, Sigel looked for help but could obtain no guidance from anyone. Unsure what to do, he set Waterloo Bridge ablaze and marched for Fayetteville at dusk. Not long after departing, Sigel received orders from Pope to march to Warrenton instead.

As the head of his column reached Warrenton, one of McDowell's staff officers met Sigel with orders from Pope: Sigel was to turn around, return to Waterloo Bridge, and "force a passage" at daylight. Of course, Sigel had burned the bridge that afternoon, meaning that he could not obey Pope's orders. Fed up, Sigel rode to Pope's headquarters to protest the orders. Pope received him hostilely, dressing down the German general in such harsh terms that Sigel asked to be relieved of command. Pope denied the request immediately. Undaunted, Sigel made his case, and Pope eventually relented, permitting the German and his weary troops to stay in Warrenton that night. Instead, McDowell's corps made the return trek to the river the next morning.[43]

However, Pope was livid. "McDowell's is the only corps that is at all reliable that I have," he complained to Stanton that night. "Sigel, as you know, is perfectly unreliable, and I suggest that some officer of superior rank be sent to command his army corps. His conduct to-day has occasioned me great dissatisfaction." He concluded, "Sigel's corps, although composed of some of the best fighting material we have, will never do much service under that officer."[44]

In fact, Sigel performed admirably during this phase of the campaign. One of his staff officers later observed, "Never was a trust more worthily bestowed and executed with more fidelity and sleepless activity. At every ford of the Rappahannock, extending for a distance of over fifteen miles, from Waterloo Bridge down to Kelly's Ford, Lee was met and foiled in every attempt to cross the river." He concluded, "Fighting him at Kelly and Freeman's Fords, Rappahannock Station, Great Run, Sulphur Springs and Waterloo Bridge, it was a wonder at the time, to those in the military family of General Sigel, how it was possible to ascertain where the enemy would strike, and in every instance to meet him with a force adequate to repel the attack."[45] As Sigel's acting chief of artillery, Ully Dahlgren played an integral role in these actions.

Pope's personal dislike of Sigel undoubtedly tainted his perceptions of the German's performance. Sigel was personally very brave, and his men liked and respected him. At least some of Pope's criticisms of Sigel were unwarranted and unfair. His animosity toward Sigel prevented the corps commander from getting credit for the things he did well and likewise kept his men from receiving their due.

Robert E. Lee knew that Pope's army grew stronger with each passing day, as more reinforcements from McClellan's army arrived. Thus, Lee had to do something dramatic to break the stalemate soon, or he would lose the opportunity and Pope's force soon would outnumber him by a substantial margin. Realizing that he had to gamble, Lee decided to split his army, sending Jackson and 24,000 men on a flanking march intended to pull Pope's army away from the Rappahannock River. If he succeeded, Longstreet, with the rest of the Army of Northern Virginia, would then close the pincers on Pope's army.[46]

By early evening on August 24, Jackson had set his command in motion, and by the next day, he had passed around Pope's flank undetected. He reached Salem, twelve miles north of Pope's right flank, after a thirty-five mile forced march. The next day, Jackson's so-called "foot cavalry" passed through Thoroughfare Gap, and made it to Bristoe Station by sunset. Jackson reached Manassas Junction on August 27, where his army enjoyed the bounty of the huge Union supply depot there.[47]

Pope had scattered the elements of his army, and he had to countermand previous orders and re-concentrate his army before he could respond. Consequently, the Army of Virginia did not pursue Jackson's bold gambit until August 27. His army, now reinforced with two corps from the Army of the Potomac, divided into three columns, with Sigel's corps marching with McDowell's and with McDowell in command of the combined column. They reached their objective, Gainesville, that night. The Army of Virginia concentrated there and then began moving to try to squeeze Jackson's corps near Manassas Junction the next day. Pope was so focused on Jackson's force that he did not look to his rear, and was utterly unaware that Longstreet, with the other half of the Army of Northern Virginia, was rapidly closing from the west, preparing to close a great pincers movement on him. Knowing that Longstreet was coming to his aid, Jackson decided to try to draw Pope's army into a decisive battle and then wait for Longstreet to arrive. He took up a concealed position on the old Bull Run battlefield, and waited for Pope to arrive and attack him there. Uncharacteristically, Jackson intended to fight a defensive battle, letting Pope bring the fight to him.

Ulric Dahlgren was his usual active and diligent self during the Army of Virginia's advance. "I am nearly worn out,—going day and night & Sigel always sends for me when anything is to be done," he informed his father on the 26th. "I have more to do than any other officer here." However, in spite of his exhaustion, he was "determined to see the matter through,—Jackson or ourselves whipped; and if they can keep us supplied with ammunition, we will fight them forever." Although Ulric Dahlgren was still only twenty years old, he had duties and responsibilities far beyond his age. As he told his father, "They think I am a regular from artillery here & I can just control the whole artillery in the fight as I have done on several occasions in the heavy fights."[48]

By this time, Dahlgren shared Sigel's views on the army commander. "General Pope is a perfect brute," he declared to his father. "Gives the most conflicting orders & scarcely knows what he does half the time." Later in the same letter, he noted, "Pope & McDowell always stay together & are both incompetent." Dahlgren related the Waterloo Bridge episode, and then told his father, "when it was too late he used such offensive language that Sigel asked to be relieved. Sigel is the man and wanted to attack in the first place, but Pope did not & so we have done nothing but fight running, occasionally making a good break."[49]

The travails of the hard campaigning season also weighed heavily on Dahlgren's mount. "My horse has been injured—he kicks very badly & in doing so strained his leg," Ulric informed his father on August 27. "Then the way we are moving would kill any horse, which I don't intend shall be my case." Ully sent the horse back to Washington with his orderly, with a request that his father take care of the horse in the hope that it would recuperate quickly. "I have used up 3 or 4 horses," he concluded. And the army still had not met Jackson on the field of battle. Plenty more hard work remained to be done.[50]

On August 28, Sigel sent Ulric to locate McDowell and obtain definite instructions from him. His current orders directed him to halt in position and form line of battle with his right resting on the Manassas Railroad about a mile from Gainesville. Dahlgren found McDowell sitting under a tree studying a map, a mile and a half to the rear of Sigel's position. Ulric told the general that an aide had brought Sigel an order to halt where he was and form line, with his right resting on the railroad. The German wanted more definite instructions. McDowell replied that he had not sent any order to halt, or any other order, for that matter, after the order for Sigel to march to Manassas. Ulric asked McDowell to elaborate on where they were to form at Manassas. McDowell, annoyed by the request, snapped, "Let General Sigel fight his own corps." As Dahlgren departed, McDowell added that Sigel should be particular to take the nearest road to Manassas, and pointed out a road on the map that went off to the right and near the railroad, and not the road that he had used.[51]

Sigel's men skirmished with small contingents of the enemy that whole day, so the presence of the enemy near Manassas Junction was no secret. From the many stragglers captured along the way, Dahlgren learned that a significant force of the enemy was near Groveton, presumably Jackson's command after leaving Manassas Junction. When Pope heard this intelligence, he began shifting troops in that direction, hoping to catch Jackson and beat his army. Thus, the stage was set for the disaster that would befall Pope.[52]

On August 28 and 29, Jackson's command took up positions on the historic First Bull Run battlefield, occupying high ground, and preparing to fight a defensive battle. Jackson intended to lure Pope into a fight, and he took steps to provoke one. Maj. Gen. Richard S. Ewell's division extended Jackson's line west along the Warrenton Turnpike to Groveton. Squabbling among Pope's corps commanders slowed his advance toward Manassas to a crawl, meaning that Jackson had a long wait and plenty of time to prepare.

However, when Confederate artillery posted at Groveton near John Brawner's farmhouse spotted the head of McDowell's column advancing east on the Warrenton Turnpike late on the afternoon of August 29, Jackson finally got the long-coveted opportunity. He waited until McDowell's troops were literally under the barrels of his guns, and then ordered the attack. Although Pope had ordered McDowell to face about in an effort to block Longstreet's approach, a large-scale infantry engagement broke out on the grounds of the Brawner farm that lasted until well after dark. Finally, the outnumbered Federals broke off and withdrew that night. Pope found Jackson, just as Jackson hoped he would. Jackson then assumed a strong defensive position along an unfinished railroad cut which offered his men a natural breastwork and excellent protection.[53]

While Jackson prepared his position, Longstreet's Corps marched toward a junction with Stonewall's men. Longstreet had to pass through Thoroughfare Gap to get to the old Bull Run battlefield, and recognizing that the Gap was a choke point, McDowell took steps to blockade it. He directed a division of infantry to hold the Gap. Troopers of the 1st New Jersey Cavalry detected Longstreet's approach and sent back word of the approach of the grayclad infantry on August 28. Union infantry came up at the double-quick, and a stiff skirmish developed as Longstreet attempted to force a passage. The Confederates finally drove off the pesky Union infantry, clearing Thoroughfare Gap. Pope failed to realize how important a stout defense of the Gap could be and thus lost an opportunity to prevent Longstreet from linking up with Jackson in time to make a difference. Longstreet pressed on, with Pope largely oblivious to the danger that awaited him if the two forces linked up.[54]

That night, Pope ordered his army to move on Jackson. The Federal believed he had intercepted Jackson's army during a retreat from Centreville. Sigel would join the division of Maj. Gen. Philip Kearny and lead the attack on Jackson's position at daylight. Sigel did not know the precise location of Jackson's army, or how strong it was, and asked Maj. Gen. John F. Reynolds to assist him. Reynolds agreed, casting the die for Sigel's advance on August 29.[55]

With Dahlgren in tow, Sigel spent several hours reconnoitering the ground to the north and west of the old battlefield near Henry House Hill. He learned that Jackson's troops occupied the wooded slopes north of the Warrenton Turnpike in force, but he could not locate the enemy's specific positions. Accordingly, Sigel planned to advance along a two-mile front, feeling for Jackson's main position. Supported by artillery on high ground to his rear called Chinn Ridge, Sigel's command lurched forward at daybreak. Before long, nearly all of Sigel's 9,000 man corps was fully engaged in fierce fighting.[56]

Sigel's corps spent all of August 29 launching uncoordinated and disorganized assaults on Jackson's position on the unfinished railroad cut. His men bore the brunt of the fighting until Pope brought up additional forces to join them, and they took heavy casualties in the close fighting.[57] Sigel committed battery after battery to the fight, with Ulric Dahlgren riding the lines, seeing to the guns under his command.[58] As the fighting lapped back and forth likes waves on a beach, elements of Longstreet's corps began arriving on the field and connected with Jackson's line, extending it to the west and beginning to even the numeric odds. The German's men fought well, but accomplished nothing of any real value. After a day of fierce fighting that saw the repulse of a Confederate counterattack, Sigel prematurely declared that he had "broken the enemy's resistance" and that "victory was on our side."[59] His exhausted men slept on their arms that night.

Pope ordered Maj. Gen. Philip Kearny to support Sigel's attacks that day. His division extended the Union right, coming into line alongside Sigel's corps. Kearny did not like Pope, and was in no hurry to support Sigel, whom he viewed as extremely arrogant. Kearny refused to attack, declaring, "To hell with General Pope, we'll march in the morning." Had he been even remotely diligent in supporting Sigel's attacks, Jackson's men would have been hard pressed to meet the threat to Jackson's flank. A properly supported attack might have pierced Jackson's line and caused a real crisis for the Confederates, who had no available reinforcements. However, Kearny's recalcitrance cost the Union army its best opportunity to defeat Jackson that day. Had Kearny not died a hero's death two days later, he probably would have faced a court-martial for his gross insubordination. Instead, Kearny frittered away the opportunity.[60]

The next morning, August 30, Pope intended to renew the attack with the Fifth Corps of Maj. Gen. Fitz-John Porter and with Sigel's battered corps. Pope had wanted Porter to attack on the 29th, but Porter spotted Longstreet's Corps moving into position on his flank and declined to attack for fear of exposing his flank to a powerful force of the enemy.[61] Pope persuaded Porter to attack on the 30th, but once he did, Porter committed his entire force to the fight, and his men fought well. Porter assaulted a portion of the unfinished railroad known as the Deep Cut (named for the depth of the sunken railroad bed) with nearly 12,000 men. Jackson repulsed the attack with heavy losses on both sides. Supporting the Fifth Corps attack, Sigel deployed his infantry atop Chinn and Dogan's Ridges. While the fighting for the Deep Cut raged, Pope received multiple reports that the enemy had been seen moving near his left flank. Believing that he had broken Jackson's corps, and that Jackson was retreating, Pope refused to listen to reports that Longstreet's infantry was massing to attack his flank in force. He did nothing but send out a cavalry patrol on the army's right flank, and he instead insisted on "pursuing" the allegedly retreating rebels.[62]

After the repulse of Porter's attack, Longstreet launched a massive counterattack that routed the Federal troops operating on Pope's flank and then slammed into Sigel's position. By 5:00 in the afternoon, his men made a desperate stand intended to hold back Lee's army long enough for the rest of the Army of Virginia to withdraw. Badly beaten, Pope abandoned the battlefield, leaving his subordinates in command while he rode off. The victorious Confederates finally drove the desperate last stand of Robert Milroy's division of Sigel's corps from Henry House Hill and sent Pope reeling back across Bull Run toward Centreville. The defeated Army of Virginia spent a miserable, rainy night there. "We have whipped them nearly back into Washington," proudly declared a victorious Southerner.[63]

Sigel himself received several wounds in this fighting. His men fought bravely, their stand on Chinn Ridge buying precious time for the bulk of the army to escape. However, Lincoln's hand-chosen commander suffered a crushing and humiliating defeat, and morale deteriorated greatly as a result. "So long as the interests of our country are entrusted to a lying braggart like Pope, or a foolish little Dutchman like Sigel, we have little reason to hope successfully to compete with any army led by Lee, Johnston, and old 'Stonewall Jackson,'" complained a disgusted Federal staff officer in the wake of the defeat.[64]

Ulric Dahlgren acquitted himself well during the ferocious fighting at Second Bull Run. "In the melee of operations, Ulric Dahlgren did the part assigned to him with his wonted zeal and gallantry," recalled his father. His steady performance earned Sigel's praise. "At the battles of Bull Run and Groveton, on the 29th and 30th of August, he was, almost without interruption, engaged in planting or relieving our batteries, under the most galling fire of the enemy," Sigel wrote.[65]

On August 31, Pope's demoralized and disorganized army hastily retreated from the chaotic battlefield. "I think confidence is lost in General Pope," declared one of his soldiers that day. "Tonight an officer of some prominence, who was in the fight, announces, after visiting the War Office, that tomorrow morning will see a new Commander in the field. Whom it can be, I can only guess."[66] Sigel spent the day pulling his scattered divisions back together and restoring some degree of unit cohesiveness. John Pope himself was a beaten man. "I should like to know whether you feel secure about Washington should this army be destroyed," he inquired of Halleck. "I shall fight as long as a man will stand up to the work. You must judge what is to be done, having in view the safety of the capital."[67]

Pope called a council of his senior commanders, who unanimously agreed that the army was in no condition to resume the offensive and that it should retreat to the outer defenses of Washington. However, as the conference concluded, an order arrived from Halleck. "You have done nobly," declared the general-in-chief. "Don't yield another inch if you can avoid it. All reserves are being sent forward . . . Can't you renew the attack?"[68] Pope announced that he had been ordered to remain at Centreville, and he declared that he would stand pat, his army still exposed and with Lee's victorious troops just five miles away. Lee was already preparing his next move—another rapid movement around his right flank that would cut the Army of Virginia off from the strong Union defenses at Centreville. Pope would either have to retreat or fight his way out.[69]

Plagued by a steady rain, Jackson's column moved out at midday on August 31. After covering fifty-four miles in thirty-six hours and then fighting a major three-day battle, Jackson's exhausted men did not make much progress that afternoon. They marched until well after dark, covering only ten miles in eight hours. Pope had no idea that Jackson's corps was on the move, and did nothing to prepare for it. Instead, he was busy blaming his subordinates—especially Porter—for his defeat and feeling sorry for himself. When Union cavalry detected the movement of a large body of Confederates around his flank, Pope finally snapped out of his reverie and began making preparations. "This movement turns Centreville and interposes between us and Washington, and will force me to attack his advance, which I shall do as soon as his movement is sufficiently developed," he informed Halleck on September 1. "The fight will necessarily be desperate. I hope you will make all preparations to make a vigorous defense of the intrenchments around Washington."[70]

He reacted quickly and had his command moving from Centreville to Germantown to block Jackson's march to Fairfax by 3:00 that afternoon. However, his whole army did not make this movement; Maj. Gen. William B. Franklin's Sixth Corps from the Army of the Potomac, Sigel's, Porter's, Banks' Corps and part of the newly-arrived Second Corps of the Army of the Potomac remained at Centreville, as did Pope and his headquarters and staff. At 5:00 that afternoon, in a ferocious thunderstorm, Maj. Gen. Isaac Stevens' Ninth Corps division attacked Jackson on Ox Hill, near Chantilly. Two hours of heavy fighting ensued that led to the deaths of Stevens and Maj. Gen. Philip Kearny. The fighting finally sputtered out when darkness fell, but Jackson's flanking maneuver had been blocked.[71] That night Pope ordered his entire army to retreat to the defenses of Washington. Only Pope's prompt reaction to learning of Jackson's flank movement saved his army from destruction and allowed it to fall back to the protection of the ring of forts surrounding the nation's capital.

On September 2, Lincoln swallowed his pride and asked George B. McClellan to assume command of the capital's defenses, and the Army of Virginia's short and unhappy life came to an end. Pope's army was absorbed into the

Army of the Potomac.[72] John Pope was unceremoniously relieved of command and exiled to Minnesota to fight Indians, never again to command troops in a major theater of the war. On September 3, Sigel, his staff, and his battered corps arrived at McClellan's headquarters near Langley, where his men now occupied a sector of the defenses of Washington.[73] The Second Bull Run Campaign, which began with so much bombast and promise, ended in catastrophic defeat.

With his pressing duties as Sigel's chief of artillery more than occupying his time, Ulric had not written to his father or let him know that he was safe and unharmed. John Dahlgren, keenly aware of the magnitude of the Union defeat at Second Bull Run, was worried sick about his favorite son. He dispatched Ulric's older brother Charley to the field to render aid to Ully if he was wounded and needed it. Charley, a third assistant engineer in the Navy, who was serving as a volunteer aide and bearer of dispatches, happily learned that his brother survived the storm of battle unharmed, and the brothers enjoyed a brief reunion.[74] On September 3, with Sigel's corps now safely ensconced in the defenses of the national capital, Ulric got permission to ride into Washington, and Charley accompanied him on the ride to the Washington Navy Yard.[75]

Ulric Dahlgren performed very well in the Second Bull Run Campaign. At the tender age of twenty, he spent the campaign serving as the chief of ordnance and *de facto* chief of artillery for Sigel's First Corps, commanding approximately sixty pieces, including veteran Regulars, in a pitched battle in spite of his lack of any formal military training whatsoever. "I gave him charge of the ordnance department," wrote Sigel, "which duties he fulfilled with great energy and ability."[76] He earned the praise of his commander and the respect of the men who served under him. Good luck seemed to bless him. "While many a brave commander and gallant soldier fell beside him, it seemed as though an invisible hand had covered him from the iron ball through which he so often rode," observed Reverend Sunderland in 1864. "He had done good work in the Mountain Department, and afterwards at Warrenton, at Gainesville, at Manassas, at Centreville, at Fairfax, in the Second Battle of Bull Run, and, in truth, over the whole seat of war in Virginia between the Potomac and Rapidan."[77]

CHAPTER SIX

Dahlgren Shows a Talent
for Scouting Missions

W HEN ULRIC AND CHARLES DAHLGREN arrived in Washington, they
headed straight for the Navy Yard, where Ulric pleasantly surprised
his father with an unexpected visit. "He was thinned indeed by hardship and
exposure, soiled with the dust of the march, and bronzed by the fervent rays of
the August sun," recalled his father, "but unhurt and in vigorous health." John
Dahlgren listened attentively to his son's accounts of his adventures, including "much to tell that was sad and unwelcome," but he noted that, in spite of
the hardships of the recent campaign, his son's spirits were good, and that his
youthful optimism remained unshaken by his experiences in the field.[1]

As father and son departed the back door of the Navy Department offices,
they encountered Abraham Lincoln, who was passing from the War Department back to the White House. Lincoln hailed them, brought them into the
entrance of the War Department, and began grilling Ulric about the Second
Bull Run campaign and battles. Lincoln intently listened to Ully's account, and
"seemed satisfied with the statements thus received; as less saddening than
others which were current; for, as yet, the details of recent operations were but
imperfectly known even at headquarters." Young Dahlgren had a gift for concise, insightful reports, and he patiently answered the President's many questions about Pope's recent debacle.[2]

Following up on his crushing defeat of Pope, Robert E. Lee sought and
obtained permission to invade the North. On September 6, the Army of Northern Virginia splashed across the Potomac River at White's Ford, upstream from
Washington, and headed into Maryland, hoping to spare Virginia from the
ravages of war and looking to gather supplies and recruits. If the opportunity
presented itself, Lee intended to cross the Mason-Dixon Line into Pennsylvania. That night, Lee's army camped in and around Frederick, Maryland, where
it rested and gathered supplies from the rich countryside until September 10.[3]

Not surprisingly, news that Lee's army had crossed the Potomac River and
lay less than fifty miles from Washington triggered panic in the national capital. Pope was formally relieved of command on September 6, and Maj. Gen.
George B. McClellan assumed command of the troops assigned to defend

the capital. He faced a daunting task—melding Pope's demoralized units into the Army of the Potomac, re-supplying those units that had raced back from the Peninsula without their wagon trains, and integrating regiments of new recruits into an effective and efficient army under crisis circumstances. Further, McClellan had to cull out those commanders he did not want, such as Irvin McDowell, who had not done well in either of the two battles at Bull Run. McClellan accomplished a great deal under intense pressure in a short period of time, restoring morale and his army to fighting trim in less than a week. This marked McClellan's finest hour.[4]

As part of this reorganization, Sigel's First Corps was absorbed into the Army of the Potomac and re-designated as the Eleventh Corps. His circumstances displeased Sigel. The German general correctly deduced that Pope had not wanted him in his army, felt that he had been in the way of both Pope and McDowell, and intimated that he would resign his commission if he did not receive an independent command.[5] Stanton took his time responding, leaving the German twisting in the breeze. The War Department's shabby treatment of Sigel did not go unnoticed; one Chicago newspaper declared, "Either dismiss Sigel as incompetent, or treat him fairly. Let us see one and same rule applied to all officers, whether they come from West Point or from over the sea."[6] No resolution or independent command was forthcoming, however. Instead, his troops assumed a position between Forts DeKalb and Ethan Allen. They were to guard the Virginia approach to the Chain Bridge across the Potomac River while acting as a corps of observation.[7] After reporting to Banks on September 7, Sigel marched to Fairfax Court House on September 21, where the Eleventh Corps added a third division.

On September 25, Sigel established his headquarters at Fairfax Court House, covering the critical Orange & Alexandria Railroad.[8] The Eleventh Corps spent the rest of September and most of October resting and refitting, enjoying a pleasant respite after the trials and tribulations of the spring and summer. His troops spent their days drilling and training and carefully observing and recording the enemy's activities and dispositions in the vicinity of Fairfax Court House. In order to keep his men sharp and ready for action, Sigel sent them out on frequent reconnaissance missions in the direction of the Rappahannock River and the Bull Run Mountains.

Ulric made regular excursions into Washington, volunteering for various errands for Sigel, or to see about obtaining additional ordnance supplies for the Eleventh Corps. While in Washington on such an errand on September 13, he stopped by the Naval Bureau of Ordnance to visit his father. When Ulric arrived, Captain Dahlgren was chatting with Maj. Gen. Joseph K. F. Mansfield, who, at fifty-nine, was one of the oldest officers still on active duty. He had previously commanded the defenses of Washington and was about to take command of Banks' old Second Corps, now designated as the Army of the Potomac's Twelfth Corps. Mansfield asked Ulric a few questions about conditions in the field, intently listening to the young man's answers. The veteran general joined his corps on September 15. Three days later, Mansfield was dead of combat wounds received while leading his troops in desperate fighting on the extreme right of the Army of the Potomac's line of battle at Antietam.[9]

The 1862 Maryland Campaign climaxed in the Battle of Antietam, fought near Sharpsburg, Maryland on September 17. In a very long day of brutal, close fighting, the butcher's bill was 12,400 Union and 10,320 Confederate casualties. "It was the hardest, most terrific and stubbornly contested battle of this war," correctly declared a member of the 15th Alabama Infantry a few days after the battle.[10] On September 19, Robert E. Lee retreated across the Potomac River and assumed a position in the Loudoun Valley of Virginia, waiting for McClellan to attack him.[11]

Ulric Dahlgren was far from the Antietam battlefield. Instead, he was in Washington for a couple of days, visiting his father and attending to details at the War Department.[12] The booming of the guns could be heard in Washington, and Ulric predictably wanted to pitch into the fray. However, the Eleventh Corps, assigned to the defense of Washington, did not march with the rest of the Army of the Potomac.[13] Thus, he missed the single bloodiest day of the Civil War. His father observed that his thoughts were focused on the ongoing battle. "Over and over, have I seen him mount his horse at my door and move at a slow pace down the street, as if with no particular purpose, when I knew that in a few hours ride he was to be in the midst of battle, for the Rebels were close to Washington," recalled Admiral Dahlgren. "He rarely spoke of the part he had taken or what he would do."[14]

He returned to the Eleventh Corps' lines on September 19, and on September 22, Sigel advanced his command as far as Centreville, where its camps blocked Lee's lines of retreat.[15] The area was bleak and desolate. "The country around Fairfax, Centreville and Manassas, has been completely devastated," observed a Confederate soldier on September 25. "One can get on a high hill and see for miles around bare fields, with not a tree or any sign of civilization; the farm houses are all deserted, and everything as silent as the grave."[16] On September 26, Ulric jotted off a quick letter to his father. "While eating our breakfast we heard that the Corps were moving so we had to fly out & found it so. We were ordered to Fairfax, so we got here last evening and have our position facing S.W. & around the town." He reported that elements of the Eleventh Corps had been sent to guard the Orange & Alexandria at Bristoe Station. "It seems the Rebels are busy fireing the bridges so as to run away with our locomotives taken at Manassas & we are trying to secure them. There is no prospect of moving farther immediately," he concluded.[17] That same day, buoyed by the victory at Antietam, President Lincoln issued the Preliminary Emancipation Proclamation.

Ulric was right. The Eleventh Corps stayed right where it was, guarding the main roads to Washington. With Milroy's division detached and sent to West Virginia, the prospects for active service in the field remained dim for the foreseeable future. They had little to do beside administrative duties and drilling, drilling, and more drilling. The young captain, full of nervous energy and always in search of another adventure, chafed. He regularly volunteered to lead scouting expeditions just to introduce some excitement into an otherwise dull routine. His chance would come—he was about to get all of the adventure that he could hope for.

General Sigel, who had been trained as an artillerist in Germany, and who recognized talent when he saw it, continued to be impressed by his acting chief of artillery. Consequently, the German wanted Dahlgren's appointment as chief of artillery of the Eleventh Corps made permanent. However, that position required a promotion to major, prompting Sigel to pen a letter to Pennsylvania Governor Andrew G. Curtin requesting Ully's promotion in a Keystone State regiment. He described Dahlgren as a "young officer of merit and usefulness, who has already distinguished himself, and reflected much credit on the service." Two eminent naval officers who knew Ulric well, Admirals Joseph Smith and Andrew Foote, endorsed the application. The note also carried another, even more remarkable stamp of approval: Abraham Lincoln's. The President, who had carefully monitored the young man's progress, endorsed the application, writing, "If the within would not violate the Rules let it be done." However, the promotion never came through due to "some difficulties of routine," and Ulric remained a captain and Sigel's acting chief of artillery.[18]

Sigel's corps stayed largely inactive. His ranks remained too depleted for his command to do much, and he had strict orders not to engage the enemy. On September 30, Sigel reported that his command had captured and paroled 1,200 prisoners at Warrenton, that his cavalry was actively patrolling and searching for the whereabouts of the enemy, and that a strong force of the enemy occupied Culpeper.[19] One of McClellan's staff officers reminded Sigel "that your troops are advanced as a corps of observation, and that, if menaced by a superior force of the enemy, you are to fall back to the lines of defense."[20] Other than sending out regular scouting expeditions and reconnaissance missions, there was little to do but to maintain a constant watch on the movements of the enemy. On October 5, a correspondent wrote, "Matters with this corps of the Army of the Potomac have been very quiet for several days past. Small scouting parties are constantly kept out in different directions to keep watch and guard, and to clear the country of rebel bands." The reporter noted, "Gen. Sigel has been promised, and in due time doubtless will receive the much-desired and much needed reinforcements. This can be relied upon."[21]

While Dahlgren chafed, Abraham Lincoln stewed. Frustrated and bitterly disappointed by McClellan's failure to thrash the outnumbered Army of Northern Virginia at Antietam, the President expected the Army of the Potomac to pursue the Confederates into Virginia. Lincoln wanted McClellan to attack Lee again before the Gray Fox withdrew into the heartland of Virginia, and before the critical upcoming mid-term Congressional elections. However, McClellan would not move until he completed the comprehensive strategic plan he was working, and his army had been re-supplied and refitted. He also worried that Lee might re-cross the Potomac River, and wanted to wait for the river to rise high enough that it could not be crossed without pontoon bridges, which Lee did not have. Finally fed up with what he viewed as an unwillingness to fight, Lincoln traveled to McClellan's headquarters in early October and urged his commander to move. Disregarding Lincoln's admonition to move, McClellan continued to work on his plan. Finally, on October 6, the President instructed Halleck to forward a direct order for the Army of the Potomac to cross the Potomac and give battle to Lee.[22] The next day, Halleck wrote, "I am satisfied that the enemy are falling back toward Richmond. We must follow them and seek to punish them."[23]

However, the Army of the Potomac really was in no shape to fight. It was desperately short on shoes, clothing, and blankets. The army "is not in condition to take the field at present. Our men are tired out, and they are out of clothing, discipline, every thing that goes to make efficient soldiers," complained one Union general on October 2.[24] McClellan resisted the order to advance for three long weeks, citing shortages in supplies and ammunition, and the need for reinforcements after the bloodbath at Antietam. He firmly believed that the army needed time to rest, refit, and complete the task of integrating both Pope's army and the raw recruits into the Army of the Potomac before taking the field again. After tackling these problems, McClellan intended to commence a decisive campaign that he hoped would end the war. But these things took time, and time was the one luxury that McClellan could not afford.[25]

Then, in mid-October, events forced McClellan's hand. The Union commander had worried about covering the Potomac River since Antietam, and Halleck rebuffed his efforts to do so. The Union high command was greatly embarrassed when Maj. Gen. J. E. B. Stuart, the Confederate cavalry chieftain, fulfilled McClellan's worst fears by leading 1,800 hand-picked troopers on a three-day raid into southern Pennsylvania, rounding up hundreds of horses and dozens of prisoners. Adding insult to injury, Stuart then safely passed back into Virginia with the loss of only two men. Finally stirred to movement by Lincoln's constant badgering and the embarrassment of what was already being called Stuart's Second Ride Around McClellan, the Army of the Potomac began crossing the Potomac River on October 26.

Little Mac had developed a good plan. Concerned that Lee might use his movement as an opportunity to cross the Potomac River again, McClellan decided to cross into the Shenandoah Valley and attack Lee's rear. If Lee did not try to re-cross the Potomac, the Army of the Potomac would march south, occupying the Blue Ridge gaps on his right until he fell on Lee's army, looking for an opportunity to defeat the Confederates in detail. If Lee fell back to Gordonsville, McClellan would move on Richmond via Fredericksburg, or try the Peninsula again if the Orange & Alexandria Railroad could not adequately supply his army. Fredericksburg, which marked the fall line of the Rappahannock River, was also a critical railroad hub that would provide a good base of supply as well as options for advancing on Richmond. As recently as October 3, Sigel's scouts had entered the town and found it lightly defended by only a few hundred cavalry and three companies of infantry.[26] McClellan's solid plan protected Washington, but still kept the Army of the Potomac on the offensive. Unfortunately, terrible weather slowed his advance to a crawl and gave Lee an opportunity to react and respond.[27]

One column, consisting of the Second and Fifth Corps, was to cross the Shenandoah River at Harpers Ferry, and then push south along the Blue Ridge, while the First, Sixth, and Ninth Corps would cross the Potomac at Berlin, Maryland, cover the Blue Ridge gaps, and operate in the Loudoun Valley between the Blue Ridge and the Bull Run Mountains. The entire command would then head for the Rappahannock River. Even if the plan succeeded, McClellan would end up in the same area where Pope's offensive had bogged down in August. The army commander realized this, but he had no choice. He had been ordered to take the field, and while he preferred operating on the

Peninsula, he had to keep his army between Lee and Washington, D. C. Thus, McClellan had few options available.[28]

The army took six days to complete its passage back into Virginia. McClellan established his headquarters in Leesburg on October 29.[29] "Very little done in the military way," noted John Dahlgren in his diary the next day. "McClellan and the Confederates occupy nearly the same positions as before, between Sharpsburg and Winchester."[30] The Union army fanned out across the Virginia countryside foraging but not doing much to bring Lee to battle. Sigel and the Eleventh Corps remained in position guarding Washington, occasionally throwing out scouting parties to check on the whereabouts of the enemy. Ulric often led these excursions.

The Loudoun Valley of Virginia was prone to guerrilla activities—it soon became the heart of the so-called "Mosby's Confederacy"—which proved a great annoyance to the Army of the Potomac. "The whole region . . . is alive with armed rebels, and not a step can be taken without its being known and announced by signals," declared a newspaper correspondent on October 14.[31] Sigel wanted to rid himself of this terrible nuisance, and sent out scouts to deal with the guerrillas. "Foremost of these dauntless young officers was Ulric Dahlgren—always cool, always reliable, ready for the most hazardous attempt, yet prudent and sagacious," recalled Reverend Sunderland. "He never went forth on these occasions without accomplishing the object designed, and returning crowned with a splendid success."[32] His father observed, "Sometimes he was with General [Julius] Stahel [commander of the cavalry forces assigned to the defenses of Washington], scouring the country in every direction, hunting out the roving marauders who were bent on pillage and plunder, or among the mountain-gaps, or down Bull Run Valley."[33] Ulric had already proven himself an able artillerist. Now, he demonstrated a real talent for the dangerous work of scouting.

Dahlgren and the contingents that he led skirmished with the enemy at Aldie and Upperville, and then fought Confederate cavalry at Warrenton. On another instance, his command fell upon and broke up an enemy camp at Berryville and fought at Gum Creek Church. "On one occasion, it is related that, riding along a solitary road, the whizzing of bullets near his person intimated his being marked by some predatory rifles, and slight puffs of smoke pointed to the ambush of these assassination," described Admiral Dahlgren in 1870. "At such times it is dangerous to pause; quick as thought he went charging to the spot, sword in hand, followed by his two orderlies, and visited prompt retribution on the dastardly miscreants."[34]

On October 25, twenty-eight-year-old Capt. Everton J. Conger of the 3rd West Virginia, a native of northeastern Ohio, along with thirty troopers, went out on a reconnaissance mission. After marching from Warrenton, they clashed with about 250 enemy cavalry near Bristoe Station, attacking and dispersing the Rebel horsemen, killing several and capturing a number of prisoners.[35] During the close, whirling melee, Conger fell from his horse, and was presumed either dead or badly wounded. His routed little band of horse soldiers left for dead. He was missing in action, and Sigel was determined to find out what had happened to the intrepid Mountaineer and his command.[36] There was just one man for a job like that—Ulric Dahlgren.

Leaving at about 11:00 p.m. on October 26, Ully led an expedition of 100 hand-picked troopers on a scout toward Warrenton Junction with the object of ascertaining the whereabouts of the enemy in that direction, and also determining the fate of Captain Conger, now missing for two days. Arriving near Manassas Junction, Dahlgren's little column found enemy pickets and drove them back toward Warrenton Junction, between Bristoe's and Catlett's Stations on the Orange & Alexandria Railroad. Dahlgren asked a resident what he knew of Conger's fight two days earlier, and learned that the wounded Union captain could be found in a nearby doctor's house.[37]

Dahlgren went straight there, finding Conger with four wounds, including one in the abdomen considered to be mortal. The wounded captain lay on a mattress on the floor, but Dahlgren convinced the family to place him on a bed and make him as comfortable as possible. After Conger related his experiences in the late skirmish, Dahlgren and his troopers moved on. Along the way, they encountered a Confederate soldier dressed in civilian clothing, whom Dahlgren arrested. Two women brandishing weapons emerged from a nearby house, threatened Dahlgren, and demanded the release of his prisoner, but he refused to back down and took the man with him when he and his troopers moved on. They returned safely and reported Conger's whereabouts. He was rescued and related valuable intelligence about the dispositions of the enemy. Conger, recovered from his wounds and returned to duty, received Sigel's praise. He later played a significant role in the events that transpired after the assassination of Abraham Lincoln in April 1865.[38]

Ulric Dahlgren's service during this period once again earned him Sigel's praise. "When the First (now Eleventh) Corps, Army of the Potomac, was acting as a corps of observation before the defenses of Washington, Captain Dahlgren was principally active in outpost duty, and with scouting-parties of our cavalry," the German general wrote in 1864. "To enumerate the great distances he rode by day and by night, the engagements in which he participated, the valuable information he brought in from his expeditions, would, of itself, fill a volume. This outpost and scouting service were the most excellent school for him; they awakened in him an almost adventurous spirit of enterprise, and prepared him for more conspicuous and important deeds."[39]

By October 30, the Eleventh Corps had advanced slightly and had established its camp on a low hill half a mile from Fairfax Court House. "The location is healthy, and has the advantage of having a fine spring of water in its immediate vicinity," noted a newspaper correspondent. The devastated countryside took on a distinctly German flavor, and the German language was commonly heard. Rumors of changes to come were in the wind.[40]

On October 31, Sigel sent Dahlgren to Albany, New York, to assist in recruiting men for the New York regiments of the Eleventh Corps. He stopped in New York City while en route, and unexpectedly encountered his father there, traveling on Ordnance Bureau business. Father and son enjoyed a brief reunion, and then Ulric went on to Albany, where he completed his mission. While he was gone, the Eleventh Corps moved to the vicinity of Centreville. Sigel had received orders to pass through Thoroughfare Gap and connect with the left wing of the advancing Army of the Potomac. Dahlgren arrived in Washington from New York on November 5, and the next day, reached the camp of the Eleventh Corps. Sigel himself was ill, and field command of the corps temporarily fell upon Brig. Gen. Adolph von Steinwehr, the senior division commander. Sigel was expected to rejoin his corps the next day. The Eleventh Corps, which now numbered about 20,000 men, was massed between New Baltimore, Gainesville, and Thoroughfare Gap, "to cover the left flank and rear of the advancing Army of the Potomac."[41]

Although Lincoln wanted McClellan to bring Robert E. Lee to battle, the Army of the Potomac's slow advance permitted the Confederate commander to avoid a general engagement on any terms but his own. Lee wanted to end 1862 without a Union victory in Virginia.[42] Most of his army lay in the vicinity of Culpeper County, occupying some of the same ground where Pope had been stalemated in August. Having the Confederate army astride his primary line of supply—the Orange & Alexandria Railroad—at Culpeper, stymied McClellan. Although McClellan did not know it, Lee's movement to block the Army of the Potomac's route of march provided the last straw for Abraham Lincoln, who resolved to relieve McClellan of command as soon as the November 4 elections ended. The President set the wheels in motion to remove Little Mac from the Army of the Potomac.[43]

Blissfully unaware of his impending relief, and with his chosen route of march blocked, McClellan set about finding another route for the advance on Richmond. He left the Fredericksburg route as the next best available option. McClellan ordered his army to concentrate at Warrenton for re-supply while he planned his next move.[44] "The army still advances, but the machine is so huge & complicated that it is slow in its motions," he complained to his wife that day.[45] However, the army's ponderous movement—it took him two weeks for his army to cover a mere forty miles—had cast the die. Changes loomed in the cold wind.[46]

The next day, November 7, proved to be a bellwether day for the Army of the Potomac. With the Army of the Potomac's advance hindered by a howling early-season snowstorm, President Lincoln, having finally grown fed up with what he perceived as George McClellan's unwillingness to advance against the enemy, relieved him of command at 11:00 p.m. Worried about the ramifications of replacing the Democratic McClellan with a darling of the Radical Republicans, such as Maj. Gen. Joseph Hooker, Lincoln instead placed McClellan's close friend, fellow Democrat, and West Point classmate, Maj. Gen. Ambrose E. Burnside of Rhode Island, in command of the army. Burnside did not want the command, and did not consider himself up to the task. "He is very slow & is not fit to command more than a regiment," McClellan correctly observed about his old friend in a letter to his wife in late September.[47] Burnside's antipathy for Hooker overrode his misgivings, so he reluctantly accepted command of the Army of the Potomac.

With Lee's Army of Northern Virginia blocking the Orange & Alexandria at Culpeper, and under orders to move, Burnside decided that continuing on with McClellan's Fredericksburg strategy offered the next best route of advance on Richmond. He immediately put the Army of the Potomac in motion. That day, the Eleventh Corps held a position on familiar ground near Waterloo Bridge over the Rappahannock River, occupying ground it covered numerous times during Pope's campaign. This movement offered Ulric Dahlgren an opportunity to make a major contribution to the war effort, and he made the most of that chance.

CHAPTER SEVEN

A Dash into Fredericksburg

A SCANT FIVE HOURS before he was relieved of command, Maj. Gen. George B. McClellan ordered a reconnaissance of the city of Fredericksburg by the cavalry forces assigned to the Eleventh Corps and Brig. Gen. George D. Bayard's cavalry brigade. Little Mac, anticipating a move on Richmond by way of Fredericksburg, wanted to see how strongly the Confederates defended the town, and to ascertain the condition of the Richmond, Fredericksburg & Potomac ("RF & P") Railroad.[1] Burnside, the new army commander, did not disturb these orders, so the mission proceeded as ordered. The choice of who would lead this expedition fell to Franz Sigel.

Bayard's brigade was camped at Rappahannock Station, and was engaged in nearly constant skirmishing with the enemy. Bayard declined to participate in this raid, leaving it entirely in Sigel's hands, commenting, "I send down toward Fredericksburg a squadron of cavalry each day."[2] The German, in turn, did not have sufficient cavalry available to send on this expedition. His horse soldiers stayed busy picketing the Blue Ridge passes and watching Stonewall Jackson's movements. As a result, Sigel turned to his favorite aide and most dependable scout, Ulric Dahlgren, to undertake this mission, much to Ulric's glee.[3]

Sigel instructed Ulric to determine the strength of the Confederate force at Fredericksburg, and then examine the railroad between the town and Aquia Creek on the way back. He was to take with him sixty troopers of the 1st Indiana Cavalry who served as Sigel's headquarters escort. Capt. Abram Sharra commanded the Hoosiers. Sharra, of Terre Haute, was only two years older than Dahlgren. He had enlisted in what became Company A of the 1st Indiana Cavalry in July 1861 and quickly rose to sergeant. He received a commission as second lieutenant in October 1861, and captain in March 1862. He had served ably and was well-respected. Only two companies of the 1st Indiana served with the Army of the Potomac; the rest of the regiment served in the Trans-Mississippi Theatre. A twenty-four year old private of the 1st Indiana named Martin Hogan also joined the expedition.[4]

Dahlgren also had the services of Maj. William Stedman and 100 troopers of the 6th Ohio Cavalry for the expedition.[5] The 6th Ohio Cavalry was part of the Eleventh Corps cavalry detachment. Forty-seven-year-old Stedman, of Granville, Ohio, the son of a veteran of the War of 1812, was active in the former

Whig Party, had served in the Ohio legislature, and was a dedicated abolitionist. He had initially commanded a militia company, and then was appointed major in the newly-formed 6th Ohio Cavalry in 1861. Stedman had already demonstrated competence in commanding horse soldiers, and eventually achieved the rank of brevet brigadier general.[6]

With the sixty officers and men of the 1st Indiana Cavalry and one of Sigel's most reliable scouts, a Confederate deserter named R. P. Brown, as a guide, Dahlgren departed Sigel's camp near Gainesville about midnight on November 8-9. They marched to Bristoe Station, where Major Stedman and his Buckeyes should have joined the column. Finding that Stedman already had marched on to Catlett's Station, Dahlgren followed the Buckeyes there. The Ohioans were tired after spending seven full days in the saddle, including nearly three straight nights. "Just as we were about to go into camp congratulating ourselves on the prospect of a good night's rest, up came Gen. Sigel's Body Guard, fresh horses and fresh men, with an order for us to accompany them on an expedition we knew not where," recounted Capt. William H. Barrett of the 6th Ohio. "There was no alternative. 'Ours not to reason why.' We went—but there were curses loud and deep."[7]

After a slight delay in preparing, the Federal horse soldiers swung into their saddles and marched all night through bad weather and over poor roads. "All night we sped away through the pine forests of Eastern Virginia," continued Captain Barrett. "The night was as black as Erebus, its darkness relieved only by the falling snow which whitened the narrow fields over which we occasionally passed."[8] They avoided the main roads wherever possible, hoping to avoid detection, which, in turn, caused them to become lost in the heavy snow and dark night. With no other options available, Dahlgren and his column followed a narrow bridle path through the dense woods.[9]

Although Dahlgren intended to arrive in the Fredericksburg area before daylight, the distance and bad roads made it impossible. The Federals stopped to rest and water their horses at Weaversville, where they barricaded the road. However, some of the Hoosiers broke into a keg of brandy and downed it enthusiastically, prompting Ulric to mount his command and get it moving sooner than he had wanted just to get away from the temptations of the alcohol.[10] The Federals finally arrived in the Fredericksburg area about 7:30 a.m. on November 9.[11] "It was no light task to ride forty miles, keep the movement concealed from the enemy, cross the river and dash through the town, especially as it was well known the rebels occupied it in force," recounted one newspaper correspondent, "it was an enterprise calculated to dampen the ardor of most men, but which was hailed almost as a holiday expedition by the Indianians."[12]

Fredericksburg was very lightly defended, even though a sortie by the enemy had been anticipated for some time. "For some days past, the authorities of Fredericksburg have been anticipating a visit from the enemy, but being but poorly sustained against such an event by the absence of any formidable force, they were illy prepared for even a slight realization of their fears," noted a Richmond newspaper.[13] When Dahlgren reached Fredericksburg, only three companies of the 15th Battalion of Virginia Cavalry, about eighty troopers, under command of Lt. Col. John Critcher, held the town. Critcher, a 41-year-old lawyer from Westmoreland County, was a graduate of the University of Virginia. He served as a Commonwealth attorney, and represented his district in the state senate. He also participated in the Virginia Secession Convention as a Union delegate, and introduced Robert E. Lee to the convention. He vowed to support his state, and enlisted as a corporal in the 9th Virginia Cavalry when Virginia seceded. In May 1862, he became a major and the commander of the 15th Battalion.[14]

On November 8, Capt. James F. Simpson and two companies of the Chesapeake Light Cavalry, part of the 14th Battalion of Virginia Cavalry, reinforced Critcher, adding another 120 men to his meager force. Many of these men wore captured blue uniforms, which caused confusion later. These 200 troopers lacked discipline, and were not particularly reliable. These new recruits were not well-armed, with each man carrying such weapons as they brought with them from home. All told, Critcher had few effective men to defend the town.[15] Critcher failed to picket the river above the town, meaning that Dahlgren's approach went undetected.

Dahlgren found the Rappahannock River too high to ford at the regular fording places when he reached Fredericksburg. "Fredericksburg is the head of tide water on the Rappahannock, and the tide was in and the ford impassable when we arrived," explained Major Stedman.[16] Two of the Hoosiers rode along the riverbank south of the town until they came to a ferry. They hailed the ferryman, who was on the opposite shore, and identified themselves as Confederate officers. The ferryman promptly pulled himself across the river to the northern bank, where the Yankees detained and interrogated him. He told the Federals that eight companies of the enemy—some five or six hundred men—held the town.[17]

Dahlgren did not want to expose his command by crossing them on ferryboats in small groups, so he sent the scout Brown to find a place to cross. Brown

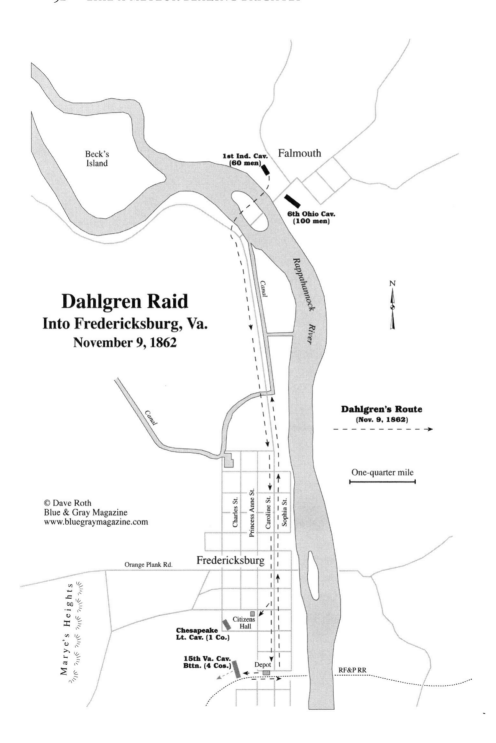

Beck's Island

1st Ind. Cav. (60 men)

Falmouth

6th Ohio Cav. (100 men)

Rappahannock River

Canal

Dahlgren Raid
Into Fredericksburg, Va.
November 9, 1862

N

Canal

Dahlgren's Route
(Nov. 9, 1862)

One-quarter mile

© Dave Roth
Blue & Gray Magazine
www.bluegraymagazine.com

Charles St.
Princess Anne St.
Caroline St.
Sophia St.

Orange Plank Rd.   Fredericksburg

M a r y e ' s   H e i g h t s

Citizens Hall

Chesapeake Lt. Cav. (1 Co.)

15th Va. Cav. Bttn. (4 Cos.)

Depot

RF&P RR

discovered a spot, well above the railroad bridge, and amid some large rocks, "by all appearances impassable," where the Union horsemen could cross in single file, although they had to "pass by taking great care and winding around among the rocks."[18]

Based on Brown's discovery, Dahlgren developed a plan of action. He intended to lead the 1st Indiana dashing through the town while the Buckeyes remained at the ford, guarding the rear and covering the route of retreat. "Captain Dahlgren resolved to fall upon them like a thunderbolt," declared one newspaper correspondent.[19] With Ulric Dahlgren leading the way, Captain Sharra and his Hoosiers splashed across the river one at a time, their crossing uncontested. About a dozen of the 6th Ohio also crossed, while the rest remained at the ford to protect the river crossing in case the Federals retreated.[20]

The crossing Federals needed to hurry. "I could plainly see the rebels gathering to meet us," reported Dahlgren, "and not wishing to give them time to collect, started for them before the Sixth Ohio were over, leaving directions for them, and supposing that they would be over by the time I would fall back as necessary." Dahlgren called for the Hoosiers to draw sabers. "Increasing his trot to a gallop, the fifty-seven dauntless men dashed into town, cheering, with sabers glittering in the sun—riding recklessly upon the enemy, who waited but a moment in the main street, then ignominiously fled," with Ulric leading the charge.[21] The townsfolk and their defenders were so unprepared for an enemy cavalry raid that quiet Sunday morning that the Federal troopers "actually passed half way through the town before their character was known, the few citizens who saw them believing them to be our men, as a matter of course," reported a Fredericksburg newspaper.[22]

Critcher quartered all of his troopers in the town. The men of the 15th Battalion stayed in a tobacco factory near the RF&P Railroad, while Captain Simpson's men used Citizen's Hall, a two-story brick building that housed a theater and meeting rooms. A stable stood behind the theater building, which was located on the west side of Princess Anne Street, midway between Charlotte and Hanover Streets.[23] "The Yankees fell upon this encampment so suddenly that the men had no time for resistance," recounted a newspaper correspondent. "It was a perfect surprise."[24] Many of Critcher's men were downtown looking for better food and quarters when Dahlgren and his command appeared. None of them could get to the perimeter of the town or prepare for the onslaught that crashed into them.[25] "It seems that the entrance of the enemy into Fredericksburg was unknown to our forces there until their fire was opened," complained a Richmond newspaper.[26]

"We found the city full of soldiers, who were almost completely surprised, and made many prisoners, whom we sent to the ford, where I supposed the Sixth Ohio to be," reported Dahlgren. The Federals charged nearly a mile from Falmouth through Fredericksburg, and Dahlgren feared blowing his horses by galloping them too far. He split his column, sending a small force under Lt. James H. Carr to dash through the town and find the main Confederate force. "We all had our sabers slung along on our wrists, and our Colt's revolvers in our right hands, our horses being controlled by our left," remembered a sergeant of the 1st Indiana Cavalry.[27] At 8:30 a.m., Carr's troopers galloped down Caroline Street, with Dahlgren and the rest of the Hoosiers following close behind. "Lieutenant Carr gallantly drove several detachments before him until they reached the main body," recounted Ulric in his official report of the action.[28] Carr ran a Rebel officer through with his saber. His orderly fenced with a determined Virginian, and "by a dexterous blow, struck him from his horse, inflicting a severe wound on his head." The orderly seized the fellow's handsome mount and grabbed his carbine and sabre as trophies. "His own sabre still bears the bloodstains—not a pleasant sight—but yet in keeping with war."[29]

After dashing through the town, the mischievous Hoosiers helped themselves to the contents of some of the local stores. They then decided to have some fun with the local residents. They reported that the Democrats had swept the recent elections in the North, that England and France had recognized the Confederacy, and then dashed on, leaving the bewildered residents wondering what was going on.[30]

Many of the men of the Chesapeake Light Cavalry "were dressed in trophies from the Yankees before Richmond in the way of coats, overcoats, &c." Consequently, when Lieutenant Colonel Critcher, who was on foot at the time, approached his headquarters from a distance of about two hundred yards off, he spotted Dahlgren's troopers drawn up mounted. Critcher understandably confused them for a company of Confederate cavalry, further delaying an effective response by the rebel horsemen. "This delusion was quickly dispelled by the rush towards him of his own cavalry, that had been at headquarters."[31]

Spotting Critcher's main body near the tobacco factory, Dahlgren formed the Hoosiers in line of battle opposite the factory. "I ordered Captain Sharra to drive them away," continued Dahlgren.[32] "As soon as Dahlgren came up and took in the situation, he gave the order to 'Draw Saber, charge!'" recounted a Yankee trooper.[33] Critcher's men panicked at the sight of Northern horsemen swarming outside the tobacco factory and fled, but not before the Federals

grabbed twenty or thirty of them as prisoners. Critcher failed to rally his terrified troopers until they were nearly a mile south of the city. He now had only
fifty or sixty men left to rally.[34]

"There was a trampling of hoofs, a clattering of scabbards, and the sharp
ringing cut of the sabers, the pistol flash—the going down of horseman and
rider—the glory gashes of the sabre stroke—a cheering and hurrahing, and
screaming of frightened women and children—a short, sharp decisive conflict,
and the town was in the possession of [Dahlgren's] gallant men," a newspaper
correspondent vividly described.[35]

The chaos created by Dahlgren's successful charge brought Captain Simpson's
troopers out of Citizens' Hall. As they emerged, fleeing Rebels warned them,
"Run for your lives! The Yankees are coming!" Horatio Haggard, one of the
Virginians, recalled, "Captain Simpson ordered us to get out in the street
with our horses and arms and to form line as quickly as possible."[36] Alarmed,
Simpson tried to cordon off Princess Anne Street with mounted men, but
merely succeeded in creating a bottleneck on the narrow, crowded street. Nine
of Simpson's troopers blocked the street, but the Hoosiers easily smashed
through their thin line, leaving one Rebel dead, another unconscious from a
saber blow, and took the remaining seven as prisoners.[37]

Sharra did not realize that the rest of Captain Simpson's troopers were mounting in the lot behind them, and that they were about to attack. The Virginians
charged into Sharra's rear and flank.[38] "The fighting was of the most desperate
nature, our men using their sabers, and the enemy in several instances, club-
bing our men with their carbines," recounted Dahlgren.[39] "We rode ahead of
many of them after giving each one a cut with the saber in passing. We actually straddled their column, and in this way chopped away all along the line,"
recalled Haggard. Simpson's determined charge in turn routed the Yankees and
liberated six of his men who had briefly been taken prisoner.[40]

Dahlgren's men dispersed about the town, chasing fleeing Confederate troopers everywhere. J. W. Gillis, a member of the 6th Ohio Cavalry who joined the
charge of the Hoosiers, spotted a Confederate trooper wearing blue pants, and
chased him into the narrow alley behind Citizens' Hall. "He turned his horse
into a stable, and just as I came to the door he came out again," recalled Gillis.
"I halted him and looking into the stable discovered some four or five more
[Confederate troopers] there who had not been out yet, and looking around
I discovered that I was entirely separated from our men, and between them
and me was a squad of rebel cavalry, who discovered me about as soon as I
did them, gave a yell and made for me." Gillis got his prisoner in front of him,

and by catching his saber on the horse's saddle, succeeded in escaping with his prisoner. "I have always wondered why those rebels who were in the stable allowed me to take their comrade away. Had they but said the word, I would have surrendered to them."[41] Sgt. Myron J. Dorn, another Buckeye, blew one Rebel from his saddle with his carbine and then cut down another with his saber.[42]

Sgt. E. T. Hebb, of Company I of the 1st Indiana Cavalry, charged with Lieutenant Carr's group. "I fired five shots from my revolver, keeping the sixth, fearing I might need it," he remembered years later. "I caught up my saber, and my first man I struck above the right ear. I suppose I knocked him about 10 feet. He was on a large sorrel horse." Hebb then set his sights on a bareheaded rebel with a bald spot on top of his head. His saber struck just to the left of the bald spot. Hebb's momentum carried him too far, and he spotted a group of Confederate troopers forming to his right. Their commander sat his horse with his pistol on the pommel of his saddle. Hebb grabbed the revolver and demanded the man's surrender. "Are you indeed Yankees?" asked the officer.

"Yes," replied Hebb. "Give up your gun."

"I give that up to no man," he responded sharply. Rebuffed, Hebb did the wise thing and galloped away to safety.[43]

While the fighting raged in the streets of the town, an erroneous report reached Dahlgren that a Confederate force had gotten behind him and threatened to take possession of the ford. "Seeing the 6th Ohio were not going to assist although I had several times given orders which I thought sufficient & which were promptly obeyed by the Ind. Cavalry, & after considering the matter with Capt. Sharra," wrote Dahlgren the day after the raid. "I determined to force a passage by the way we had come, which I was confident the Ind. Cav. would do, so exultant were they after having driven greatly superior numbers in a hand to hand contest."[44] Sharra pulled back, bringing along the colors of the 15th Battalion of Virginia Cavalry, which he had found in the tobacco factory. The Federals also carried away about thirty prisoners and two wagonloads of gray cloth as the spoils of the raid.[45]

"We had a beautiful race up Main Street, in which some 5 or 6 shots were exchanged, much to the amusement of the boys who made the welkin ring as the captured Yankeys were led back," noted a Fredericksburg resident.[46] With Captain Simpson's Virginians hot on their tails, the Northerners fell back to the ford above Falmouth, the blueclad troopers fighting a spirited rearguard action the whole way. "On several occasions, Captain Dahlgren's men were completely surrounded, and all avenues of retreat were apparently cut off; but they were not to be conquered," wrote one newspaper correspondent.[47] One of Simpson's troopers, a man named Oney Brock, spotted Critcher's captured colors and demanded that they give up the flag to him. When they ignored him, Brock killed the Yankee carrying the flag, and then carried the colors to safety.[48] "With their sabers they fought brilliantly, and after a short but decisive combat they succeeded in cutting their way through the enemy," observed a Philadelphia newspaper correspondent.[49]

Even civilians joined in. One angry young woman, waving a pistol, blocked the route of one of the Hoosiers, who was escorting two prisoners up Caroline Street. "Directly after two of Capt. Simpson's men coming up, she called on them to follow and rescue the Confederates which they proceeded to do at once," reported a Richmond newspaper. "The Federal hearing them approaching turned on his horse and took six deliberate shots at them but none took effect. The firing took place on the square on which we live and some of it immediately in front of our residence. The Confederates were released and soon thereafter the Federal captured."[50]

Other Federals complained that civilians attacked them with stones, and one man was captured when a well-aimed rock knocked him from the saddle.[51] Most of the women of the town did not join in the fighting, but instead stood on their porches, waving their handkerchiefs and cheering on Simpson's hard-charging horsemen. When he heard that a regiment of enemy soldiers was lying in ambush ahead, Simpson wisely broke off the pursuit at the north end of Caroline Street.[52]

Arriving at the ford, Ulric found it still safely in the hands of the 6th Ohio Cavalry. The Buckeyes had a dilemma of their own. Some of the Ohioans joined the Hoosiers in town and several of them dashed back, reporting that the enemy were six hundred strong. They claimed that all the Hoosiers had been killed or captured, and that they should leave quickly if they wished to avoid being captured. Several of the Buckeyes fled, but about sixty of them, led by Major Stedman, decided to stand and hold the ford, hoping to save any survivors of the dash into the town. "Soon we had the satisfaction of seeing our friends return and covering their retreat across the river," noted Captain Barrett. "They had had a desperate encounter." Upon the return of the Hoosiers, the Ohio troopers learned that Dahlgren had ordered them to cross, too—no order to do so had arrived, although a few of them had pitched into the fray of their own accord.[53]

The Federals splashed back across the river. Then Dahlgren divided his command again, and some of them buried a dead man under some pine trees on the north bank of river.[54] While they toiled, Dahlgren led twelve hand-picked men off toward Aquia Creek to examine the railroad line. Dahlgren found the road in "tolerable condition," and set the bridges over the Potomac and Accokeek Creeks ablaze. They surprised and captured the four-man picket post at Accokeek Creek, "our surprise having been so effectually accomplished that not one of the pickets was aware of our entering Fredericksburg." In burning the bridges, Dahlgren exceeded his orders and destroyed important transportation links that unnecessarily caused problems for the Army of the Potomac and the U. S. Military Railroads later.[55]

While Dahlgren and his little band rode off on their reconnaissance, the rest of the raiders marched back to the Union lines with their prisoners and prizes in tow. When the wagons stalled a couple of miles from Falmouth, they were set ablaze after Major Stedman "gave the cloth to any one who would carry it, and the men took it all."[56] Ulric made his way back to Sigel's headquarters after firing the bridges, arriving that evening. "The enemy's loss was considerable, but it is impossible to state the exact number," Dahlgren reported. "I know of 3 being killed, several wounded, and 39 prisoners. Our loss, 1 killed and 4 missing. We also captured two wagon loads of gray cloth, about to be sent south."[57]

The men—especially the Buckeyes of the 6th Ohio, who had already spent the better part of a week in the saddle—were exhausted by their ordeal. "We arrived at our camp the next morning about four o'clock," recounted Stedman. "We were tired out. The men slept in their saddles while marching. We had been four nights on duty and were 'fagged out' entirely." The march took a heavy toll on both horses and men, but it also uncovered important intelligence about Confederate dispositions in the city.[58]

Franz Sigel heard rumors that Dahlgren's expedition had been captured. ""The reconnoitering party sent to the Aquia Creek and Fredericksburg Railroad has been captured when making an attack on Fredericksburg," he reported to Burnside. "No information in regard to the bridges over the Potomac and Accokeek Creeks has been received."[59] Dahlgren and his command dispelled all doubts when they showed up in camp during the early evening hours. "Gen. Sigel is in ecstasies tonight," reported a correspondent."[60]

A relieved Sigel reported on the raid to his superior, Maj. Gen. Samuel P. Heintzelman, the commander of the forces assigned to the defenses of Washington. "The reconnoitering party from Fredericksburg has just returned," he wrote breathlessly. After describing what happened on the expedition, Sigel wrote, perhaps a bit disenguously, "[Dahlgren] reports the bridges on the Potomac Creek and Accokeek Creek (of the Aquia Creek and Fredericksburg

Railroad) destroyed."[61] Sigel did not inform Burnside that the bridges over the creeks had been destroyed until November 13, and then he did not tell Burnside that Union troops had destroyed them.[62] While the German passed on the critical intelligence that the bridges had been destroyed, he neglected to tell either Burnside or Heintzelman that Dahlgren had destroyed them, a critical piece of information that Heintzelman did not learn for several days.

That night, Sigel sent a second scouting party to Fredericksburg, which found a small force of Confederates still holding the city. "No train of cars has been there since the attack," Sigel reported to Burnside, implying that the Confederates had neither evacuated nor reinforced the city—instead, things quickly returned to normal in Fredericksburg. The success of these expeditions convinced Burnside that road to Richmond via Fredericksburg remained open.[63]

Things, however, had not returned to normal. Dahlgren's unexpected dash into the city rattled the townsfolk. "We spent the week after in anxiety and fear with continued reports of the enemy approaching our halcyon days were drawing to a close," observed Fredericksburg resident Jane Howison Beale, who had no idea just how accurate her prediction would be.[64] In fact, a Charleston, South Carolina newspaper reported on the raid and observed, "either the enemy are coming upon Richmond from Fredericksburg, or are about to be transported to the Suffolk line of advance. It indicates work, however, one side or the other."[65]

An extremely irate resident of Fredericksburg, one Mrs. Ford, followed the raiders all the way back to their camp to retrieve her slave boy, who had been seized by Dahlgren's troopers. When the slave came forward and said that he wanted to go home with the indignant Mrs. Ford, the Federals let him go with her. She returned to her home in Fredericksburg by evening, still complaining about her poor treatment at the hands of Dahlgren's men.[66]

A tired but elated Ulric sat down the next day, November 10, and penned a report of his adventure. General Heintzelman endorsed Dahlgren's report, declaring it "a very gallant affair." However, he also stated ominously, "The burning of the bridges was very unnecessary."[67] Characteristically, Ulric's enthusiasm had caused him to exceed his orders without realizing that there would be far-reaching ramifications. This trait re-surfaced in 1864, bearing a much worse result.

A correspondent of the *Baltimore American* criticized Ulric for his decision to leave before destroying the cloth mill. "Unfortunately, Capt. Dahlgren neglected to destroy a large woolen factory in Fredericksburg, which was manufacturing

cloth for the Rebel army at the rate of 1,000 yards per day," noted the correspondent. "His raid was regarded as prophetic of the advance of our army, and
immediately after he left all the machinery was removed to Richmond."[68] In
truth, Dahlgren probably did not have sufficient time to torch the cloth factory,
but burning it would have had military value. However, his unfortunate decision to burn the railroad bridges lacked any military value, and the loss of these
bridges actually created substantial problems for a large Union army trying to
supply itself in the Fredericksburg area.

At the same time, Dahlgren benefited from good fortune. At least one of
Simpson's Virginians believed that they had faced at least 500 enemy troopers that day, not just 160.[69] Critcher himself was not impressed. "Exclusive
of Simpson's company, which had not reported for duty, I question whether
we had as many men in Fredericksburg at the time as Dahlgren, and of these
several were sick and others without arms," he later wrote. "So that, knowing
our position and our weakness as he must have done, and as he could have
learned from any one along the road or at Falmouth, the exploit of this youthful
hero, though very creditable to him, seems not so distinguished by its boldness
or success."[70]

A Confederate court of inquiry convened to investigate why Dahlgren simply
marched into the town unopposed determined "that there was great negligence
on the part of the pickets in allowing a surprise; that there was an absolute want
of discipline, if not want of courage, evinced upon the part of the men of the
Fifteenth Battalion; that the officers seemed to have done their duty in trying
to get the men to stand, but utterly failed." The court of inquiry also found that
Simpson's men acquitted themselves well in attacking the Federal rearguard.
The court of inquiry absolved Critcher himself of any wrongdoing, blaming
the incident on the demoralization of his command as a result of being forced
to do provost duty in Richmond, its poor equipment, and the raw nature of the
troops involved. The court of inquiry concluded, "The panic, which, under such
circumstances, might, and in all probability would, affect any raw and undisciplined troops."[71] Critcher's command was "very much ashamed" for having been
driven from the town by a smaller force of the enemy.[72]

A correspondent from the *Boston Evening Journal* raved about the results
of the expedition, assigning it more significance than it probably warranted.
"Stuart has his compeers—Pleasonton and Dahlgren. We are beginning to
learn war," he effused. "We have had Southern dash and valor against inexperi-
ence, in horsemanship; but the cool intrepidity, determination and bravery of

the Northern soldier is beginning to be felt. We shall hear more from Capt. Dahlgren and his men."[73]

"It appears, from all accounts, to have been a daring raid, and one worthy of imitation by our cavalry," crowed the *New York Times*.[74] "For real daring, perhaps nothing which has occurred during the present campaign ran equal to it," declared the *Philadelphia Inquirer*.[75] Another correspondent from a New York newspaper declared, "Great credit is due Capt. Dahlgren and the officers of the body-guard above named."[76] The exclusion of Major Stedman and his Buckeyes from the praise being lavished upon Dahlgren and the Hoosiers did not sit well with the Ohioans, who grew hostile toward their comrades as a result.

Dahlgren's accomplishment did not impress everyone. "The early hour and the virtually undefended condition of the city does not render this 'feat' of the Yankees as daring as it was audacious," sniffed one Richmond newspaper. "They had but a short road and a clear one to travel, expected to meet no resistance and met with but little; came in and went away, no wiser and somewhat worse off than before they started."[77]

The expedition covered about one hundred miles, including nearly thirty miles behind enemy lines, and it succeeded, even if Ulric exceeded his orders by destroying the two railroad bridges.[78] He lost only ten men captured, one man dead, and a few wounded.[79] He brought back important first-hand intelligence about the strength and dispositions of the Confederate garrison in the city, and he confirmed that the railroad was operable, save for the two bridges that he burned on his way out of town. Whether this intelligence impacted Burnside's plans for a move on Fredericksburg is unknown; the army commander had already completed his plan of operation by the time of the expedition. However, the intelligence probably reinforced the idea that a movement on Richmond by way of Fredericksburg provided the best route. At the same time, Confederate Brig. Gen. Daniel Ruggles was preparing to leave on horseback when the Federal horse soldiers dashed into the town, and barely had time to make his escape from a squad approaching on a cross street.[80] Thus, an opportunity to grab an important prize slipped through Ulric's fingers.

Dahlgren's men conducted themselves well under difficult and stressful conditions. "They behaved very well," grudgingly admitted a resident of Fredericksburg. "Aleck Green, whom they took prisoner and discharged, told me that they were the most respectable set he had seen of all the Yankees."[81] A Richmond newspaper noted, "Citizens were not interfered with nor their property injured."[82]

A Confederate officer observed Dahlgren's conduct while leading the street fighting in Fredericksburg, and admiringly declared the young man "the bravest Union officer he had ever seen."[83] Sigel described the expedition as "one of the most brilliant and daring expeditions since the breaking out of the war," and praised Ulric's performance lavishly in a letter to John Dahlgren. "His modesty is as commendable as his skill and bravery. I esteem his soldierly and manly qualities very highly, and think you have much to be gratified at in him."[84]

However, some of the newspaper accounts improperly blamed the 6th Ohio for failing to obey orders and cross into the town. This caused a great deal of indignation among the Buckeyes, who already felt slighted. "Had any such order reached us, or any information that we were wanted, we would not have been slow in hastening to the rescue. The truth of the matter is that the Guard expected to find a small force to oppose them, and finding more than they bargained for, they sought to escape censure for their rashness and to set their bravery in a stronger light by claiming that we refused to assist them," declared an angry Captain Barrett. "They did a gallant deed, but their injustice lowered them much in our estimation."[85]

Major Stedman was likewise miffed. "I hear that certain of the good people of Randolph think that I am not much of a fighter," he wrote on December 9. After justifying his actions in prior campaigns, he took aim at Ulric Dahlgren. "At Fredericksburg, not only myself, but all of the Sixth Ohio, except a few with carbines, were cheated out of an opportunity to achieve any honors by Captain Dahlgren, who wished to reap the whole laurels himself, after he learned that there were only sixty or seventy there."[86] Of course, Stedman incorrectly assessed the strength of the enemy, but there was no denying that the idea that a twenty-year-old staff officer was getting all of the credit while his command was being accused of cowardice infuriated the major.

General Sigel maintained a regular correspondence with John Dahlgren. "Captain Ulric Dahlgren, sent yesterday to reconnoiter the Fredericksburg and Aquia Railroad, has been captured, with forty men, in making a dash on Fredericksburg; the particulars not known yet," he wrote on November 10, 1862, to his father's abject horror. That evening, the arrival of a second telegram alleviated his concerns somewhat. "Allow me to congratulate you upon the brilliant success and gallant behavior of your son, Captain U. Dahlgren," wrote Sigel somewhat cryptically. Dahlgren was left hanging until the next day, spending a sleepless night worrying about the fate of his son. Finally, good news arrived the next morning. "Information has been received that your son is not captured but will be here tonight," wrote one of Sigel's staff officers. "Our reconnoitering party made, under command of your son, a gallant charge into Fredericksburg, and routed the rebels. Shall send you more particulars when Captain Ulric arrives." Finally, the best news of all arrived. "I have just arrived from Fredericksburg—all right," telegraphed Ulric that night, much to his father's great relief.[87]

The next day, John Dahlgren wrote to his son. "Your friends are all pleased with your <u>coup</u> at Fredkbg, and you are duly credited," he declared. He then advanced an interesting idea for his son's consideration. "It seems to me that with a couple of hundred men, and a roving commander, still on staff of Gen. Sigel, you would do more for some really good promotions in the end than as a Major of Artillery. A regiment of Rangers would be the thing."[88]

Impressed by the *New York Tribune's* coverage of the raid, President Lincoln sent for Halleck to arrange a promotion for Ulric as a reward for his daring dash on Fredericksburg. However, Halleck reminded the President that certain rules prevented Lincoln from promoting young Dahlgren. The President told John Dahlgren that he had been overruled and claimed "he was only the lead horse in a team, and must not kick out of traces."[89] Although Ulric was a skilled artillerist, his father recognized that his real gift was for cavalry and small unit operations. Even greater success with this sort of oeration lay ahead for Ulric Dahlgren.

CHAPTER EIGHT

Campaigning with Burnside and Hooker

O N NOVEMBER 13, Sigel provided Burnside with an extremely detailed report on the status of things in his sector. He concluded by making a sensible recommendation: "It seems to me that the line of Culpeper-Gordonsville is the best line of operation under the present circumstances, although the line from Fredericksburg to Sexton's Junction and Richmond is naturally shortest, yet this is not really so, if we consider that our army would be detained before the entrenchments of Richmond, now probably strengthened by a second and more exterior line of defense." He also correctly observed, "It is also evident that a direct advance upon Richmond, by way of Fredericksburg, would leave the greatest part of Virginia under the control of the enemy, and would not separate his armies of the east and west, while an advance upon Gordonsville would force them to fight at that point, or to retreat either toward Richmond or Lynchburg."[1] Although Sigel made reasonable and prudent recommendations, the decision had already been made to implement McClellan's plan for an advance upon Richmond via Fredericksburg. That Ulric Dahlgren's daring reconnaissance found the town lightly defended only reinforced that decision.

On November 14, Halleck dashed off an urgent dispatch to Burnside. "It is reported that Dahlgren is about going on another raid to Fredericksburg," reported the general-in-chief. "You had better direct General Sigel to stop this, or it may interfere with your purposes. Look out for a cavalry raid to cut off your supplies." Burnside complied, issuing the necessary orders to cancel any further plans for another expedition to Fredericksburg by Ulric.[2]

On that same day, Burnside re-organized his army. He created three Grand Divisions, consisting of two corps each. Franz Sigel's Eleventh Corps and Maj. Gen. Henry W. Slocum's Twelfth Corps were specifically designated as the army's reserve force, which would be augmented by other miscellaneous commands.[3] Once again, the Eleventh Corps would not be a front-line combat unit, just as it had been left out at Antietam. Perhaps it was because Burnside and Halleck had no faith in Sigel; Halleck referred to the German as a "damned coward" and complained about his corps. "Although it was comprised of some of the best fighting men we have," he claimed, "it wouldn't do much under Sigel."[4] Perhaps his troops still carried the taint of Frémont's legacy. "From the tenor of the order, it is more than likely that this is done to give [Sigel] time to fill his command from the new regiments sent forward," observed a correspondent of the *Philadelphia Inquirer*. "It is not likely that the General will be long kept inactive. His worth is too well known, and therefore the position in which he is at present placed must be only temporary."[5] No matter what the reason, the Eleventh Corps would not be one of the Army of the Potomac's primary combat forces. Instead of marching toward Fredericksburg with the army, the Eleventh Corps remained at Fairfax. This did not sit well with the ever-restless Ulric Dahlgren.

Sigel rightfully believed that Stanton had mistreated him, and considered resigning his commission. Ambrose Burnside, an officer junior to him, had been elevated over him to army command, he had been denied command of a Grand Division in favor of officers junior to him, and he was fed up with continually receiving the short end of the stick. Sigel's days with the Army of the Potomac were clearly numbered. Ulric Dahlgren was closely associated with Sigel, and an ambitious young man like him had to be concerned for the future of his own army career.

On November 15, the Army of the Potomac began its movement toward Fredericksburg. Confederate scouts shadowed the Federal cavalry, but learned little about the movements of the main body. Lee did not respond quickly when he learned that the Federal cavalry was on the move, because he was convinced that it was too late to hold Fredericksburg. Instead, he headed for the North Anna River. So far, Burnside's plan was working well, and it looked like he might steal a march on Lee. However, the November weather did not cooperate—it was cold and snowy with high winds and frigid temperatures—conditions that did not favor a major campaign. "For several days past the corps in the advance of us have been moving," reported a newspaper correspondent on November 16. "The headquarters of General Sigel are still here, but there is considerable speculation on all hands to know what will transpire in the next forty-eight hours. Evidently there will be a move, but which way, none, except those in high authority, know."[6] It began raining incessantly, turning the roads into bottomless quagmires that made moving large bodies of troops difficult.[7]

The Eleventh Corps remained in the vicinity of Fairfax Court House. "As this corps is composed of fighting men—soldiers who are serving a country and not an individual—it is not the least demoralized by the recent change in commanders," observed a newspaper correspondent assigned to army headquarters, "and is, therefore, as ready as ever to discharge any duty that it may be called upon to perform with alacrity." While the rest of the Army of the Potomac marched, Sigel and his men waited for orders that might never arrive.[8]

Sigel reorganized his staff on November 20. He reappointed Ully as an aide-de-camp, the role he had filled since the German assumed command of the corps in June. While the Eleventh Corps awaited orders to march, new regiments continued to arrive, replenishing its depleted ranks and bringing it back up to combat readiness.[9] On November 23, Sigel's staff, including Ulric, presented the general with a new horse and all the accouterments as a birthday present.[10]

With the Eleventh Corps still conveniently camped close to Washington, Ulric regularly visited the city. "Captain Ulric occasionally visits the home he loves so well," wrote his father, "and in its quiet finds a pleasing contrast with the bustle of camp-life."[11] No doubt, the thought of a warm bed and a home-cooked meal held a great deal of appeal for a soldier accustomed to the travails of service in the field. While Ulric traveled back and forth to Washington from Fairfax, the Army of the Potomac marched toward its date with destiny at Fredericksburg.

Sigel's command, although not participating in the advance on Fredericksburg, nevertheless occupied a strategic location near Fairfax. Sigel stood between the Loudoun Valley, where Stonewall Jackson and his command were operating, and the main body of Lee's army at Fredericksburg. Sigel thus blocked the direct route of march from the Valley and prevented Jackson's infantry from easily joining the Army of Northern Virginia. Sigel pulled back only after forcing Jackson to take a more roundabout route to join Lee.[12]

Brig. Gen. Julius Stahel commanded the cavalry division assigned to the defenses of Washington. Stahel, a Hungarian immigrant, was a competent officer whose horse soldiers effectively covered a large area with a relatively small force. On November 28, Stahel led a reconnaissance in force to Ashby's Gap, Snicker's Gap, and beyond, into the Shenandoah Valley, monitoring the activities of Stonewall Jackson's corps. After marching from Middleburg to Rector's Cross Roads, Stahel sent two detachments off on a scouting expedition. Ulric Dahlgren, who volunteered for the expedition, led one of those detachments, and took his command to Salem, ten miles away. They found no enemy.

While on the way to Salem, they overtook a farmer struggling with a large load of corn. Ully's horses desperately needed rations, so he directed his men to take a few ears for their mounts. The farmer protested, but when he realized that he would not win the argument, took another tack. He declared that several of his horses had developed a debilitating disease from eating the corn. "Oh," retorted Dahlgren, "all of our animals have that disease, so there is no risk to run." This unexpected response turned the tables and alarmed the farmer, who begged to be left alone because he feared that his horses might catch distemper. However, his pleas fell on deaf ears. The corn fed the hungry Union horses.

With no enemy at Salem, Dahlgren and his little column headed back to rejoin Stahel's main body. Ulric rode at the head of the column with two other men. As they approached Stahel's position, one of the Union pickets mistook the three horsemen for the enemy and fell back upon the main command, causing alarm that the enemy had snuck up on them and were about to attack. Fortunately, the picket quickly discovered his mistake and rushed back to his post red-faced. Ulric reported his findings to Stahel, and the column pressed on.[13]

The Union cavalry then pulled back to a position near Middleburg and halted for the night. The next day, November 29, they moved to Snickersville through a heavy snowstorm. Passing through Snicker's Gap, they skirmished with enemy videttes at a ford across the Shenandoah River and then pushed across the river. Advancing a short distance beyond the river, they located an enemy camp and scattered the Confederate soldiers they found there. With twenty-five men, Dahlgren headed off to the right from Middleburg, marched to Mt. Gilead, Circleville, Goose Creek Church, and the Leesburg Pike. He arrived at Snicker's Ford about 3:00 that afternoon and captured several prisoners along the way. Hearing that small squads of the enemy were hanging upon the flanks and rear of Stahel's main body, Dahlgren assembled all of the men who could be spared from the command guarding the river ford and pursued the enemy, scattering them. Dahlgren's little command then rejoined the main body.[14]

The rest of the column marched to Berryville, and drove a superior force of enemy cavalry through the streets of the town with a spirited sabre charge. Stahel captured nearly thirty Confederate riders in the process. That night, having accomplished his objective, Stahel ordered his command to fall back in a northeasterly direction toward Leesburg, all the way to Chantilly. The Hungarian decided to camp at Mt. Gilead that night.

The next morning, November 30, Stahel headed for Goose Creek and followed it to Leesburg. The Federals ended their march at Chantilly after a fatiguing night and three long days in the saddle. The successful expedition ascertained the dispositions of the enemy while suffering only one man killed and fifteen wounded in severe skirmishing. They killed four of the enemy, and wounded no less than thirty in the various skirmishes.[15]

By December 11, Burnside's army already had been at Fredericksburg for nearly three weeks, waiting for the arrival of pontoon bridges the Federals needed to cross the Rappahannock. Had the bridges been there when Burnside arrived, he would have crossed the river and moved past Fredericksburg before Lee could concentrate his entire army there. Burnside instead sat and waited for them. By the time they arrived, Lee's entire army had dug in on the high ground beyond the old river town, the heights frowning with Confederate artillery.

On December 11, Burnside ordered Sigel to move his corps and the Twelfth Corps as rapidly as possible toward Fredericksburg.[16] Sigel quickly complied. The Eleventh Corps crossed Bull Run at Wolf Run Shoals and headed toward Dumfries, on its way toward the Rappahannock River and Burnside.[17]

Sigel dispatched Dahlgren to ride to Burnside's headquarters before moving out of his camps. Ulric arrived in time to watch the army preparing to assault the town. Always eager for action, Dahlgren sought permission to serve on the army commander's staff.[18] Burnside, who needed active and diligent staff officers for the coming battle, agreed and ordered him to be temporarily assigned to the personal staff of the commanding general. Once again, the fates smiled on Ulric Dahlgren—this turn of events meant that he would take part in the coming battle after all. Given his pugnacious nature, this result undoubtedly pleased him.[19]

Union engineers bridged the Rappahannock at three places before dawn on December 11. The Confederates did not oppose the construction of the left and center bridges, but contested the laying of the right bridge, which was immediately in front of the town itself. By the time that the Northern engineers made it halfway across the river, Confederate riflemen of Brig. Gen. William Barksdale's Mississippi brigade, concealed in houses, opened fire on them, making it impossible for the engineers to work safely. Union artillery replied but failed to drive out the sharpshooters. Barksdale held the Federals at bay for the better part of the day.

As darkness fell over the city, the 7th Michigan, and the 19th and 20th Massachusetts crossed the river in pontoon boats in order to drive off the sharpshooters. Ulric Dahlgren occupied one of the first boats to make the crossing. The severe and accurate fire of the Confederates dropped a number of bluecoats just as the boats made landfall on the western shore.[20] Bullets whizzed all around Dahlgren, but he remained impervious to the danger. Undaunted, the Federal infantrymen swept forward, driving out the enemy sharpshooters, permitting the completion of the last bridge. Thus, with the final piece of the puzzle now in place, the Army of the Potomac prepared to make its main thrust that came two days later, on December 13.[21]

Early on the morning of December 12, most of the Army of the Potomac crossed the Rappahannock on its pontoon bridges. They spent December 12 preparing to assault the Confederate lines and skirmishing with the enemy.

Forming up on the morning of December 13, they moved out to assault the long lines of Confederate infantry arrayed on the high ground in their front. At Prospect Hill, on the Union left, the blueclad soldiers briefly punched through Jackson's line, but a determined counterattack shoved them back. On the right, the Confederates repulsed assault after assault on a sunken road near the base of Marye's Heights with heavy losses until darkness brought the short winter day to a cold and unpleasant close. The Army of the Potomac suffered extraordinarily heavy losses compared to the relatively light casualties of the enemy, but Burnside resolved to continue trying to bull his way through. He intended to resume the attack the next morning.[22]

After the day's heavy losses, Burnside realized that he would need the Eleventh Corps after all. He had sent Ulric to Sigel with a dispatch to prepare his corps to march late in the day on December 11 or perhaps shortly after midnight on December 12.[23] Sigel's corps reached Dumfries, about twenty miles from Fredericksburg, on the afternoon of December 13. "We are hotly engaged," wrote Burnside's chief of staff. "The commanding general wishes you to move up as rapidly as possible, without exhausting your troops."[24] Burnside decided that Dahlgren, as the German's own staff officer, was the best person to carry orders to Sigel. Always eager to pitch into the fray, Ully happily accepted the mission.

Dahlgren exchanged uniforms with a private to make himself less conspicuous, got a fresh horse, swung into the saddle, and headed out at 4:00 p.m. Accompanied by a single orderly, Dahlgren covered the twenty miles to Dumfries in about two hours, personally delivering the order to Sigel. A cavalry detachment had been assigned to join him, but most of them could not keep up. An officer managed to catch Ulric as he crossed a stream. The officer saluted him and said, "This is a good gait for us but a bad one for the escort." Dahlgren nodded. "True, but I have important dispatches for General Sigel at Dumfries and time is precious." The two officers and the orderly left their escort behind, struggling to catch up.[25]

The German corps commander wondered what had happened to his aide. Hearing a report of the day's fighting from Dahlgren pleased him. After a hasty meal and an hour-long nap, Dahlgren found a remount and headed back to Burnside's headquarters.[26] The inky darkness of the cold December night made rapid riding difficult, and he had no reason for extreme haste. At five o'clock the next morning, Dahlgren finally arrived at headquarters, announcing that he had successfully completed his mission. Once again, Dahlgen had demonstrated his remarkable endurance in the saddle.[27]

However, nearly twenty-four hours in the saddle left the young captain exhausted. He was so tired, in fact, that "he came well nigh falling from his horse" on the ride back.[28] He slept through the day's intermittent fighting, giving him a chance to recuperate a bit from his ordeal. Burnside finally decided to break off the battle and withdraw on December 14. His badly beaten and battered army safely re-crossed the Rappahannock on December 15 and returned to its camps around Falmouth to lick its wounds. The Battle of Fredericksburg was over.

On December 17, with his corps still near Falmouth, Sigel sent Dahlgren to Burnside's headquarters with a proposal to make more effective use of the reserve division that would shift it to the right, closer to the main body of the army and shortening the lines of communication. Ulric delivered the message to Burnside and then returned to Eleventh Corps headquarters.[29] This dispatch demonstrated that Sigel really did not understand Burnside's plans. The proposed movement would have placed the Eleventh Corps in the middle of the area where Burnside intended to attempt another stealthy advance on Fredericksburg. The movement of the Eleventh Corps would have drawn attention to a quiet sector precisely when Burnside did not want the enemy to focus on that area.

On December 19, Ulric and Sigel caught a train to Washington. In the wake of the debacle at Second Bull Run, rumors swirled that Irvin McDowell was a traitor and that he had taken steps to insure Confederate victory. McDowell immediately demanded a court of inquiry to clear his name, and got his wish. The court convened in Washington on November 21, 1862, and lasted for sixty-five days before clearing McDowell of the charges. As a critical witness in the case, Sigel testified at length. Ulric testified before the court of inquiry on December 30, 1862, answering a handful of questions and giving his account of his one interchange with McDowell during the battle. He testified that McDowell was curt to him and that he seemed annoyed when Dahlgren approached him on Sigel's behalf to relay a message.[30] After testifying, Ulric enjoyed ten days' leave, permitting him to spend the holidays at home with his family, to his father's delight. It proved to be the last time he spent the holidays at home.

When the holiday furlough ended, Ulric returned to the Eleventh Corps' camp at Stafford Court House. "The camp is filled every day with rumors of all kinds—particularly of rebel raids upon the line between this point and Alexandria," reported a newspaper correspondent assigned to Sigel's headquarters. "If Madame Rumor could be believed, this corps has been destroyed in detail several times; but I imagine that if the enemy act upon such a belief, they will find themselves woefully mistaken."[31] Sigel, recently appointed to command a reserve grand division consisting of the Eleventh and Twelfth Corps, had just completed another reorganization of his staff, and Ulric re-joined the German's staff as an aide-de-camp. His tenure in that role was short, as Sigel's remaining time with the Army of the Potomac was also short. Maj. Gen. Carl Schurz, another German immigrant, assumed command of the Eleventh Corps upon Sigel's promotion.[32]

Trying to redeem himself after the crushing repulse at Fredericksburg, Burnside attempted a winter campaign along the Rappahannock. The Army of the Potomac tried to flank Lee out of his strong positions above Fredericksburg. However, the campaign quickly bogged down in the horrendous January weather. "Mud up to horses' knees. Army stuck in the mud," observed Capt. Isaac Ressler of the 16th Pennsylvania Cavalry.[33] "An indescribable chaos of pontoons, wagons and artillery . . . supply wagons upset by the roadside, artillery stalled in the mud, ammunition trains mired by the way," recalled a member of the 6th Pennsylvania Cavalry. "Horses and mules dropped down dead, exhausted with the effort to move their loads . . . A hundred and fifty dead animals, many of them buried in the liquid muck, were counted in the course of a morning's ride."[34] As the Confederates watched and waited for the Army of the Potomac to slog through the mud, they enjoyed a good laugh at the expense of the Northerners. The Rebels posted a placard near Army of the Potomac headquarters bearing the inscription, "Burnside's army stuck in the mud six miles above Falmouth."[35]

The sullen and angry Northerners felt humiliated. Burnside himself wrote, "I moved the greater part of the command, with a view to crossing above, but owing to the severe storm which began after the concerted movement commenced, we have been so much delayed that the enemy has discovered our design. The roads are almost impassable, and the small streams are very much swollen. I shall try not to run any unnecessary risks. It is most likely that we will have to change the plan." A second storm soon followed, and more than six inches of snow covered the ground, making the movement of an army impossible.[36] Instead, the unhappy Army of the Potomac went into its winter encampment.

Morale in the Federal army reached its nadir after the Mud March. The men sank into the depths of despair when they realized that they were being misused and wasted. "Army matters in general appear blue," reported Capt. George N. Bliss of the 1st Rhode Island Cavalry, "there have been 10,000 deserters from the army since the battle of Fredericksburg. Some of our leading generals appear determined to ruin General B[urnside] at any cost. It is always darkest just before day, ergo our day ought to be near at hand. Every dog has his day, I hope we have not had ours."[37] A trooper of the 3rd Indiana Cavalry ominously noted in his diary, "A dissatisfaction [is] making its appearance in the North which promises serious results."[38]

Capt. Charles Francis Adams, Jr. of the 1st Massachusetts Cavalry, grandson and great-grandson of American presidents, inherited the Adams family talent for the written word. "The Army of the Potomac . . . will fight yet, but they fight for defeat, just as a brave, bad rider will face a fence, but yet rides for a fall," he reported on January 26. "There is a great deal of croaking, no confidence, plenty of sickness, and desertion is the order of the day. This arises from various causes; partly from the defeat at Fredericksburg and the failure, but mostly from the change of commanders of late. You or others may wonder or agree, as you choose, but it is a fact that McClellan alone has the confidence of this army. They would fight and rally under him tomorrow and under him only. Burnside has lost, and Hooker never had their confidence."[39]

Rumors flew. The men still adored McClellan and enthusiastically embraced even the slightest hint that he might return. In mid-January, a trooper of the 16th Pennsylvania Cavalry gleefully noted, "It is reported that Genl. McClellan had been appointed commander-in-chief of the Armies."[40] Just the name generated enthusiasm among the demoralized Northern soldiers. However, the high command had other ideas for the army. On January 26, Burnside was relieved of command of the Army of the Potomac, and Maj. Gen. Joseph Hooker assumed command of the army in his stead.

Forty-eight-year-old Joseph Hooker, grandson of a Revolutionary War captain, graduated midway in the West Point Class of 1837. He had an outstanding career in the pre-war Regular Army, demonstrating both leadership and administrative abilities. He received brevets of all grades through lieutenant colonel for gallant and meritorious service in the war with Mexico, a record not surpassed by any first lieutenant in the United States Army. After the Mexican War, he served as assistant adjutant general in the Pacific Division of the Army and finally resigned his commission in February 1853. Regretting this decision, he unsuccessfully sought reinstatement five years later. However, on August 6, 1861, he received a commission as brigadier general of volunteers.

The following spring, Hooker's division fought several hard battles during McClellan's Peninsula Campaign, and Hooker received the moniker "Fighting Joe" from a newspaper headline. During the coming months, he demonstrated solid leadership skills, commanding a corps at Antietam and a grand division at Fredericksburg. In the aftermath of the Mud March, Hooker schemed for the removal of Burnside as army commander. When he learned of Hooker's efforts, Burnside preemptively tried to relieve Hooker. If that failed, Burnside threatened to resign from command, a solution readily embraced by Lincoln and Stanton.[41]

The brash, brave, and arrogant new army commander understood the importance of logistics. He firmly believed that the nation needed him to lead it to victory, and he energetically set about overhauling the Army of the Potomac for a grand spring campaign to end the war. Fighting Joe immediately instituted sweeping reforms. He made sure that the men had ample rations, including fresh bread and vegetables. They also received all of the clothing they needed. He instituted a system of furloughs, allowing men to go home and see their families for a few precious days, and he made a strong effort to recruit replacements to fill the ranks of regiments depleted during the brutal fighting of 1862.

He eliminated Burnside's ponderous grand division system, and instituted corps badges to develop *esprit de corps* in the ranks. Army hospital facilities improved dramatically, and the new commanding general held frequent inspections and reviews to restore the men's pride. He ordered that regular drills be held, and soon, the morale of the entire Army of the Potomac improved dramatically. "Our new commander took hold of the reins with a firm hand, and the army, if not united in believing his nomination to the position the best that could have been made, was at least ready and anxious to obey his orders, and to do its whole part in the solutions of the problems all were called upon to face," observed a Regular cavalry officer.[42]

With the elimination of the grand divisions, Sigel reverted to command of the Eleventh Corps, which remained the smallest corps in the army. The German general was extremely dissatisfied with the duties assigned him, and threatened to resign more than once. With Sigel's duties waning, Ulric Dahlgren found himself looking for things to keep him occupied. He spent part of his time working on developing new ordnance for use by the cavalry, utilizing the training he had received while working for his father. This work led to frequent trips to Washington and nights spent quietly at his father's home at the Navy Yard. "Once only did he allow himself to participate in any gay assemblage, and then simply as a mark of respect for the request of a lady, whose exalted words and refined taste had rendered her friendship, during a long period of time, much prized by his parents," noted Captain Dahlgren.[43]

In mid-February, Ulric returned to the Eleventh Corps camp near Falmouth, where great changes had occurred during his absence. Still frustrated that he led the smallest command in the Army of the Potomac, and with no prospects for the size of his command being increased, Sigel continued agitating. The German did not respect Hooker, meaning that his days with the Army of the Potomac were definitely numbered. He also experienced health problems that left him in no shape to command.

On February 12, Sigel asked to be relieved of command of the Eleventh Corps. When this request was denied, he instead took medical leave, traveling to New York City to rest and recuperate. Maj. Gen. Oliver O. Howard, who had lost an arm to a terrible combat wound suffered during the 1862 Peninsula Campaign, assumed command of the Eleventh Corps, and the War Department substantially increased the size of the corps in Sigel's absence. When Sigel reported for duty in April 1863, Halleck declined to give him back the Eleventh Corps. The German's tenure with the Army of the Potomac was over.[44]

With Sigel's departure, Ulric received a new assignment. On February 20, he visited Hooker at army headquarters. "Hello, Dahlgren," said the new army commander. "Sit down." Hooker asked after Ulric's father, and declared himself to be one of John Dahlgren's admirers. "He told me to always stop to see him when over that way," wrote Ulric to his father. Dahlgren informed Hooker that Sigel had applied for Ulric's promotion to major of artillery so that he could receive a formal appointment as chief of artillery for the Eleventh Corps. After hearing about the rejection of the application, Hooker told Ulric to make a written statement and to provide him with a copy of it. He would then do everything that he could to bring about the promotion, although the army commander stopped short of promising it. "He remarked that I deserved promotion for the Fredericksburg fight, that he considered it the handsomest thing of the whole war," reported Ulric.[45]

Ulric asked his father to forward a copy of the letter of endorsement from Sigel as quickly as possible. "I want to bring the matter before Hooker immediately," he wrote. Hooker would be traveling to Washington in a few days, and Dahlgren wanted his promotion to be on the army commander's agenda. Hooker inquired as to how long Ulric had been in the service. The brash young man made a point of the fact that, despite his relatively brief length of service, he had not yet received any sort of a promotion. Just to make certain of the timely arrival of the letter, Ulric sent his father a telegram the next day requesting the letter.[46]

John Dahlgren responded promptly, sending the letter down by rail. It arrived the next day. Ulric immediately forwarded the letter to Hooker and then lamented, "Gen. Sigel has treated his staff very shabbily." He complained, "The General has offered his resignation & goes tomorrow to Washington on leave until his resignation is accepted, but has not said anything to us about it, me only knowing by accident. The cause I think of his resignation are that he is kept in such a small command," concluded Ulric very perceptively.[47]

Instead of a promotion, Ulric received an appointment as an aide-de-camp on Hooker's staff on March 21, 1863.[48] "His active nature was soon engrossed with the labor that fell to his share," noted his father. "His genial and manly qualities were appreciated by his new comrades, and he found himself on the most friendly terms with the whole staff."[49] He enthusiastically pitched into his new duties while Hooker reorganized and rejuvenated the Army of the Potomac. By April, the army's morale was restored, and more than 125,000 men filled its ranks.

Hooker designed a campaign modeled along the lines of Burnside's failed Mud March.[50] He intended to steal a march on Lee's army, cross the Rappahannock, and sidle around the Army of Northern Virginia's flank. He hoped to draw Lee out of his stout defenses at Fredericksburg, and then make a bold move on Richmond by way of Culpeper. In mid-April, Hooker sent a strong force to hold the Rappahannock River fords while the newly-formed Cavalry Corps prepared to make a raid deep behind enemy lines intended to interdict Lee's lines of communication and supply with Richmond. Unfortunately, atrocious weather intervened and delayed the departure of the 15,000-man Cavalry Corps for two weeks while its commander, Maj. Gen. George Stoneman, waited for the flooded river to recede far enough to permit them to cross.[51]

His plans dashed by the terrible weather, Hooker met with Lincoln at Aquia Landing on April 19 to discuss how best to proceed. Ulric accompanied the army commander to the meeting and retrieved his mare, sent down from Washington by his father. Even though the element of surprise was lost, the Union high command decided to continue the movement, and by April 22, the Army of the Potomac was ready to break its camps and begin its grand spring campaign.[52] On April 27, a clear, warm spring day, the Second, Fifth, Eleventh and Twelfth Corps splashed across the Rappahannock and the campaign began in earnest.

As the Army of the Potomac marched, Ulric spent his days dashing about the countryside, scouting and delivering messages, including swimming a fast and swollen river in one instance. On a couple of occasions, he ascended in an observation balloon in an attempt to examine the Confederate dispositions. Sometimes, he assisted Hooker's chief of staff, Maj. Gen. Daniel Butterfield, and other times, he rode by the army commander's side, always ready and willing to gallop off to deliver a message or to report on events. He was "always a keen and zealous observer of passing events."[53]

Hooker ordered his staff to be ready to move the next morning, April 29, so the spring campaign finally got underway. Hooker had difficulty with the two-year units whose terms of service were expiring. With so little time left to serve, these men understandably wanted no part of fighting that could cost them their lives. "There has been some trouble among the men whose time is nearly out in regard to the day the U. S. place of registration," noted Ulric in his diary. "It will be a blessing to get rid of these men as they do nothing in a fight."[54] Three days later, he keenly observed, "Mistakes are crimes in this army."[55] Always aware of the politics of a situation, Ulric waited and bided his time, patiently looking for another opportunity to advance his own ambitions.

On April 30, the Fifth, Eleventh, and Twelfth Corps reached Chancellorsville, named for a large white brick tavern located along the Orange Turnpike. Ulric rode to and from Chancellorsville that evening, reporting to Hooker on the dispositions of the troops. "Met Genl. Hooker and made report, which he did not think much of," observed Ulric in his diary that night.[56] He also swam the frigid waters of the Rapidan River to communicate with Maj. Gens. George G. Meade and Darius N. Couch, the commanders of the Second and Fifth Corps, respectively, before returning to army headquarters.[57]

The battle began on May 1. With only about 60,000 men available—Longstreet's First Corps was then besieging Union troops at Suffolk, Virginia—Robert E. Lee assumed a strong defensive position and waited for Hooker to attack. Hooker advanced from the west, but pulled back after meeting stout resistance beyond Chancellorsville. Instead of remaining on the offensive, he fell back and assumed a defensive posture, ceding the initiative to Lee. This decision, made over the vociferous objections of several of Hooker's corps commanders, had far-reaching implications for the outcome of the battle. "Hooker was brave and determined, but seemed tired with the responsibility," Dahlgren observed in his diary. "His thoughts were not about him, and he took suggestions from any one. His want of capacity for such a large command was clearly shown this evening. He should have moved upon Fredericksburg as soon as he arrived. We lay here and let the enemy do most anything he pleased."[58]

The next day, Stonewall Jackson executed a daring and dangerous flanking maneuver by two-thirds of Lee's available force (part of his army had to remain on Marye's Heights in Fredericksburg to defend against Hooker's demonstrations there). Leaving only 13,000 men to demonstrate in Hooker's front, Jackson took 27,000 men on a twelve-mile flank march that was intended to crash into the lightly defended Union right flank, held by the Eleventh Corps. Ully Dahlgren, out carrying messages, rode out toward the Union right, where he detected signs of the presence of the enemy from the shouted commands of the hard-marching Confederate officers. "I went down the turnpike and watched their movements," wrote Ulric in his diary, "saw that they were passing us, and could hear their orders." At about this time, he saw Maj. Gen. Daniel E. Sickles' Third Corps engaged with Jackson's infantry near Catharine Furnace. Dahlgren galloped back to headquarters to report his intelligence, including news of Sickles' fight, prompting Hooker to say that he "had not ordered it." It was, however, too late—the initiative had already been snatched from Hooker's hands.[59]

By the time Dahlgren reported his findings, Jackson's savage flank attack had already commenced. His troops slammed into the Eleventh Corps and rolled it up. Hearing the guns booming from the Union right, Hooker sent Ulric to see what exactly was going on. "I went there, and found the Eleventh Corps running and the enemy pressing them on the flank and rear, which I reported to General Hooker." Hooker shifted troops to meet the threat, thus saving his army after taking heavy losses.[60] The Army of the Potomac, badly beaten by a much smaller enemy force, drew up in a defensive perimeter around the Chancellor house. A Confederate shell dazed Hooker when it struck his headquarters on May 3, leaving the Union army leaderless.

While the main forces fought it out at Chancellorsville, the Army of the Potomac's Sixth Corps, commanded by Maj. Gen. John Sedgwick, finally drove the Confederate defenders from their strong position along Marye's Heights, and advanced toward Hooker's position from the east. Robert E. Lee shifted Maj. Gen. Lafayette McLaws and Richard H. Anderson's divisions to Salem Church to meet the threat, leaving only Stonewall Jackson's command, now under command of his cavalry chief, Maj. Gen. J. E. B. Stuart, in Hooker's front. Heavy fighting erupted around Salem Church, and the Confederate defenders repulsed Sedgwick. As darkness fell on May 3, Ulric rode east, carrying messages for Sedgwick from Hooker.[61]

Two days later, Hooker sent Dahlgren to the Army of the Potomac's chief engineer, Brig. Gen. Gouverneur K. Warren, who was building a second line of defense. Ulric rode to Warren with orders to stop and return to army headquarters. He then escorted Warren back. "I had a horse killed & a whiskey flask broken in my saddle bags," Ulric informed his father about his ride that day.[62] After another day of desultory skirmishing, Hooker broke off and withdrew across the river unmolested on the night of May 6, soundly beaten even though two full corps of the Army of the Potomac did not engage in the fighting. "Nothing in sight," observed Ulric in his diary, "singular that the enemy did not follow us."[63] Hooker began withdrawing, and by the next night, the entire Army of the Potomac had safely crossed the river, leaving Lee's victorious army in control of the battlefield. Ully dashed off a quick telegram to his father: "Headquarters near Falmouth—All right."[64] That night, an exhausted Ulric Dahlgren, worn out from his constant labors, fell asleep on the floor of a telegraph office.[65]

Ulric had once again performed well under fire. As he always seemed to do, he kept himself near the front for most of the battle, keenly observing and recording events as they unfolded around him. His duties were somewhat humble; such is the lot of a staff officer in combat. However, his efforts in detecting Jackson's flank march might have made a difference in the outcome of the battle if the Union high command had been inclined to respond to the threat in a timely fashion.

While Hooker faced Lee at Chancellorsville, Stoneman's great raid finally got underway on April 30, with the element of surprise completely lost. The Federal horse soldiers bogged down well behind enemy lines, and two of the three divisions did not make their way back to the Army of the Potomac until well after the end of the Battle of Chancellorsville. The other division, unable to force its way through a large force of Confederate cavalry, instead joined the Army of the Potomac at Chancellorsville on the night of May 2. After a hard winter of picketing, the raid further took a severe toll on the men and horses of the Cavalry Corps, and it took several days for the horsemen to be ready to undertake another significant mission. As Stoneman made his way back to the army, Hooker sent out scouts, including Ully Dahlgren, to try to locate his missing horsemen. Dahlgren made a fifty-mile roundtrip from Falmouth to Kelly's Ford on May 8, carrying a message to the Cavalry Corps commander. "This most dangerous mission he performed, riding from Falmouth to Kelly's Ford, and back again, untouched by the countless balls that had whistled all around him."[66]

Always ambitious, Ulric continued pressing for higher rank. On May 21, he reported on the status of his efforts in a letter to his father. "I have written to Gen. Sigel stating that the President has now authority to brevet volunteers, that he is doing so for past action, that it is necessary that the application originate with the General with whom an officer has served." Hooker, Ulric reported, intended to recommend that the young man receive brevets to major and lieutenant colonel "for special services which were recognized on the battlefield at Cedar Mountain," and also for the Fredericksburg raid, respectively.[67]

Ulric Dahlgren had a plan in mind. "The rebel cavalry are again feeling along our lines, probably to find a weak point to enter at, as is their custom," wrote Dahlgren on May 23. "If they should attempt a raid, this would offer a fine chance for a small body of cavalry to penetrate their country." If the Southern horsemen launched a raid, Dahlgren proposed a counterpunch. He would take the 6th U. S. Cavalry across the Rappahannock and Rapidan Rivers, march to Louisa Court House, pass between Columbia and Goochland, and cross the James River to destroy the arsenal at Bellona. He would then either burn the bridges across the James at Richmond, dash through the city and on to White House Landing on the Pamunkey River, or after burning the bridges, go on to the crucial railroad junction city of Petersburg and then into the Federal lines at Suffolk. "The greatest obstacle would be passing their picket line on the Rappahannock," commented Dahlgren, "which, if accomplished without being discovered, would leave the roads open before us; but I know several men in the provost-marshal's service who feel confident of guiding such an expedition."[68] The aggressive young captain knew that his plan could succeed only if the Confederate cavalry went off on a raid of its own. "The object of the expedition would be to destroy everything along the route, and especially on the south side of the James River, and attempt to enter Richmond and Petersburg," he concluded.[69] "Hooker thought it too desperate," Ulric grumbled in his diary that night.[70]

On May 26, General Hooker visited Washington, taking Dahlgren with him. Ulric's proposed expedition undoubtedly occupied part of the agenda for Hooker's meeting with Stanton and Lincoln. The young man may even have presented his plan directly to the President and the secretary of war. The Union high command did not approve the proposed raid, and the two officers returned to Army of the Potomac headquarters the next day. Uric Dahlgren remained undaunted in spite of the rejection of his grand scheme. He continued refining his ideas for leading a cavalry raid on Richmond. That day would come. For now, though, hard duties lay ahead.[71]

On May 29, he made an ominous note in his diary, observing unusual activity among the rebels across the river. Later that same day, there was a review of twenty-five regiments and four batteries by some dignitaries from Richmond. Ully noted that "the artillery is in excellent order, but too many white horses," which made excellent targets. On June 4, Union scouts discovered empty enemy camps across the river.[72] Although they had no way of knowing it, another invasion of the North loomed, and Ulric Dahlgren stood poised to play a very important role in the unfolding of those evens.

Brig. Gen. Alfred Pleasanton
LIBRARY OF CONGRESS

Brig. Gen Julius Stahel
LIBRARY OF CONGRESS

CHAPTER NINE

The Gettysburg Campaign

Ulric Dahlgren's Finest Hour

IT WAS PROBABLY A GOOD THING that the Union high command rejected Ulric's proposed cavalry raid. Not long after his dramatic victory at Chancellorsville, Robert E. Lee began planning a second invasion of the North. In anticipation of that expedition, he ordered the concentration of all of his available cavalry forces in Culpeper County, where it spent a couple of weeks resting, refitting, and preparing for the coming invasion. Dahlgren's proposed raid would have run right into Stuart's assembled horse soldiers, likely leading to a most unhappy result.[1]

Within a month of its dramatic victory at Chancellorsville, the Army of Northern Virginia broke its camps and began advancing toward its date with destiny in Pennsylvania. "All quiet except now and then a shot. The enemy had filled up their rifle pits and stood on the R.R. as if they had not men enough over to hold the place but then moved up and were replaced by others," scrawled Dahlgren in his diary on June 6. "Their movements are very mysterious." He noted that deserters from Longstreet's corps reported that their command was on the move near Culpeper.[2] Finding out Lee's intentions became Hooker's primary concern.

Hooker dispatched the entire Cavalry Corps of the Army of the Potomac to break up the large concentration of Confederate cavalry forces in Culpeper County, Virginia. Brig. Gen. Alfred Pleasonton, the acting commander of the Army of the Potomac's Cavalry Corps (Stoneman was absent on medical leave), intended to lead the expedition himself. On June 6, Dahlgren noted in his diary, "Pleasonton preparing for a move. I will join him in the morning."[3] The perpetually restless Dahlgren was not about to miss such a grand adventure.

At 5:00 in the afternoon on June 7, Ully swung into his saddle and headed off to find Pleasonton's headquarters. He arrived there about 1:00 a.m. on June 8, and spent the day carrying messages to arriving Federal cavalry units.[4] That morning, he wrote to the cavalry chief, "General Hooker directs me to remain here for your instructions until he knows the result of Colonel [Alfred] Duffié's reconnaissance yesterday and until he can learn whether General [Julius]

Stahel's cavalry can assist."[5] He therefore served as an acting aide-de-camp to Pleasonton.

Pleasonton envisioned a pincers movement on the concentration of Southern horsemen. Two columns of Yankee troopers would attack Maj. Gen. J. E. B. Stuart's Confederate force, then thought to be concentrated at Culpeper Court House. Brig. Gen. John Buford commanded the northern wing, consisting of the Army of the Potomac's First Cavalry Division and 1,500 select infantry. Pleasonton ordered Buford to cross the Rappahannock River at Beverly's Ford and advance to Culpeper. The southern column, commanded by Brig. Gen. David M. Gregg, consisting of the Second and Third Divisions of the Cavalry Corps and another brigade of 1,500 elite infantry, would cross at Kelly's Ford and attack Stuart from the south.

This plan, while sound, was based on faulty intelligence. Rather than being concentrated at the town of Culpeper, the Confederate cavalry force lay just across the Rappahannock, so Buford's opening attack immediately encountered stiff resistance on the southern side of the river. Surprised by the resolve of the grayclad horsemen and stunned by the death of one of his brigade command-ers—Col. Benjamin F. Davis of the 8th New York Cavalry, who was killed in the opening moments of the battle—Buford's attack bogged down near the small wooden St. James Church, where most of Stuart's horse artillery battalion was concentrated.

In response, and not knowing how strong an enemy force held the ridge near the church, Buford ordered five companies of the 6th Pennsylvania Cavalry, also known as Rush's Lancers, to charge about 800 yards across a wide field under heavy artillery fire.[6] The Lancers contained many Philadelphia blue bloods, and Ulric knew many of them. Maj. Robert Morris, Jr., the great-grandson of the financier of the American Revolution, commanded the unit. Their colonel. Richard H. Rush, grandson of Dr. Benjamin Rush, had recently resigned his commission due to persistent illness, and Lt. Col. C. Ross Smith, next highest in rank, was permanently detailed to Pleasonton's staff. The last two compa-nies of the regiment had only turned in their lances just after the Battle of Chancellorsville.[7]

Unable to resist, Ulric Dahlgren pitched into their midst and together, they "made a dash of conspicuous gallantry" across the field and into the teeth of the Southern artillery. They "charged the enemy home, riding almost up to the mouths of [the] cannon," nearly capturing two of the Confederate guns.[8] One of the Rebel gunners admired, "Never rode troopers more gallantly . . . as under a fire of shell and shrapnel and finally of canister, the dashed up the very muzzles, then through and beyond our guns."[9] Maj. Gen. Henry C. Whelan of the 6th Pennsylvania reported, "The rebel cavalry, being much superior in number to us, closed in on [our] front and both flanks thus completely surrounding us."[10]

Charging across the open fields amidst the storm of shell and shot, Dahlgren rode boot-to-boot with Major Morris.[11] The men of the Keystone State galloped across an open field nearly a mile wide. A deep ditch bisected the field. On the opposite ridge stood St. James Church. A line of Confederate horse artillery, unlimbered along the ridge, supported by two brigades of cavalry, became the target of the charge. "We charged in column of companies. When we came out of our woods they rained shell into us, and as we approached nearer, driving them like sheep before us, they threw two rounds of grape and canister, killing as many of their men as ours; upon which they stopped firing and advanced their carbineers," Ulric reported to his father. "All this time we were dashing through them, killing and being killed; some were trampled to death in trying to jump the ditches which intervened, and, falling in, were crushed by others who did not get over."

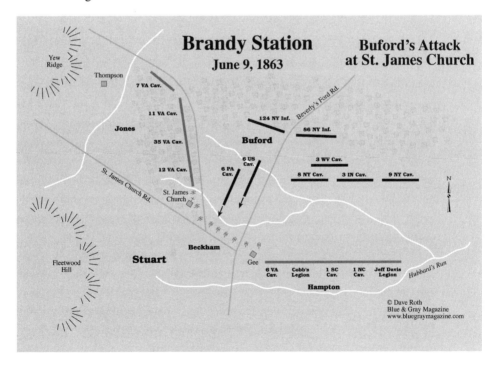

Brandy Station, July 9, 1863

"We dashed at them, squadron front with drawn sabres, and as we flew along-our men yelling like demons-grape and cannister were poured into our left flank and a storm of rifle bullets on our front," recalled Maj. Henry C. Whelan of Rush's Lancers. "We had to leap three wide deep ditches, and many of our horses and men piled up in a writhing mass in those ditches and were ridden over. It was here that Maj. Morris's horse fell badly with him, and broke away from him when he got up, thus leaving him dismounted and bruised by the fall. I didn't know that Morris was not with us, and we dashed on, driving the Rebels into and through the woods, our men fighting with the sabre alone, whilst they used principally pistols. Our brave fellows cut them out of the saddle and fought like tigers, until I discovered they were on both flanks, pouring a cross fire of carbines and pistols on us, and then tried to rally my men and make them return the fire with their carbines."[12]

As Dahlgren and Morris tried to jump the ditch, canister from one of the Confederate guns ripped into Morris' horse. The mortally wounded horse went down, falling on top of the major, trapping him underneath it. Ulric "could not tell if he was killed or not, for at the same instance my horse was shot in three places. He fell, and threw me, so that I could see nothing for a few moments." The Lancers found themselves hemmed in by the horse artillery. When the Confederate cavalry rallied and countercharged, the Pennsylvanians desperately fought their way out and dashed back toward the trees from which they came. "I saw the rear passing me, and about to leave me behind, so I gave my horse a tremendous kick and got him on his legs again," Dahlgren recounted. "Finding he could still move, I mounted and made after the rest—just escaping being taken." In the process, Ulric suffered a heavy blow to his arm from the back of a saber that nearly unhorsed him, leaving him painfully bruised. He rallied the remaining Lancers and led them back to the safety of the tree line. "After that, Buford made five successive charges against their line before he could break them, losing two hundred and fifty men."[13]

Dahlgren's coolness under fire and his courage in rallying and leading the Lancers back to safety impressed the Pennsylvanians. Likewise, the ferocious fight put up by the Lancers impressed him. "Capt. Dalgrean one of Gen Hookers staff officers . . . says that he never seen men fight so well in his life," recounted a sergeant of the 6th Pennsylvania Cavalry. "He says that when they charged and had their horse disabled they took to bushwhacking and fought with the infantry and their carbines. Major Morris led our men to the charge and when they were surrounded and Morris fell, it was Capt Dalgrean who rallied our men on their Collors, and charging the Enemey cut their way out again."[14]

Later that morning, the same five companies of the Lancers made a second mounted charge into the midst of the Confederate horsemen, fighting on until Gregg's command arrived on the field several hours later. All told, the combat at Brandy Station lasted for nearly fourteen hours, and was the greatest cavalry battle of the war. At the end of the day, the battle-weary Federals withdrew across the Rappahannock. Stuart was content to let them go. "So we fought fourteen hours, finally driving the enemy four or five miles off. Night coming on, and the enemy whipped, we crossed the river," Ulric concluded. "We are all delighted . . . . I have just had the balls extracted from my horse . . . . He was my best horse, and the bone in his foreleg is so shattered that I am afraid he must be killed."[15]

Dahlgren's gallant service did not go unnoticed by his temporary commander. When Pleasonton penned his report of the great battle, he wrote, "Captain Dahlgren . . . aide de camp of Major-General Hooker, [was] frequently under the hottest fire, and [was] untiring in [his] generous assistance in conveying my orders." He continued, "Captain Dahlgren was among the first to cross the river and chargedwith the first troops; he afterwards charged with the Sixth Pennsylvania Cavalry when that regiment won the admiration of the entire command, and his horse was shot four times. His dashing bravery and cool intelligence are only equaled by his varied accomplishments."[16] John Buford similarly lauded Dahlgren, writing, "To Captain Dahlgren, General Hooker's staff, I tender my thanks . . . for volunteering his services in carrying messages to different parts of the field."[17] A correspondent from *The New York Times* reported, "Captain Dahlgren, of General Hooker's staff, a model of cool and dauntless bravery, charged with the regiment, and his horse was shot in two places. He describes the charge as one of the finest of the war."[18]

"Ulric Dahlgren had that day given another earnest of fervent devotion to the Union case. To have ridden, as he did, near the head of that proud array of horsemen, breast to breast with its leading files, when it dashed like a thunderbolt on the foe, was a memory worth preserving," declared Admiral Dahlgren. "How narrowly he escaped in limb, perhaps in life, is best seen from the wounds which his horse received; a little higher speed, and he would have been left on the field, a wounded captive, perhaps to wear out the remains of life in one of those horrible dungeons where perished some of the gallant men near whom he rode that day,—among them Major Morris, who he saw fall with his horse."[19] In fact, Major Morris died a miserable, lonely death of illness while a prisoner in Richmond's dank Libby Prison, a fact not lost on Ully Dahlgren.

There was no rest for the young staff officer, who climbed back into his saddle at ten o'clock that night to ride to army headquarters to report on the fighting. He arrived the next morning, reported to Hooker, and then finally took a well-earned rest.[20] The respite lasted a day. He woke to the sad news that his badly wounded horse, Dick, had died during the night.[21] On the 11th, he was back in the saddle, scouting again. That evening, he reported his findings to Hooker:

> Last night (1 o'c a.m.) the signal officer here saw fires southeast—about where [Brig. Gen. James J.] Archer's brigade seems to have been—at the same time the enemy's pickets were withdrawn, excepting about 10 or 12 men along a line about 3 miles opposite here. This morning the pickets were strengthened, but not as strong as at first. The officer of the day thinks they were altogether withdrawn farther down, but I don't think he knows anything about it. He thought, also, that they were replaced near here by cripples, but he has not been down far; it is not yet reliable. The signal officer here has just discovered that 6 camps are missing where the fires were last night—they seem to be Archer's from the general direction.
>
> The artillery has not yet moved, only the six regiments of infantry. The signal officer at o'c P.M. reported no changes from the Fitzhugh House station. The pickets along the river seem to be nearer the water than usual, + also nearer together towards Fredericksburg + and with scarcely any supports. I will continue around the whole line, and go to the next station below, to see if there is anything moving.[22]

With a new campaign about to begin, both father and son continued looking for ways to gain a promotion for the ambitious young man. That day, Admiral Dahlgren dashed off a quick note to his son. "I have just sent a note to Gen. Hooker asking his consent to have you detailed for special duty in the Navy Department, for I want to give you a commission," he wrote, still unaware of the important role that his son had played at Brandy Station two days earlier.[23]

The next day, unaware that his father had made such a request, Ulric penned a lengthy description of the action at Brandy Station. "Pleasonton thanked me for my services & I suppose if he makes a written report will acknowledge them," Ulric concluded. In a postscript, he asked his father if Sigel had obtained the brevets for him, and then told his father, "I have a chance to be Lt Col of the 6th Ohio Cavalry Regmt which I am working for. Have to wait a week & will then get a letter from Hooker to give & then get it endorsed by the President." Had the commission as lieutenant colonel of the 6th Ohio come through, Ulric's commanding officer would have been William Stedman, now colonel of the Buckeye regiment. Given Stedman's bitterness about not receiving recognition for the previous fall's raid on Fredericksburg, this would have made for an interesting command dynamic. However, the coveted commission never materialized.[24]

On June 13, Dahlgren carried dispatches from Hooker to the headquarters of Maj. Gen. John F. Reynolds, commander of the Army of the Potomac's First Corps. Included was an order appointing Dahlgren as Reynolds' guide for the advance northward.[25] On June 16, Dahlgren rode into Washington with a letter for President Lincoln. "The cabinet seemed ignorant and anxious—great excitement about the invasion," he noted in his diary.[26]

Navy Secretary Gideon Welles recounted Ulric's thorough briefing on the situation at Army of the Potomac headquarters. Describing the young captain as "intelligent and gallant," Welles asked where the army was located. "He says between Fairfax and Centreville, or most of it was there; that Lee and the Rebel army are on the opposite side of the mountain fronting Hooker. He knows little or nothing of the reported Rebel advances into Pennsylvania, and thinks Hooker does not know it."[27] After delivering his message, he spent an hour visiting with his father, who observed, "He is well, but well rid of flesh."[28]

Ulric then turned around and headed back, carrying a letter from Lincoln to Hooker regarding the army commander's relationship with General-in-Chief Halleck. "You state the case much too strongly. . . . I believe Halleck is dissatisfied with you to this extent only, that he knows that you write and telegraph ('report' as he calls it) to me," wrote Lincoln. "I need and must have the professional skill of both, and yet these suspicions tend to deprive me of both. . . . Now, all I ask is that you will be in such mood that we can get into our action the best cordial judgment of yourself and General Halleck, with my poor mite added, if indeed he and you shall think it entitled to any consideration at all."[29] With the Union high command rapidly losing patience with Hooker, changes loomed. Several days later, Ulric led a reconnaissance to search for the Confederate infantry, which was advancing down the Shenandoah Valley toward Winchester. The town, however, fell to Lt. Gen. Richard S. Ewell's Second Corps infantry on June 14.

Ulric remained active while the Army of the Potomac groped for the Army of Northern Virginia. The Federal cavalry went out to try to find the whereabouts of Lee's army. Hooker had instructed Pleasonton to reconnoiter the Loudoun Valley on June 17, but then changed his mind. Hooker sent Ully Dahlgren to find Pleasonton to order the cavalry chief to halt wherever Dahlgren found him, as Hooker expected "to receive battle from the enemy in that position at

Manassas." Ully found the cavalry chief between Sudley Springs and Aldie and informed Pleasonton that he was to hold the cavalry corps at Gum Springs, east of Aldie. Pleasonton protested, sending Dahlgren back to Hooker suggesting that it would be better to advance the main body beyond the Bull Run Mountains at Aldie. Ully rode to the telegraph office in Centreville. "Gen'l Pleasonton is between Sudley Springs and Aldie and will halt near Gum Springs," reported Ulric at 1:00 that afternoon. "He reports nothing between Thoroughfare Gap and Ashby Gap and wants to push his whole command on to Aldie. I will wait here for answer."[30]

Hooker's chief of staff, Maj. Gen. Daniel Butterfield, replied promptly. "Under no circumstances advance the main body of your cavalry beyond [Aldie]," instructed Butterfield.[31] Ignoring the order to remain in place, Pleasonton continued his march toward Aldie. Pleasonton then ordered his lead brigade "to go on immediately, and not stop until we got through" Aldie Gap.[32]

On June 18, as the armies jockeyed for position on their way toward their date with destiny in Pennsylvania, John A. Dahlgren received a promotion to rear admiral and an appointment to command the fleet of ironclads assigned to the Southern Atlantic Fleet. His specific task was to command the Atlantic Blockading Squadron and to capture Charleston. He wanted to appoint Ulric as an aide-de-camp and take his son with him to South Carolina, but he never got the chance. That same day, Hooker told Ulric that he would not release him go with an invasion of the North underway.[33] Leaving the Navy Yard was a bittersweet experience for John Dahlgren—the family had spent many happy days there. "I expect to leave here on Wednes. (24th) and New York on the 29th or 30th," wrote Admiral Dahlgren on June 22. "So my son, goodbye. If we should not meet before that, our future is in hands that will provide better than we can. So never be discouraged however beset by the ills of life." Admiral Dahlgren had no idea how prophetic his words of fatherly advice actually were. His assignment to duty at sea meant that the Admiral could not be there when Ulric made an unplanned and unhappy visit home in July.[34]

On June 23, Admiral Dahlgren paid a final call upon President Lincoln before departing for Charleston. Ulric's future was on his mind, and he mentioned to the President that he was looking for ways to arrange a promotion for his son. He showed the President the letters from Sigel and Hooker, and Lincoln expressed his approval. The Admiral then visited Stanton, who indicated that he would make Ulric a major on Pleasonton's or some other corps commander's staff. The Admiral offered his son the option of either taking the promotion to major, or transferring to Charleston, where he could serve as assistant to the chief of ordnance. "I asked Mr. Stanton to send for you and see what you wanted," wrote the Admiral. However, this would have to wait until the end of the coming campaign, which was already well under way.[35]

As the armies headed north, Jeb Stuart faced a daunting task—keeping the active and diligent Union cavalry from finding the main body of the Army of Northern Virginia. Stuart's horsemen fought a series of stubborn delaying actions in the Loudoun Valley of Virginia at Aldie, Middleburg, and Upperville, on June 17, 19, and 21, respectively, as the two armies jockeyed for position. The Upperville fight, in particular, marked a first—it was the first time that the Army of the Potomac's Cavalry Corps defeated Stuart's troopers on the field of battle, driving them back to the mouth of Ashby's Gap, where the Southern horse soldiers came under the protection of Longstreet's infantry, then passing north on its way to Pennsylvania on the west side of the Blue Ridge. In spite of several days of hard fighting, Stuart prevented the Federal cavalry from finding the main body of Robert E. Lee's army.[36]

Dahlgren missed these fights, having ridden off with the division of Maj. Gen. Julius Stahel, whose independent cavalry command was still assigned to the defenses of Washington. Stahel's command had the primary task of patrolling the banks of the Potomac River and eradicating the guerilla forces of the notorious raider, Maj. John S. Mosby.[37] Rumors soon reached Admiral Dahlgren that Ully had been captured during one of the fights. Fortunately, they were just that—rumors. Reflecting on the fate of other young officers he knew who had been captured, young Dahlgren dreaded the very thought of being held prisoner. "Father, they shall never take me alive," he prophetically declared.[38]

On June 22, Hooker sent Dahlgren to Warrenton to search for Rebel forces left behind during the advance. He found only a single brigade of Confederate cavalry there, proving that Lee's army had already passed north on its way to Pennsylvania. "The brief and fragmentary memoranda of the young soldier evince his usual intentness on the work in hand," observed Ulric's father, "he is in the saddle constantly, and by following the scout of General Stahel's cavalry, loses the opportunity of being in the combats about Aldie."[39]

In the meantime, Admiral Dahlgren wrote to Hooker, seeking to have his son transferred to the Navy Department. Hooker replied that he would not object, but that "justice to the merits and services of Captain Dahlgren requires me to state that I consent to his withdrawal from me at this time with very great reluctance."[40] Fortunately for Ully, receipt of this letter changed Admiral Dahlgren's mind, and he rescinded the request for transfer. Instead, Ully remained with the Army of the Potomac.

The advance elements of the Confederate army entered Pennsylvania during the last week of June; Maj. Gen. Jubal A. Early's division of the Confederate Second Corps terrorized the town of Gettysburg on June 26. Lee's columns fanned out across south-central Pennsylvania, with elements of Ewell's corps reaching the outskirts of Harrisburg and occupying the important market town of York. Desperately searching for the Confederate army, Hooker asked to have the independent garrisons at Harpers Ferry and from the defenses of Washington assigned to his command. When the War Department denied this request, Hooker asked to be relieved of command, hoping that Halleck and Stanton would give in rather than relieve him. To Hooker's surprise, the Union high command promptly accepted his resignation on June 28. Lincoln ordered Maj. Gen. George G. Meade, Ulric's fellow Philadelphian, to assume command of the Army of the Potomac. Hooker, however, did not forget the outstanding service of his gallant young aide. He later praised Ulric's service during the early stages of the Gettysburg Campaign to Admiral Dahlgren, declaring, "I cannot too highly commend the zeal, efficiency, and gallantry which have characterized the performance of his duties while a member of my staff."[41]

Eager for accurate intelligence about the disposition and whereabouts of Lee's army, Alfred Pleasonton dispatched several scouting parties to try to locate it. He carefully selected the leaders of these reconnaissance missions from his small circle of trusted staff officers. Pleasonton's assistant adjutant general, Lt. Col. Andrew J. Alexander, commanded one force, made up of 40 Regulars of the 2nd U.S. Cavalry.[42] Capt. Frederic C. Newhall of the 6th Pennsylvania Cavalry,[43] led a second force.[43] Once again, Ulric Dahlgren saw an opportunity to "harass and as far as possible cut off the rebel communications."[44]

While at Army of the Potomac headquarters at Frederick, Maryland on June 30, Dahlgren wrote to the army's new commander, Meade, proposing "to take some men and operate on the rebel rear." Ulric actually intended to take 100 men and ride around the Army of Northern Virginia, cut its lines of communication with Richmond, and destroy the pontoon bridges across the Potomac River at Williamsport, Maryland, a most auspicious plan.[45] Meade, distracted by the weight of his new duties and worried about moving the Army of the Potomac quickly, did not pay the proposition much attention. Dahlgren "then applied to General P[leasonton] who ordered a sergeant and fifteen men to report—only ten came. With these and four scouts under Sergeant [Milton] Cline, we started out."[46] With only fifteen men, Ulric obviously would not be able to pull off as ambitious a scheme as he originally planned, but his little

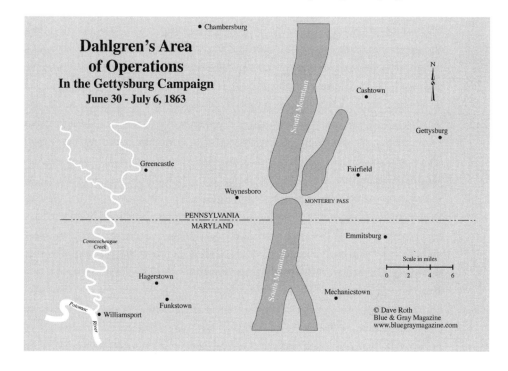

Map: *Dahlgren's Area of Operations in the Gettysburg Campaign*

command nevertheless would have a significant impact on the outcome of the campaign.

The raiding party was instructed by Pleasonton to operate on Lee's lines of communications and to kill, capture, and destroy whatever might be of use to the Confederacy. The tiny force consisted of the four scouts, two men of the 1st U. S. Cavalry, three from the 2nd U. S. Cavalry, three from the 5th U. S. Cavalry, and two men from the 6th U. S. Cavalry, including Pvt. Daniel A. Carl. The best men available, with the best mounts, accompanied Dahlgren on the expedition.[47]

Sergeant Cline was an excellent choice for a mission of this nature. Cline, thirty-nine-years-old, served in the 3rd Indiana Cavalry. He was a short, red-headed man with gray eyes, and had served as a sailor on Lake Champlain in his home state of New York before the war. In 1862, Cline joined the Bureau of Military Information as a scout, where he demonstrated a real flair for intelligence gathering.[48] The other four scouts were probably also members of the Bureau of Military Information. While they have not been specifically identified, historian Edwin C. Fishel believes that they included Capt. John

McEntee, and his scouts, Henry W. Dodd, Benjamin F. McCord, Ed Hopkins, and Anson Carney.[49]

Dahlgren dressed his little detachment in civilian clothing, and immediately set out for the rear of the Rebel army with his tiny force. They paused in Hagerstown to eat breakfast and feed their horses before moving on. They reached the Maryland village of Funkstown later that morning.[50] Two Pennsylvania infantrymen, separated from their command during the march north, spotted Dahlgren's approach. One of them declared, "I'll bet five dollars they are Union men."

Dahlgren overheard the exchange and inquired, "How can you tell Union men from rebels?" One of the Pennsylvanians responded, "We are Union soldiers and ought to know." The men exchanged information about the lay of the land and the disposition of the nearby Confederate forces. Dahlgren and his men then marched fifteen miles to the Pennsylvania town of Greencastle, arriving there late in the afternoon of July 1. They spent the rest of the day hovering around the town looking for stray Confederates, as a large force of Confederate cavalry and then most of Ewell's infantry had occupied Greencastle in the days prior to the battle already raging at Gettysburg.[51]

On July 2, after donning their uniforms once more, Dahlgren and his little command entered Greencastle and rode into the town square. Soon, the entire town knew that Yankee troopers had arrived, even though there was a squad of grayclads nearby. The townsfolk, who briefly saw Confederates on June 15 and were occupied by Rebel infantry on their first advance across the Mason-Dixon Line on June 22, were thrilled to see friendly soldiers. "If a band of angels had come down into the town they could not have been more unexpected or welcome," commented a local citizen. "It required only a few minutes to apprise the people of their presence, when all Greencastle seemed to be in the street." He continued, "Hats flew into the air and cheer followed cheer. Even the old and staid ministers forgot the proprieties and many wept for joy."[52]

Dahlgren quickly ordered the streets cleared of civilians and then climbed to the top of a nearby church tower to survey the area. Private Carl's uncle, Dr. Adam Carl, lived in the town, and Carl asked permission to visit his uncle. Dahlgren granted the permission. After carefully scanning the surrounding area, he spotted a detachment of Confederates obliviously riding into the outskirts of the town. Carl was feeding his horse in the alley behind his uncle's house when Dahlgren rode up and said, "Get ready; there is a squad of rebels coming, and we are going to fight." The two men mounted quickly and rode back to the town square.[53]

Dahlgren ordered his men to mount and form line of battle. "Boys, there is something important in that party, for there are two men mounted and a lot of infantry guarding them," declared Ulric. "Now, boys, how will we take them? Will we ride into them with the sabre, or will we depend upon our pistols and carbines?" They cried, "We will take them with this!" They drew their sabers, executed a left half-wheel, and charged the surprised Southerners with a "ringing cheer."[54]

"[Dahlgren's men] did not fire a shot, but some shots were fired by some rebel soldiers who were in the rear," observed one local civilian eyewitness. "Two bullets . . . struck the Carl house . . . and the marks are to be seen to this day."[55] They captured twenty-two rebel infantrymen and two couriers, along with two bags of mail destined for the Army of Northern Virginia. Dahlgren spotted a valise tied to the saddle of one of the nervous couriers. The man's discomfiture piqued Dahlgren's interest. He removed the valise from the saddle and searched it. Tucked inside a shirt, to his surprise, Ulric found letters to Robert E. Lee from President Jefferson Davis and Adjutant General Samuel Cooper.

These letters, which were not sent in cipher or any other form of encryption, responded to a proposal by Lee that during the invasion of the north, coastal defense garrison forces be moved from North and South Carolina to reinforce Lee's army. Lee wanted these troops to assume a blocking position in Culpeper County, near Brandy Station, where they either could quickly join Lee's invading army, or protect Richmond if the Northerners attempted a counterstroke. Gen. P. G. T. Beauregard would command this pick-up force, and would be charged with relieving the pressure being placed on the Confederate capitol from the east by Union forces commanded by Maj. Gen. John A. Dix. Because of strong Federal pressure on all fronts, these coastal defense troops could not be spared. Davis vehemently denied the request while Cooper suggested that Lee detach a portion of his force to guard his lines of communication with Richmond.[56]

"Boys, here is an important dispatch from Jeff Davis to Gen. Lee," Ulric declared triumphantly. "I must leave you and endeavor to place it in Gen. Meade's hands as quickly as possible. Serg't. Cline, take charge of these men; make your way to Emmitsburg and deliver all prisoners to the nearest Union forces. If any of these fellows attempt to escape, shoot them."[57] Dahlgren detailed several of his men to remain in Greencastle and barricade the Waynesboro Road on a hill east of town in order to prevent pursuit and recapture. The scouts piled hay wagons, hay ladders, and other impediments across the road.[58] Leaving the scouts to guard the barricade, Dahlgren galloped nearly thirty miles to

Gettysburg, arriving late in the evening of July 2.[59] "A ride of thirty miles over mountain roads, through a country covered by the enemy, must have been no insignificant addition to a day's work," commented his father. "No doubt, too, it was late in the night when he reached the battlefield, for the last assault of the rebels had been made about dark."[60]

Ironically, Robert E. Lee eventually learned of these missing dispatches in an article that appeared in *The New York Times* on July 8, after his retreating army passed through Hagerstown, Maryland on its way to the Potomac River crossings and the safety of Virginia. "I see it stated in a letter from the special correspondent of the New York Times that a bearer of dispatches from Your Excellency to myself were captured at Hagerstown on the 2d July, and the dispatches are said to have a great bearing on 'coming events,'" wrote Lee on July 8. "I have thought proper to mention this, that you may know whether it is so."[61] The Confederate high command made a critical error in sending such important dispatches in the clear. Col. Edward Porter Alexander, sometime chief of artillery for the Army of Northern Virginia's First Corps, and a former Signal Corps officer, leveled an appropriate criticism: "How careless it is to send valuable military information around without putting it in cipher."[62] Likewise, "it was inexcusable in Mr. Davis to make no effort to carry out General Lee's wish," noted a member of the 9th Virginia Cavalry. "Instead of doing this, he wrote General Lee telling him it was impossible to do what he wished, and trusted it to a single cavalryman to carry it through a hostile country to General Lee."[63]

There is much controversy over the effect that Dahlgren's intelligence had on the outcome of the battle of Gettysburg. Most traditional accounts of the story claim that when Dahlgren arrived on the field, Meade was conducting a council of war with his corps commanders to decide whether to continue to hold the line at Gettysburg, or to fall back to a pre-selected position along Pipe Creek in northern Maryland. Under this version of events:

> [Meade] had been consulting with his corps commanders, and had resolved to withdraw his army to Pipe Creek, the position that had been previously selected by General Warren, his chief of engineers, and in pursuance of that plan was then engaged in retiring his heaviest pieces of artillery from the front. A perusal of the dispatch captured and presented by Dahlgren wrought a sudden change in Meade's plans and the artillery was quickly ordered back to the positions from which it had been withdrawn, and the Federal army made ready to recommence the battle on the following morning.[64]

In fact, there is no evidence to support the contention that Meade ordered the artillery to leave the field at Gettysburg at any time prior to the council of war. More likely, the author of this account heard Brig. Gen. Henry J. Hunt, the Army of the Potomac's chief of artillery, repositioning his guns for the coming day's fighting and mistook those noises for the beginning of a full-scale retreat by the Army of the Potomac.

Meade needed operational intelligence, not strategic intelligence. Dahlgren's prize provided critical strategic intelligence—it made it clear that Lee would not receive any reinforcements, and that the Gray Fox would have to make do with his available force. This, in turn, meant that Meade could focus on the Army of Northern Virginia without worrying about threats to his rear. That knowledge undoubtedly gave Meade confidence as he planned for the third day's fighting. Additionally, Dahlgren did not mention attending or briefing the council of war in his diary; such an important event would have received notice in Ully's daily journal. However, Dahlgren's coup did not provide the tactical intelligence Meade required.[65]

Recent research suggests that the council of war ended before Dahlgren arrived at Gettysburg. On the morning of July 3, the Army of the Potomac's Adjutant General, Brig. Gen. Seth Williams, sent a dispatch to Maj. Gen. O. O. Howard, commander of the Eleventh Corps, reporting the intelligence brought in by Dahlgren. This means that Howard left the council of war prior to Dahlgren's arrival, or else he already would have been aware of Dahlgren's coup. It is unlikely that Howard, who commanded the battlefield at Gettysburg for much of the day on July 1, left the council of war early, so it becomes apparent that the council was already over prior to the young captain's arrival.[66]

Regardless of whether Dahlgren arrived in time to influence the results of the council of war, his feat was nevertheless a *coup de main*. His intelligence provided irrefutable proof that Lee could expect no reinforcements and that Army of Northern Virginia had been left to fend for itself in Pennsylvania. Unaware of the monumental nature of the intelligence he had captured, the tired young officer got a richly deserved respite that night. He needed it. More adventures awaited him the next day.

Waking early on the morning of July 3, Dahlgren again swung into his saddle and rode ten miles down the Emmitsburg Road towards Mechanicsville, Maryland, looking for Brig. Gen. Wesley Merritt's Reserve Brigade of the Army of the Potomac's First Cavalry Division. Merritt's command spent the first two days of the battle of Gettysburg guarding supply wagons in Maryland, hearing the guns booming a few miles away.[67] Dahlgren carried an order from Pleasonton instructing Merritt to give the young captain some officers and one hundred handpicked horse soldiers to make a second raid toward Greencastle.[68]

Reading the orders, Merritt detailed one hundred men of Companies D, F, K, and L of the 6th Pennsylvania Cavalry, which included many of the same men that Ully had rallied during the charge on the guns at St. James Church. Capt. William P. C. Treichel commanded the contingent of Lancers, with Lts. Albert P. Morrow, Edward Whiteford, Bernard H. Herkness, and Charles White joining the expedition. The small column set out to cover the twenty-five miles to Greencastle, reached Waynesboro, Pennsylvania late that afternoon, and stopped there to bivouac for the night.[69]

Dahlgren roused the men from their slumbers shortly after 1:00 a.m. Less than an hour later, the horse soldiers resumed their course for Greencastle, which was briefly occupied by Brig. Gen. John D. Imboden's Northwestern Brigade of Confederate cavalry. Imboden and his Virginians advanced through the town on their way to Gettysburg on the morning of July 3. Dahlgren's weary horse soldiers were alone, operating far behind enemy lines, and with a large force of the enemy not far away. They were in a very precarious situation, and they knew it. "Soon this fine detachment . . . bearing away to the left and crossing the Blue Ridge at Monterey Pass," observed an officer of the 6th Pennsylvania, "was thrashing around in the enemy's rear, on the wrong side of the mountains for safety or comfort, or for any reasonable hope of accomplishing with such a small party, anything to compensate for the risk they ran."[70]

Ulric's column marched, using the same roads that Lee's army would have to use in order to retreat toward the Potomac River. On the morning of July 4, word reached Greencastle that Lee's great assault on the Union center on the previous afternoon had failed. A Confederate wagon train of wounded men, a seventeen-mile-long traveling sea of misery which wound its way from Gettysburg through the Cashtown Gap south toward Greencastle, south to Hagerstown, and ultimately to the Potomac River ford at Williamsport, was headed their way. Robert E. Lee gave the critical assignment of defending this wagon train of wounded to Imboden. It was a daunting task at best, with torrential rains and roving parties of Federal cavalry only making the mission all the more challenging. The 18th Virginia Cavalry, commanded by the general's brother, Col. George Imboden, led the train's advance. Imboden had a battery of horse artillery as additional support.[71]

As Ully's horsemen marched, a large number of mounted civilians joined them, armed with shotguns and axes that they intended to use to destroy the wheels of the Confederate wagon. When they arrived near Greencastle, a local citizen informed Ulric that Imboden's cavalry held the town, covering the passage of the wagon train. Undaunted, with the first pink fingers of daylight creeping across the horizon, Dahlgren ordered his men to draw sabers and charge. Their blades flew from their scabbards, and the Pennsylvanians put spurs to their horses. "Our little band, led by Captain Treichel, charged through the streets, surprising the enemy," proudly declared the regimental historian of the 6th Pennsylvania. "Lieutenant Morrow received a slight wound while leading a portion of the force in this charge, while his horse was killed under him."[72] The Pennsylvanians took seventeen Confederate infantrymen and another seven cavalrymen prisoners in this daring charge.[73] They also captured a Rebel paymaster and the money he carried.[74] "Passed the 4th in Greencastle. The enemy's communications entirely destroyed," Ulric proudly wrote in his diary that evening. "Remained in the town all day, feeling proud of our work. Citizens very uneasy about our being there."[75]

A Rebel staffer, McHenry Howard, recalled that when he and a few other mounted men were about a mile from town, they "heard a shot and then met a mail carrier galloping down the road, who reported that he had been attacked while passing through the town." When Howard and his comrades rode into Greencastle that day, the town "seemed sullenly quiet, doors and windows closed and nobody on the street." Instead of hospitality from the townspeople, the blazing carbines of the Pennsylvania horse soldiers met them. There, "about fifty of the Southern Cavalry came down South Carlisle Street, demanding to see the town authorities, but just before they reached the square, the Federal soldiers made a dash and drove them out in splendid style, capturing a considerable number. Though the shots whistled in close proximity to our ears, the citizens remained on the street to witness the result." Howard later commented, "So much for my twenty hours in Maryland and Pennsylvania and so much for my only cavalry experience. I had fired but one shot . . . and this was one of the only two shots I fired during the war. I should add that in this little campaign, we had three men captured—at Greencastle—and one wounded, who got off."[76]

The Federals got an early start again the next morning, July 5. They took a long and dangerous route to get to Greencastle, riding to Emmitsburg, on to Fairfield, through the Monterey Pass, and then on to Greencastle, some 21 miles away. Not far from Greencastle, Dahlgren happened upon a train of six hundred wagons, accompanied by Imboden's 18th Virginia Cavalry, a regiment of infantry, and supported by a battery of horse artillery. Dahlgren's force laid in wait until about three hundred of the wagons had passed. Detachments commanded by Lieutenants Albert P. Morrow and Bernard H. Herkness then attacked opposite ends of the train, briefly seizing the Confederate artillery.[77] "The Yankees broke into our lines and captured the battery," recounted Imboden's adjutant, John Hyde Cameron. "Captain [Francis M.] Imboden charged the Yankees and we recaptured the battery. I can now see how my old friends Carter Berkeley, Dr. Willis, and Dr. Ware were delighted at being recaptured."[78]

"Dahlgren ordered a charge, to which the party responded with all their might, and in a moment they were in the midst of the wagons banging away and trying to capture the train," observed an officer of the 6th Pennsylvania, "but the infantry and cavalry escort was entirely too strong for them and they were obliged to beat a retreat, and finally to scatter to avoid the enemy's close pursuit."[79]

"The command was moved near to the road and lay concealed until about 300 wagons had passed, when, the force being divided between Lieutenants Morrow and Herkness, they charged to the front and rear of the train at the same time," recounted the regimental historian of the 6th Pennsylvania Cavalry. "With the assistance of citizens they destroyed 130 wagons and run the horses off to the woods, captured two iron guns, and 200 prisoners." When the train's infantry detachment appeared, a severe firefight ensued wherein the Pennsylvanians lost nearly all of the prisoners previously taken by them. In addition, the Lancers lost a number of men captured, including Lieutenant Herkness, who was captured after receiving a severe sabre cut in the skirmish with Imboden's Virginians. It was "very romantic fighting," as Ulric later described this fighting.[80] "Our men fled to the woods and were scattered in small squads during the night," concluded the regimental historian of the Lancers. "They rendezvoused at Waynesboro, Pa. On the following morning they succeeded in bringing to Waynesboro about thirty prisoners."[81]

"After the advance—the 18th Virginia Cavalry—had passed perhaps a mile beyond the town, the citizens to the number of thirty or forty attacked the train with axes, cutting the spokes out of ten or a dozen wheels and dropping the wagons in the streets. The moment I heard of it I sent back a detachment of cavalry to capture every citizen who had been engaged in this type of work, and treat them as prisoners of war," recalled General Imboden. "This stopped the trouble there, but the Union cavalry began to swarm down upon us from the fields and cross-roads, making their attacks in small bodies, and striking the column where there were few or no guards, and thus creating great confusion." Imboden narrowly escaped capture by some of Dahlgren's men, relying upon blasts of canister from two of Capt. John H. McClanahan's guns to drive off his pursuers. "They would perhaps have been too much for me, had not Colonel Imboden, hearing the firing turned back with his regiment at a gallop, and by the suddenness of his movement surrounded and caught the entire party."[82]

Dahlgren's horse was shot out from him during the fracas, and "it was only by dispersing his men in different directions amid the deep forest, that he avoided close pursuit and contrived to reach the vicinity of Boonesboro."[83] The combined force of Union cavalry and civilians destroyed 130 wagons, ran the horses into the woods, and captured two guns and 200 prisoners, including Maj. William M. Lock of the 18th Virginia Cavalry.[84] However, a counterattack by Companies F and I of the 18th Virginia Cavalry drove the bluecoats off, recaptured the guns, and took a number of prisoners.[85] "The Federals had cut the train," noted a Virginian. "My company turned back and Company I came forward; we struck the Yankees in both flanks and drove them away, getting back all they had taken, together with some prisoners."[86]

"The infantry and cavalry escort was entirely too strong for them and they were obliged to beat a retreat, and finally to scatter to avoid the enemy's close pursuit," recalled Capt. Frederic C. Newhall of the 6th Pennsylvania Cavalry. "Lieutenant Herkness of our regiment was severely wounded and captured, with ten or more of the men, and the whole command was badly cut up, while before [Capt. William P. C.] Treichel could get the remnant together again the country about him was swarming with rebels retreating now from their bitter defeat at Gettysburg."[87]

C.S.A. Maj. Alfred H. Belo of the 55th North Carolina Infantry, wounded on the first day of the Battle of Gettysburg, later wrote, "In passing through Greencastle quite a number of citizens came around the wagon, and soon after leaving there a body of Federal cavalry attacked the wagon train. I had on a fatigue jacket with a Major's star. The wreathed star in their army showed the rank of Brigadier General. They asked 'Where's that General?' My servant, who was riding one of my horses and leading the other, hearing this, urged me to try and mount my horse and escape, but before this was done, a body of our cavalry came up and repulsed the Federals."[88]

The intense fight at Greencastle took its toll on Dahlgren's little column. By the morning of July 6, only about eighty of the original 100 men remained with him. Dispersed about the Pennsylvania countryside, the young cavalryman's command was "greatly scattered, being secreted by loyal citizens." Lieutenant Whiteford, along with his squad of ten Lancers, hid in Hagerstown while Longstreet's infantry corps passed through the town.[89] Despite the disorganization of his command, Dahlgren learned that some of Brig. Gen. Albert G. Jenkins' cavalry had demanded a ransom from the town of Waynesboro. Once again putting spurs to his horse, Ulric dashed off, leading his horse soldiers on another reckless head-long charge, surprising and scattering the Rebel troopers in the streets of the town. After a pursuit of nearly six miles, Dahlgren finally gave up the chase, instead choosing to attack another wagon train. His men destroyed a large number of wagons and took more prisoners along the way.[90]

On the morning of July 6, Dahlgren joined Brig. Gen. Judson Kilpatrick's Third Cavalry Division's advance on Hagerstown. The dangerous and taxing raid far behind enemy lines was finally over. They had destroyed over two hundred wagons, loaded with valuable supplies stolen from the farmers and merchants of Pennsylvania. "At one time they held more than double their number of prisoners, many of whom escaped during their several engagements," proudly declared the regimental historian of the 6th Pennsylvania Cavalry, "although they succeeded in bringing in to General Buford's headquarters between seventy and eighty of them."[91] Although costly in terms of men and horseflesh, Dahlgren's expedition succeeded. However, his career was about to take an entirely different, and not altogether happy, turn.

July 6, 1863 proved to be, as Admiral Dahlgren later described it, "the last day of service that Ulric Dahlgren shall render to his country for a long time."[92] That morning, Kilpatrick learned that a train of Southern wagons was passing through Hagerstown, and he decided to try to bag it. On the night of July 4-5, he pounced on a large Confederate wagon train as it headed through the Monterey Pass through South Mountain, bagging nearly 1500 wagons. He decided to add the Hagerstown train to his already impressive tally of booty. Kilpatrick's initial advance into the town was largely unopposed, to the surprise of the Federal horse soldiers. They entered the town from the south, while the Southern defenders expected the Federals to approach from the north. However, the Northerners soon discovered that the town's streets had been barricaded, and that Confederate riflemen occupied church steeples and cupolas, sniping at the Yankee horsemen as they tried to enter the city. The grayclad cavalry brigades of Beverly H. Robertson and John R. Chambliss, Jr. held the town.[93]

Dahlgren and his contingent of tired Lancers arrived just as Kilpatrick made his dispositions to attack two brigades of Confederate cavalry, the vanguard of which had arrived in Hagerstown's public square. Finding enemy pickets in force, Kilpatrick decided to recall his forces and avoid an uneven fight in the streets of the town. It was too late, however, for the gallant young cavalryman. Joined by the remnants of his raiding party, and always eager to pitch into the fray, Dahlgren fell in with a squadron of the 18th Pennsylvania Cavalry, which was already advancing to attack the Confederate positions.

With the Pennsylvanians at his side, Ulric Dahlgren made a head-long dash down the main street of Hagerstown—Potomac Street—crashing into pickets of the 9th Virginia Cavalry posted there, and driving all resistance back toward the public square in the middle of town. Reinforced by most of Col. John R. Chambliss Jr.'s brigade of Confederate cavalry, the grayclad troopers made a stand there, and the two forces went saber-to-saber, boot-to-boot, in brutal and bloody urban hand-to-hand combat.

A local citizen, who had an eyewitness view of the action in the streets below, recalled, "The cutting and slashing was as beyond description; here right before and underneath us the deadly combat was waged in a hand to hand combat, with the steel blades circling, waving, parrying, thrusting, and cutting, some reflecting the bright sunlight, others crimsoned with human gore; while the discharge of pistols and carbines was terrific, and the smoke through which we now gazed down through and on the scene below, the screams and yells of the wounded and dying, mingled with cheers and commands, the crashing together of the horses and fiery flashes of the small arms presented a scene such as words cannot portray."[94] The commander of the company of the 18th Pennsylvania, Captain William C. Lindsay, was killed in this fighting, and his small command took heavy casualties. Dahlgren spotted the Rebel trooper responsible for killing Lindsay and "immediately cut the man down with his saber."[95]

Having avenged Lindsay's death, Dahlgren left the remnants of Company A in the alleys on both sides of the town square, and went in search of reinforcements, which he found in the form of Company D. Dahlgren called on twenty men of Company D to dismount, leave their sabers on their saddles, and to proceed on foot. He placed ten troopers on each sidewalk, while riding along in the middle of the street. Dahlgren stayed even with the advance of the squads, and told the Pennsylvanians not to fire until he gave the order. When they approached to within 300 yards of the town's square, the dismounted Confederate horse soldiers opened fire on them, using the mounted captain as a convenient target. Dahlgren rode on, oblivious to the danger and the bullets whizzing by his ear.

Responding, Ulric hollered, "Now boys, give it to them!" The Yankees fired a volley from each sidewalk, driving the Southern cavalrymen from their position. The Rebels fell back to the Zion Reformed Church, where, supported by artillery, they made a stand. The Confederate troopers, sheltering behind walls and tombstones, opened fire on the advancing Federals. The men of the 18th Pennsylvania incurred heavy losses, "in consequence of having to face, with sabers, in a narrow street, an enemy who was using pistols."[96] An unexpected and fierce flanking fire caused Dahlgren to wheel and face the new threat. He sat his horse on the west side of the street, coolly directing his men to meet the flanking attack by the Rebels, when, "the rebels behind the church shot him."[97] Capt. Frank A. Bond of the 1st Maryland Cavalry is often credited with firing the shot that hit Ully Dahlgren.[98] Although unaware of the severity of his wound, Dahlgren turned to *New York Times* correspondent E. A. Paul, who was riding at his side, and called out, "Paul, I have got it at last!" He remained in the saddle for a full half hour until he fainted from loss of blood.[99]

"Meanwhile, showers of bullets came on the devoted party from every direction—from streets, alleys, and houses. Several of our men were killed, others were wounded and left behind, and it only remained to get out of town as quickly as possible," recounted Paul. "Captain Dahlgren was already wounded; the sensation was so slight, that he thought it was nothing more than a glancing ball, and little dreamed that his heavy boot and foot had been pierced. But he must now turn with the remnant of his party and ride for life. His good steed once more bears him from captivity or death, and then he falls from the saddle, exhausted by loss of blood. Friendly hands are near to receive the wounded soldier and bear him to an ambulance."[100]

Maj. Luther Trowbridge of the 5th Michigan Cavalry watched the injured young captain ride up to Kilpatrick and report on his role in the fighting. After hearing the report, Kilpatrick gave the young officer further orders. Interrupting, Dahlgren responded, "General, I am hit," and pointed out the wound in his leg. Trowbridge saw the wounded captain dismount his horse, and watched him lay down on the ground, where he evidently passed out from the shock and loss of blood.[101] Some nearby troopers carried the gravely wounded captain to a nearby ambulance, where he spent the night. Coming to, Dahlgren had the strength to pull out his diary and scribble in it, "Did not consider it more than a ball glancing—had no idea that it went through. Foot not very painful. Slept well."[102] However, he probably did not realize that his wounded foot was mangled.

After the Gettysburg Campaign, Judson Kilpatrick praised Dahlgren lavishly in his report of the fighting at Hagerstown. He wrote, "I cannot pass over this engagement without mentioning a few among the many individual cases of gallantry that came under my own observation: . . . Captain . . . Dahlgren . . . was wounded, leading a daring charge through the streets of Hagerstown."[103]

The next day, his ambulance reached shelter in the town of Boonsboro, where a surgeon removed several bone shards from the wound. The injured captain nevertheless maintained a positive attitude, writing in his diary, "Foot easy and comfortable. Slept well."[104] The next day, his journey continued on to Frederick. Dahlgren was still not in much pain, but he also had a realistic view of his condition, noting in his diary, "Foot easy—no fever; the foot had better come off."[105] He was right. And what remained of his short life would never be the same.

Capt. Charles E. Cadwalader, whose commission was in the 6th Pennsylvania Cavalry, served with Dahlgren on Meade's staff. The two Philadelphians, who had a great deal in common, became close friends over the past few months. "I am sorry to lose him as we had become very intimate and I liked him very much," Cadwalader informed his mother a few days later. Cadwalader correctly guessed that the serious wound suffered by Dahlgren would leave Ulric "on the shelf for months," as he put it.[106]

The Confederate retreat continued while Dahlgren recuperated from his Hagerstown wound. In the early phases of the Gettysburg Campaign, Secretary of War Edwin M. Stanton dispatched Brig. Gen. Lorenzo Thomas, the adjutant general of the United States, to Harrisburg, Pennsylvania, so that a steady and professional hand joined Maj. Gen. Darius N. Couch in supervising the emergency troops gathered there. Late in the afternoon of July 4, Secretary of War Stanton relayed Dahlgren's intelligence coup to Thomas:

> We have sure information, by intercepted dispatches from Jeff. Davis and General Cooper, that on last Saturday Lee made an urgent appeal for re-enforcements from Beauregard, Bragg, and from Richmond, and they were refused, because Beauregard had sent all he dared part with to Joe Johnston, and so had Bragg; that the force in North Carolina and at Richmond was too small to defend Richmond and protect Lee's communications, and that they could not spare a man. The story about Beauregard coming, no doubt, has been told by Lee to keep up the spirits of his men. Davis' dispatch is the best view we have ever had of the rebels' condition, and it is desperate. They feel the pressure at all points, and have nothing to spare in any quarter, so that Lee must fight his way through alone, if he can. Everything here will be employed to best advantage, and it is of the utmost importance to push forward from Harrisburg and harass the enemy.[107]

Likewise, Maj. Gen. Samuel P. Heintzelman, commander of the troops assigned to the defenses of Washington, D.C., realized the significance of the intelligence captured by Dahlgren. "The news from General Meade is good. . . . We captured very important dispatches from Jefferson Davis to Lee and from General Cooper. The letters go into minute details of the situation," Heintzelman scribbled in his diary on July 4. "With the knowledge we have of our situation and this information of theirs, our prospects are decidedly flattering."[108]

Thus, Dahlgren's intelligence coup provided Washington with the necessary impetus to push the pursuit of Lee's beaten army, even if that information came at a staggering price. Vicksburg was in the process of falling—the beleaguered garrison would surrender that day—the substantial Union garrison at Fortress Monroe, at Hampton Roads, kept the rebels assigned to defend Richmond pinned down, and Federal forces under Maj. Gen. Quincy Gillmore were pressuring the Confederate defenders of Charleston. No reinforcements could be spared to rescue Lee's army, which was now pinned with its back against the flooded banks of the Potomac River and apparently ripe for the picking. Further, the Army of the Potomac's high command knew that Lee's army was outnumbered and desperately short of artillery ammunition.[109] After hearing of the escape of Lee's army across the Potomac on July 13-14, a mortified Lincoln lamented, "We had them in our grasp. We had only to stretch forth our hands and they were ours. And nothing I could say or do could make the army move."[110]

Bad weather and Meade's seeming hesitation at pushing the issue with the Confederates further exasperated Abraham Lincoln. The Army of Northern Virginia crossed the Potomac River on the morning of July 13 before Meade could attack Lee's army while it was still pinned against the banks of the swollen river. Knowing that Lee had no available reinforcements and that he would have to fight it out along the banks of the flooded Potomac River, it came as no wonder or surprise that Lincoln grew terribly frustrated with George Meade's seeming unwillingness to pursue Lee's army. Ulric Dahlgren's intelligence gave Meade a clear understanding of the state of the Confederate forces. Thus, while Dahlgren's capture of the correspondence intended for Lee may not have played a role in the decision of the Army of the Potomac to stay and fight it out at Gettysburg, it played a crucial role in the pursuit and the opportunity to destroy Lee's army; an effort which, however, was lost along the banks of the Potomac River.

CHAPTER TEN

The Slow Road To Recovery

SOMETIME DURING THE EVENING of July 9, a train delivered the wounded soldier to Washington, D.C., where a few friends greeted him. Several soldiers also waited at the station with a stretcher to carry him to his father's house. Admiral Dahlgren was absent—he had arrived at Port Royal, South Carolina on July 4 and then assumed command of the South Atlantic Blockading squadron on the 6th—and Ulric's brother Charley lay ill in Cincinnati after contracting malaria during the Vicksburg Campaign. His brother Paul, a midshipman, was at the Naval Academy, temporarily located in Newport, Rhode Island. Ulric was in bad shape. However, he still understood the effect that seeing him in such a state would have had on his father. "If my father had been here I could not have consented to be brought home, because this bloody wound would have tortured him, and that would have been more than I am able to bear!" he declared to a family member.[1]

"Loss of blood and pain, and discomfort have made sad inroads already on his hardy frame," later wrote his father, "but the sight of old familiar faces recalls something of the past, and his eye once more beams with pleasure as it ranges over the objects that revive past memories." A surgeon attended him carefully, urging Ulric to try to rest. However, the wound caused him great pain and suffering. The heat and humidity of the Washington summer further sapped his energy and will, causing his condition to deteriorate quickly.[2] His Aunt Patty "took charge of him & nursed him as his own mother would have done had she been living," noted Charley after the war.[3]

Friends crowded around him, offering their sympathy. Even President Lincoln visited Ulric's bedside. "As he looks upon the youth in whom he has ever evinced so much interest, now tortured with agony which no words can describe, tears unbidden come. Well for both it is, that the misty veil that hides the future is impenetrable to mortal eye!" commented Admiral Dahlgren of Lincoln's visit.[4] General Hooker called. One evening, Secretary of War Stanton, a frequent visitor, paid an unexpected call. Upon his arrival, he asked for Ulric's Aunt Patty. When she came down to see him, Stanton handed her an envelope and said, "I have promoted Ulric to a colonelcy."[5] Stanton left the commission with Patty Read, making Ulric Dahlgren the youngest full colonel in either army. Stanton's letter said:

Enclosed you have a commission for colonel, without having passed through the intermediate grade of major. Your gallant and meritorious service has, I think, entitled you to this distinction, although it is a departure from general usage which is only justified by distinguished merit such as yours. I hope you may speedily recover, and it will rejoice me to be the instrument of your further advancement in the service.[6]

The promotion, a reward for Ully's brilliant service during the Gettysburg Campaign, came as a complete surprise to all. However, he lingered on death's doorstep and did not know about the honor bestowed upon him for several days.[7]

"I was at his bedside day and night," recalled his Aunty Patty. "His sufferings were terrible and it seemed a miracle that his life was spared." She continued. "Our dear sufferer had been at the point of death all day and I dared not give him the commission without consent of his physicians," she added. "They came in soon after, and feared the result. One said 'no' the other 'yes, it will do him good,' so it was given and the next morning early he asked for a magistrate. One was sent for and I shall never forget the solemn scene when dear Ulric with all the strength he could command, raised his right hand and said, 'So help me God, Amen.'" However, nobody expected that he would ever be able to don the colonel's eagles. Instead, they expected him to die. However, Ully was strong-willed, and perhaps the commission arrived at precisely the right moment. It gave Ulric a reason to want to live.[8]

His uncle, S. Abbott Lawrence, elderly himself and in poor health, came from Newport, Rhode Island, to help care for the dangerously ill young man. Ulric sweltered in the brutal heat of the summer, which depleted his strength as the days passed. In spite of his sufferings, he was not bitter. Upon hearing that a former schoolmate from the Rittenhouse Academy, fighting on the Confederate side, had been wounded and captured, he put aside his own travails and expressed sympathy for his friend's plight.[9] The patient's condition did not improve appreciably; rather, it worsened to the point that all traffic in front of the house was prohibited and a sentry was placed at the front door to prevent anyone but medical personnel from entering.

Ulric suffered from excruciating pain. Surgeons examined the wound carefully, and reported the news that all dreaded: gangrene had set in and the foot would have to be amputated. On July 21, fifteen days after he was wounded, a surgeon removed Ulric's mangled lower right leg below the knee. For three days, the young man's life hung in the balance and it appeared that he would not survive. Finally, on the third day after the surgery, he showed some improvement, and then gradually got better with each passing day.[10]

Something had to be done with Ulric's severed limb. In the summer heat, it could not be transported back to Philadelphia for burial in the family plot. An old friend of Admiral Dahlgren came up with an unusual solution to the problem: the limb would be sealed in the Dahlgren Gun Foundry building being erected at the Washington Navy Yard. The severed limb received a full military funeral, complete with honor guard and casket. A plaque on the wall marked the burial place: "Within this wall is deposited the leg of Col. Ulric Dahlgren, U.S.V. Wounded July 6, 1863, while skirmishing in the streets of Hagerstown, with the Rebels after the Battle of Gettysburg."[11]

On July 22, correspondent Noah Brooks of the *Sacramento Daily Union* reported that Ulric was in Washington due to being seriously wounded in battle. Brooks called Ully a "hero," and described him as being as "brave and gallant a soldier as ever lived" who had "distinguished himself by various exploits of arms." Not realizing that the foot had already been amputated, Brooks reported that Ulric was "now very low in health in consequence of the wound, and will lose his foot, if not worse." Thanks to Brooks, word of Ully's wound soon reached California.[12]

On July 25, the fourth day after the amputation, his uncle informed Ulric of the long-coveted promotion to colonel. That long-awaited news stirred something in the young man, who rallied from death's door. "The eye of the youthful warrior again gleamed with its former fire, and his whole face glowed as with a light of transfiguration," recalled Reverend Sunderland.[13] Then, his brother Charley arrived, joining Ully. The young man was still suffering from malaria, which left him weak and very sick. "Both are but wrecks of the active, care-free lads who went out from their home and offered their mite to the great cause," lamented Admiral Dahlgren. "One is wasted by disease, the other by wounds; but they have been repaid by looking upon grand events."[14] With each other as company, the two brothers gradually got better.

Their father still did not know that Ully had suffered a grievous injury. A combined arms campaign to make an amphibious landing on Morris Island, capture Battery Wagner, and compel the surrender of Fort Sumter was underway. John Dahlgren commanded the naval portion of this ambitious campaign. As Ulric smashed into Imboden's wagons at Greencastle on July 5, his father met with Maj. Gen. Quincy Gillmore to plan their campaign to reduce the city's defenses.[15] His duties kept him occupied—On July 17, the Admiral wrote to his sister Patty, "Some one sent me a slip about Ully—which shows he is active."[16] Little did he know of the true state of his favorite son's health and well-being.

Admiral Dahlgren finally learned of Ulric's plight on July 20 when he received a letter from his sister Patty. "An anxious day with me," he noted in his diary that day. "News that Ully has been wounded." Two days later, he wrote, "My mind is with my poor boy. I do wish to know how it fares with him. Oh, that he may escape any permanent injury!"[17]

"I have been concerned beyond expression to hear of your misfortune," John Dahlgren wrote in a letter to Ulric that day. "It was almost a foreboding with me, and hence my anxiety to have you assigned to duty with me. I trust most sincerely that it will have no ill consequences." Doing all he could with his duty intervening, Admiral Dahlgren declared, "You will have the whole house at your disposal, and all that I have to make you comfortable."[18] The Admiral's misery at not being there to care for his son was palpable.

Ulric turned to the Bible for comfort while he recuperated. He spent long days reading its verses and quietly singing hymns to bolster his spirit. He could hear the sounds of services being conducted in Reverend Sunderland's church on Sunday mornings, and one Sunday afternoon, sent for the minister. The Reverend had not seen the young man since he was wounded, and the sight surprised him. "Oh, how beautiful, and brave, and grand he seemed, as in his waste and woe-worn plight of fleshly torture, at length I beheld him stretched out, and saw the signals of that fearful maiming," recalled Sunderland. "In spite of all, my tears ran down, as he lifted up to my salutation one sweet smile of greeting from that couch of physical agony." Sunderland and Ully prayed together, leaving the minister impressed with the conviction of the young man's faith.[19]

Ulric also maintained a regular correspondence with his Aunt Patty when she returned to her own family in Philadelphia after the crisis passed. His letters provide insight into his state of mind as he lay in his sickbed. "Often while lying down in my room, I think over what I have seen and what has taken place since I first came home wounded," he wrote. "It seems like a dream and puzzles me to think of 'Death' and wonder what it is." This young man who so frequently laughed in the face of danger suddenly recognized his own mortality, and it must have come as a great shock. "How little we know who will go next," he correctly observed.[20]

When they heard of his wound, his uncle Charles, now back in Natchez after the fall of Vicksburg, and his cousins all wrote to him, expressing their concerns about his wound and their hopes for his full recover. Family bonds still proved stronger than regional sectionalism.[21]

By August 1, he had improved enough for his doctors to declare him out of danger. On August 4, Admiral Dahlgren finally learned of the severity of Ulric's wound. "News from Ully," he scrawled in his diary that day. "Poor child! He had to lose his leg to save his life. Sad loss. He receives every attention from the President down, and has a Colonel's commission. I feared the result, and have been kept in extreme anxiety since I heard of his wound."[22]

On August 19, the Admiral found time to write to Ulric. "I have had nothing so welcome as your letter," he declared. "It is not so much what we have in this world as the use we put our means to. You can do a great deal more minus a foot than most men who have two. It is no small matter to have fought your way to a colonelcy at 21, and that must lead to more."[23] Although his duties at Charleston Harbor were all-encompassing, John Dahlgren was still a father, and his favorite son had been badly wounded. His parental anxiety came as no surprise, and the burden weighed heavily on him. A few weeks later, a recovered Charley joined his father's staff. Having one of his sons nearby comforted the Admiral, who continued worrying about Ully.

As Ulric got stronger, he began learning to walk with crutches. For a young man as active and athletic as Ulric, walking with the assistance of crutches proved a difficult proposition. It took him a long time to master the process, and even then it proved difficult. In addition, the raw stump caused him constant discomfort.

By August 13, he felt well enough to travel. Some of the Navy Yard sailors bore him to the train station on a litter and then loaded him on a train north. On August 15, Ulric arrived at his uncle S. Abbott Lawrence's cottage at Newport, Rhode Island. He spent several weeks enjoying the pleasant ocean breezes as he continued to regain his strength. However, his uncle, who had been in poor health, suddenly died during Ully's visit, casting a pall upon the young colonel's respite by the sea. "Tears that his own afflictions could not excite were to flow freely over the sudden death of his beloved uncle, whose guest he now was."[24]

Finally leaving Newport on September 21, he spent a week visiting old friends and family in Philadelphia. He donned his new colonel's uniform and sat for a photographer in the City of Brotherly Love, still looking sallow, pale, and gaunt from his recent ordeal.[25] Two days later, his brother Paul, who had been at sea on a frigate on a midshipman cruise, came home. He had not heard of Ulric's wounding "and was naturally much shocked to behold the great change which it had occasioned." During October, Ulric spent a week visiting friends in Harrisburg before returning to his father's house in Washington.[26]

When he arrived, he was surprised to find his brother Charley there. Once

Charley recovered from his bout of malaria, he joined their father's staff as an aide at Charleston. However, he got permission to go to Washington, where he paid a call upon Lincoln's personal secretary, John Hay.[27] Ulric and Charley also visited, and Ulric may have told his brother that he was bored and was considering making a trip to Charleston to visit Admiral Dahlgren.

Ulric also visited Secretary Stanton. "It was really ludicrous to see him holding my horse by the head while I got in the wagon, trying to jump away from him & he holding on like grim death," he told his father. The restless young man spent his days reading, writing, exercising, and at the dentist's office. He was bored to tears, and desperate for some change to his routine. "My health is fine," he wrote to his father on October 28. "I may come down and see you at Charleston."[28] Although he had only one leg, he still possessed a powerful will, and nothing so trifling as losing a leg was about to slow him down. Dahlgren began planning the trip, including making arrangements for passage south on a Navy steamer.

On November 6, Ulric wrote to the commander of a Federal steamer that was about to leave the New York Navy Yard for Charleston. "I had made arrangements to go down with you on the 10th to the Flag Ship 'Philadelphia' & a Boat would have been sent off for me per prior arrangement with [Admiral Dahlgren]," he said. "Will you lunch there? And if any inquiry is made, would you please send word that I did not come over but will do so soon."[29] The final preparations for the trip were now well under way. Ulric eagerly looked forward to leaving the tedium of his convalescence and joining his father at sea; as he later put it, "I came out thinking I could be of some assistance not being able to take the field."[30]

While he got ready for the ordeal of ocean-going travel, Ully resumed his social life. Finally able to get around, albeit with difficulty, he began enjoying life's simple pleasures again. On November 11, Dahlgren, John Hay, and two other young gentlemen went to the theater to see the renowned actor John Wilkes Booth perform *Romeo and Juliet*. After the show, the four men went out drinking, and they had a grand time. "Dahlgren was very funny by the one legged enterprise he displayed in making a night of it," noted Hay in his diary that night.[31]

On November 19, Ulric left his father's house in Washington and caught a train to Philadelphia. He arrived in Philadelphia that night and spent the next day visiting with friends and relatives and then attended a German opera with an old friend that night.[32] On November 21, Ulric boarded the steamer *Massachusetts*, carrying supplies from the City of Brotherly Love to Charleston.

The passage took sixty-five hours through heavy seas, meaning "all green hands sea sick."[33] The steamer appeared off Charleston bar about eight o'clock on the morning of November 24. Admiral Dahlgren had no idea that his son was coming, so no arrangements had been made for the arrival of the one-legged cavalryman. The *Massachusetts* crossed the bar and approached the inshore squadron, consisting of ironclads and the Admiral's flagship, a river steamer carrying the appropriate name of the *Philadelphia*.

The *Massachusetts* dropped anchor, and the commanding officer's gig approached the flagship. When Admiral Dahlgren looked down, he was stunned to see Ulric seated therein. The gig reached the *Philadelphia* and pulled alongside her. The heaving seas made it dangerous for the crippled soldier, who declined all offers of help and pulled himself up into the low gangway. His father and brother Charley greeted him there. Six months had passed since the Admiral last saw Ulric, and much had happened. Ulric earned the respect of the Army of the Potomac's high command, demonstrated great courage and leadership in battle, and suffered a crippling wound that cost him a leg.[34] However, Ulric still possessed the benefit of youth and the remarkable powers of recuperation peculiar to young people. He slowly regained his strength. "Massachusetts in sight at 8 a.m. To my surprise and pleasure, Ully came in her," Admiral Dahlgren recorded in his diary that night. "Poor fellow! with but one leg. I wish I could have borne the loss for him. But a Colonel at twenty-one!" he concluded proudly.[35]

Likewise, the Admiral had a difficult time of it. He and Maj. Gen. Quincy Gillmore, who commanded the land forces assigned to Charleston, did not get along, and the stress of being in charge took a fearful toll on his health. The Admiral's haughty attitude and prickly personality did not earn him many friends. "Because of his ordnance work, Dahlgren rarely had an opportunity to exercise authority which denied him an opportunities to develop a command presence and friendships within the navy's officer corps," astutely observed historian Stephen R. Wise. "His promotions came from his expertise with ordnance and not from sea duty. This lack of experience with his peers often haunted him in his relations with his officers and the army."[36]

Dahlgren and Gillmore inevitably clashed. "Dahlgren's lack of command experience, combined with a tremendous ego, also affected his relations with the equally prideful Gillmore," continued Wise. "While the campaign dragged on, these two war machines lost track of the jointness of their venture."[37] Their combined efforts to take Battery Wagner, on Morris Island, failed repeatedly until the Confederates finally evacuated the fort, further deepening the schism between the two commanders.

The Admiral's fleet was presently shelling Fort Sumter, trying to reduce it from sea by a virtual blizzard of hot metal rained from above.[38] "Dahlgren has been in wretched health, dyspeptic, distraught, and overworked. His brain seems to be a little affected," wrote John Hay in his diary on October 21. "He seems to have lost his continuity of thought. His dispatches have lost coherence. The business of the fleet is in chaos."[39] No doubt, part of his stress resulted from being worried sick over Ulric's condition. John Dahlgren needed a break from his burdens, and his son's unexpected arrival provided just the lift his spirits so desperately needed.

After spending a few minutes catching up, Dahlgren and his two sons boarded a skiff that carried the family out to the ironclad *Weehawken* so that Ulric could get a good view of the rebel batteries, Fort Sumter, Fort Moultrie, and the city of Charleston beyond. Union long-range artillery regularly rained shells upon Charleston, hoping that the terror they caused would break the morale of the citizenry. The shells arcing across the sky made quite a spectacle for the young cavalryman, who watched intently.[40] The *Weehawken* bore the scars of many Confederate artillery shells. Her captain took a few moments to show Ulric the damage and battering it had undergone; two weeks later, she foundered and slipped to the bottom of the sea.[41] "The impression made by first seeing a monitor is that of a vessel nearly submerged, the water washing over the deck and looking as uncomfortable as one can imagine," Ulric recorded in his notebook that night. "The monitors have been well battered and look leaky from some tremendous hits about the water-line."[42]

Ulric settled into his father's spacious quarters aboard the *Philadelphia*. He enjoyed just being near his father and older brother, and his presence worked wonders for his spirit and his father's as well. A few days later, Ulric accompanied Admiral Dahlgren on a review of the fleet's Marine Corps battalion, which included Lt. Charles H. Daniels, his old comrade from the Harpers Ferry expedition a year earlier. This force was encamped on Folly Island, an uninviting, malaria-ridden barrier island south of Charleston, where the men passed their days drilling and training. More than 10,000 Union troops garrisoned Folly, which was nothing but a large armed camp. One Northern wag commented, "it did look like a piece of Folly to try to live on such an island."[43]

"Folly Isld looked very desolate & the troops are doing nothing," Ulric noted in his diary.[44] However, they were there for a review of the Marines, who snapped to. Resting on his crutches, Ully watched with great amusement as the men struggled through the evolutions of the training manual in the heavy sand. That night, Admiral Dahlgren dined with the officers, and Ulric proposed a toast to his former commander, General Hooker.[45]

The loss of his leg caused him to reassess his role in the great conflict. Although the missing limb crippled him, it did not weaken his resolve. "I stay to take part in the great fight; if I die, what death more glorious than the death of men fighting for their country?" he wrote in a letter to a friend. "Life is only the vestibule to real existence; a state of preparation for the future. Every one has something to fulfill in this world as in a school. The duty must be faithfully performed here, or the penalty be paid hereafter."[46]

At the same time, Ully remained concerned about his reputation and, in particular, about how his actions might be perceived. "I never like any one to call me rash, for you must remember now I do none of those things which some call daring, without thinking well over the object to be attained, and if it be worth the risk involved; for I feel the responsibility of other lives more than my own," he continued, giving real insight into his nature. "There is no excuse for exposing those unnecessarily. But where a great object requires considerable risk, of course, no one is to hold back then." He concluded with great foreshadowing, "I always feel a conviction that in going into battle I may never return alive. I think over my sins and pray God to pardon them. I never go down to the fight without first offering prayer to the Almighty for forgiveness and acceptance!"[47]

A few days later, Ulric did something for the first time since that terrible day at Hagerstown—he rode a horse. He slowly moved to the horse's side on his crutches. Strong helping hands lifted his one foot into the stirrup and he then rose into the saddle with ease. He sat assuredly, gathered up the reins, quickly put his horse into an easy canter, and vanished. He rode about three miles to see the Confederate stronghold of Fort Wagner, finally abandoned by its stalwart defenders in early September. He surveyed the fort as best he could without dismounting.[48]

On November 28, word of Maj. Gen. Ulysses S. Grant's decisive victory at Chattanooga on November 25 reached the fleet. On December 1, once the news was confirmed, there was a "salute by army & navy & ships dressed in honor of Grant's victory," a stirring spectacle that Ully thoroughly enjoyed.[49] The next day, the *Philadelphia* left the inlet and anchored farther out. Ulric had a clear view of the movements of the Union naval ships and he could see the Federal batteries shelling Fort Sumter from the north end of Morris Island. The next day, he took the barge to see the wreck of the *Keokuk*, a lightly armored vessel that sank during the unsuccessful April 1863 attack on Fort Sumter. Ulric wanted to see Port Royal, South Carolina, described by his father as "probably the finest harbor on our Southern coast," so the next day he boarded the *Sonoma*, which was headed there. She steamed out late in the day, and then made good time when a howling nor'easter blew in.[50] "Heavy sea and blowing hard," noted Ully in his diary. "Schooner in tow; had to cast her off early next morning, on account of the weather." In spite of the storm, he declared, "Had a very pleasant trip."[51]

The *Sonoma* anchored in the Port Republic harbor, and Ulric disembarked. He found the place commanded by Capt. William Reynolds, an old shipmate of his father's, and a brother of Maj. Gen. John F. Reynolds, who was killed during the first day's fighting at Gettysburg. They spent several pleasant hours visiting. The next day, Ulric went over to Hilton Head, the military depot on the southern shore of the bay, where he enjoyed a brief reunion with his old commander, Maj. Gen. Rufus Saxton, who was now responsible for recruiting and training Negro soldiers.[52] Dahlgren dined with a friend and then headed for Beaufort, which he reached in the evening.[53]

On December 10, he penned a letter to an acquaintance. "I received your kind invitation to partake of a baked opossum on Nov. 24th, a few days since—too late to participate in that glorious affair or to acknowledge the receipt in time," he wrote. "I am sorry indeed that I was not in Washn., for I should certainly have been present to hear the story of the melancholy but honorable death of the aforesaid 'possum'. I hope for his own name that he gave up his precious life fully aware of the necessity which demanded it."[54]

"I hope to live to see the destruction of Charleston," he declared. He then addressed his father's ongoing conflict with Gillmore, blaming all of the trouble on the Army officer. "The truth is this Gillmore is an able engineer, but so eager for advancement that he would sacrifice most any friend to his own ambition. He is an able man to be sure, but he has been playing a very cunning game here—while the Navy have acted openly & honorably." He concluded, "Gillmore could not hold his position here 24 hours were it not for the Navy." Thinking better of such intemperate language, he added a postscript. "Please do not mention what I saw here, as it is merely *'entre nous'*."[55] After posting this letter, Ulric boarded a steamer bound for Charleston.[56]

The journey took a full day due to a severe storm at sea. "Went on board the Philadelphia; rough getting from one steamer to another," he noted in his diary. "Thought the small boat would be swamped."[57] Admiral Dahlgren did not expect Ully to return in such horrible weather. "I felt sure he would not come here until the bad weather was over, for the boat has labored so much that it seemed as if she could not last through it."[58] The storm battered his father's flagship, an ordinary river steamer, which nearly swamped after a heavy swell broke her rudder.

The next day, as the *Philadelphia* struggled its way toward the inlet to Charleston Harbor, General Gillmore boarded for breakfast with Ulric and the Admiral. They chatted about operations. Gillmore had proposed an ambitious attack on Savannah, Georgia, and he wanted Dahlgren's support and approval. The Admiral readily assented. Ulric dutifully took notes, recording the contents of the discussion for posterity. Later that day, the *Philadelphia* anchored in the Folly River, close enough to open on the rebel batteries on Folly and Morris Islands. She stayed there for several days.[59]

Ully remained particularly concerned for his father, who continued receiving harsh criticism for his failure to take Charleston. "Father is a little impatient to go in," he wrote to the Admiral's friend Henry A. Wise, who succeeded Dahlgren as chief of ordnance. "It is rather hard . . . to have all the abuse which has been heaped upon him without a word in reply . . . Our attack here must be perfectly successful—we cannot afford to lose or be checked in the smallest way. The power of the Iron Clads must not be shown at a disadvantage— Suppose we should fail—Foreign nations would see our weak points & take advantage of them as quickly as we do. But let more Iron Clads be sent here & Father is confident of perfect success."[60]

Ulric now shared a cabin with his brother Charley, enjoying the company of his family. Occasionally, he went ashore to ride the lines on horseback, keenly watching anything of interest play out in front of him. He recorded his thoughts and observations in his diary, and the days passed quickly. The soldiers and sailors waited for the spring campaigning season to come. "Let us hope, if Grant does not steal a march on us by one of his famous rear attacks, that Charleston will then fall, and the long-suffering soldiers and sailors of this army and squadron reap the reward they have well merited of complete and decisive triumph," wrote an anonymous newspaper correspondent in late December.[61]

Soon, it was Christmas—his last—and Ulric spent a quiet day with his father. As Admiral Dahlgren observed, Christmas "is, in truth, a home festival only,—without the family circle it cannot be enjoyed with real zest." The two men made the best of their holiday together, missing the rest of the family but reveling in simply enjoying each other's company.[62]

Four days later, Admiral Dahlgren ordered an expedition to Murrells Inlet, a small arm of the sea near the northernmost point of South Carolina. The narrow Inlet only admitted small, light-draft vessels at high tide. Normally, part of Admiral Dahlgren's squadron guarded the Inlet, but one of his crews was captured while attempting a landing. The Admiral dispatched an expedition to try to rescue the prisoners. The rescue force included two gunboats, two light-draft steamers, and two sailing vessels, along with four howitzers and one hundred Marines.

Once Ulric heard about the upcoming expedition, his aggressive juices kicked in. Not only did he want to join the expedition, he asked permission to command the landing force. The combination of his crippled condition and the fact that he was not a Marine officer made it impossible for him to command the landing force, but Admiral Dahlgren granted him permission to accompany the expedition as a volunteer. "Father has for several days been perfecting his plan of attack," Ully noted in his diary on December 28, "and I think nothing is wanting but the iron clads to arrive."[63] The expedition departed on the afternoon of December 29.[64]

The voyage to Murrells Inlet took a day. The little fleet arrived there on the afternoon of December 30 and began preparing for the landing. "Good fishing. Preparations for landing complete. Everybody eager to take part," wrote Ulric in his diary.[65] However, a storm roared in that night, causing the sea to become rough and forcing the little Union fleet to move away from Georgetown. "Refugees report that the rebels expected us, and had reinforcements from Savannah and Georgetown waiting for us," noted a disappointed Dahlgren the next day.[66]

The landing finally occurred on New Year's Day. One of the gunboats opened on a Confederate schooner and set it ablaze, the thick black smoke of nineteen barrels of burning turpentine filling the sky. Boatloads of Marines followed, presenting a pretty sight as the men rowed across the Inlet. They landed successfully, freed the prisoners, and scattered two hundred Confederate cavalrymen, "a happy New Year doubtless to them," observed a gleeful Ully in his diary.[67]

After successfully completing its mission, the expedition returned to Charleston. Ully resumed his place in his father's cabin, passing the short winter days reading or observing events as they transpired in front of him. If the weather permitted, he went ashore for a horseback ride. "The subject always present to him, however, was the pending military and naval prospect, of which there was no closer observer there," noted his father. "His eye never failed to notice any changes that might occur, and notwithstanding his disability and as yet unconfirmed health, he even joined the scouting parties that went up at night to reconnoiter the rebel movements at the front."[68] He also went out on the barge from time to time. "Came unexpectedly on Ully in a tug, bound up on a scout, and in such weather," Admiral Dahlgren noted in his diary on January 10.[69]

Now that he was missing a leg, Ulric's career path obviously had to change, and he spent a lot of time contemplating his future. On January 10, he sat down and composed a lengthy letter to Secretary Stanton to advise him as to the state of affairs in Charleston. He described the condition of the enemy defenses in great detail, and pointed out that taking Charleston posed a major challenge for the commander of any military force trying to attack the city, building up to a request for more ironclad ships to add to the Admiral's fleet. He declared, "my wound is quite well but it will be some months before I will be able to use an artificial limb, as my knee is very crooked 'contracted'. I can be of much use here & have already taken part in an expedition up the coast where we destroyed a schooner with a valuable cargo of Turpentine & Cotton." Having set the stage by demonstrating that his health was good enough for him to serve in the field, Ulric concluded, "I would therefore ask your permission to accept a Volunteer appointment without pay as Aid to my Father, in order to allow me to take part in the coming fight with the Iron Clads. It is merely a nominal appointment without which my authority would be little."[70] Stanton did not grant Ulric's request.

On January 12, Ully attended a flag-raising ceremony at Battery Wagner, watching the Union colors rise above the stout fort. Speeches were made, and the Federals waited for the enemy to join the celebration by opening fire, but they never did. "Considerable drunkenness," sniffed Ulric in his diary.[71] Four days later, Ulric again attended a meeting between his father and General Gillmore, carefully taking notes of their discussions. That same day, he went for a ride along the beach, and was horrified when he was mistaken for an orderly.[72] On January 20, he attended a review of Federal troops, commenting upon their good appearance.[73]

Since Secretary Stanton had not given him permission to join his father's staff as a volunteer aide, the time finally came for Ulric to return to Washington. His stump was healing nicely, and he was finally ready to be fitted with an artificial limb. On January 22, 1864, he bade farewell to his father for the last time. About four o'clock that afternoon, Ully rested on his crutches in the gangway of the *Philadelphia* and said goodbye to his many new friends, who had gathered there to see him off. He carried a small box, containing "a valuable memorial of hard service." He grasped the rope ladder and began descending to the unsteady boat waiting for him below. Still unsteady, many hands reached out to help him down into the boat, and he settled in. The oars dropped into the water, and as the barge glided away, Ully raised his cap in farewell to his new friends. His father turned and waved his cap in an affectionate farewell, and watched the barge steadily but slowly get smaller as it headed off. Ulric boarded an ocean-going steamer that bore him away.[74] "A brave boy, that, and none the worse for losing a foot," noted his father in his diary that night, "he rides as well as ever, and gets about in odd places surprisingly." Admiral Dahlgren never saw his son alive again.[75]

The steamer arrived at Fortress Monroe late in the afternoon of January 24. "Beautiful sight," Ulric noted in his diary. "Moon rising full & vessels with lights &c."[76] The anchor dropped, and the young colonel debarked to pay his respects to Maj. Gen. Benjamin F. Butler, the commander of the Federal garrison there. During the night, the voyage resumed, and the steamer entered the Delaware River the next day, arriving at the Philadelphia Navy Yard about midnight on January 25. On January 26, Ulric caught a train to Washington, arriving at his father's house that evening. "Everything looks well," he noted with satisfaction. "Eva has fine piano & improves."[77]

A newspaper correspondent reported, "Colonel Ulric Dahlgren has returned from his visit to Charleston, with his health very much improved. Hopes are entertained by him that his limb will allow him to enter the field again in a very short time."[78] Ully spent the next three weeks returning the calls and acknowledging the attentions of friends who had shown him great kindness during his recuperation, including influential Republican Rep. Schuyler Colfax of Indiana and others.[79] He also paid a visit to the White House, calling upon President Lincoln and Secretary Stanton, where he reported on the state of affairs at Charleston. Wherever he went, he got a warm reception, and was constantly the object of attention. He left the impression of "an unobtrusive and modest young man, whose thoughts were earnestly and enthusiastically bent on the future of his country."[80]

On January 30, Ulric again visited the White House. "I called at the White House matinee yesterday," he informed Admiral Dahlgren. "Abe told me to come up soon, he would like to have a talk with me and I intend to call ever day until I find him in."[81] Two days later, February 1, Ulric arrived about 4:00, and found Lincoln at home. He went to the President's private quarters and the two men chatted about "military and political matters" while Lincoln's barber shaved him. No one knows specifically what the two men discussed.[82]

Another night, Ulric attended a fancy dress ball at the National Hotel, decked out in new colonel's dress uniform and wearing his new wooden leg. Before his wounding, Ulric was known as an expert at the waltz, but he could no longer dance. Pretty girls from good families—described as "the young princesses and duchesses and countesses of America"—surrounded him, refusing to dance with the other eligible young men at the party. Instead, they clustered "around him merrily, as if they were trying to keep him from thinking of his lost leg ad his vanished dancing days." They stayed by his side all evening, spurning all invitations to dance, in tribute to the handsome young colonel's sacrifice for the Union cause. "He used to be such a beautiful waltzer," they lamented. "Poor fellow! We must not let him feel neglected!" One of Lincoln's secretaries recalled that Ully was "a sort of vision of splendid, generous youth, bright young manhood and brilliant young womanhood, will always come up in company with your memory of the hero who could not dance."[83] A Federal officer left this description of Ulric in February 1864: "Dahlgren was a boyish looking young man, of middle height, thin, and with light hair, moustache and imperial."[84]

During this time, he also penned a detailed account of the operations around Charleston he had observed during his visit there. He wrote the article under the anonym "Truth," in a calm and comprehensive tone intended to set the record straight and to silence some of his father's many critics. Reverend Sunderland described it thusly: "a paper freighted in every line with a candor, a majesty, and self-evidencing power which only belongs to the truth itself—and which, being at the same time a work of filial affection, as well as a patriotic and public defense of the national prowess, might well stand for the crowning work of all his intellectual efforts." The article was published after his death.[85]

The whole time, Ulric longed to return to duty in the field in spite of his handicap. Newly fitted with a hand-carved wooden prosthetic leg, he believed that he could handle whatever duty might come his way. He watched and waited for an opportunity to strike a blow for his country, answering any suggestion that he was too enfeebled to take the field again with a kind but resolute determination. Instead, he heard the constant and irresistible call to duty that claimed his young life a few weeks later.[86]

Brigadier General Judson Kilpatrick
LIBRARY OF CONGRESS

CHAPTER ELEVEN

An Untimely End to a Promising Life and an Unending Controversy Spawned

BRIG. GEN. JUDSON KILPATRICK, commander of the Army of the Potomac's Third Cavalry Division, was a man possessed of boundless ambition, a young man in a hurry. Born in Deckertown, New Jersey, on January 14, 1836, he was the second son of Simon and Julia Kilpatrick. The elder Kilpatrick served as a colonel in the New Jersey state militia and cut an imposing figure in his fine uniform. This martial image was not lost on little Judson, who quickly decided that he wanted to be a soldier. To that end, he spent his childhood attending good schools and reading about military history, eagerly learning all he could about the great captains of history.[1]

The boy's most ardent wish came true in 1856 when he received an appointment to the United States Military Academy at West Point, New York. He graduated in the Class of 1861, ranking seventeenth in a class of forty-five. "His ambition was simply boundless," recalled a fellow Cadet, "and from his intimates he did not disguise his faith that . . . he would become governor of New Jersey, and ultimately president of the United States."[2] A few days after graduation, he married his sweetheart, Alice Shailer, the niece of a prominent New York politician. He carried a personal battle flag emblazoned with her name into battle for the entire war, which lasted longer than his marriage to Alice. The young lieutenant and his bride spent only one night together before he rushed off to begin his military career.[3]

Recognizing that volunteer service would lead to quicker promotions than the Regular Army, Kilpatrick asked his mathematics professor from West Point, Gouverneur K. Warren, to recommend the new graduate for a captaincy in the newly-formed 5th New York Infantry, which Warren would command. On May 9, 1861, Kilpatrick received a commission as captain of Company H, 5th New York. Shot in the hip at the June 10, 1861, Battle of Big Bethel, the Civil War's first full-scale land battle, Kilpatrick was the first Regular Army officer to be wounded in the war.

When Kilpatrick returned to duty, he did so as lieutenant colonel of the 2nd New York (Harris) Cavalry. His departure from the 5th New York was not happy—Kilpatrick took sick leave instead of returning to duty with his regiment, all the while angling for higher rank in a cavalry regiment, and angering

Warren in the process. Now second in command of a regiment of horsemen, Kilpatrick and his troopers served in Maj. Gen. George B. McClellan's Army of the Potomac, taking part in the 1862 Peninsula Campaign. That summer, the unit left the Virginia Peninsula to serve with Maj. Gen. John Pope's Army of Virginia, while their lieutenant colonel eagerly searched for opportunities to gain fame and rapid promotion to ever-higher levels of rank.

He almost never got that chance. In the fall of 1862, Kilpatrick was jailed in Washington, D.C.'s Old Capitol Prison, charged with conduct unbecoming an officer. He was accused of taking bribes, stealing horses and tobacco and then selling them, and impropriety in borrowing money. In January 1863, friends in high places and the exigencies of the war prevailed, and Kilpatrick returned to his regiment without the scandal of a court-martial.[4] For most young officers, such charges would have been career-ending. Somehow, Kilpatrick not only survived unscathed, but in December 1862, he received a promotion to colonel of the 2nd New York Cavalry while still in prison.

On June 14, 1863, largely as a result of his good performance at the Battle of Brandy Station, Maj. Gen. Alfred Pleasonton, commander of the Cavalry Corps, had Kilpatrick promoted to brigadier general. Two weeks later, Maj. Gen. Julius Stahel was relieved of command and his independent cavalry division was merged into the Army of the Potomac's Cavalry Corps. Kilpatrick assumed command of the newly designated Third Cavalry Division. At Gettysburg, on the afternoon of July 3, he ordered a fool-hardy mounted charge by Brig. Gen. Elon J. Farnsworth's cavalry brigade which accomplished little but the pointless death of Farnsworth.[5]

Because of the Union victory at Gettysburg, Kilpatrick was not censured for his poor choice in ordering Farnsworth's brigade to charge over terrible ground. When bloody draft riots broke out in New York City a few days later, Kilpatrick went there to assume command of the Federal cavalry forces gathered to help quell the disturbances.[6] Then, after visiting with his wife and newborn son for two weeks, Kilpatrick returned to duty in Virginia.

The Federal and Confederate armies spent a long and bloody fall jockeying for position. Kilpatrick suffered a crushing defeat at the hands of Maj. Gen. J.E.B. Stuart's cavalry at the battle of Buckland Mills on October 19, 1863. The precipitous rout known to history as "the Buckland Races" provided a sour ending to Kilpatrick's active campaigning season in 1863. He went into the winter encampment searching for ways to redeem himself and restore his name to the good graces of the army high command and the general public. Kilpatrick soon came upon an idea.

In the spring of 1863, while still the colonel of the 2nd New York Cavalry, Kilpatrick led his regiment and the 12th Illinois Cavalry on an expedition toward Richmond during the Stoneman Raid. His force reached the outer defenses of Richmond before Kilpatrick wisely drew off, recognizing that his small command could not overcome the stout defenses ringing the Confederate capital. Kilpatrick's column came so close to Richmond that it engendered panic in the Confederate capital, and prompted Abraham Lincoln to ponder the possibility of a lightning raid on the city. Based on information obtained from a prisoner of war, Lincoln wrote to Joseph Hooker that he believed that "there are not a sound pair of legs in Richmond, and that our men, had they known it, could have safely gone in and burned everything and brought in Jefferson Davis."[7] Northern newspapers disseminated the same thoughts. "There were hours, from what we hear, any one of them might have captured Richmond, bagged the whole administration, and set the Union prisoners free, for the city was wholly undefended," declared the *Philadelphia Evening Bulletin* on May 9, 1863.[8] Kilpatrick certainly understood the nature of the missed opportunity, and continued to harbor and cultivate the idea of a bold dash into Richmond to free the Union prisoners of war being held at Libby Prison and on Belle Isle. Hence, he came up with a specific plan to rescue them and shower himself in glory in the process.

These Union prisoners suffered under horrific conditions. Belle Isle was a hellish place, packed beyond its capacity with prisoners. It offered only rudimentary shelter and sanitary facilities, and the men never had enough food—in January 1864, for example, the prisoners went eleven days without a single meal. J. Osburn Coburn, a member of the 6th Michigan Cavalry who had been captured in the fall of 1863, was a prisoner at Belle Isle. On January 18, 1864, he wrote an especially telling entry in his diary that succinctly describes the mental and physical state of the prisoners of war that awful winter.

> It is three months since I was captured. Then I expected that all enlisted men would be paroled and exchanged, and returned to our lines. We were full of health, heart, hope, and spirits. We were fleshy, having known but little of hunger. We were confident of our ability to endure almost anything. Now we are down, clear down, starved out. Our flesh as well as hope and spirits are all broken or nearly so. We get peevish and irritable, cross, dirty and careless. Eat like beasts, our faces and hands begrimed with dirt and pine smoke and but little inclination to wash them or strength if we had. The

Libby Prison and Belle Isle

LIBRARY OF CONGRESS

weather has been so cold and we with so little wood that we cannot wash but on warmer days.

Coburn died of chronic diarrhea on March 8.[9]

Col. Luigi Palma di Cesnola, an Italian count who commanded the 4th New York Cavalry, was badly wounded and captured during the June 17, 1863 Battle of Aldie. Cesnola spent ten long months as a prisoner of war, and visited Belle Isle several times during his captivity. He left a chilling description. "Of these six thousand four hundred and thirty-four prisoners, over seven hundred were at the time I first visited Belle Isle, without tents or any shelter whatever at night, lying in ditches, or digging holes in the sandy ground in which they slept in a bundle, one over the other, and I heard on the top were found frozen to death, and I actually saw men wrapped up in blankets brought out of the enclosure who were found dead and frozen in ditches outside of the tents!"[10]

Libby Prison was an old warehouse that had been converted to use as a prison for officers only, and it was, if anything, even worse than Belle Isle. "From the day of our capture dates a sad history of privation and misery, far surpassing in bitter reality anything which the pen of novelist has produced," noted Capt. Willard Glazer of the 2nd New York Cavalry in November 1863. "Rather than to experience what we have suffered, there are few who would not embrace a speedy death. Yes, death would be to them a welcome release."[11]

"Time here is a burden, a tormentor, a bore," fretted a Pennsylvania captain on February 9, 1864. "There are few officers here who would not willingly have stricken from their lives the portion that is still to be spent in this hole."[12] That night, 102 prisoners, led by Col. Thomas E. Rose of the 77th Pennsylvania Volunteer Infantry, escaped from Libby Prison, using a tunnel they had dug.[13] Bucking the odds, a handful of these men made it safely back to the Union lines, where they recounted the horrors of their captivity, stirring up passions and raising calls for action. The Federal prisoners were suffering mightily, with men dying by the hundreds of disease and exposure to the elements. When the public read the accounts of the escaped prisoners, a hue and cry went up across the North, trying to find a way to end the misery of the captives. Calls for action rang out.

A wealthy spinster named Elizabeth Van Lew ran an extremely effective Union spy ring in Richmond. Van Lew regularly communicated with Maj. Gen. Benjamin F. Butler, commander of the Department of Virginia and North Carolina. An extract of a report from a member of Van Lew's organization, written in early 1864, provided critical information that may have played a role in the decision to take action. "Now is the time to capture Richmond," the author declared, and it "can be done either by forcing Lee to retreat there to winter, or by the capture of Davis, which would not be a hard feat to accomplish." The author suggested that since "Davis is the head and front of the rebellion," his capture would cause the fall of the Confederacy and the surrender of Richmond. "He has many enemies (all Union men) who, with his fall, would be glad to welcome again the stars and stripes."

After pointing out that there were many Union men who would be glad to welcome the starts and stripes again, the author continued, "One or two thousand men (mounted) could land on the Pamunkey at dark, and ride unmolested to Richmond, by getting into the Mechanicsville Pike, and before day burn the government buildings, release the federal prisoners, and carry of Jeff Davis. This could be effected with less risk than would appear at first glance." He concluded, "A well digested plan would succeed." This call for action from deep within the Confederate capital may well have triggered the decision to take military action, both to free the prisoners and also to decapitate the Confederate government.[14]

Because of the abject misery endured by the prisoners of war and aspiring to be president some day, Butler concocted a bold plan to free the captives. Brig. Gen. Isaac Wistar led a combined arms force of about 4,000 infantry and 2,200 cavalry on a raid on Richmond at the beginning of February. Wistar agreed that the plan had merit. "It seemed to me that if a quick and secret concentration could be effected on the Williamsburg peninsula, a surprise of Richmond itself, by a sudden cavalry attack, might be possible," he wrote in his post-war memoirs. Wistar planned to march his infantry from his headquarters at Williamsburg on the night of February 5, followed by his cavalry force the next morning. The infantry would take and hold Bottom's Bridge over the Chickahominy River. His cavalry would arrive on February 7, repair the bridge, dash into the city of Richmond, surprise its defenses, and free the prisoners. They would then withdraw, with the newly-liberated prisoners in tow.[15]

A Union private named William J. Boyle, 1st New York Mounted Rifles, condemned to death for murder, escaped from Fortress Monroe and fled to the Confederate defenses of Richmond. Upon arriving within the enemy lines, Boyle told the Confederate authorities everything he knew, which effectively spoiled any possibility of surprise and gave the Confederates plenty of time to reinforce their positions and prepare for the coming attack. With his surprise ruined, Wistar only advanced as far as Bottom's Bridge on the Chickahominy River and wisely elected not to attack. "A passage could doubtless have been forced at some point above and the position turned, but instead of a ten-mile gallop to Richmond, the crossing and fighting, however, successful, must have consumed most of the day, long before the expiration of which the Richmond redoubts would have been fully maanned, the town safe from a *coup de main* and the Hanover division moving on our rear," wrote Wistar. "There remained no object to be gained commensurate with the loss and jeopardy to be incurred by delay, and my orders were explicit—that if the *surprise* failed, the command was not to be risked for any new object."[16]

Consequently, Wistar withdrew. "Thus failed an enterprise prepared with care in all its details, which had engaged the liveliest interest and expectations of those to whom it was confided, and which but for a minute accident which none could have foreseen, might have accomplished memorable results."[17] Butler added a note to Wistar's report of the failed expedition. "The whole result of the expedition, in addition to the prisoners captured and a few refugees, escaped Union prisoners, and negroes picked up and brought in," he wrote, "is the obvious demonstration that a small force in this vicinity, actively handled, can and should hold a much superior force of the enemy in the immediate vicinity of Richmond inactive, except for its defense." Thus, the idea for a raid on Richmond to free the prisoners of war continued to germinate.[18]

During the middle of February, after the failure of the Wistar expedition, Maj. Gen. George G. Meade, the commander of the Army of the Potomac, conferred with Secretary of War Stanton. The Secretary informed Meade that Lincoln was very anxious to have an amnesty proclamation distributed in the Virginia countryside. Stanton informed Meade that he had summoned Kilpatrick to discuss the practicability of doing so via a cavalry expedition. It was extremely unusual for Stanton to summon Kilpatrick for a high-level conference outside the regular chain of command. Normally, Maj. Gen. Alfred Pleasonton, the commander of the Cavalry Corps, participated in decisions involving his subordinates. Here, Stanton went outside the chain of command to consult with a division commander without including the corps commander in that process.[19]

Kilpatrick met briefly with the president on February 16, and then Lincoln sent him on to the War Department. He proposed to take no less than 4,000 cavalrymen and six pieces of artillery, cross the Rapidan River at Ely's Ford and proceed to Spotsylvania Court House. Once there he would detach part of his force under command of Brig. Gen. George A. Custer to destroy the Virginia Central Railroad in the vicinity of Fredericks Hall Station, and another force to destroy the RF&P Railroad near Guinea Station. Meanwhile, the main column would cross the North Anna River near Carmel Church, destroy the railroad bridge three miles below, and then proceed to Hanover Junction. The Guinea Station task force would then join the main body at Carmel Church and proceed to Richmond via the Brook Pike. In conjunction with troops from Butler's commanding advancing from the direction of West Point (the confluence of the Mattaponi and Pamunkey Rivers, which there form the York River, northeast of Richmond), they would dash on Richmond to try to free the Union prisoners of war, and then return by way of Fredericksburg.[20]

Lincoln expressly approved two of Kilpatrick's proposed objectives—freeing the prisoners on Belle Isle and in Libby Prison, and severing Confederate communications. He also proposed that Kilpatrick distribute the president's recent amnesty proclamation, which was aimed at persuading secessionists to return to the Union fold. Stanton then ordered Kilpatrick to return to Stevensburg to develop a detailed plan.[21]

When Meade returned to camp, Kilpatrick submitted his plan. "From the information I have but lately received, and from my thorough knowledge of the country, I am satisfied that this plan can be safely and successfully carried out," he concluded.[22] Meade's intelligence reports suggested that only about 3,000 local militiamen, a few field batteries, and a small force of cavalry defended Richmond. Maj. Gen. Wade Hampton's division of cavalry, consisting of about 1,500 men, was the only other force available to defend the Confederate capital. "I thought it practicable by a rapid and secret movement that Richmond might be carried by a *coup de main*, and our prisoners released before re-enforcements from either Petersburg or Lee's army could reach there," reported Meade. Kilpatrick then assured Pleasonton that the plan would succeed or he would die trying. These assurances were not enough to persuade the Cavalry Corps commander.[23] The plan was approved over the stated objections of Pleasonton, who did not believe that the plan was feasible at that time. Pleasonton, it turns out, was correct.[24] The plan failed to address what would be done with the freed prisoners, many of whom were sick and malnourished; there was no means of transporting them back to the Union lines short of making them walk. One modern historian has described the plan as "myopic at the least, harebrained at the worst." Nevertheless, the appropriate orders issued, and the die was cast.[25]

Jefferson Davis recognized the threat posed by the plan. Had the plot worked, including Brig. Gen. George A. Custer's expedition to Charlottesville, the Federals would have severed all lines of communications between Lee's army and Richmond. "This movement, with the destruction of the railroads by General Kilpatrick, and of the Central Railroad and the James River Canal by Colonel Dahlgren, would have isolated that army from its base of supplies," observed the Confederate president in his memoirs.[26]

Meade was initially optimistic about the raid's chances. "I trust they will be successful; it will be the greatest feat of the war if they do succeed and will immortalize them all," he wrote to his wife on February 29. The Union high command staked much on the success of this daring and terribly risky plan.[27]

Kilpatrick would lead the main column and approach Richmond from the north. Ulric Dahlgren, just returned to active duty, would lead a secondary column of 500 men, making a wide swing, and approaching Richmond from the south.[28] The selection of Dahlgren surprised a lot of people. Dahlgren received the most important and most dangerous assignment, commanding men who were not familiar with him. The young man, still recuperating from his Hagerstown wound, had never commanded a force as large as 500 men in his life. "It was well known that he was in no condition to take the field just then," declared his father, "for, the maimed limb not being yet healed, he moved on crutches, and his emaciated frame gave token of unrestored vigor; wherefore his friends strove to dissuade him from the undertaking."[29] Ulric boarded a train in Washington on February 22, and arrived at Kilpatrick's camp at Stevensburg, in Culpeper County, Virginia, that afternoon.[30]

The choice of the one-legged colonel, still carrying the pallor of his near-death experience, and obviously no longer the hale and hearty adventurer he once was, did not please everyone. Some questioned whether he was fit for duty and had the strength for such a rigorous expedition. "Col. Dahlgren is scarcely well of the loss of his leg," noted one of Meade's staff officers on February 29.[31] He had to demonstrate that he could safely sit a horse, and that he possessed the stamina for arduous duty in the field. General Meade, suspecting Ulric's inability to withstand the vicissitudes of a prolonged expedition in the inclement weather of February, was disinclined to give him permission; but Dahlgren, determined to go, mounted his horse, and proceeded to a review of the men of the Second Corps, rode so fearlessly over the fields, and under his frank smile, so well hid all traces of bodily suffering, that Meade reluctantly granted his permission for Ulric to go on the expedition. He apparently satisfied his detractors, but at what cost?[32]

However, the men of the Third Division, who did not know him, preferred one of their own instead of an unknown commodity like Ulric Dahlgren. "But why was Col. Dahlgren selected?" inquired one of Kilpatrick's scouts years after the war. "I believe it was one of the many cases during the war where it was intended that the tail should wag the dog; that is, if the dog caught the rabbit.

Does any soldier who knew or served under General Kilpatrick believe, had the selection been left to him, he would have gone outside of his old Third Cavalry Division for a leader?"[33] Thus, it appears likely that Ulric's political connections got him the position, and it remained to be seen whether he was up to the task.

Kilpatrick himself apparently harbored some doubts about whether Ulric could handle such a severe test. A cryptic statement by him suggests that the Union high command forced Dahlgren on him. Kilpatrick's good friend from New Jersey, Maj. Edwin F. Cooke, served in 2nd New York Cavalry, Little Kil's old regiment. He assigned Cooke to accompany Dahlgren's column—perhaps to keep an eye on the young man. As Kilpatrick took his leave of his old friend, an enlisted man heard him call out, "Good-bye, Major, do this thing up clean for me, and then ask anything you like." Cooke, seeking to assure his friend, responded, "You will find it all right General, depend on me."[34] This odd exchange between two old friends suggests that not only did Kilpatrick have doubts about Dahlgren, there also may have been some hidden agenda for the mission that only Kilpatrick, Dahlgren, and the high command knew.

By this time, the fact that a raid intended to free the prisoners loomed was no longer a secret. "There was a congregation of high mandarins today, Sedwick, Warren, Newton, Merritt, Kilpatrick, Chapman, &c., for an expedition is plainly on foot," recorded one of Meade's staff officers in his diary on February 27.[35] "There was a rumor for some time that some unusual expedition was contemplated in which only picked men and horses would be taken," noted a member of Kilpatrick's headquarters escort.[36] Brig. Gen. Henry E. Davies, who commanded one of Kilpatrick's brigades, was more direct. "General Kilpatrick made no secret of his plan which became a subject of common talk about the Camps and the important element of secrecy so essential on such an enterprise was entirely disregarded," recounted Davies.[37]

The lack of security for a supposedly secret operation appalled Lt. Col. Theodore Lyman, who served on Meade's staff. Lyman described the preparations as being "like a picnic, with everybody blabbing and yelping." In a letter to his wife, he reported, "the idea is to liberate the prisoners, catch all the rebel [Members of Congress] that are lying around loose, and make tracks to our nearest lines."[38] Word of the impending raid even reached civilians in Washington, D. C.[39] If civilians in Washington knew, then the Confederates certainly knew about it, too.

"I venture beforehand to prophesy that it will fail, for the following reasons," noted Lyman in his diary, "1st, I believe that Kilpatrick is an incompetent officer for such a thing; he is a great talker & manager, but has no head or skill, so far as proved; as to his dash & physical courage, *peutêtre*. 2d, Geographical difficulties, & rivers, and roads bad or hard to find. 3d, Military difficulties; the home-guards must be poor indeed if, behind some breastwork or stone wall, they fail to drive off our cavalry." The staff officer's predictions proved accurate.[40]

Once Dahlgren demonstrated that he could handle the travails of extended service in the field, events began moving quickly. He left his father's house at the Washington Navy Yard on February 18, crossed the Potomac River, and boarded a train of the Orange & Alexandria Railroad, riding it to the Army of the Potomac's winter encampment around Brandy Station. He mounted his horse there and rode over to Kilpatrick's headquarters at Stevensburg, some five miles farther on. He soon fell back into the familiar routine of an army in camp, spending the next ten days consulting with Kilpatrick and fine-tuning the plan for the raid.[41]

On February 26, Pleasonton officially informed Kilpatrick that Dahlgren would accompany the expedition. "Col. Ulric Dahlgren is authorized to accompany you, and will render valuable assistance from his knowledge of the country and his well-known gallantry, intelligence, and energy," instructed Pleasonton.[42] Interestingly, nothing in this order indicates that Dahlgren was to command a column of the expedition, only that he was to accompany the expedition and render assistance. Somehow, he ended up in command of the flanking column. Therefore, the logical question of why arises.

If Admiral Dahlgren is to be believed, the suffering of the prisoners of war motivated him. "It awakened his deepest indignation," wrote the Admiral. "War in its mildest form is cruel enough to sate a tiger, and he had ever been most careful to avoid aggravating these sorrows by inflicting needless pain on any."[43] Reverend Byron Sunderland echoed a similar note. Ully rode alongside Maj. Robert Morris, Jr. at Brandy Station, and rallied the regiment when Morris went down and was captured. In August 1863, Morris died a lonely death of disease in Libby Prison, and other members of the Lancers remained locked up there, suffering abjectly. "Stirred by the tidings of their anguish, which, borne on every breeze, were filling the heart of the whole nation with heaviness, causing every cheek to tingle with shame, and every soul to heave with the sighing of bitterness, he could no longer be restrained," Reverend Sunderland poetically recalled a few weeks later.[44]

Lt. Reuben Bartley, a signal officer who accompanied the expedition, also reinforced this explanation for Ulric's participation in the expedition. "When an opportunity offered to try and release our prisoners he joined in it with his whole soul as he had often advocated such a step long before it was tried," recalled Bartley, "and always was ready to volunteer in an expedition having that object in view."[45]

In addition, Ulric knew the terrain well, having traversed it numerous times, and none disputed his courage under fire. He had amply demonstrated that he was a tireless and courageous raider. No one doubted these things. However, the fact remained that he was still an inexperienced, twenty-one-year-old colonel with one leg.

Ully had proposed a raid on Richmond in May 1863, just after the Battle of Chancellorsville, and he apparently continued to harbor the dream of leading such a raid. His overarching ambition has been described at length, and such an expedition, if successful, would be spectacular and a real feather in his cap. He also enjoyed unparalleled access to Stanton and Lincoln, perhaps more so than any other junior officer in the history of the United States Army. He socialized with Lincoln's two personal secretaries, John Hay and John Nicolay. His father was a close friend of Lincoln's.

Some have speculated that Lincoln had a far more nefarious plan for this expedition, and that the real object of the raid was not just the liberation of the prisoners of war, but also the decapitation of the Confederate government through a surgical strike intended to eliminate President Jefferson Davis and his cabinet. According to one theory, Lincoln developed the plan and decided to use Ully Dahlgren as his weapon of choice to implement it.[46] This issue will be addressed in detail in the next chapter.

Whatever the reason, Ulric Dahlgren was selected to command the 500-man flanking column, a hand-picked force selected from the 1st Maine, 1st Vermont, 5th Michigan, 5th New York, and 2nd New York regiments of Kilpatrick's division.[47] His column would go by the Fredericks Hall Station route, and would then re-join the main body near Richmond, hoping to enter the city from the south. His men diligently prepared for the upcoming expedition.

Writing from the headquarters of the Third Cavalry Division at Stevensburg on February 26, young Dahlgren penned a remarkable letter to his father. He had some intuition that this excursion would be his last. He also hinted vaguely at the purposes of the expedition, and he could hardly contain his excitement over being permitted to play a major role in it. "I have not returned to the fleet, because there is a grand raid to be made, and I am to have a very important command," he wrote. "If successful, it will be the grandest thing on record; and it if fails, many of us will 'go up.' I may be captured, or I may be 'tumbled over;' but it is an undertaking that if I were not in, I should be ashamed to show my face again. With such an important command, I am afraid to mention it, for fear this letter might fall into wrong hands before reaching you." He told his father that he felt able to take the field in spite of his grievous wound, and concluded by saying, "I think we will be successful, although a desperate undertaking. Aunt Patty can tell you when you return. I will write you more fully when we return. If we do not return, there is no better place to 'give up the ghost.'"[48]

He also sent a similar letter to his Aunt Patty, enclosing the letter to his father. "I have written a letter to Father. When it comes, keep it until you hear whether we succeed in our raid or not," Ulric instructed. "If I do not return, then give it to him. We will start soon, and I think, will succeed, and, if so, it will be the grandest thing on record. I have not the slightest fear about not returning, but we can't always tell, so don't be uneasy nor say a word to anyone." Having said goodbye to his loved ones, Ulric prepared in earnest for his last ride.[49]

He then engaged in controversy over a scout assigned to help lead his column. A man named J. R. Dykes came highly recommended by the Bureau of Military Information, but for some reason, Dahlgren neither wanted the man nor trusted him. Dykes was delinquent in arriving at the Brandy Station encampment, triggering a flurry of telegrams searching for him. Even if he arrived in time to make the march, Dahlgren did not seem to want him.[50] "Cline and men are now on their way to Genl Kilpatrick, with Capt McEntee," wrote Col. George Sharpe, the commander of the BMI, in a letter to Dahlgren. "We have no reason to doubt Dykes loyalty. You can inquire fully about him from Cline and others of our men, who consider him above suspicion." Whatever it was about Dykes, Dahlgren never agreed to his accompanying his column, meaning that a dependable scout did not make the journey with his command. That failure may have had serious implications for the success of the expedition.[51]

The next day, Kilpatrick received his orders: the raid was on. He was to "move with the utmost expedition possible on the shortest route past the enemy's right flank to Richmond, and by this rapid march endeavor to effect an entrance into that city and liberate our prisoners now held there and in that immediate vicinity."[52] A powerful diversionary column under Custer would march for Charlottesville the next day, February 28. Kilpatrick would move out the same day.[53]

The Federals mounted up and marched out of their camps at Stevensburg at 7:00 in the evening on February 28, with 3,582 men and six pieces of artillery.[54] With 460 men, Dahlgren took the advance, leading the way to Ely's Ford, his crutch strapped to his saddle. Ulric's force included six members of the

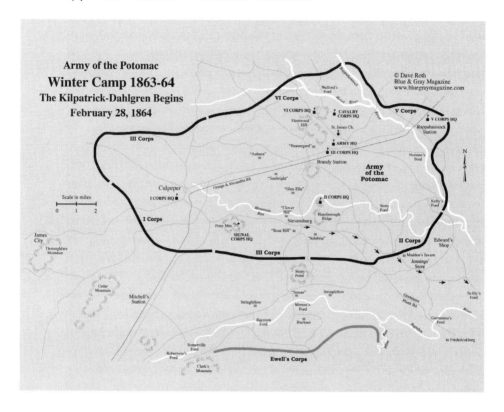

Bureau of Military Information ("BMI"), including Pvt Martin E. Hogan of the 1st Indiana Cavalry, Sgt. William R. Wood of the 6th U. S. Cavalry, Jake Swisher, Anson Carney, J. R. Dykes, and William Chase. Carney and Dahlgren knew each other well; Carney went on the first Greencastle raid on July 2, 1863. Another three BMI men, including Capt. John McEntee and Sgt. Milton Cline, both of whom rode to Greencastle with Ulric Dahlgren, accompanied Kilpatrick's column. The precise reason why so many BMI men went on this expedition remains unknown.[55] These men wore Confederate uniforms to mask their identity and to permit them to move freely through the countryside. If they were captured, they would be hanged as spies, so the stakes were high for the BMI agents.[56]

The enemy heavily picketed the ford—an important one—and it had to be taken quietly for the Federals to retain the element of surprise. With Hogan skillfully leading the way, the Hoosier and Sgt. Wood each captured a Confederate picket at Ely's Ford at 11:00 p.m. Then, with a detachment of twenty-three members of the 5th New York Cavalry under command of Lt. H. A. D. Merritt captured the entire picket reserve—2 officers and 14 enlisted

men of the Cobb Legion Cavalry of Georgia—and crossed the Rapidan undetected.[57] "Never in the history of the war, perhaps, was the need of vigilance
and protection against surprise by men on picket more signally illustrated than
on this occasion," noted an officer of the 9th Virginia Cavalry.[58] As a reward
for surprising and capturing the pickets, Dahlgren honored Merritt and his
detachment by assigning them to lead the advance of the expedition.[59]

"It is with regret that I am compelled to say anything disparaging of our
cavalry," noted Col. Walter H. Taylor, who was one of Robert E. Lee's staff
officers, "but sad to relate the entire picket at Ely's ford on the Rapidan river
were captured by the enemy. No one was left to give intelligence of their having
crossed. In this direction the cavalry were our sole reliance, so the enemy actually reached the [Virginia] Central railroad before we were aware of their
having crossed to this side of the river."[60] The expedition was off to the best
start possible.

"Myriads of stars twinkled in heaven, looking at us as if in wonder why
should we break the laws of God and wander at night instead of seeking repose
and sleep," recounted Capt. Joseph Gloskoski, the signal officer accompanying
Kilpatrick's command. "The moon threw its silvery light upon Rapidan waters
when we forded it, and it seemed as if the Almighty Judge was looking silently
on our doings."[61]

The entire column crossed the river unmolested. Once on the other side,
Kilpatrick ordered Dahlgren to march rapidly to Fredericks Hall Station on the
Virginia Central by way of Spotsylvania Court House, and then to continue on
to a point above Goochland, where he was to cross the James River, move down
the opposite bank, and, if possible, be in position to seize the main bridge that
led to the city of Richmond by 10:00 a.m. on Tuesday, March 1.[62]

The sky was very dark and overcast on the night of February 28, but it did not
rain, and the column made excellent time. Ulric had not spent so much time
in the saddle in quite a while, and it showed. One officer of the 5th Michigan
Cavalry noted that he "was much emaciated, his wooden leg seemed to annoy
him during the march, and in mounting he needed assistance."[63] However, he
still possessed an iron will, and he was determined to fulfill his mission and his
destiny. So, he gritted his teeth and pressed on. His courage impressed the men
who rode with him.

About 2:00 a.m. on the 29th, one of Dahlgren's men accidentally discharged
his carbine, the blast shattering the quiet night. Ulric galloped back to the man's
position in line, ordered him to dismount, and forced him to lead his horse on
foot until after daylight the next morning. BMI agent Anson Carney felt sorry

for the man, and interceded with Dahlgren on his behalf. His plea fell on deaf ears. Dahlgren told Carney that such carelessness ought not to be overlooked, so he decided to make an example of the man. Ulric's point was well-taken, but he employed harsh disciplinary methods. Hopefully, though, the rest of his command would learn from the incident and avoid such conduct for the rest of the expedition.[64]

They reached Spotsylvania Court House by early dawn on February 29. The blueclad horsemen finally halted to cross a stream. As the ambulances that accompanied the column struggled their way up a steep bank, Dahlgren inspected his command. The men formed into two lines for this purpose, and he rode twice along the line. "Many had never seen him before," noted an officer. "His appearance, however, gave general satisfaction, and expressions of confidence were heard all around." A member of the 2nd New York Cavalry echoed a similar note, "I think that any soldier living who was with him (Col. Dahlgren) will say that he was a brave and fearless leader."[65] Once Dahlgren completed the inspection, the march resumed and continued steadily on with the exception of a single halt to feed the horses.[66] They reached the vicinity of Fredericks Hall Station about 11:00 on the morning of February 29, narrowly missing an opportunity to capture a train carrying Robert E. Lee that passed through the area less than an hour before Dahlgren's arrival. "The train upon which he traveled was very last one that made the through trip," reported a relieved Walter Taylor.[67]

The Federals captured sixteen Maryland artillerists, who told the raiders that three different camps, including eight different batteries in each camp, numbering eighty-three total guns, were arrayed around the station. These guns made up the entire artillery reserve of Lt. Gen. Richard S. Ewell's Second Corps, commanded by Lt. Col. Hilary P. Jones, who was then presiding over a court-martial of one of his men. A regiment of infantry and a battalion of sharp-shooters also camped there. Some of the gunners were drilling, firing their guns at targets. Spotting Dahlgren's cavalry column and mistaking them for friendly horse soldiers, the artillerists held their fire and let the cavalrymen pass by unmolested.[68]

After interrogating the prisoners, Dahlgren wisely determined not to attack the camps at the station and moved around them instead cutting the Virginia Central Railroad and telegraph lines at Gunnell's Crossing, about a mile south of the station. While the men tore up the tracks and bent the rails, a train approached from the north. Spotting the fires blazing to generate the heat to bend the rails, the engineer wisely retreated, pulling back to safety as quickly as he could.[69]

Moving about three miles beyond the station, Dahlgren spotted a house on a nearby hill that seemed to be a hub of activity. Lieutenant Colonel Jones was presiding over a court-martial there. The artillerists spotted the approach of the Yankee horsemen, and panic ensued. "Running to the windows and doors of the house and looking out they saw a number of Yankee cavalry galloping toward the house firing their pistols and shouting as they came, pointing their large pistols into the windows" recalled one Confederate. They rather rudely demanded the surrender of the occupants. Because none of his men were armed, Jones ordered them to surrender, nearly thirty in all, including several girls and thirty-seven-year-old Capt. William F. Dement of Charles County, Maryland, who commanded the 1st Maryland Artillery. Although most of them escaped later that night, they provided quite a haul of prisoners and a feather in Dahlgren's cap.[70] With only 500 men in his entire command, Dahlgren was unable to guard the prisoners properly. He also did not need them hindering the advance of his quick-moving raid. He told Lieutenant Bartley that he did not want them along the next day, as they might slow down the column or get in the way when the time came to enter Richmond. He also declared that he did not want to spare the men necessary to guard them. Thus, Dahlgren made it easy for the Confederates to escape, which compromised the secrecy of the expedition.[71]

However, Dahlgren made a good impression on his captives. He treated them well, sharing his food and even a nip or two of whiskey with them. "He was most agreeable and charming," noted Captain Dement, "very fair-haired and young looking with manners as soft as a cat's."[72] However, Ulric could be cold, hard, and calculating when he needed to be, and he could also be thoroughly ruthless, making for an interesting dichotomy. Later that day, and for no apparent reason, Dahlgren inexplicably permitted Jones to visit his wife at a private residence called Chantilly along the Federal route of march.[73]

Although the raiders destroyed the telegraph lines around Fredericks Hall Station, their doing so did not prevent word of the Federal cavalry expedition from reaching Richmond. That afternoon, Robert E. Lee informed Gen. Samuel Cooper, the Confederate adjutant general, that "enemy's cavalry appears to be moving by our left and right, one column in the direction of Charlottesville, the other Frederick's Hall." He also notified Maj. Gen. Arnold Elzey, commander of the defenses of Richmond, that Union cavalry raiders were headed in his direction. Thus, the Confederate authorities had plenty of time to make their dispositions to receive the Northern horse soldiers. The Yankee troopers lost the element of surprise for good.[74]

Dahlgren turned south, heading for the South Anna River. They arrived at the banks of the river about 10:00 p.m. on the night of February 29. By then, it was raining, and the men were cold and wet to the bone. "The night of the 29th was one of the most dismal nights that ever was witnessed in Va.," complained Lieutenant Bartley. "The rain fell in torrents and it was so intensely dark that one could not discern a man riding at his side. It was with the greatest difficulty that the column could be kept together. Everything had to be done by sound, and it was unsafe to make any noise for we were now entirely cut off from any support and liable at any moment to be attacked, but our very boldness saved us."[75]

The weary horse soldiers, including Dahlgren, suffered. "Who could complain of weariness when he looked at the colonel, still weak from his wound, riding along quietly, uncomplainingly, ever vigilantly watching every incident of the march?" wrote one of the men to Admiral Dahlgren after the end of the expedition.[76] The intensely dark night and the rain made it impossible to keep the column closed up. "More than half the men were asleep on their horses," recalled an officer of the 5th Michigan Cavalry. "I slept soundly at least half the night while marching."[77] About fifty of his troopers got lost in the darkness, but caught up to the column again at Goochland Court House in the morning.[78]

His men crossed the frigid South Anna at Turkey Creek Ford, a few miles from the town of Vontay. They crossed in the inky darkness by torchlight, offering some of Dahlgren's captives a perfect opportunity to escape, and they slipped away silently into the night. The escapees included Lt. Col. Hilary P. Jones, the commander of the artillery battalion whom Dahlgren permitted to pay a call upon his wife.[79]

Ully finally halted the column around midnight, about nine miles from Goochland. A small grocery store stood by the roadside. By a stroke of luck, the Yankees captured several wagons loaded with corn and meal on their way to the Army of Northern Virginia, providing feed for the poor, hungry horses of Dahlgren's command.[80] With assistance from an orderly, Ulric dismounted. When one of the men asked if he was tired, he replied, "We'll have some supper and two hours' sleep, then you'll see how bright I am." The men gratefully ate what they could find and then bivouacked for two hours, trying to steal a few moments of sleep in the cold rain.[81]

"We were now directly between Lee's army and Richmond in a part of the country where no hostile Yankee had been since the war commenced," correctly observed Lieutenant Bartley. "This with the small number of men and the success we had met since we first set together with the important of the mission we were on made it intensely exciting. I never before or since experienced the sensation of that night's march. The liberty of ten thousand of best and bravest men was depending on our success."[82] The Federal horse soldiers carried quite a burden as they slogged on through the cold, wet night.

Every man was in the saddle again by daylight on March 1, moving out in spite of the cold rain that continued to fall. About 10:00 that morning, the column reached the James River Canal at a spot about twenty-one miles from Richmond. Dahlgren ordered Capt. John F. B. Mitchell of the 2nd New York Cavalry to take 100 men of his regiment, the ambulances, prisoners, extra horses, and proceed along the Kanawha Canal, destroying locks, burning mills, canal boats, and all the grain he could find. He also instructed Mitchell to send the ambulances, etc. forward to Hungary Station, and to proceed down the river road or the canal with a local black man named Martin Robinson as their guide. B.M.I. agent John Babcock had recommended Robinson and represented to Dahlgren that the black man was both knowledgeable and reliable. Dahlgren told Robinson that if he misled the column or could not or would not give a satisfactory answer to any question, he would instantly be hanged on the spot.[83] Dahlgren intended to lead the rest of the column to a ford on the James River and then dash into Richmond by way of the Mayo Bridge.[84] Mitchell was to either join them, or march to join Kilpatrick and the main column.[85]

So far, things were going as well as anyone could have hoped. "Up to this, our success had been remarkable—two nights and one day in the Confederate lines and not a shot had been fired at us," observed Dahlgren's signal officer. "We were beginning to think we would go right through with the whole program." However, things were about to take an ominous turn, and Dahlgren would spend too much time looting and burning in Goochland County, meaning that his command would not reach Richmond until several hours after Kilpatrick's column appeared at the outer defenses of the Confederate capital.[86]

Along the way, they came upon some of the largest plantations in that part of Virginia. One, called "Sabot Hall," was the home of James A. Seddon, the Confederate Secretary of War. Brig. Gen. Henry A. Wise stayed there the night before, and would have made quite a catch for Dahlgren's raiders. Some of Mitchell's men torched the barn, corn houses, and stables. Ully rode up to the handsome house, and struggled from his saddle. Grabbing his crutches, he hobbled to the front door and knocked loudly. Seddon's wife, Sarah Bruce "Sallie" Seddon, answered the door. "I'm Colonel Dahlgren," declared the young man.

"Are you related to Admiral Dahlgren?" inquired the lady of the house.

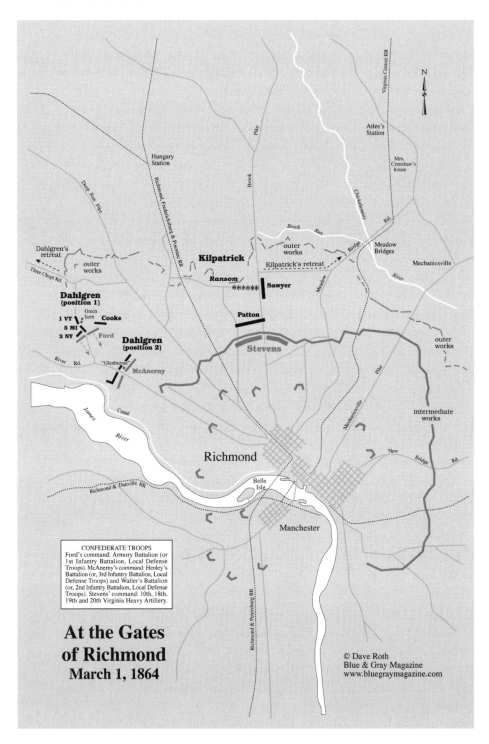

At the Gates of Richmond
March 1, 1864

CONFEDERATE TROOPS
Ford's command: Armory Battalion (or 1st Infantry Battalion, Local Defense Troops). McAnerny's command: Henley's Battalion (or, 3rd Infantry Battalion, Local Defense Troops) and Waller's Battalion (or, 2nd Infantry Battalion, Local Defense Troops). Stevens' command: 10th, 18th, 19th and 20th Virginia Heavy Artillery.

© Dave Roth
Blue & Gray Magazine
www.bluegraymagazine.com

"I'm his son, Ulric."

"Then I knew you as a boy, and I knew your father when I was one of your mother's schoolmates in Philadelphia. He was a beau of mine." She invited the young man in and asked her manservant to go to the cellar for a bottle of blackberry wine.

Before long, Mrs. Seddon and Dahlgren were toasting each other, laughing and reminiscing. She and Ulric visited for quite a while before the young man realized he had to move on. He pulled himself up, hobbled to the door, and bid Mrs. Seddon a fond farewell. As he left, he told her that he would see to it that no harm came to her handsome home.[87]

Mrs. Seddon, however, had not forgotten that her courteous visitor was the enemy. When she sent for the bottle of blackberry wine that provided the pleasant diversion, she also sent another servant galloping off to Richmond to warn her husband that a large party of enemy cavalry was on its way. After the episode ended, she was, perhaps properly, credited with saving Richmond.[88] The next day, she wrote to her husband, "In front, I saw the raging flames which were consuming our own property, I thought I hated the Yankees with all my heart before, but the feeling was intensified by this spectacle."[89]

Mitchell did as ordered, leaving Dahlgren and the rest of the column behind. His troopers nearly captured General Wise, who fled across the James River to make good his escape.[90] Along the way, Mitchell's men burned a gristmill and some barns belonging to a man named John Morson, destroyed a few locks along the canal, and damaged other structures. Some of his men looted nearby homes as they marched, prompting one resident of Richmond to write, "His men, in the meantime, were allowed to amuse themselves by destroying furniture, pilfering plate, and doing other mischief to the farm-houses in the vicinity."[91] The delay engendered by these activities proved fatal.

Reaching Mannakin Town, Dahlgren tried to cross the James at Jude's Ferry but could not due to its being swollen by the overnight rains. The inability to cross made it impossible for the Yankees to enter Richmond from the south. Martin Robinson told Dahlgren that the river could be crossed at the chosen spot. Angered by his inability to get across the river, which he blamed on the incompetence of the guide, Dahlgren handed over one his bridle straps and ordered that Robinson be hanged, in spite of John Babcock's vouching for the man. His men used the bridle strap to lynch Robinson and left his body hanging on a nearby tree before trying to find another route. They left the unfortunate guide's body behind, still swinging from the tree.[92] One of his men later claimed that the guide had intentionally steered the raiders off course:

"Dahlgren was deceived by a negro guide," he wrote, "and, at midnight found himself ten miles from where he should have been."[93]

Not all of Dahlgren's command believed that the guide had intentionally deceived the Federals. One of the BMI men traveling with his column later wrote that he believed "that the hanging of that poor black man was a cruel and cowardly murder. The negro was taken from the plantation where he lived; did not know the country; did not profess to know. Probably he had never been five miles away from his home region." The same man also noted, "It has always seemed strange to me that an officer of Col. Dahlgren's ability should have been so misled. The route he was to take was not a difficult one to follow; and, aside from this, one would suppose that some of Gen. Meade's scouts would have been selected to accompany him, on account of their knowledge of the country between the Rapidan and Richmond."[94]

Tuckahoe Plantation, located on the River Road a few miles west of Richmond close to the spot where Dahlgren hanged Martin Robinson, was the boyhood home of Thomas Jefferson. The handsome 1714 H-shaped white frame house was also the home to various generations of Virginia Randolphs. In 1864, Maj. Richard S. Allen and his wife Virginia owned the handsome plantation along the banks of the James River. As local legend has it, as Dahlgren headed east along the River Road, he came upon Tuckahoe Plantation. Word of the burning of barns and mills elsewhere in Goochland County preceded his arrival. When the one-legged colonel rode down the long cedar-lined lane to the main house at Tuckahoe, Virginia Allen stood in the yard waiting for him with a couple of pistols strapped over her finest dress. She intended to defend her home at all costs. Fortunately, she did not have to. Dahlgren recognized her from attending balls and other social events in the north, and, instead of burning the house, he reportedly came inside for tea. Mrs. Allen's lovely and historic old home survived unscathed.[95]

After leaving Mrs. Allen, Dahlgren marched to a crossroads about eight miles west of Richmond. He sent several men and an officer to try to find Kilpatrick with the news that Dahlgren intended to attack at dusk, and to suggest that they coordinate their attacks. However, Confederate cavalry patrols captured these men, so word of Dahlgren's whereabouts never reached Kilpatrick. Mitchell and his detachment rejoined the main column there about 3:30 that afternoon.

Dahlgren sent off the ambulances, extra horses, and prisoners under guard. They also captured three militiamen who were picketing the approaches to the city after hearing of the approaching Federals. Both men and horses were near the limits of their endurance, and Ulric knew it. He ordered a halt near dark near a Baptist church for an hour and a half to feed the horses and to boil coffee for the men.[96] About half an hour later, while his men enjoyed their coffee and ate what meager rations they had, Dahlgren gathered his officers around and informed them of the mission's objective. He told them that their goal was to attack the city's south side, free the prisoners of war at Belle Isle, and "capture the city, its officials and archives, if possible."[97] This was the first suggestion that there was more to the mission than just freeing the prisoners of war, and it was an ominous suggestion.

Suddenly, he heard Kilpatrick's guns barking. The Yankee horsemen quickly mounted up and headed east on the Three Chopt Road to Westhampton, and then turned east on the Westham Plank Road. Eager to pitch into the fray, Ulric failed to take necessary precautions by deploying scouts and flankers with his column, meaning that his men advanced blindly, and headed straight for the defenses of the city.[98]

Kilpatrick's column arrived in front of Richmond about 10:00 on the morning of March 1. His troops seized an unoccupied section of the outer defensive works of Richmond along the Brook Turnpike. His dismounted troopers continued advancing toward the intermediate line of defenses, coming within about a mile before drawing fire from Confederate artillery. Kilpatrick decided to attack, but the Confederates repulsed his dismounted troopers after some fairly heavy skirmishing. Southern cavalry under command of Bradley T. Johnson was operating in his rear, and Kilpatrick still had not heard from Dahlgren, whose column was supposed to arrive in the Richmond area at about the same time his had. Six hours had passed, and there was still now sign of Dahlgren's command. When Kilpatrick heard train whistles—suggesting the arrival of reinforcements—he decided to break off and withdraw, pulling back toward Atlee's Station. That evening, while Dahlgren's command was finally engaging the Confederates on the west side of town, elements of Maj. Gen. Wade Hampton's Confederate cavalry division arrived and pitched into the 7th Michigan Cavalry, routing it, wounding its commander, Lt. Col. Allyn C. Litchfield, and capturing the wounded colonel. That did it. Kilpatrick recognized that he would not be able to enter Richmond and withdrew, and, instead of moving toward the pre-arranged rallying point at Hungary Station, Little Kil's troopers headed east, moving to meet up with Butler's command on the Peninsula. That decision meant that any possibility of linking up with Dahlgren was forever lost, a fact that had serious implications for the 500 men of the one-legged colonel's command.[99]

Kilpatrick's signal officer launched two rockets into the dark, rainy night, trying to communicate with Dahlgren's command. "Here I had time to look for Colonel Dahlgren's signals," recounted Capt. Joseph Gloskoski, Kilpatrick's acting signal officer. "None could be seen, however, owing partly to woods, mist, and smoke, and want of knowledge of his whereabouts." He and Dahlgren's signal officer, Lt. Reuben Bartley, had arranged a specific sequence of signals. He believed that the sounds of Kilpatrick's guns and the answering guns of the enemy should have made it easy for Dahlgren to find Kilpatrick's command, but Dahlgren failed to do so.[100]

Dahlgren had sent out various scouts, including BMI member Sgt. James R. Wood and another man named Ed Magee, as his column approached the city, hoping they would locate Kilpatrick's command. When none of the scouts reported back, Dahlgren sent Lieutenant Bartley and a few men rode off to try to find the main Federal force near Hungary Station. Bartley traveled cross-country to the Brook Pike and approached within a few miles of the city, but without success.[101] He ascertained that a large force of enemy cavalry of Hampton's division was patrolling, searching for the Union horsemen, and had several close calls with being captured by Hampton's scouting parties. Because of the roving bands of Confederate cavalry, Bartley dared not use his signal rockets, for fear that Confederate cavalry would use them to hone in on him and his little command.[102]

The horsemen entered the city's outer ring of defenses, crossed the railroad, and traveled another three miles before a volley from the woods blasted the 5th Michigan Cavalry, which led Dahlgren's advance. "It was now growing dark, but we pushed on," recalled Captain Mitchell. "At first there was some wavering. Every now and then a volley was poured into the ranks. It grew rapidly darker and darker; soon you could see nothing but the flash of the enemy's muskets."[103]

That afternoon, the bells of Richmond began tolling, calling out the home guard. Every available man took to the field for the defense of the city.[104] In spite of the alarms sounding, "there was very little excitement in Richmond," noted resident Sallie Brock Preston. "So suddenly and unexpectedly did this adventure occur, that we wee scarcely aware of our danger until it was over."[105] A Union man had a different recollection. "Kilpatrick's raid around Richmond in 1864 created, seemingly, more consternation in the city than did the seven days' battles with McClellan around Richmond," he wrote. "Every bell rung out long and loud."[106] While the civilian population was not alarmed, the home guard understood the nature of the threat, and it turned out to defend the Southern capital.

Three hundred Confederate home guards, commanded by Maj. Charles H. Ford, a veteran of the British cavalry, deployed to meet Dahlgren's troopers on the grounds of "Roselawn," the farm of Benjamin W. Green.[107] They waited in the rain until the 2nd New York Cavalry charged them with their sabers drawn. A volley split the Federal column, which peeled off after being repulsed. The infuriated Dahlgren responded with "threats and expostulations," and then ordered the 1st Maine Cavalry to go in along the road. The Maine men attacked, driving the enemy from their position. Downed timber and other obstacles made rapid movement impossible. However, the 1st Maine pressed its attack until it encountered stout breastworks in its front.[108]

Dahlgren turned to Lt. Robert Haire of the 5th Michigan and ordered him to charge. Haire deferred to a more senior officer, Lt. Samuel Harris, who had spent most of the war serving as a staff officer. Harris, in turn, deferred to Haire, who ordered his Wolverines to draw sabers and charge. Although Harris suffered a severe shoulder wound in this charge, the Michiganders broke the home guards and drove them from their position. Dahlgren also sent Major Cooke off to try to flank the Confederate right with nearly 200 mounted men.

The dismounted Confederates stubbornly resisted Dahlgren's advance, forcing the Federals to charge each successive skirmish line. Cooke's mounted men crashed into the Confederate right flank, routing it. "It was a scrub race—across fields, fences and stone walls, we pressed after them, rallying and scattering them repeatedly as they attempted to dispute our advance whenever a wall or house afforded shelter," recalled a Yankee horseman. "Between formidable works, over rifle pits, ditches, and every obstruction, with a cheer, a run and a volley from our Spencers, we crowded them back to the edge of the city. It was now dark and the gas lights burning. We were inside the city limits, though the houses were scattered."[109]

Capt. John H. McAnerny commanded home guard troops of the Henley Battalion (3rd Infantry Battalion, Local Defense Troops). McAnerny, commissioned an officer in the 3rd Alabama Infantry, had been badly wounded at the 1862 Battle of Gaine's Mill, during the Seven Days' Battles, and was not yet well enough to return to duty with his regiment. His motley force of clerks, reinforced by men of Lt. Col. Richard P. Waller's 2nd Infantry Battalion, formed a line of battle on a brow of high ground across the intersection of the Three Chopt and Westham Plank Roads, with their right resting on a hill that descended into swampy ground. "Don't a man fire a shot until he hears my voice," ordered

Captain McAnerny. "Remember, two volleys." The Federal horsemen pounded down on them, with bareheaded BMI agent Martin Hogan leading the way, their officers spurring them on, telling the men that they faced only militia. When the blueclad horsemen reached the top of the hill, silhouetted against the gathering dusk, McAnerny ordered his men to open fire. They loosed a withering volley, staggering the Federals. A second volley stopped the blueclad horsemen in their tracks with heavy losses.[110]

Ully Dahlgren had a close call during this intense fighting. Miles Cary, who served in the home guard, spotted Dahlgren in the gloaming. Dahlgren rode right by Cary, who recognized him. "When they met our main line, they turned; and as the lights from Richmond hung low at their backs, I could plainly see Dahlgren, as he was mounted," remembered Cary. "I ran possibly twenty yards to cut him off." Fortunately for Ully, Cary's powder was wet. "My bayonet could not have been three feet from his chest when my cap burst, my powder being wet. In an instant he knew that an enemy was in his front, and, rising in his stirrups, with a downward stroke of his saber, he cut for my head." Cary raised his rifle, which absorbed the blow. Dahlgren's saber deflected off the barrel of the gun, slashing through Cary's cape, and deep into the left breast of his overcoat. The sharp saber sheared the skin off his left wrist. "Then, spurring his horse, he struck for my chest, but his horse, striking against me, swerved me aside, and I caught the point of his saber deep in the bone of my left forearm, midway between shoulder and elbow." As Ully's horse passed Cary, it trampled his leg and sent the Virginian sprawling, permitting Dahlgren to escape unharmed.[111]

John B. Jones, who worked in the Confederate War Department, recorded this fighting in his diary. "The Department Clerks were in action in the evening in five minutes after they were formed in line. It rained fast all the time, and it was very dark. The enemy's cavalry charged upon them, firing as they came; they were ordered to lie flat on the ground," he wrote. "This they did, until the enemy came within fifteen yards of them, when they rose and fired, sending the assailants to the right and left, helter-skelter. How many fell is not known."[112] One Federal account indicated that Dahlgren suffered twenty-two killed, twenty-six wounded, and thirty-two captured in this engagement.[113] The Confederates later claimed they captured 100 horses and accouterments, a number of small arms, and one three-inch cannon in this fierce fighting.[114]

"Finally, from the increased fire it appeared that the enemy had received reinforcements, and the colonel gave the order to retire after we had driven the enemy 2½ miles," reported Captain Mitchell. With the enemy's right resting on a hill that descended into as swamp, Dahlgren realized that the Confederate flank could not be turned. Thus, he decided that he had already gone "far enough", and elected to break off and withdraw.[115] Dahlgren called for the 2nd New York and ordered Captain Mitchell to take command of the rear guard, and to keep it well closed up with the main column. The defeated Yankees marched in "perfect silence and good order." Dahlgren retreated about six miles and halted the column to try to determine how best to proceed.[116]

Lieutenant Bartley, Dahlgren's signal officer, might have made a final attempt to communicate with Kilpatrick's column by his signal rockets, but he dared not use them. Enemy soldiers surrounded Dahlgren's beleaguered troopers, and the Southerners mistook Bartley for one of their own in the darkness. If he fired his signal rockets, the enemy would have known the Federals were there, and the whole column might have been captured. Instead, Dahlgren ordered Bartley to abandon his rockets and torpedoes. Unless Dahlgren could break through to Kilpatrick's command, the last chance to communicate with the main body was now gone.[117]

Weather conditions deteriorated badly as they retreated. "No one engaged in that night's search will ever forget its difficulties," shuddered Lieutenant Merritt of the 5th New York Cavalry. "The storm had set in with renewed fury. The fierce wind drove the rain, snow, and sleet. The darkness was rendered intense by the thick pines which overgrew the road, and which dashed in our faces in an avalanche of water at every step." The defeated Federals suffered intensely as they marched silently through the night.[118]

Ulric had failed. He had failed to cross the James River, he had failed to enter the city of Richmond from the south, and he had failed to break through the enemy to reach Kilpatrick's main body.[119] Foiled by the heavy rains and the poor choice of a guide, his expedition was utterly routed, marking what was perhaps the first major failure of his life. He expressed his disappointment, but "so quietly was this said, that, but for a sad glance from his eye, one would not have known how much he felt it," as one of his officers remembered.[120] He could have withdrawn and gone back the way he came, but that was not Ulric Dahlgren's nature. He had been given an important task, and he was determined to fulfill his mission if at all possible. He decided to go on and attempt to enter Richmond anyway. As he mounted again, he told the man assisting him, "We are going on, and if we succeed, I'd gladly lose the other."[121]

Cold rain poured down, drenching and chilling the exhausted horsemen to the bone. It was "dark as a stack of black cats" that night, and men and horses picked their way along infrequently used wood roads, frequently stopping to remove fallen trees and tracing the course of the road with their hands, as it was too dark to see. His "tired and exhausted men fell asleep on their horses," as one recalled. "It became necessary to march by file, the jaded animals stumbling and falling down." In the chaos of the repulse and in the inky darkness, Dahlgren failed to obtain a guide, which created real problems for his defeated column.[122]

When the advance elements of Dahlgren's column reached the area of Atlee's Station, they found a small wagon train of wounded Federals taken prisoner during the repulse of Kilpatrick's troopers. Dahlgren briefly questioned a wounded officer of the 7th Michigan Cavalry, Lt. Col. Allyn C. Litchfield, to learn what he could about the whereabouts of Kilpatrick's command, and then permitted the Confederate wagons to take the wounded men on into Richmond for treatment. He now knew that Kilpatrick had been repulsed from the defenses of the Confederate capital and had then been driven off by Hampton's cavalry.[123]

Dahlgren and fewer than 100 men rode ahead of the column. He failed to tell anyone what his intentions were, leaving his officers "without any knowledge of our commander's intentions," as one later noted.[124] As a result, he became separated from his main body, and they never saw him again. Led by the intrepid Captain Mitchell, the main body eventually found Kilpatrick's column by following the trail of amnesty proclamations from Old Church, northeast of Richmond. His men found Kilpatrick's command near Tunstall's Station on the James River Railroad and punched their way through a force of Confederate cavalry. They then made their way to Yorktown, where the weary horsemen finally got to rest a bit.[125]

Leading his little command, which included only about ninety-five men and four commissioned officers, Dahlgren headed for the city's defenses once more, skirmishing along the way. "The skirmishing was heavy, the enemy's fire was very annoying; but I stopped in admiration of the colonel's coolness," admired one of his men. "He rode along the line, speaking to the men, so calm, so quiet, so brave, that it seemed to me the veriest coward must needs fight, if never before." He ordered his men to draw sabers and charge, and scattering the enemy and driving them back into their stout works. Having done so, there was now nothing left to do but to try to make their way back to Kilpatrick's main body.[126]

Had Butler's troops come up the Peninsula, as the original plan contemplated, Dahlgren might have succeeded in bringing his beleaguered little command out safely. However, Butler ordered his command not to go past New Kent Court House, thirty miles east of Richmond, leaving Dahlgren to try to make his way to safety at Gloucester Point on the northern bank of the York River, across from Yorktown, nearly sixty-five miles north and east of Richmond.

Dahlgren and his men rode on through the dark, rainy night, their clothing coated by ice as the chilly rain froze upon contact. They had spent three solid days in the saddle, with only a few breaks, and they had reached the limits of their endurance. "In all the history of the war there is no more pathetic figure— with crutches strapped to the saddle, and in the stirrup an artificial limb to take the place of the leg lost but a few months before—none more dramatic than young Ulric Dahlgren as he led his handful of exhausted men through the roused country," as one early historian of clandestine missions of the Civil War noted.[127] They rode on through the night, and at midnight, the last day of Ulric Dahlgren's life began.

The pelting rains finally ended on the morning of March 2. It was still cold and blustery, but the dim late winter sun helped to warm the weary troopers a bit. Dahlgren had less than one hundred men with him, and all were exhausted from having spent more than sixty straight hours in the saddle. Ully rode at the head of his column, ignoring his own infirmities and exhaustion. Within a few hours, they reached the banks of the swollen and fast-running Pamunkey River at Hanovertown.[128] The river was too deep to ford, and a rope-drawn ferry provided the only means for crossing it. Men and horses crossed in small groups, proving to be a time-consuming process. When the entire command was finally across, Dahlgren called a halt to feed men and horses. They had little in the way of forage or rations, but they hungrily ate whatever they had. After a brief rest, the men swung back into their saddles and moved out once again.[129]

A Confederate captured that morning escaped and made his way to safety among the men of the 9th Virginia Cavalry near Hanover Court House. "One of our pickets sent in a man taken under such suspicious circumstances as to induce the belief that he was a Yankee," noted Col. Richard L. T. Beale of the 9th Virginia Cavalry. Beale interrogated the man, learned that he was an escaped prisoner, and that Dahlgren and his command were attempting to cross the swollen Pamunkey. Beale sent out patrols, a move that ultimately claimed Ully Dahlgren's life.[130]

They clung to the riverbank for three or four miles and then headed off onto the main road. Before long, an enemy soldier emerged from his hiding place. Although the Confederate did not fire a shot, the Federals dispatched him. They reached the north bank of the Mattaponi River by mid-afternoon. By now, troopers of Co. H of the 9th Virginia Cavalry, also known as Lee's Rangers, and commanded by Lt. James Pollard, dogged the Federals, harassing them at every step. When they arrived at Walkerton, they used another ferry to cross the wide Mattaponi. Dahlgren deployed a few vedettes and his command began crossing, their horses swimming the chilly currents of the deep river.[131]

Soon, the crack of a rifle rang out, and then another and another. The enemy was closing in on Dahlgren's beleaguered little column. The Northern vedettes returned fire, holding their positions until the rest of the Federals were safely across. The rear-guard then crossed and rejoined their comrades on the south side of the river. Ulric Dahlgren had dismounted and was watching and directing the passage of his men. His men called out to him to cross before the enemy closed in on them, but he remained there, leaning on his crutches, waiting until the last man had made it to safety on the other side of the river. "He stood alone and erect, disregarding the bullets which struck near him on all sides, and calmly awaiting the return of the ferry-boat," recounted his father. "It must have been as plain to the rebels that he, whom they made the target for their rifles, was crippled—as it was that the river rolled between him and his men, separating him from all assistance. Any resolute man of their number could have rushed forward and borne away, by main force, the enfeebled frame of the young soldier." Dahlgren was impervious to their bullets, instead drawing his revolver and calling on the Confederates to come out of their hiding places. Finally, once all of his men and horses were safely across, he boarded the ferry and was the last man to step on the south bank of the Mattapony. It was 2:00 p.m.[132]

The grayclad troops watched the Federals cross, counting them as they passed. Realizing that Dahlgren had less than one hundred men with him, the word went out to round up parties of local men to try to stop the Union horsemen. Before long, a force of nearly four hundred men had gathered to oppose Dahlgren's passage. "So soon as it was known that Colonel Dahlgren was crossing the river above, the defense began to gather in squads," recounted a local civilian.[133] Trackers plagued their every step, forcing the Yankee horse soldiers to open fire at bushes and clumps of trees, using up all of their ammunition, slowing their rate of march and further wearing on already exhausted men and horses. "We were continually under fire, but the casualties were few, owing to the inferior arms of our opponents," observed one of Dahlgren's men. "We were able to keep them at a good distance with our carbines." The harassing fire of the bushwhackers prevented the weary Federals from watering their horses.[134]

The Confederates captured flankers as soon as Dahlgren sent them out, meaning that the column advanced blindly with no screen.[135] Dahlgren dispatched the scout Hogan with a small party of men to act as a rear guard, a thankless but necessary job.[136] He also gave orders that any house used by bushwhackers was to be set ablaze, a harsh response intended to limit the harassing fire that took its toll on the sagging morale of Dahlgren's bedraggled little command.[137]

As darkness fell, they crossed a bridge over Anseamancock Creek and continued for another half mile before Dahlgren called a halt to feed and rest his tired men and animals. His men ate their first meal in thirty-six hours. While the rest was desperately needed, it told the Confederates where Dahlgren's men were. "It being about nine o'clock in the evening, and very dark, our fires enabled the rebels (that were secreted all about us) to come near enough to even count the number of our force," recalled one of the raiders. "This they told me after we were captured."[138] Maj. Edwin F. Cooke, the second ranking officer on the expedition, used the opportunity to determine how much ammunition the men had left. They were nearly out, and most of the seventy remaining men had none left at all. They were in dire straits, and if challenged, they would be incapable of putting up much of a fight.[139]

Dahlgren's manservant pulled down a nearby rail fence, spread the rails out on the ground, and laid out a blanket on them, creating a rudimentary bed for the exhausted and gaunt young colonel. He and his little command had marched nearly 150 miles with virtually no rest, and all were at the limits of their endurance. Dahlgren dismounted, lay down, and slept for a few minutes, the only sleep he had had in several days. Half an hour later, he awoke and climbed back in the saddle. His column moved out again, slogging along through the gathering darkness of the cold Virginia winter. It was dark and overcast, but it did not rain that night. The densely wooded countryside offered numerous opportunities for a determined foe to stage an ambush.[140] In order to discourage ambushers from opening fire, Dahlgren required Captain Dement, the Maryland artillerist captured at Fredericks Hall Station, to ride by his side at the head of the Federal column.[141]

A scratch force of Confederates, consisting of the dogged Lieutenant Pollard and his twenty troopers, twenty-eight men of the 5th Virginia Cavalry under command of Capt. Edward C. Fox, seventy men of the 42nd Virginia Battalion under a Captain McGruder, thirty-four home guards, and some home guard cavalry, totaling 150 men, gathered at King and Queen Court House. This scratch force included a group of local schoolchildren whose ages ranged from thirteen to seventeen, commanded by their schoolmaster, Edward W. Halbach, whose poor health had prevented him from serving in the Confederate army.[142]

Pollard and his men followed along, harassing the rear of the Union column

The Death of Colonel Dahlgren
HARPER'S WEEKLY

*Dahlgren's bloodstained gauntlet and
sash. Note the bullet hole in the sash.*
DON TROIANI

by keeping up a running skirmish. When Dahlgren halted to feed, the Confederates dashed ahead to plan and set up an ambush at the northeast corner of a road junction, hidden by woods and the slope of a hill a couple of miles ahead. Pollard designed the well-planned and well-hidden ambush at a spot where four-foot high banks lined the road on either side. The Confederates built a barricade of fence rails across the road, took their positions behind the barricade and on either side of the road, and waited patiently for the Federals to arrive.[143]

"At last we heard them moving with all the noise of a cavalry command," recounted Henry C. Pendleton, one of the local civilians manning the ambush. "Our little force of volunteers had increased to sixty-five men and boys. We were restless, anxious, nervous. Nearer and nearer they came. We were not to fire till the head of the column should reach our barricade. To us it was a moment of fearful suspense, but every man at present stood at his post ready to do his duty."[144]

Dahlgren remained at the head of his column, leading the way with the two BMI men, Martin Hogan and Jake Swisher, at his side. By now, it was about 11:00, and the inky darkness masked the density of the woods lining the road. Suddenly, Dahlgren heard a rustling of leaves or branches, which instantly put him on guard. Dahlgren ordered Hogan and Swisher to see what lay ahead. Swisher spurred ahead, cried, "Halt!" and cocked his revolver.[145] "Who are you?" called out Lt. H. A. D. Merritt of the 5th New York Cavalry, who, along with Captain Dement, rode by Dahlgren's side.[146] The young colonel drew his revolver and demanded the surrender of those in his front. He pulled the trigger and snapped his pistol in the dark, but the damp cap sputtered and failed to fire. Instead, Confederate muzzle flashes lit the night. Ulric Dahlgren toppled from the saddle, killed instantly by multiple gunshot wounds, his body unceremoniously dumped face down in the thick mud of a roadside ditch. A full colonel at twenty-one, he was dead a month and a day before his twenty-second birthday.[147]

However, this story does not end with Ulric Dahlgren's tragic and untimely death. Instead, his death triggered a controversy that still rages to this day. One final adventure also remained for his mortal remains.

CHAPTER TWELVE

Ulric Dahlgren's Final Adventure

The CONFEDERATE VOLLEY KILLED Ulric Dahlgren instantly, but his men did not realize it in the inky darkness of the winter night. "A bullet, grazing my leg and probably striking my horse somewhere in the neck, caused him to make a violent spring sideways," recounted Lt. Henry Merritt of the 5th New York Cavalry. "I was aware of someone dropping beside me and attracted by a movement from the ground, demanded who it was. Major Cooke replied that his horse had been shot. Neither of us knew, at the moment, of the death of Dahlgren, though he was not four feet from us when he fell."[1] Ulric's prisoner, Capt. William F. Dement, went down under the weight of his dead horse. Dement pulled himself free and made for the safety of the woods.[2] The Confederates immediately captured many of the disoriented Federals, and the rest surrendered the next morning. Instead of reducing the number of prisoners being held at Belle Isle and Libby Prison, Dahlgren's command instead swelled the ranks of those already overcrowded facilities.[3]

Ully's body lay face down in the roadside ditch, resting against a fence, with a bullet hole in the temple, probably the killing shot.[4] Thirteen-year-old William Littlepage from nearby Stevensville came down to the site of the ambush to search for souvenirs.[5] Groping along in the dark, he stumbled upon Dahlgren's body. The boy noticed a handsome gold watch on the body, so he decided to search the dead Yankee's pockets. He found a cigar case, a notebook, and some folded papers, all of which he put in his pocket. With his newfound treasure safely stashed, Littlepage went to find his schoolmaster, Edward W. Halbach.

"Mr. Halbach, will you have a segar?" asked Littlepage.

"No," replied the teacher, "but where did you get segars these hard times?"

The boy replied that he had found them in the pocket of a dead Yankee, and that he also took a memorandum book and some papers.

"Well," said Halbach, "William, you must give me the papers, and you may keep the segar-case." The boy then remarked that the dead Yankee also had a wooden leg. This prompted a Confederate lieutenant who had been one of Dahlgren's prisoners for most of the march, and who had escaped in the thick darkness, to ask Littlepage how he knew that the dead man had a wooden leg.

"I know he has," replied Littlepage, "because I caught hold of it, and tried to pull it off."

"There!" responded the lieutenant, "you have killed Col. Dahlgren, who was in command of the enemy. His men were devoted to him, and I would advise you all to take care of yourselves now, for if the Yankees catch you with anything belonging to him, they will certainly hang us all to the nearest tree."[6]

Interested in his student's find, Halbach scanned the papers found by young William, and discovered that they spelled out a plan for Dahlgren's column to dash into Richmond, burn the city, free the prisoners of war, capture Jefferson Davis and his cabinet, assassinate them, and then free the local slaves so that they could wreak havoc on their former masters. Appalled, Halbach shared the contents with several friends, who told him to turn them over to nearby Confederate troops. Halbach refused at first, thinking that simply mailing them to Richmond would suffice. However, Halbach's friends prevailed upon him to surrender the papers to Lieutenant Pollard because they would reach Richmond much more quickly through his efforts than through a semi-weekly mail. Convinced, Halbach sought out Lieutenant Pollard and showed him the documents.

Pollard, astonished by what he read, took them to his commanding officer, Col. Richard L. T. Beale. Pollard turned over the documents, Dahlgren's notebook, and his wooden leg to the colonel. Beale read the documents and then instructed Pollard to take them to Maj. Gen. Wade Hampton, or if Hampton could not be located, to Maj. Gen. Fitzhugh Lee.[7] Pollard delivered them to Fitz Lee, who immediately took them to Richmond and delivered them personally to Jefferson Davis.[8] "Admitted to his private office, I found no one but Mr. [Judah P.] Benjamin [the Confederate Secretary of State], with him. The papers were handed him, and he read them aloud in our presence, making no comment save a laughing remark, when he came to the sentence, 'Jeff. Davis and Cabinet must be killed on the spot,'" recalled Fitz Lee. "That means you, Mr. Benjamin." Lee then took them to the office of Gen. Samuel Cooper, the adjutant general of the Confederate army, and he never saw them again.[9] Cooper eventually released the contents of the documents to the Richmond newspapers, which reproduced them verbatim. Before long, a great hue and cry went up. "Richmond had been trembling in horror and dread for many days," recalled one civilian, "and so the news of Dahlgren's capture and death was indeed good news."[10]

In the meantime, outraged local citizens desecrated Ulric's body. They cut off his finger to steal a ring that had belonged to his deceased sister. They stripped his body naked but for his stockings. They then left the body lying in a field, placing the corpse so that hogs could not get to it. They gave his crutches to a local member of the home guard who was wounded in the leg.

The Confederates marched their prisoners past the body. "I passed within ten feet of him," recalled one of the raiders. "He was stripped of every thread of clothing, his false leg taken off, and a finger cut off to get his ring. He had three balls through him, and was almost covered with mud—this was about eight o'clock in the morning."[11] Later that day, the local citizens buried Dahlgren in a crude and hastily dug muddy grave at the intersection where he fell. There was no fanfare, and no ceremony. A couple of locals were about to disinter the body to give it a decent burial when a squad of soldiers showed up with orders from Jefferson Davis to bring the body to Richmond.[12] They took the body to Walkerton.

At Walkerton, they loaded the corps on a train that carried it to Richmond, where it was dressed in a clean, coarse cotton shirt, dark blue pants, and wrapped in a heavy U. S. Army blanket. They then placed Dahlgren's remains in a plain white coffin with a flat top that had his name stenciled on top. The final humiliation occurred at the York River train depot on March 7. They removed the top of the coffin and placed the mutilated body of Ulric Dahlgren on display for most of the day.[13] The body was then removed from the depot and buried in an unmarked grave in a Richmond cemetery late at night to protect the remains from further depredations. The grave was leveled down so that no one could tell where it was.[14] Only two men—one a freed black man—knew the location of the burial, and they were sworn to secrecy. "Where that spot is no one but those concerned in its burial know or care to tell," crowed a Richmond newspaper. "Friends and relatives at the North need inquire no further; this is all they will know—he is buried a burial that befitted the mission upon which he came."[15]

Jefferson Davis later downplayed the disposition of Dahlgren's remains. "Many sensational stories, having not even a basis of truth, were put in circulation to exhibit the Confederate authorities as having acted with unwarranted malignity toward the deceased Colonel Dahlgren," he wrote. "The fact was, his body was sent to Richmond and decently interred in the Oakwood Cemetery, where other Federal soldiers were buried."[16] Davis wrote these words in 1881, and they may reflect an attempt to rewrite history. At the time, the desecration and then display of Dahlgren's body was the subject of a media frenzy.

The first hint that anyone in Washington had of the failure of the expedition came on the evening of March 3. That night, Maj. Gen. Benjamin F. Butler, who maintained his headquarters at Fortress Monroe, informed Stanton that Kilpatrick had safely made it to Fort Magruder, near Yorktown, but that Dahlgren and Major Cooke were missing and presumed to be prisoners. This unhappy news caused a great deal of concern for Stanton as a result of the close relationships between the Dahlgrens and the White House.[17] The next day, Butler sent a force of 2,000 infantry and 1,000 cavalry, and a battery of artillery under Wistar's command to meet and assist Kilpatrick.

The Richmond newspapers then published the contents of the documents verbatim. As they are reproduced in their entirety in the appendix to this book, they will not be repeated here. All of them were written in Ulric's hand on official Third Cavalry Division stationery. Among the instructions Dahlgren wrote to his men were to release prisoners on Belle Isle, and then the Federal horse soldiers were to "destroy and burn the hateful city." Most chilling of all was the following instruction: "Do not allow the Rebel leader Davis and his traitorous crew to escape."[18]

A second document, written on the same stationery, was titled "special orders," in which Dahlgren ordered the destruction of Richmond. "The bridges will be burned and the city destroyed," he wrote. "The men must keep together and well in hand, and once in the city it must be destroyed and Jeff. Davis and Cabinet killed." In addition to decapitating the Confederate government, Dahlgren also ordered that "horses and cattle which we do not need immediately must be shot rather than left . . . Men will stop at Bellona Arsenal and totally destroy it, and everything else but hospitals . . . Everything on the canal and elsewhere of service to the Rebels must be destroyed." He also prepared an itinerary for the raid on a third sheet of the official stationery.[19]

Finally, Dahlgren's pocket notebook was filled with notes and comments. It indicated that once captured, Davis and his cabinet "must be killed on the spot." It also included an earlier draft of the speech to the soldiers that included the lines, "You must encourage the prisoners to destroy the city; make one vast flame of it."[20]

When these documents were made public, a huge controversy erupted that continues to rage to this day. "Henceforth the name of Dahlgren is linked with eternal infamy," declared the *Richmond Whig* in response, "and in the years to come defenseless women and children will peruse, with a sense of shrinking horror, the story of Richmond's rescue from the midnight sack and ravage led by Dahlgren."[21] On March 5, 1864, the *Richmond Inquirer* ran the following editorial:

> Soldiers, read these papers and weigh well their purpose and design. Will not these documents take off the rosewater sentimental mode of making . . . .campaigns? Should our army again go into the enemy's country,

will not these papers relieve them from the restraints of a chivalry that would be proper with a civilized enemy, but which only brings upon them the contempt of our savage foe? Decidedly, we think that these Dahlgren papers will destroy, during the rest of the war, all rosewater chivalry, and that Confederate armies will make war afar and upon the rules selected by the enemy.[22]

Other papers ran similarly inflammatory editorials. The editor of the *Richmond Whig* asked:

Are these men warriors? Are they soldiers, taken in the performance of duties recognized as legitimate by the loosest construction in the code of civilized warfare? Or are they assassins, barbarians, thugs who have forfeited (and expect to lose) their lives? Are they not barbarians redolent with more hellish purposes than were the Goth, the Hun, or the Saracen?[23]

After describing the content of the papers, the editor of the *Richmond Daily Dispatch* wrote:

And thus concluded the grand plot which was to have achieved results which Dahlgren assured his men would "write their names on the hearts of their countrymen in letters that can never be erased." Their failure deprives them of any such inscription on the pages of history which will hand them down to the execration of mankind through all future ages . . . Let us redouble our energies and our vigilance to guard against the schemes and plots of a foe who has proved himself to be the most unscrupulous as he is the most brutal and fiendlike that ever made war on a people.[24]

The Richmond newspapers excoriated him as Ulric the Hun. Some of the editorials even called for the immediate execution of Dahlgren's men as punishment for their participation in such a nefarious scheme.[25] His wooden leg was displayed in the front window of a Richmond shop, held out as a trophy.

In fact, Jefferson Davis and his cabined discussed that very subject. Secretary of War Seddon was the most vocal supporter of the execution of the prisoners, and so was Davis' military advisor, Gen. Braxton Bragg. However, Davis did not agree. He wanted Robert E. Lee's opinion, and permitted Lee to decide the question.

On March 5, Seddon wrote:

> I inclose to you herewith a slip from one of the morning papers containing
> an account of the disposal of a portion of the enemy's force which recently
> attacked this city, and a copy of the papers found on the body of Colonel
> Dahlgren, who was killed. The diabolical character of those papers and of
> the enterprise they indicate seems to require at our hands something more
> than a mere informal publication in our newspapers. My own inclinations
> are toward the execution of at least a portion of those captured at the time
> Colonel Dahlgren was killed, and a publication of these papers as its justi-
> fication. At any rate, a formal publication from the highest official position
> should issue, calling the attention of our people and that of the civilized
> world to the atrocious modes of warfare adopted by our enemies. General
> Bragg's views coincide with my own on this subject. The question of what is
> best to be done is a grave and important one, and I desire to have the benefit
> of your views and any suggestions you may make. It is not for the purpose
> of evading or sharing any responsibility which may attach to the action to be
> taken that I seek to know your views, but simply that in determining what
> is best to be done I may have the aid of your wisdom and experience, as well
> as your judgment of what would be the sentiment of the army on a course
> of severe but just retribution. You will, of course, appreciate to what conse-
> quences such a course may not rightfully, yet not unnaturally, considering the
> unscrupulousness and malignity of our foes, lead, and estimate such results
> in forming your judgment.[26]

Thus, Seddon left the momentous decision in the wise and careful hands of
Robert E. Lee. Lee's decision would have significant consequences for the rest
of the war, no matter which course he chose.

Fortunately, Lee selected the course of caution. The next day, he responded.

> I concur with you in thinking that a formal publication of these papers should
> be made under official authority, that our people and the world should know
> the character of the war our enemies wage against us, and the unchristian
> and atrocious acts they plot and perpetrate. But I cannot recommend the
> execution of the prisoners that have fallen into our hands. Assuming that the
> address and special orders of Colonel Dahlgren correctly state his design and
> intentions, they were not executed, and I believe, even in a legal point of view,
> acts in addition to intention are necessary to constitute crime. These papers

can only be considered as evidence of his intentions. It does not appear how far his men were cognizant of them, or that his course was sanctioned by his Government. It is only known that his plans were frustrated by a merciful Providence, his forces scattered, and he killed. I do not think it right, therefore, to visit upon the captives the guilt of his intentions. I do not pretend to speak the sentiments of the army, which you seem to desire. I presume that the blood boils with indignation in the veins of every officer and man as they read the account of the barbarous and inhuman plot, and under the impulse of the moment many would counsel extreme measures. But I do not think that reason and reflection would justify such a course. I think it better to do right, even if we suffer in so doing, than to incur the reproach of our consciences and posterity. Nor do I think that under present circumstances policy dictates the execution of these men. It would produce retaliation. How many and better men have we in the enemy's hands than they have in ours? But this consideration should have no weight provided the course was in itself right. Yet history records instances where such considerations have prevented the execution of marauders and devastators of provinces.[27]

That settled it. Lee's wise counsel immediately ended any further discussion of executing the prisoners. Lee understood the implications of this decision. His son, Brig. Gen. William H. F. "Rooney" Lee, was a prisoner of the Union from June 1863 to February 25, 1864, before he was exchanged for a Northern brigadier general, Neal Dow, who came very close to being a victim of a retaliatory hanging after the failed raid by Dahlgren and Kilpatrick.[28] However, General Lee's wise counsel certainly did not end the controversy.

On March 30, Gen. Samuel Cooper, the Confederate Adjutant General, conveyed an order from President Davis to Robert E. Lee. The Confederate President wanted Lee to make certain inquiries of Maj. Gen. George G. Meade, the commander of the Army of the Potomac, to determine if the plan set forth in the Dahlgren papers, had, in fact, been sanctioned by the Union high command.[29]

The next day, Lee complied, opening an extraordinary correspondence. Lee's letter read:

I am instructed to bring to your notice two papers found upon the body of Col. U. Dahlgren, who was killed while commanding a part of the Federal cavalry during the late expedition of General Kilpatrick. To enable you to understand the subject fully I have the honor to inclose photographic copies of the papers referred to, one of which is an address to his officers and men, bearing the official signature of Colonel Dahlgren, and the other, not signed, contains more detailed explanations of the purpose of the expedition and more specific instructions as to its execution. In the former this passage occurs:

We hope to release the prisoners from Belle Island first, and having seen them fairly started, we will cross the James River into Richmond, destroying the bridges after us and exhorting the prisoners to destroy and burn the hateful city; and do not allow the rebel leader Davis and his traitorous crew to escape. The prisoners must render great assistance, as you cannot leave your ranks too far or become too much scattered, or you will be lost.

Among the instructions contained in the second paper are the following:

The bridges once secured, and the prisoners loose and over the river, the bridges will be secured and the city destroyed. The men must keep together and well in hand, and once in the city it must be destroyed and Jeff. Davis and cabinet killed. Pioneers will go along with combustible material.

In obedience to my instructions I beg leave respectfully to inquire whether the designs and instructions of Colonel Dahlgren, as set forth in these papers, particularly those contained in the above extracts, were authorized by the United States Government or by his superior officers, and also whether they have the sanction and approval of those authorities.[30]

A staff officer carried the letter across Union lines under a flag of truce. It did not reach Meade until April 15.

Two days, April 17, later Meade responded:

I received on the 15th instant, per flag of truce, your communication of the 1st instant, transmitting photographic copies of two documents alleged to have been found upon the body of Col. U. Dahlgren, and inquiring "whether the designs and instructions contained in the above extracts, were authorized by the United States Government or by his superior officers, and also whether they have the sanction and approval of these authorities." In reply I have to state that neither the United States Government, myself, nor General Kilpatrick authorized, sanctioned, or approved the burning of the city of

Richmond and the killing of Mr. Davis and cabinet, nor any other act not required by military necessity and in accordance with the usages of war.[31]

As support for his position, Meade included a letter by Judson Kilpatrick.

In accordance with instructions from headquarters, Army of the Potomac, I have carefully examined officers and men who accompanied Colonel Dahlgren on his late expedition.

All testify that he published no address whatever to his command, nor did he give any instructions, much less of the character as set forth in the photographic copies of two papers alleged to have been found upon the person of Colonel Dahlgren and forwarded by General Robert E. Lee, commanding Army of Northern Virginia. Colonel Dahlgren, one hour before we separated at my headquarters, handed me an address that he intended to read to his command. That paper was indorsed in red ink, "Approved," over my official signature. The photographic papers referred to are true copies of the papers approved by me, save so far as they speak of "exhorting the prisoners to destroy and burn the hateful city and kill the traitor Davis and his cabinet," and in this, that they do not contain the indorsement referred to as having been placed by me on Colonel Dahlgren's papers. Colonel Dahlgren received no orders from me to pillage, burn, or kill, nor were any such instructions given me by my superiors.[32]

And with that, the United States Army disavowed Ulric Dahlgren.

The repudiation did not sit well with General Meade. The army commander later told one of his staff officers that he considered the weight of the evidence in favor of the authenticity of the documents and that he did not consider Kilpatrick to be a trustworthy person.[33] "This was a pretty ugly piece of business; for in denying having authorized or approved 'the burning of Richmond or killing Mr. Davis and Cabinet,' I necessarily threw odium on Dahlgren," Meade wrote to his wife in explaining his actions. "I, however, enclosed a letter from Kilpatrick, in which the authenticity of the papers was impugned; but I regret to say Kilpatrick's reputation, and collateral evidence in my possession, rather go against this theory. However, I was determined my skirts should be clear, so I promptly disavowed having ever authorized, sanctioned, or approved of any act not required by military necessity, and in accordance with the usages of war."[34] Meade undoubtedly understood the magnitude and implications of a failure to disavow Ulric's actions, and his determination to clear his skirts meant that the true answer has never come out.

Lee's adjutant, Col. Walter H. Taylor, was not impressed by the Federal response. "That rascal Kilpatrick in his letter says that the copies (photographic) of the address which we sent were verbatim copies of an address which Col Dahlgren had submitted to him & which he had approved <u>in red ink except</u> that they lacked this approval and had that about burning the city & killing the high officials, thereby intimating that we had forged these copies & interpolated the objectionable exhortations," his sniffed in a letter home. "The low wretch—he approved the whole thing I am confident <u>now.</u> Gl. Meade's disclaimer is much more decided and candid—that I had expected."[35] Kilpatrick's hollow disclaimers did little to settle the raging controversy.

Mary Chesnut, whose husband was a Confederate general, kept a diary filled with her many pithy observations of life and especially of politics in Richmond. "Now that Dahlgren has failed to carry out his orders, the Yankees disown them; they disavow it all," she wrote disdainfully. "He was not sent here to murder us all, hang the President, and burn the town. There is the notebook, however, at the Executive Office, with the orders to hang and burn."[36] The disavowal, although politically necessary and expedient, did not ring true to indignant Confederate citizens.

Varina Davis, wife of the Confederate president, knew Ully as a child, and she could not come to grips with the enormity of what those documents meant. She found the contents of the documents shocking and tried to reconcile them with the boy she knew. A visitor inquired, "Did you believe it?" She responded that there had been insufficient time to forge the documents, and that there was also an itinerary written in the same hand. When the visitor expressed disbelief, Mrs. Davis offered to send for the memorandum book. She said that the memorandum book had been photographed and sent to General Meade "with an inquiry as to whether such practices were authorized by his government; and also to say that if any question was raised as to the copies, the original paper would be submitted. The denial was accepted." The visitor laughed again and said, "Now, the fact is I do not want to believe it, and if you could convince me I would rather not look at it." Mrs. Davis noted, "I had felt much the same unwillingness, having been intimate with his parents. Once Commodore Dahlgren had brought the little fair-haired boy to show me how pretty he looked in his black velvet suit and Vandyke collar, and I could not reconcile the two Ulrics."[37]

Despite the official disavowal, Ully's death deeply grieved many throughout the North. "A more gallant and brave-hearted fellow was not to be found in the service," Secretary of the Navy Gideon Welles wrote in his diary. "His death will be a terrible blow to his father, who doted on him and not without reason."[38] General Meade wrote to his wife, "You have doubtless seen that Kilpatrick's raid was an utter failure. I did not expect much from it. Poor Dahlgren I am sorry for."[39] President Lincoln's personal secretary John Hay, who was one of Ully's favorite companions for a night out in Washington, was in Florida when he received the news. "I was much shocked at hearing today of Ulric Dahlgren's death," he wrote in his diary. "A great future cut off and a good fellow gone."[40]

Col. Charles Wainwright, an accomplished Union artillerist who kept a detailed and candid diary, commented on Ulric's death. He properly assessed the reasons why the raid failed, and why Ulric paid the ultimate price for the failure. "Poor Dahlgren is killed," he wrote. "He had let his men disperse into small bodies; nearly all of them got in safely, but he is said to have been betrayed by his negro guide, and murdered in cold blood. All who knew him regret his loss exceedingly."[41]

The *Philadelphia Inquirer*, Ulric's hometown newspaper, which called him a "hero," also described him as "one of the bravest sons of America, and his death will be regretted by all who knew him." The *Inquirer's* coverage concluded, "It is hoped that the means taken will secure the body of the gallant Colonel, who knew no such words as fear or fail."[42] Word of Ully's death did not reach the West Coast for more than a month. "Young Dahlgren leaves a spotless name and a gallant record to his country and his wife, sisters and family," declared the *Sacramento Daily Union* on April 9.[43]

E. A. Paul, a correspondent of the *New York Times*, and Dahlgren were old friends. In fact, Ulric was riding alongside Paul when he received his wound at Hagerstown. Of his friend, Paul wrote, "He has fallen, and the grave has closed over one of the most manly forms that has succumbed during the present war. He died just where he would have wished most to die—fighting the enemies of the Union." The correspondent composed a lengthy biographical sketch of Ulric and concluded his essay with a flourish. "Col. Dahlgren was only about 22 years old, tall in stature and sparely built; a warm friend, but resolute and quick to resent a real insult. Admired by all for his manly traits, he was loved by all for his genial, social qualities. His name will ever be fresh in the memory of all who knew him, and his untimely end will nerve the arms of his old associates to strike harder blows than ever for the cause of the Union."[44]

"A grateful people will shrine his memory in their hearts, and keep green forever the brave boy's name!" proclaimed *Harper's Weekly.* "His sublime daring on every field to which he was called after that time justified fully the sanction which the Government gave him in its first appointment to an honorable position. His temper and character as a soldier remarkably resembled that of the lamented WINTHROP, and his career affords another illustration, beautiful and significant, of that sturdy and courageous manhood which these troublous latter days are maturing as the future hope of the Republic."[45]

A man named S. C. Roonce, of Clarksville, Pennsylvania, wrote to the editor of the *Saturday Evening Post* "relative to some plan by which the young men of this state could raise money to erect a monument to the memory of this noble and chivalric young officer, who has been so vilely slandered by the rebel press." The men of Dahlgren's Howitzer Battery passed a resolution proposing the erection of a monument to his memory in his home town of Philadelphia, but it never happened. Instead, the local Grand Army of the Republic chapter for downtown Philadelphia was named in his honor in the years after the war.[46]

Admiral Dahlgren learned of the expedition on the day Ully died. He went home to Washington for a few days and was surprised to find his son gone on a mission. "Ully is away with General Kilpatrick, which I regret, for his crippled leg is not well," he noted in his diary that night.[47] On March 4, President Lincoln sent the Admiral a note informing him that his son was missing in action. Dahlgren went to the White House to see what more information might be available. At the Admiral's behest, President Lincoln telegraphed for further news.[48] He could get none, leaving the sailor fretting. Later that evening, Butler telegraphed the White House that a one-legged colonel had been captured, which renewed the Admiral's flagging hopes.[49] On March 6, Butler reported that Ully was not a prisoner, but rather at King and Queen Court House, and that he would send out an expedition to recover him.[50]

By March 7, the Admiral was nearly frantic with worry. "No tidings today of Ully," he wrote in his diary. "Nothing from the President, who would, of course, send me word. Oh, how I wish this painful anxiety were at an end?" The next day, the worst news arrived. Lincoln sent for him to tell him that his beloved son was dead. The waiting made the Admiral even more frantic. "Merciful Father! Am I to lose my brave son? Not yet, not yet, I pray," he while he waited for his appointment with the President. "Le me see him once more." When his steamer was finally ready, it carried him to Fortress Monroe. "How precious now are the two months he spent with me, and how I missed him when he went! My son, my son!" wrote the anguished father. He arrived at Fortress Monroe that night and went ashore immediately to meet with General Butler. Butler handed him a package of Richmond papers, proving the horrible rumors true. "The exact facts are not known, only that he separated from the main body, was overtaken, and a conflict ensued. So ends a career too brilliant to last long," he wrote. "And yet the scoundrels had no regard for the body of one so young and so brave. It was stripped, the finger cut off to get the ring, and every vile epithet bestowed by the Richmond press.—May an avenging God pursue them! And yet how glorious, though he lost a leg at Gettysburg, and was not well enough to be on his horse!"[51]

"The young hero has fought his last battle for his country," Admiral Dahlgren wrote this sister Patty on March 10. "He fell at the head of his men. It is incredible that such savage perversity should have been allowed to his remains, and yet it has the deliberate approval of the Richmond press—a mutilated corpse exposed to the gaze of the whole city, without one word for his youth or his gallantry." He continued, "My son fell like a true man in the lead of his men,—no one in advance of him, having risked all in an attempt to rescue his fellow soldiers from a horrible captivity." He concluded, "He has given limb and now life for his country."[52]

Admiral Dahlgren now turned to the task of obtaining his son's body to bring it home for burial in Philadelphia. "So terrified was Richmond that I have little hope, especially as the Richmond press affirm that nothing shall be known, even where his grave is, and they approve of the brutality offered to the inanimate body."[53] Butler penned the Admiral a sympathetic letter. "I will have sad pleasure in doing everything I can to enable you to recover his remains," wrote the Massachusetts politician. "I would send a special flag of truce for this if I though that mode the most effectual, which I do not in the present state of exasperation of the rebels at Richmond. My regular flag of truce will go up tomorrow morning with prisoners, and I will then make such an appeal to the Commissioner Judge as I can, to have your request complied with."[54] The next day, Butler made good on his promise.

Butler addressed his letter to Robert Ould, the Confederate commissioner for exchange.[55] Butler composed a subtle and diplomatic plea on Admiral Dahlgren's behalf on March 11. "I have the honor to request that the body of Col. Ulric Dahlgren, late of the U. S. Army, which we learn is buried in Richmond, be permitted to be forwarded by flag-of-truce boat, to be delivered to his afflicted father, who is waiting here to receive it," he penned. "As remains of officers have been forwarded to their friends in this manner I trust this request may be granted; specially so, because I see by the Richmond papers that some circumstances of indignity and outrage accompanied the death. You do not war upon the dead as these papers would imply, and would it not be desirable to prevent all supposition that your authorities countenance such acts by delivering the remains to the bereaved family?" Butler informed Ould that funds to reimburse any expenses incurred had been authorized.[56] The waiting continued, tormenting Admiral Dahlgren.

The next day, March 12, Judson Kilpatrick came to see the grieving father. Kilpatrick spoke in "unbounded terms of my dear son, who seemed, as usual, to have been the very soul of the operation." The cavalryman addressed that aspect of Ully's death that bothered him most: the reports of the contents of the Dahlgren Papers. "The General said it was basely false that his orders contained anything of killing Davis or burning the city. The General had read it over with Ully more than once."[57]

That same day, General Butler ordered an expedition by a portion of Kilpatrick's cavalry as well as the small mounted command and some of the black infantrymen assigned to his department to march to King and Queen County and punish the citizens who participated in the death of Ulric Dahlgren. He called them "those citizens who, claiming to be non-combatants when any force of ours is there, yet turned out and ambushed Dahlgren."[58] Brig. Gen. Isaac J. Wistar commanded the expedition, along with Kilpatrick, who commanded the mounted troops. They destroyed the public buildings in the town of King and Queen Court House, and then discovered an enemy force consisting of the 9th Virginia Cavalry, the 42nd Battalion of Virginia Cavalry, a portion of the 5th Virginia Cavalry, as well as some armed civilians, nearly 1,200 men in all, awaiting them. The Federal cavalry charged and scattered the gray-clad horsemen, pursuing them until Kilpatrick finally ordered them to break off the pursuit. With the Mattapony rising quickly and already unfordable due to heavy rains, Wistar called off the expedition and ordered Kilpatrick and his troopers to return to Yorktown.[59] With his typical bluster, Kilpatrick declared, "The people about King and Queen Court-House have been well punished for the murder of Colonel Dahlgren."[60] Kilpatrick undoubtedly overstated the case (as he often did), but his words gave Ulric's tormented father little solace. He continued to wait for the return of his beloved son's body.

No news came, increasing the grieving father's torment. "The bright, beautiful Sabbath. Another day of solemn suspense," he wrote in his diary on March 13. "When I left Washington it seemed as if dear Ully's death was the greatest possible affliction. Now, I hardly know if I can recover his body. How thought of him flit by me. The last evening he was with me I have him my last memorandum in case I fell. Dear boy, he goes before me! Here, too, I have a whole life to contemplate, from the baby in the cradle to the distinguished Colonel falling in battle; and yet I am in the vigor of life. My son!"[61] On March 16, unable to bear the inactivity and the waiting for something that might never come, Admiral Dahlgren boarded his steamer and returned to Washington on March 16. He poured out his grief in his diary, tormented by his inability to provide his son with a decent burial.[62]

The next day, President Lincoln sent explicit orders to Butler. "If you obtain the remains of Col. Dahlgren, please notify me instantly so that I can let his afflicted know." Butler issued the necessary instructions, and then the waiting game began anew. The Admiral's torment continued unmitigated.[63]

A few weeks later, still unable to release his grief, he wrote in his diary, "Occupied in collecting every item about dear Ully—old letters &c. every day some extracts sent me showing how deeply the grave fellow had taken hold of the feelings everywhere." That same day, April 5, Admiral Dahlgren received a letter from Captain Mitchell, who wrote to share his views of Ully's fate and the outcome of the failed raid. "Took his meals with him and assisted him off & on his horse—writes in glowing terms of the noble boy so brave under fire,— so enduring of hardship—and his presence so influent with the men—Dear Ully you have fought your last battle—Rest my son in peace."[64]

He also spilled out his grief in a letter to his sister Patty. "My son fell like a true man in the lead of his men,—no one in advance of him,—having risked all in an attempt to rescue his fellow soldiers from a horrible captivity—But neither this, nor the evidence of having been maimed in previous battle, nor his humanity at Fredericksburg could create a kind or generous sentiment in the hearts of those terrified cowards who had been too much exasperated by their fears to forgive," he declared. "The bravest might be proud of young, brief, blazing career—And so am I—Would that I had a dozen such to stand up before the world and do battle for a good cause, as he has done—He has given limb and now life for country."[65] He was so deeply mired in his grief that others began worrying about the Admiral's sanity. Secretary Welles called on the Admiral on April 8 and advised him "to get abroad and mingle in the world, and not yield to a blow that was irremediable."[66] Secretary Stanton encountered Dahlgren on the street on April 18. That Dahlgren only spoke about the loss of his son greatly disturbed the Secretary of War.[67]

Even Ulric's Uncle Charles, by now a Confederate general without a command, attempted to help retrieve the body. He implored the government to relent, locate his nephew's body, and forward it through the lines for a proper burial. "I am glad you are going to try and I hope will succeed in recovering the body of Ully," Charles Dahlgren's son Bernard wrote to his father. Sadly, Charles, who lost his command due to incompetence, had no better luck than Butler. Only two men knew where the body was buried, and they were sworn to secrecy. The storm of controversy still raged, and disinterring the body for return to Union authorities risked further desecration. Thus, Charles Dahlgren's efforts to help also came to naught.[68]

A week later, there was still no word. "We have not received Colonel Dahlgren's body, for reasons which I believe are not within the control of the Confederate officers," reported Butler to Stanton on March 23.[69] He was right. On March 23, the Confederate authorities decided to return Ully's body to his father in a show of compassion. However, when they went to disinter the body, a great shock awaited them. The unmarked grave in the Richmond cemetery was empty.

Elizabeth Van Lew, a forty-six-year-old Richmond spinster, was a devoted Unionist. With the coming of the Civil War, Miss Van Lew decided that she could provide a great service to the Union cause by forming a spy network that passed along critical information. She shuffled along the streets, mumbling to herself, successfully convincing the citizenry of Richmond that she was insane. They named her "Crazy Bet," and largely ignored her. Consequently, she passed among the people of the city gathering intelligence that she forwarded to the Union authorities. She became an effective and reliable source of extremely useful information.[70]

Her network of spies had not only located the unmarked burial site, they had disinterred the body and removed it to a nearby farm owned by William S. Rowley, described by Van Lew as "the bravest of the brave and truest of the true."[71] They hid the body there until it could be moved to a safer place to await its eventual return to Admiral Dahlgren for a proper burial in the North. "The heart of every loyal person was stirred to its depths by the outrages committed upon his inanimate body," she wrote, "and to discover the hidden grave and remove his honored dust to friendly care was decided upon." She chose F. W. E. Lohmann, one of her most dependable men, for the task, and, after talking with the black gravedigger who had buried the body, Lohmann disinterred the body from its unmarked grave in Richmond's Oakwood Cemetery.[72]

On April 5, Martin M. Lipscomb, another member of Van Lew's network, accompanied the body on a cold, dark, and rainy night. Along with an African-American helper, Lipscomb opened the coffin and identified the body by the missing leg. He loaded the coffin into a wagon and drove it to Rowley's farm, where they carried it into a workshop. Rowley sat with it all night, and then loaded the body into a new metallic coffin the next morning. A few saw the body. "Sad and sorrowful were their hearts and tender wailing fell from their lips," wrote Van Lew in a post-war account. "Col. Dahlgren's hair was very short, but all that could be spared was cut off and sent to his father before Richmond fell. Gentle hands and tearful eyes examined his breast to see if there was any wound there, but nothing of the kind could be perceived. The body, except the head, was in a perfect state of preservation, fair, fine and firm the flesh . . . here and there a purple spot as if mildew." Given the fact that he had been buried in damp ground with little care, the good state of the body surprised everyone who saw it.[73]

They sealed the new coffin, placed it in Rowley's wagon, and then covered the coffin with young peach trees to conceal its presence. F. W. E. Lohmann and his brother John accompanied Rowley until he reached the defenses of the Confederate capital. Rowley boldly drove the wagon through the Confederate picket lines, including those in the area where Dahlgren's command had fought the home guard the day before his untimely death. When he approached this picket post, Rowley finally recognized the peril he faced. He drove up to the tent and stopped, casually dropping the reins. The lieutenant of the guard told one of his men to inspect the wagon and then went back into his tent. Fortunately, another wagon going the opposite direction pulled up at that moment, distracting all. However, the guard recognized Rowley, and said, "Whose peach trees are those? I think I have seen your face before."

"Yes," replied Rowley, "and I have yours."

"Where?" asked the guard.

"At your own house," replied Rowley. That jogged the man's memory, and he acknowledged their meeting in that fashion. "But whose peach trees are those?" he asked again, more insistent this time.

"They belong to a German in the country to whom I am carrying them," said Rowley. With that, the conversation turned to the difficulties involved with raising peach trees. The discussion dragged on until the lieutenant finally emerged from his tent and told the guard to "get through searching that wagon and let the man go on. Not to keep him there until night."

Responding, the guard said that it would "be a pity to tear those trees all up, when you have them packed in there so nicely."

"When I packed them," retorted Rowley, "I did not expect them to be disturbed, but as it is . . . ." With that, another cart pulled up that also required inspection, and the lieutenant again called for the guard to pass Rowley on. "I don't want to hinder you any longer," the guard finally said. "I think it all right, at any rate your honest face is guarantee enough for me—go on." Rowley quietly heaved a sigh of relief and continued on his way.[74] The Lohmanns, who jumped off the wagon and sneaked around the picket post, rejoined Rowley. They passed Yellow Tavern, where Jeb Stuart fell a few weeks later, and then drove ten miles further west into the country to the farm of a German named Robert Orrick, who lived near Hungary Station. They quickly dug a fresh grave and buried the body there under a freshly planted peach tree to mark the grave. "The two Lohmanns then returned home in the wagon, and every true Union heart, who knew of this day's work, felt happier for having charge of this precious dust," concluded Miss Van Lew.[75]

Their mission of mercy completed, Miss Van Lew sent a coded message to Butler informing him that the body had been recovered. Word soon filtered back to Admiral Dahlgren. On March 29, he wrote in his diary that an inferior officer had paid him a call, carrying a mysterious message. The officer told Admiral Dahlgren "some Union men had secretly disinterred my son, and transferred the remains to a metallic coffin, and intended to remove them from Richmond. I replied as before to similar hints, that I looked to the Rebel authorities for my son, and would not at this time admit to any other course." He expressed skepticism, but similar rumors continued filtering in.[76]

On April 14, the *Richmond Examiner* reported that the Confederates, in compliance with Butler's request, had opened Ully's grave "under the direction of the officials who interred the remains, but the grave was empty—Dahlgren had risen, or been resurrected, and the corpse was not found." The disappearance of the body sent chills through Richmond's citizens, who remained in an uproar over the alleged plot spelled out in the papers found on Dahlgren's body.[77]

His hopes buoyed by these rumors, Admiral Dahlgren again traveled to Fortress Monroe to receive his son's remains for burial. Again, he left empty-handed. However, this time, he left with good news. On April 17, Butler sent the Admiral a telegram after the truce boat departed. "Mr. Ould assured Major [John] Mulford [the Union commissioner] that upon going to the grave of Colonel Dahlgren it was found empty, and that the most vigorous and persistent search fails to find it. That the authorities are making every exertion to find the body, which shall be restored if found."[78]

Three days later, Butler informed Admiral Dahlgren, "I have reliable information from Richmond that Colonel Dahlgren's body has been taken possession of by his Union friends, and has been put beyond the reach of the rebel authorities."[79] The next day, Butler forwarded additional information:

The remains are not so far within my control as to be able to remove them from Richmond, where every effort is being made by the detectives to find them; but they are, I am informed and believe, in the hands of devoted friends of the Union, who have taken possession of them in order that proper respect may be shown to them at a time which I trust is not far distant.

I hardly dare to suggest to Ould, when he reports to me, as he will, that he cannot find them, that I can put them into his possession, because that will show a correspondence with Richmond as will alarm them, and will redouble their vigilance to detect my sources of information. I am, however, under the direction of the president.[80]

This was very good news, but on April 26, Robert Orrick called upon Admiral Dahlgren bringing even better news. Orrick "said that my Ully's remains were on his farm. They had been removed privately by one or two persons. He says the body cannot be removed until our troops get that far."[81] Finally satisfied that his son's remains were safe, Admiral Dahlgren prepared to return to duty at Charleston. The formal burial would have to wait. One important task remained undone.

Before leaving for Charleston, the Admiral arranged for a memorial service for his son, which was held on April 24, 1864. Dignitaries including Secretary Stanton and President Lincoln gathered at Washington's First Presbyterian Church to honor the fallen hero. Rev. Byron Sunderland, the rector of the church, presided. Sunderland had known Ully Dahlgren since boyhood, and watched him grow up. He ministered to the desperately wounded young man during the summer of 1863, and knew well Ulric's frail condition. He selected II Samuel, 3:34 as a fitting reading: "Thy hands were not bound, nor Thy feet put into fetters: as a man falleth before wicked men, so fallest thou. And all the people wept again over him!" Reverend Sunderland began his stirring eulogy by declaring, "A brave man had fallen by assassination. He had not died as a felon or a coward. No earthly power could bind his hands or put his feet in fetters. None had ever been able to take him captive, or confine him in chains and prisons." He went on for nearly two hours, summarizing Ulric's life and accomplishments. He closed by asking that those present share with him "a pious and reverential awe" at just how much the young man had accomplished in his short but very full life.[82]

Years later, Reverend Sunderland gave an interview to a reporter of the *Washington Post*. "I preached a requiem sermon when Col. Ulric Dahlgren was killed while making a raid in Virginia. On this occasion, it was in 1864,

I defended and vindicated the character of the dead soldier, against whom false and cruel charges had been made," he said. "His body had not then been found."[83] He did an excellent job of it.

Knowing that his son's body was safe, Admiral Dahlgren had one final battle to fight. He was determined to restore Ully's good name and reputation, and he launched a vigorous campaign to dispute the validity of the papers found on his son's body. He spent the rest of his life decrying the documents as forgeries. His campaign to rehabilitate his son's reputation began the day after the memorial service.[84]

The next day, April 25, Admiral Dahlgren penned a letter his friend, Charles C. Fulton, the editor of the *Baltimore American* newspaper, defending himself against criticisms of his command at Charleston. He also addressed Ulric's death. "I had some hopes of seeing you—but you know how heavy an affliction has fallen on me," he wrote. "A more brave & gentle spirit never gave limb & life to the cause than my son. They take care at Richmond to ignore entirely the real purpose of the expedition, which was to release from their vile dungeons the Union soldiers who are there dying the most horrible death. But [they] lie and desecrate the remains of the mere youth, whom in life they never faced with impunity." Dahlgren concluded with a flourish, albeit an inaccurate one. "The 9th Vir. that murdered him in midnight ambush is the same brave chivalry that he scattered like chaff in [Fredericksburg] and drove out thought twice his number."[85]

When Admiral Dahlgren examined the photographic reproductions of them, he noticed that the signature apparently read "U. Dalhgren." The name was apparently misspelled, and the first name was not spelled out, using an initial instead. "I always told him," Admiral Dahlgren wrote to his sister Patty in 1867," that I gave him no middle name in order that he should write his name in full."[86] He later spelled out his argument in defense of Ulric's reputation:

> The document alleged to have been found upon the person of Colonel Dahlgren is utterly discredited by the fact that the signature attached to it cannot possibly be his own, because it is not his name,—a letter is misplaced, and the real name *Dahlgren* is misspelled *Dalhgren*; hence it is undeniable that the paper is not only spurious, but is a forgery. Evidence, almost as positive, is to be found in the writing of the Christian prefix of the signature. The document is signed "U. Dalhgren," whereas Colonel Dahlgren invariably signed himself "*Ulric* Dahlgren," *never with the bare initial of the first name.* Among all the letters of his writing which can be collected, not an instance

to the contrary occurs, down to the last that he ever wrote, just before starting for Richmond.[87]

On July 24, 1864, the *New York Times* published a lengthy letter penned by
Admiral Dahlgren. "I have patiently and sorrowfully awaited the hour when
I should be able to vindicate fully the memory of my gallant son, Col. Ulric
Dahlgren," he declared, "and lay bare to the world the atrocious imposture of
those who, not content with abusing and defacing the remains of the noble
boy, have knowingly and persistently endeavored to blemish his spotless name
by a forged lie." The letter spelled out the Admiral's arguments as to why the
Dahlgren Papers were forgeries and could not be authentic documents.[88]

Lt. Reuben Bartley, the signal officer who accompanied Dahlgren's command,
also defended the dead hero. In a letter that was published in a newspaper on
December 29, 1864, Bartley declared:

> I pronounce those papers a *base forgery* and will give some of my reasons for
> doing so. I was with the expedition in the capacity of signal-officer, and was
> the only staff-officer with him. I had charge of all the material for destroy-
> ing bridges, blowing up locks, aqueducts, etc. I knew all his plans, what he
> intended to do and how he intended doing it, and I know that I never received
> any such instructions in those papers are said to contain. I also heard all the
> orders and instructions given to the balance of the officers of the command.
> Men cannot carry out orders they know nothing of. The colonel's instruc-
> tions were, that if we were successful in entering the city, to *take no life except
> in combat*; to keep all prisoners safely guarded, but to *treat them with respect*;
> liberate all the Union prisoners, destroy the public buildings and govern-
> ment stores, and leave the city by way of the Peninsula.[89]

The issue of the authenticity of the Dahlgren Papers will be addressed in
the appendix to this book, and will not be explored in depth here. Admiral
Dahlgren went to his grave adamantly defending his lamented son's reputation.
The controversy over the authenticity of the Dahlgren papers still continues
today.

Richmond finally fell on April 2, 1865, when the Confederate government
abandoned it after the crushing defeat of Lee's army at the Battle of Five Forks
on April 1. The evacuation of the city meant that Ulric Dahlgren's body could
finally be recovered and returned to his father for a proper burial in the family
plot in Philadelphia. "The abandonment of Richmond by the Rebels will at

least enable me to discharge my last duties to the remains of dear Ully," Admiral Dahlgren declared to his sister Patty. "It would be a satisfaction to me that the high place of these miserable wretches should witness the honors that will be so fittingly paid to the young martyr."[90]

Maj. Gen. William T. Sherman wrote to Dahlgren on April 5. "I hear you are relieved at your own request and gone home," he wrote. "I trust your health is better, and that you soon may realize another hope which I Know you Cherish, to go to that other proud but doomed city [Richmond], and remove thence all that is left to earth of your soon Ulric. May we meet soon in Peace." Sherman's warm letter demonstrates the depth of empathy for the Admiral's plight and the esteem in which he was held among the highest levels of the Union military.[91]

On April 9, efforts to recover Ully's body began in earnest. "Yesterday a train went out on this road as far as Hungary station," reported a correspondent of one of the New York newspapers the next day. "On it went a surgeon who had come from Washington to secure the body of Colonel Ulric Dahlgren, who was killed during the famous Kilpatrick raid against Richmond. Colonel Dahlgren's body was found buried near Hungary station."[92]

Two days later, Secretary Stanton ordered Maj. Gen. Godfrey Weitzel, who was in command of the city, to "take immediate measures to . . . secure the remains and send them with a guard of honor to Washington. Care should be taken to identify them with certainty. If not there spare no effort to find them and report speedily."[93] The remains were recovered quickly and were then taken to Washington by boat on April 11. A new metallic coffin held the body, which was accompanied by a military escort consisting of one sergeant and six privates of the 11th Connecticut Volunteer Infantry, under command of Lt. U. Walker.[94]

Although Ully's mortal remains were finally safe, a proper burial had to wait for nearly six more months. When his duties permitted him to leave Charleston for a few days, Admiral Dahlgren came to Washington to identify his son's remains. After a careful inspection, he was persuaded that his son's body lay in front of him. "The intense heat of the weather rendered it inadvisable to attempt their transference to the burial lot of the family, near Philadelphia," observed Admiral Dahlgren. "The obsequies were necessarily postponed until cold weather."[95]

While the Admiral waited for the heat to break, a concerted effort to recover Ulric's personal effects began. F. W. E. Lohmann, who played such an important role in the rescue of Dahlgren's body, also helped to track down his personal property. Lohmann traced Ulric's ring to one Cornelius Martin, formerly of Company H, 9th Virginia Cavalry. When confronted by Lohmann, Martin finally admitted that he took the ring after stoutly denying it at first. Martin then told Lohmann that he gave the ring to a Dr. Saunders, and Lohmann tracked Saunders down, too. The authorities paid Saunders a visit, and "after some difficulty caused him to produce the ring which Martin vouched was the one he took from Col. Dahlgren's fingers." The precious ring, which had belonged to Ully's dead sister Lizzie, was safely back in family hands.[96]

Other detachments recovered Ulric's wooden leg, his pocketwatch, and his uniform coat, which had four bullet holes in the left side and carried the bloodstains of his mortal wounds. Interestingly, Lieutenant Pollard, who had played such an important role in Ulric's death, lost a leg during the campaigns of 1864, and tried to use Ulric's prosthetic leg. However, he was unable to do so, as the wooden leg—of high quality—was too long to be useful. The irony is striking.[97]

The Admiral stored Ulric's body in a Washington vault, awaiting the cooler weather of autumn. On October 30, 1865, Admiral Dahlgren personally supervised the removal of the remains from the vault. A military honor guard transported the remains to the City Hall of Washington, where they lay in repose that night under the watchful eye of several commissioned officers. The body remained there until noon on October 31, and numerous mourners paid their respects.[98]

An honor guard consisting of battalions from the 10th Veteran Reserve, 18th Regiment Hancock's Corps, and the 195th and 214th Pennsylvania Volunteer Infantry escorted the coffin, which was carried by eight non-commissioned officers. Two generals and six colonels served as the pallbearers. "Close behind walked the father and the younger brother [Paul], the latter having been permitted to leave West Point for the melancholy occasion; the other brother [Charley] was far distant. Last came the officers of the army and navy."[99]

They took the remains to Reverend Sunderland's First Presbyterian Church. Reverend Sunderland was in Europe, so he did not preach the services, which were held on October 31. Instead, Rev. Henry Ward Beecher, the prominent abolitionist minister, came from New York to conduct the services.[100] President Andrew Johnson and all of his cabinet ministers attended, as did various army and navy officers. Secretary Stanton's letter of July 1863, enclosing Ulric's commission as a colonel, lay on top of the coffin. "As long as our history lasts," thundered Beecher, "Dahlgren shall mean truth, honor, bravery, and heroic sacrifice." A procession carried the coffin past silent crowds to the railroad depot, where it was loaded onto a special train to Philadelphia.[101]

The train stopped in Baltimore, where a body of troops awaited it. They loaded the body onto a hearse and carried it through the city so that the silent throngs lining the streets could also pay their respects to the fallen cavalryman. They then returned the casket to the train, which proceeded north to its final destination.[102]

Upon arrival in Philadelphia, soldiers carried the body to Independence Hall to lie in repose. "Few dead are honored by resting there," noted Admiral Dahlgren in his diary, most recently "Ulric's friend, President Lincoln."[103] Black bunting hung from the central chandelier and extended to the sides of the room. The catafalque—the same one that had held Abraham Lincoln's remains earlier that year—was covered with a beautiful silk flag. The funeral occurred on November 1, 1865. The mayor and many other dignitaries, including Generals Meade, Andrew A. Humphreys, Alexander Webb, and others paid their respects. "An exquisite cross of white flowers, having a centre of violet heliotrope surrounding a large white tuber-rose, and a wreath of laurel leaves, white and yellow roses, white bachelor buttons, lying upon the flag, cast a sweet scent around." The 7th Regiment of U. S. Veteran Volunteers served as the honor guard.[104]

Rev. Dr. J. P. Wilson, who baptized Ulric as a baby, presided over his funeral, and gave another stirring eulogy. "The expedition in which he laid down his life was not an enterprise of mere adventure and chivalrous daring," declared Reverend Wilson. "No holier human mission ever was or could be undertaken. Tidings of the sufferings of our starved and dying soldiers in the prisons of Richmond, within the very sight and hearing of the Chief of the Rebellion and of the leaders of his armies, reached the ears of Congress and smote the heart of the nation, and it was hoped that by a sudden and bold movement their release could be effected." He continued, "I said the mission was a holy one. There was a double motive, each laying the highest claim on true manhood for all that hand can do and heart can dare, the claim of country and the claim of humanity."[105]

The body was then loaded onto a hearse and taken to Laurel Hill Cemetery. An escort of 196 men drawn from the Philadelphia Navy Yard, the First Troop Philadelphia City Cavalry, and a detachment of the 7th U. S. Infantry escorted the hearse on its slow march. The Marine Band also accompanied the body as it moved out Walnut Street to Ridge Avenue, and then on to the cemetery. "The coffin is borne as before in front of the line of soldiers, presenting arms, drooping flags, while the solemn dirge alone breaks the stillness. The day is beautiful, the sky is unclouded, and the lovely tints of autumn are all around. The trees have their rich varied coats of scarlet, brown and green. Had she been intent to welcome the hero to a bridal couch rather than to a grave, nature could not have decked herself in a sweeter, more beauteous attire." Reverend Wilson said a graveside prayer, and the metallic coffin was lowered into the grave with the cross of white flowers still atop it. Admiral Dahlgren stood sorrow stricken as the chief mourner, watching his beloved son's mortal remains being lowered into the ground. The honor guard fired three volleys over the grave and the mourners left.[106]

Ully was buried in the north part of Laurel Hill Cemetery, not far from the main gate. A very small marble stone marks his grave, with the simple inscription "Colonel Ulric Dahlgren" and inscribed with the dates of his birth and death. It is a very modest marker, particularly considering that there were numerous proposals to erect a monument to his memory. He rests next to his mother, and a few feet from the remains of his beloved little sister Lizzie and the two little boys who died in infancy. "A mother & four children from my home group,— how sad!" lamented Admiral Dahlgren in his diary. The Admiral himself joined them just five years later. He was buried in the same grave with Ully.[107]

"Thus is laid to rest, in his native city, a brave youth, whose duty to his country and to his God were the guides of his short lifetime," concluded the report of the *Philadelphia Inquirer*. "His name is on history's pages by the side of Greble, Lyon, Ellsworth, Baker, our gallant patriots, and our noble martyred President, and like them is immortalized for the guidance of coming generations."[108]

Ulric Dahlgren's adventure finally ended a year and a half after he met his destiny on a nondescript, muddy road in King and Queen County, Virginia. His restless soul was, at last, at peace.

CHAPTER THIRTEEN

An Incomplete Life Assessed

B Y TURNS Ulric Dahlgren has been described as a Hun, a martyred hero, a bloodthirsty assassin who intended to decapitate the Confederate government, and as a genteel, educated, well-bred young man who was the youngest colonel in the Army of the Potomac. The contrast between Northern and Southern perceptions of Dahlgren really is stunning. Varina Davis's comments that she could not reconcile the two Ulrics are, perhaps, the most telling of all.

Obviously, these extremely simplistic black and white views do not accurately describe a complex young man such as Dahlgren. His was an incomplete life, snuffed out suddenly and unexpectedly at the very young age of 21 years, 11 months. A long and productive life lay ahead of him, and one can only speculate what this brilliant young man might have accomplished if he had lived to ripe old age. Members of his family, including his father, had a genius for science—a son of his brother Charles, named Ulric in honor of the dead hero, became a world famous biologist and researcher at Princeton University—and the young colonel seems to have inherited some of the family's genius.[1] That he was permitted to make presentations to the prestigious Franklin Institute at the tender age of nineteen amply demonstrates his intellect and the respect for it shown by others. Fate intervened and prohibited him from fulfilling his promise, instead leaving the modern reader to evaluate his incomplete life and wonder whether he might have achieved greatness.

There is no doubt that politicians at the highest levels of the Union government greatly esteemed Ulric Dahlgren. "How he was beloved by those who knew him you all do know," declared powerful Republican Congressman Schuyler Colfax of Indiana, who served as vice president during the administration of Ulysses S. Grant. "Manly, warm-hearted, brave in battle, and generous in victory, with a patriotism and devotion worthy of himself, he left here with a heart full of sympathy for his gallant comrades pining in the prisons of Richmond, and forgot that he was crippled in the trying day and night rides of Kilpatrick's raid on the rebel capital."[2]

No other junior officer in history has enjoyed more unfettered access to the Oval Office than did Dahlgren, meaning that he cultivated close relationships with the President's secretaries and with the Chief Executive himself. "He was decidedly the most gallant and daring cavalry officer of the war," boldly

declared John G. Nicolay, personal secretary to Abraham Lincoln, upon learning of Dahlgren's death, "and his loss will be mourned here as widely and deeply
almost as was [Col. Elmer] Ellsworth's."[3] While Nicolay obviously overstated
the case, he did have a point. Few officers—either Regulars or volunteers—had
a more distinguished record as a daring scout than did Dahlgren.

Ulric Dahlgren was born to be a soldier. Raised among the heavy guns of his
father's ordnance department, he spent his childhood sighting and firing large-
bore cannon and had the keen eye of a natural artillerist. That an unschooled
and untrained youth of twenty was sent on a critical mission to defend Harpers
Ferry in the midst of an unprecedented crisis and that he commanded artillery
there while still a civilian is nothing short of remarkable. That Sigel chose him
as chief of ordnance and acting chief of artillery for an entire infantry corps,
commanding West Point-trained career soldiers, speaks volumes for the natural talent Dahlgren had for gunnery.

Sigel praised him amply in an account of the Second Bull Run Campaign
that he penned. His words ably capture the essence of Dahlgren the soldier.
"In every respect one of the best and noblest soldiers born on the American
soil. In the prime of youth, of tall and fine stature, vigorous, energetic, and
of extraordinary courage, well educated, the son of an Admiral, animated by
a just but modest pride to act and to excel with a thorough knowledge of all
kind of ordnance and ammunition, no better officer could be found the branch
of service entrusted/ to him and for the many other special duties which her
performed as aide-de-camp. He was so able to select and assort his ammunition and to find out the quality and range of his guns has he was to scout and
reconnoiter, or to gout out on a raiding expedition," wrote the German general.
"He was as prompt to plant a battery under the most galling fire of the enemy,
as he was eager to ride for many miles during the death of night and under
the greatest difficulties and personal danger, to carry a dispatch to or from his
commander. He remained with the I and XI Corps until Spring 1863 when
he was transferred to Genl. Hooker's staff. He was severely wounded in an
engagement and afterwards killed at the head of a cavalry detachment, belong
to a raiding expedition under command of General Kilpatrick. His death was
deeply felt in the North, especially as it was accompanied by the most dismal
circumstances."[4]

As Sigel noted, Dahlgren possessed an obvious talent for dangerous missions,
quickly proving to be one of the most reliable and daring scouts in the entire
Army of the Potomac. Personally fearless, no mission was too dangerous for
Dahlgren, and he seldom disappointed. Instead, he could be relied upon to bring

Captain Ulric Dahlgren in 1862
LIBRARY OF CONGRESS

back accurate intelligence. The intelligence coup that he scored at Greencastle, Pennsylvania on July 2, 1863, was the crowning accomplishment of his scouting career. The dispatches he captured provided uncontroverted evidence that Robert E. Lee would receive no reinforcements while north of the Potomac River, and that George G. Meade could focus on Lee's army without having to worry about his rear or lines of communication and supply being caught off guard by the unexpected arrival of Confederate reinforcements.

The young man was extremely bright, eager to learn, morally grounded, strong in his religious faith, outgoing, and social. He apparently made friends quickly and easily. A quick study, he first mastered surveying and then the law before finding his real talent, soldiering. He reveled in the company of other bright young men, and he loved Army life. He impressed senior and junior officers alike with his intelligence, dash, and *joie d'vivre*, prompting Maj. Gen. Henry W. Halleck, the army's chief of staff, to call him "an officer of great promise."[5] He was a superb and tireless horseman. In short, he had nearly unlimited potential as a soldier, and might well have accomplished great things had he lived.

Admiral Dahlgren, who was hardly an objective observer, recounted his son's virtues in a letter written almost six months after Ully's demise. "Ulric Dahlgren was to the type of an American in its best form. He had all the fervor & religious bent of the Puritan, with none of his sternness—on the contrary he was all gentleness,—and I have often heard veteran officers remark that they could hardly believe what they heard of his daring qualities in the field," he declared.[6] These were indeed admirable traits, and they made the Admiral's son a fine soldier who might have been a great one under different circumstances.

Ully Dahlgren possessed all of the tools to have become a truly great soldier. In many ways, his life and personality mirrored that of George Armstrong Custer, another fearless cavalryman who lost his life on the field of battle. Like Custer, Dahlgren was a man who loved war, who dared death to look him in the eye, and who was completely reckless with his own safety. And, like Custer, his character flaws ultimately cost him his life. Like Custer, he met a sad and lonely end, his mutilated body unceremoniously buried in a crude unmarked grave. The parallels are, indeed, striking.

At the same time, Ulric Dahlgren was very young and inexperienced. He was an extremely brash and egotistical young man. Nearly limitless ambition plagued him, and probably cost him his life. His father, Rear Admiral John A. Dahlgren, was also a man of boundless personal ambition whose conduct demonstrated a constant desire for promotion and higher rank in a lifelong quest for personal glory. These personality traits undoubtedly rubbed off on his son. In fact, their correspondence makes it difficult to determine who was more ambitious for Ully to reach high rank at a precocious age—the father or the son. This unrelenting quest for personal glory often drove Ully Dahlgren to make rash decisions, and the final one—to try to fulfill his mission to free the prisoners of war even though his force had been badly beaten and was nearly out of ammunition—ultimately caused him to pay the ultimate price, his life.

The truth was that Dahlgren was in no condition to consider taking the field in February 1864. He had only had his prosthetic leg for a few weeks and was not accustomed to wearing it. His stump was barely healed, and the young man clearly had not recovered from the ordeal that nearly claimed his life in the summer of 1863. He had no business trying to lead troops in the field, but was too proud and too ambitious to realize it, or to exercise the good judgment to decline the mission. Instead, he insisted on joining the raid irrespective of his health or inability to withstand the travails of active winter campaigning. Perhaps a more mature or less ambitious man would have recognized this and declined to participate, but such was not Ully Dahlgren's nature, and doing so was not in keeping with his personality.

He was also an arrogant young man who was prone to poor judgment. "Dahlgren was a daring, dashing young fellow," declared Fitzhugh Lee, "but was too enthusiastic."[7] "Brave almost to rashness," concurred Ulric's friend E. A. Paul, a correspondent for the *New York Times*.[8] He undoubtedly inherited the trait of arrogance from his father; Admiral Dahlgren felt superior to common seamen, Latin Americans, and Arabs.[9] Ulric was also prone to exceed his orders if he saw an opportunity for glory and personal advancement. The best example of this trait was the November 1862 foray into Fredericksburg when Dahlgren needlessly destroyed the railroad bridges around the town and ultimately made supplying the Army of the Potomac far more difficult than it needed to be.

Likewise, Ulric Dahlgren made poor decisions in the field. His giving Lt. Col. Hilary P. Jones permission to visit his wife and the subsequent social calls on Sallie Seddon and Tuckahoe Plantation, by example, demonstrated poor judgment and a distinct lack of concern for the secrecy of the mission. Mrs. Seddon, in particular, had the poise and wherewithal to distract Dahlgren with her social graces while sending word of the advancing Federals to her husband in Richmond, allowing ample time for the mobilization of the home guard. Had Dahlgren focused that same attention on maintaining mission integrity and secrecy, the mission to free the prisoners of war might have succeeded. Likewise, the hanging of poor Martin Robinson was entirely unnecessary and was an abomination. While Dahlgren's frustration is understandable, the execution of the guide served no purpose other than to further inflame the Southern public against Ulric and his men.

Ulric's failure to destroy the Dahlgren Papers is the best possible example of his poor judgment. Once he was repulsed from the defenses of Richmond, and it became obvious that it would be impossible to fulfill the objects of the mission, Ulric should have destroyed the damning papers he carried in order to prevent just the sort of chaos that developed once their existence became known. However, he had been awake for nearly seventy-two hours without any meaningful sleep, and he was undoubtedly in agony from the unfamiliar prosthetic leg. The combination undoubtedly impaired his judgment significantly, as there simply was no justification for the failure to destroy the Papers. Dahlgren's signal officer, Lieutenant Bartley, by comparison, destroyed his cipher book and codes when it became obvious that the command was in dire straits, and that sensitive information never fell into enemy hands as a result. Ulric should have destroyed the Dahlgren Papers, but he did not, and his men suffered as a consequence of his poor judgment.

Maj. Gen. Fitzhugh Lee, the Confederate cavalryman who delivered the Dahlgren Papers to Jefferson Davis, wrote a long letter about the episode that was published in 1870. Lee wrote an interesting valediction made all the more intriguing by Lee's prominent role in the events that played out after Dahlgren's death. "Personally, as a man educated to be a soldier, I deplore Colonel Ulric Dahlgren's sad fate. He was a young man, full of hope, of undoubted pluck, and inspired with hatred of 'rebels,'" wrote Lee. "Fired by ambition, and longing to be at the head of 'the braves who swept through the city of Richmond,' his courage and enthusiasm overflowed, and his naturally generous feelings were drowned."[10] With that, Fitz Lee summed up both the strengths and flaws of Ulric Dahlgren's character.

And what of the ill-advised mission that ultimately cost Dahlgren his life? The plan was deeply flawed from the beginning. First, and foremost, there were too few men sent to Richmond to accomplish a difficult task; just ninety days later, Maj. Gen. Philip H. Sheridan determined that 12,000 men—three times as many as Kilpatrick and Dahlgren took to Richmond—were not sufficient to pierce the stout defenses of the Confederate capital. Second, the plan made no arrangements for what would happen to the prisoners of war if they were liberated. With many of them sick and malnourished, they were in no condition to undertake an arduous overland march, but there seemed to be no real plan for what would happen to these men if they were actually freed. Finally, there was no coordination with Butler's command, meaning that there was no pressure on Richmond from the east, and no force nearby for Kilpatrick and Dahlgren to link up with.

Even if his column had maintained the element of surprise and had it entered Richmond proper, would Dahlgren have been able to liberate the prisoners of war? Maj. Thomas P. Turner, the commandant of Libby Prison, had long worried that Union soldiers might attempt to free the prisoners of war, and he took precautions to prevent it. The failed Wistar raid of February 1864 convinced him that he had to act. Turner stored huge quantities of gunpowder in the basement of Libby Prison, and he intended to detonate that gunpowder if it looked like Federal troops might succeed in reaching the prisoners of war. Turner made sure that the Northerners imprisoned there knew about the existence of his booby-trap, and that he was serious about using it if necessary. A monstrous explosion would not only destroy the building, it would instantly kill all inside it. "The fullest preparations" were made to "blow the Yankees out of existence," as one Richmond newspaper colorfully put it.[11] Thus, even if Dahlgren had managed to enter the city, instead of freeing the prisoners, he actually might have caused their collective deaths in a huge conflagration.[12]

The failure of the expedition ultimately made things worse for the Union prisoners being held in Richmond. Dahlgren's officers, in particular, suffered mightily. They were placed in a single 12 by 15 foot room in the cellar of Libby Prison where as many as fifteen men huddled. The dank room had almost no ventilation or light, and the only latrine was an open tub. At mealtime, they ate under the watchful eye of their guards and had neither plates nor utensils. If a man became ill, he received no medical care. Efforts to alleviate their suffering were limited to men trying to pass crumbs of food to these poor wretches through a hole in the ceiling. For nearly five months, these men endured conditions that horrify readers removed from these events by more than 140 years. They were punished terribly just for being along on the expedition.[13]

Recognizing that the presence of such a large contingent of prisoners of war offered an extremely tempting target for the Union, the Confederate high command decided to transfer the prisoners to a newly-opened prison camp in Georgia called Andersonville. Ultimately, conditions at Andersonville proved to be even more vile than those at either Libby Prison or Belle Isle. In short, the failed raid actually increased the suffering of the Union prisoners of war.[14]

Their suffering was so intense, in fact, that another ill-advised cavalry raid was launched in an effort to free them in the summer of 1864. Maj. Gen. George Stoneman, formerly the commander of the Army of the Potomac's Cavalry Corps, assumed command of a division of cavalry assigned to Maj.

Gen. William T. Sherman's Army of the Ohio that spring. Stoneman's attempt to free the prisoners failed just as miserably as the Kilpatrick-Dahlgren Raid failed, and Stoneman ended up as a prisoner at Andersonville himself.[15] The irony is striking.

Thus, it becomes clear that the mission that cost Ulric Dahlgren his promising life was ill-advised, and probably had no real prospect of succeeding. The crippled young colonel had no business even trying to make the expedition in the first place, but the opportunity to seek glory—" it will be the grandest thing on record," to use Dahlgren's own words—proved irresistible. Dahlgren had to be where the action was, and it cost him his life.

The Kilpatrick-Dahlgren Raid was apparently not the first Union attempt to kidnap and carry off Jefferson Davis. There were actually two prior failed attempts. In the spring of 1862, four Frenchmen who served in the 53rd New York Infantry (including one who was awarded a Medal of Honor in 1865) apparently concocted a scheme to kidnap Davis and carry him off, thereby ending the war early. Their plan was not approved by the government or by their superior officers, and they acted pretty much on their own. Not surprisingly, their scheme failed and the four Frenchmen ended up in Libby Prison. Although there is little historical evidence to support this story other than a memoir by one of the alleged participants, if it was true, it demonstrates beyond dispute that Union soldiers had been incubating the idea of kidnapping Jefferson Davis for some time. Perhaps the Confederate authorities were aware of this scheme and made contingency plans to deal with the inevitable next attempt.[16]

Then there was Wistar's failed attempt to kidnap Davis, part of Butler's daring plan, which was specifically approved by President Lincoln. Due to Private Boyle's treachery, the plan was fully disclosed to the Confederate authorities, who probably also learned of the plot to kidnap Davis in the process. Thus, the Kilpatrick-Dahlgren Raid was the third and final unsuccessful attempt to kidnap Davis.

Many have speculated upon the overall effect of the failure of the Kilpatrick-Dahlgren Raid on the outcome of the war. Some allege that the failure of the Kilpatrick-Dahlgren Raid actually set into motion events that strayed far beyond the wildest imagination of the men who planned and executed it. Author Duane Schultz claimed that the failure of the raid triggered the Confederate raid on St. Alban's, Vermont, a campaign of terror throughout the north, and that Jefferson Davis authorized the use of terrorism against civilians in the form of guerrilla raids, bank robberies, arson, acts of sabotage, and a war directed at the civilian population of the north, all in retaliation for the failed Kilpatrick-Dahlgren Raid.[17] This seems a bit far-fetched, as there is little evidence that the Confederate government intended to engage in such nefarious conduct.

In *Come Retribution: The Confederate Secret Service and the Assassination of Lincoln*, authors William A. Tidwell, James O. Hall, and David Winfred Gaddy allege "the so-called Dahlgren's raid of February and March 1864 provided the motive [to assassinate Abraham Lincoln] that could have persuaded the Confederate government to consider retaliation against Lincoln personally." The authors claim that the failure of the Kilpatrick-Dahlgren Raid set into motion the series of events that ultimately led to the assassination of President Lincoln, and that rather than a deranged crackpot who assembled a conspiracy of ne'er-do-wells, John Wilkes Booth was actually an agent of the Confederate secret service operating with the sanction of Jefferson Davis and the Confederate government.[18] Again, this probably overstates the case, and it seems very unlikely that such a link existed. However, it remains no stretch of the imagination to conclude that the failure of the raid and the discovery of the Dahlgren Papers undoubtedly caused an already unpleasant war to turn even more so. And the blame for that must rest with Ulric Dahlgren, as the author of the papers.

There is also a great deal of irony in the fact that Dahlgren and his putative classmate from Rittenhouse Academy, Davey Herold, both died as a consequence of their participation in plots to assassinate heads of state. In perhaps the greatest irony of all, Herold was hanged on the grounds of the Washington Navy Yard—probably within sight of the large brick home where he grew up—along with the other surviving conspirators. Herold and Ulric Dahlgren undoubtedly crossed paths during the early years of the Civil War. Davey worked in the pharmacy at the Washington Navy Yard during Admiral Dahlgren's tenure in command there, and Herold probably brought the gravely wounded Ulric Dahlgren medication during his post-wounding recuperation. Perhaps they reminisced about their common childhood or their days as students at Rittenhouse Academy.[19] One has to wonder whether Herold's knowledge of Ulric Dahlgren's participation in a plot to kidnap and assassinate Jefferson Davis influenced his decision to participate in John Wilkes Booth's successful conspiracy to assassinate Abraham Lincoln.

There remains one great, daunting question that any biographer of Ulric Dahlgren must tackle before finally leaving the subject. The ultimate question to be determined is whether Abraham Lincoln knew of Ulric Dahlgren's plans in advance, and whether Lincoln approved them. In other words, what did Lincoln know, and when did he know it, to borrow the parlance of the Watergate era.

There are five possible scenarios:

+ That Lincoln himself came up with the plan an its bloody components, and selected the trusted young colonel, Ulric Dahlgren, to execute it.

+ That Stanton got hold of Kilpatrick's plan to free the prisoners of war and corrupted it by adding the assassination of Davis and his staff to the plot, and that Kilpatrick willingly went along with it.

+ That Kilpatrick and Dahlgren added the murder and arson component to the plan.

+ That Dahlgren himself added murder and arson to the otherwise innocent but doomed plot to free the prisoners of war.

+ That Dahlgren was recruited to join the plot developed by Stanton and Kilpatrick, and that Kilpatrick recognized that Dahlgren was the proper weapon to execute the plan and gave Dahlgren the instructions that the young colonel carefully copied into his notebook.

Although I believe that the fifth scenario is the most likely one—the evidence certainly supports it—a full and fair analysis must include all of the possibilities. Consequently, I will do so.

Southerners certainly believed that Lincoln not only knew of the plot, but that he approved it. After all, he had previously approved Butler's plan to kidnap Davis, which the Confederate authorities probably knew after the failure of Wistar's expedition. Lincoln's close relationship with Admiral Dahlgren was well known, and the esteem in which Lincoln held John Dahlgren was also common knowledge. It was no stretch, therefore, for the average Southern citizen to conclude that Lincoln had something to do with the mission, given the choice of one-legged Ulric Dahlgren to lead the critical portion of the expedition. At the very least, they speculated, Lincoln knew of Ully Dahlgren's plan, and his choice of Ully to command a portion of the expedition constituted a tacit endorsement of the plan.

These conclusions are understandable, and they are also logical. The question is, how well grounded in truth are they? This question is simultaneously fascinating and frustrating, as we will never know the true answer. Attempting to answer this question is much like peeling an onion: one peels away a layer and finds many more beneath it. However, no biographer of Ulric Dahlgren can truly claim to have written a full account of his life without delving into this quagmire.

Lincoln understood that a harsh Reconstruction policy, combined with an aggressive prosecution of Jefferson Davis for treason, would ultimately do the country more harm than good. In a conversation with Maj. Gen. William T. Sherman at City Point, Virginia at the end of March 1865, Lincoln used one of his favorite tactics, telling parables to make his point. Sherman specifically asked what Lincoln wanted to see happen to Davis once the war ended. "A man once had taken the total-abstinence pledge. When visiting a friend, he was invited to take a drink, but declined, on the score of his pledge, when his friend suggested lemonade, which was accepted," Lincoln said. "In preparing the lemonade, the friend pointed to the brandy-bottle, and said the lemonade would be more palatable if he were to pour in a little brandy; when his guest said, if he could do so 'unbeknown' to him, he would not object." From this story, Sherman concluded that Lincoln's thinly veiled desire was that Davis be permitted to slip out of the country "unknowingly" rather than to have him prosecuted for treason.[20]

Admiral David Dixon Porter, who also attended the City Point conference, had a similar recollection. "My opinion is, that Mr. Lincoln came down to City Point with the most liberal views toward the Rebels," he wrote in 1868. "He felt confident that we would be successful, and was willing that the enemy should capitulate on the most favorable terms."[21] Lincoln reportedly said, "Let 'em up easy" in responding to a question about what his intentions for bringing the Confederate states back into the fold.

Given these declarations, it seems implausible that Lincoln would have approved the assassination of Davis and his cabinet. Lincoln was a brilliant and politically astute man, and he had to have known that such a policy would have dire ramifications for his own presidency. It defies logic, therefore, to conclude that Lincoln knew of and approved of Dahlgren's plan before it was put into motion.

Likewise, on April 24, 1863, the War Department issued General Orders No. 100, which spelled out the laws of war, styled as Instructions for the Government of Armies of the United States. Francis Lieber, a noted German-American jurist and political philosopher, assisted in the preparation of this system of the laws of war, which became known as the Lieber Code. Article 148 of the Lieber Code provides:

> The law of war does not allow proclaiming either an individual belonging to the hostile army, or a citizen, or a subject of the hostile government an outlaw, who may be slain without trial by any captor, any more than the modern law of peace allows such international outlawry; on the contrary,

it abhors such outrage. The sternest retaliation should follow the murder committed in consequence of such proclamation, made by whatever authority. Civilized nations look with horror upon offers of rewards for the assassination of enemies as relapses into barbarism.[22]

Thus, while the kidnapping of Davis remained a legitimate military objective, political assassination was expressly made illegal pursuant to the code of the laws of war propounded by the Lincoln Administration. Thus, if Lincoln ordered the assassination of Davis, he would have violated the law and could have been impeached for doing so. As a lawyer, Lincoln would have understood the implications of this, and it is difficult to conceive that he might have committed acts that might have led to his impeachment for committing felonies.

Dahlgren visited the White House twice in the weeks just before the commencement of the raid, and on both occasions, he had extended private audiences with the President. There is no record of those conversations, and we will never know precisely what they discussed. However, at least one of those visits, where they discussed political and military matters, was in the presence of the Presidential barber, so it seems unlikely that the details of a secret plan to assassinate Jefferson Davis would have been discussed under such circumstances. It therefore seems unlikely that they discussed the plan, or that Lincoln approved it. There certainly was no written record of a Presidential approval that could be traced back to him. Since neither Dahlgren nor Lincoln survived, and because neither of them left a record of their discussions, we will never know the truth. However, it seems unlikely that Lincoln approved the plan, as doing so would not only be illegal, it would contradict Lincoln's well-documented position on Reconstruction.

A more likely scenario is that Secretary of War Edwin M. Stanton not only knew of the plan, but approved it and maybe even concocted it. Stanton was well aware of the suffering of the prisoners of war, and he was under a great deal of pressure to do something about their plight. It is entirely conceivable that Stanton not only knew of and approved the plan, but that he might even have thought it up, alone, or in conjunction with Kilpatrick, selected Dahlgren to implement it, and that he never told Lincoln about it in order to permit the President to plausibly deny any role in the scheme.

The similarity between the failed Wistar expedition of February and the plans set forth in the Dahlgren Papers also suggests strongly that someone high up in the administration knew about the plan and authorized it. Otherwise, why was Kilpatrick summoned to Washington for consultations with Lincoln and Stanton? And why else was Ully Dahlgren selected, other than that he was known to be a reliable confidant of the President?[23]

The unlikely choice of Dahlgren to command the critical portion of the expedition provides further evidence of Stanton's probable involvement in conceiving and ordering the plan for the kidnapping and assassination of Jefferson Davis and his cabinet. It is important to remember that Dahlgren had never commanded anything larger than the detachment of 100 troopers who accompanied him to Greencastle on July 4, 1863, that the men of the Third Cavalry Division did not know him, and that he was clearly not in physical condition to undertake such a difficult mission. But for Stanton's patronage, how else could Dahlgren have gotten such an unlikely appointment and such a critical role in the planning of the raid?

Had Stanton been aware of the true plan for the expedition in advance, and had Dahlgren assassinated Davis and his cabinet, it is entirely possible that Stanton would have disavowed Dahlgren anyway to avoid the taint of such a monstrous act. Even if he did not disavow Dahlgren, he probably never would have admitted his role in public (or at least not until after the war ended) for fear of bringing about retribution in kind.

It seems likely that once Kilpatrick and Stanton came up with their scheme and then selected Dahlgren to implement it, Kilpatrick then sat down with Dahlgren in the days prior to the commencement of the raid and gave him specific instructions for the conduct of the raid. Dahlgren apparently carefully copied those instructions into his pocket notebook, which he then used as the basis for developing the text of the address to his men and the orders for the expedition. The contents of the notebook (which are related verbatim in the appendix to this book) certainly sound like notes that someone would have scribbled down during the course of a number of intense discussions between Kilpatrick and Dahlgren. Kilpatrick evidently forgot to tell Dahlgren to memorize these orders and destroy the notes in order to prevent a paper trail, meaning that the notes were still in the pocket notebook when found by young William Littlepage. Dahlgren compounded that error by choosing not to destroy the damning documents when it became obvious that the expedition had failed, setting the stage for the controversy that followed. That Dahlgren was killed, in turn, then enabled Stanton and Kilpatrick to keep their skirts clear, to borrow a phrase from George Meade, by claiming that they had no knowledge of the orders, and, with Dahlgren dead, there was nobody to dispute the claim.

Likewise, and as set forth in detail in the appendix to this book, the Dahlgren Papers themselves disappeared after the war, probably at either Stanton's direct order or, more likely, by his own hand. Unless he had something to hide, why would Stanton have destroyed important historical evidence? Dahlgren was already dead, and the controversy had already raged for a year, so there was nothing to gain by destroying the documents other than protecting Stanton's own reputation and legacy. If it could be proved that Stanton conceived of the plan, then he would become the target of the controversy, and not Dahlgren.

In the wake of the Lincoln assassination in April 1865, Stanton's power grew even greater. He would have done anything to protect and preserve that power, and destroying the Dahlgren Papers would have been a wise move under those circumstances in order to prevent his role in the nefarious scheme from becoming known. I therefore believe that Stanton and Kilpatrick modified the plan to free the prisoners of war to include the kidnapping and assassination of Davis and his cabinet, and that they either recruited Dahlgren as the instrument to execute the plan, or that Dahlgren, once he heard of the poorly-kept secret, eagerly joined the cabal himself. Either way, there simply is no tangible evidence that Abraham Lincoln knew of or approved such a plan.

As a third possibility, Lincoln might have authorized a plan for the kidnapping of the Confederate leadership, and that Stanton and Kilpatrick together modified the plan to include the assassination of the Southern leaders without telling Lincoln. In this scenario, Lincoln would have authorized the basic concept, but could then plausibly deny having known that the true plan was the assassination of Davis and his cabinet. Given Kilpatrick's aggressive advocacy of his plan for the raid, this seems an unlikely explanation for the genesis of the Dahlgren Papers.

There remains a final possibility: that there is nothing more here than what meets the eye. It is entirely possible that Ulric Dahlgren dreamed the whole thing up himself without the authority or even knowledge of his superiors. Perhaps the Dahlgren Papers represent the desperate attempt of a crippled but brilliant young man to achieve further military glory that probably would have been denied him otherwise. Ulric was addicted to danger, and he probably saw this expedition as a prime opportunity to indulge that addiction and to strike a decisive blow for the Union at the same time. Although he was a victim, he was a victim of his own ambitions and poor judgment in the field. Dahlgren's propensity for exceeding his orders is well-documented, and has already been discussed in some detail earlier in this chapter. Perhaps the Dahlgren papers represent the best-known episode of ill-advised opportunism of the war, and perhaps the Union high command properly disavowed him and his scheme.

Some support for this position arises in the transcribed post-war memoir of William W. Patteson, Company C, 43rd Battalion of Virginia Cavalry, also known as Mosby's Rangers. Patteson served under the command of the legendary Confederate partisan, Col. John Singleton Mosby. He left the following tantalizing tidbit in his post-war memoirs:

> Genl. Lee's Army had taken up its winter quarters on the Rapidan River. Grant came in with 165,000 men & camped in Culpeper Co. until Spring. A Union Genl. John C. Robinson of Binghamton, New York took our remaining house for his headquarters only allowing us one room for eight persons. He & his staff taking eight rooms (his wife came & spent the winter.) She was a sister or sister in law of Admiral Dahlgren (an Aunt of the infamous Ulric Dahlgren) who was attached to Grant's army as Col. of Cavalry, and I often saw him at our house. He had lost a leg in one of the fights and wore a cork one. He conceived the idea of burning Richmond and freeing many thousand of union prisoners through the advice of spies and a woman traitor in Richmond Va. This he had told the Genl and his wife as they passed by our door which was open a little but a curtain hung over it & they did not see me—that they would hear in a few days of the burning of <u>that place</u> (meaning Richmond Va.), he had in his pocket this order from Washington with him. How I did wish to get that information to Genl. Lee. Well he left that night never to return. Our boys settled his hash.[24]

Patteson's teasing memoir suggests that Ulric told Brig. Gen. John C. Robinson, who commanded a division in the Army of the Potomac's Fifth Corps, that he was the sole author of the plan. The problem with this account is that Ulric only spent one week in the Army of the Potomac's winter encampment in Culpeper County before the raid kicked off, so it is questionable how many times Patteson could have seen Ulric at Robinson's winter headquarters. Nevertheless, Patteson's tantalizing account raises real issues as to whether Ulric was, in fact, the sole author of the plan.

If one accepts Occam's Razor as a truism, then this explanation makes the most sense. Occam's Razor states that the explanation of any phenomenon should make as few assumptions as possible, eliminating, or "shaving off," those that make no difference in the observable predictions of the explanatory hypothesis or theory. In short, when given two equally valid explanations for a phenomenon, one should embrace the less complicated formulation. In other words, the principle may be stated as "all things being equal, the simplest solution tends to be the best one."[25] It is certainly easier to conceive of the idea that

Dahlgren alone was responsible for the plot, which is also the conclusion that casts the fewest aspersions.

The evidence, however, does not support this conclusion. As set forth fully above, it seems obvious that Judson Kilpatrick and Edwin Stanton cooked up this scheme, and that they either recruited Dahlgren to be the instrument to execute it, or that the young man, addicted to danger and always on the lookout for opportunities to advance his boundless personal ambition, eagerly joined once he heard about it. It is doubtful that the inexperienced Dahlgren came up with such a scheme on his own initiative, and it is likewise doubtful that the scheme can be traced to Abraham Lincoln.

What is much more clear is that Judson Kilpatrick was not entirely truthful in disavowing Dahlgren's orders. Capt. John McEntee, a tall, gaunt merchant, served in a Union infantry regiment during the early days of the war. When the Army of the Potomac's Bureau of Military Information was formed, McEntee proved himself to be a very competent and reliable scout and gatherer of intelligence whose reports carried a great deal of credibility.[26] McEntee accompanied Kilpatrick's column to Richmond.

General Marsena Patrick was the Army of the Potomac's provost marshal. As such, he worked closely with the Bureau of Military Information, and had an opportunity to discuss the failed raid with McEntee. Patrick recorded his recollections in his diary, noting that McEntee shared the same low opinion of Kilpatrick as Patrick, and "says he managed as all cowards do—He further says that he thinks the papers are correct that were found upon Dahlgren, as they correspond with what D[ahlgren] told *him*."[27] General Meade made no real secret of his personal belief that the documents were real and that Kilpatrick's disavowal of them rang hollow.

Martin Hogan, the BMI man who led the advance of Dahlgren's column, wrote a strong letter to a Chicago newspaper in 1875. "For ten years I have read the abuse which had been heaped upon the grave of Ulric Dahlgren," he declared. "I took it as a matter of course until Jeff Davis, over his well-known signature, says that Col. Dahlgren had orders on his 'Richmond raid' to burn Richmond and murder Mr. Davis and his Cabinet. I am fully prepared to denounce this statement of ex-President Davis as false in every sense. I had the honor to command the advance guard of that raid, and I know personally that Col. Dahlgren had no orders to murder anybody." At the end of that strong statement, Hogan invited anyone with knowledge of raid to come forward and prove him wrong.[28]

Similar statements also surfaced. An anonymous author who wrote a paper entitled "Memoranda of the War Commenced Too Late" recorded a conversation that he allegedly had with George A. Custer. Custer supposedly denied "Federal claims that the Dahlgren papers were forged or altered. Custer allegedly said that the night before he and Dahlgren parted, Dahlgren told him 'that he would not take Pres. Davis & his cabinet, but would put them to death, and that he would himself set fire to the first house in Richmond & burn the city.' He, Custer, did not think this purpose right."[29] The author's identity is unknown, the context of the document is likewise unknown, and it is of questionable credibility. It only warrants noting because it adds some weight to the claims of McEntee that the true purpose of the raid was known.

A much more interesting and more credible account has recently surfaced. In 1871, John Singleton Mosby, the noted Confederate partisan leader, wrote a letter to a friend. "On a recent visit to Philadelphia I met socially with General Isaac Wister (*sic*) of the Federal army," recounted Mosby. "He informed me that the infernal purposes of Kilpatrick and Dahlgren were correctly disclosed in the papers found on Dahlgren's body; that he was in command at Yorktown at the time, that Kilpatrick after his retreat from Richmond spent several days at his headquarters, that Kilpatrick, who was then ignorant of Dahlgren's death, told him all his plans which were identical with what was stated in the Dahlgren papers. He also said that [General Benjamin] Butler once ordered him on a similar expedition but that he positively refused to go."[30]

This letter has some credibility. Wistar was in command at Yorktown, Kilpatrick did end up in Yorktown for several days after being repulsed from Richmond, and Butler had indeed ordered Wistar to advance on Richmond to free the prisoners of war prior to the Kilpatrick-Dahlgren Raid. It appears, therefore, that Wistar's claim that Kilpatrick in fact knew of and approved the plan to kidnap and assassinate Jefferson Davis and his cabinet ring true. It bears noting that both General Meade and Col. Walter H. Taylor, Robert E. Lee's adjutant, plainly expressed their skepticism about the credibility of Kilpatrick's politically necessary denial within days of it occurring, which lends further credibility to Wistar's account. It seems likely, therefore, that at the very least, Judson Kilpatrick knew of and approved the plan and that he later denied it out of political expediency. At the same time, Mosby might have misunderstood Wistar, or Wistar may have been a bit misleading in describing his role in this episode.

Lincoln was certainly familiar with Judson Kilpatrick. In the fall of 1862, Col. Lafayette C. Baker, head of the Union's secret service, unceremoniously clapped then-Lt. Col. Judson Kilpatrick into Old Capitol Prison in Washington, and left him there for several months without even so much as informing Little Kil why he was being held. At the end of November, Kilpatrick penned a long letter to Lincoln complaining of his treatment. Lincoln himself acted upon the letter, eventually leading to Kilpatrick's release and his return to his regiment, the 2nd New York Cavalry.[31] Perhaps Lincoln knew that Kilpatrick was beholden to him as a consequence of the president's intervention in the fall of 1862, and he may have approved Kilpatrick's proposed raid on Richmond with the caveat that the kidnapping and execution of Davis and his cabinet be the object of the expedition. It is, therefore, entirely possible that Kilpatrick was fully aware of the plan, but used the death of Dahlgren as a reason to hide his role in the nefarious scheme.

It is, therefore, clear that Judson Kilpatrick was intimately involved in the planning of this operation, that the plot might have originated with him, and that the untimely death of Ulric Dahlgren provided him with a perfect opportunity to disavow his role and protect his own reputation. The most likely scenario, I think, is that Kilpatrick and Stanton hatched this scheme themselves, that they did not tell Lincoln, and that they either recruited Ully Dahlgren, or that Dahlgren, once he heard about the poorly-kept secret, readily joined in the scheme, hoping to do something spectacular that would feed his addiction to danger, do the dirty work for Kilpatrick in the process, and perhaps win the ambitious young colonel another promotion.

We will never know the truth about who knew what and when they knew it. We do know that Ully Dahlgren's boundless ambition cost him his life in an ill-advised and ultimately hopeless attempt to free the Union prisoners of war from the charnel houses of Richmond. It appears that Dahlgren was a willing participant in a scheme cooked up by Judson Kilpatrick and Edwin Stanton, and that his willing participation led to tragedy along a dirt road in King and Queen County. Dahlgren's poor choices in the field compounded the failure and ultimately led to the fatal confrontation. His arrogance and courage made it impossible for him to do the smart thing and break off after being repulsed from the defenses of Richmond. His failure to destroy the Dahlgren Papers brought down the wrath of the Confederate government on his men once they became prisoners of war. All of the personality traits that caused him to shine in the early days of his military career converged on that cold March night in King and Queen County, and their synergy spelled disaster for Ulric Dahlgren and the brave little band that followed him unquestioningly across the Virginia countryside.

Ulric the Hun. The martyred Northern hero. The true Ulric Dahlgren lies somewhere between these two extreme perceptions. Like Varina Davis, we will probably never reconcile these two diametrically opposed perceptions of this young man whose unfinished and too short life will forever be linked with the controversy that raged after his untimely death. He was, ultimately, a brilliant but fatally flawed young man who possessed all of the tools to have achieved greatness. Instead, he fell victim to his own ambitions, which cost him his life. The youngest colonel in the Union army at twenty-one, he was dead before the age of twenty-two. He blazed spectacularly across the night sky like a meteor, burning out almost as quickly as he lit the heavens. His incomplete life's legacy, including all of his deeds of daring and all of his many accomplishments, were all swept away by a tsunami of controversy.

Were the Dahlgren Papers Authentic?

T HIS APPENDIX deals with the question of whether the documents found
on Ulric Dahlgren's body were authentic. Before addressing the question
of whether the documents were authentic, their contents will be recounted
here, verbatim.

First comes the address to the men of Dahlgren's command:

Headquarters Third Division Cavalry Corps

_____, 186_

Officers and Men:

You have been selected from brigades and regiments as a picked command
to attempt a desperate undertaking—an undertaking which, if successful,
will write your names on the hearts of your countrymen in letter that can
never be erased, and which will cause the prayers of our fellow-soldiers now
confined in loathsome prisons to follow you and yours wherever you may
go. We hope to release the prisoners from Belle Island first, and having seen
them fairly started, we will cross the James River into Richmond, destroying
the bridges after us and exhorting the released prisoners to destroy and burn
the hateful city; and do not allow the Rebel leader Davis and his traitorous
crew to escape. The prisoners must render great assistance, as you cannot
leave your ranks too far or become too much scattered, or you will be lost.
Do not allow any personal gain to lead you off, which would only bring you
to an ignominious death at the hands of citizens. Keep well together and
obey orders strictly and all will be well; but on no account scatter too far, for
in union there is strength. With strict obedience to orders and fearlessness
in the execution you will be sure to succeed. We will join the main force on
the other side of the city, or perhaps meet them inside. Many of you may fail;
but if there is any man here not willing to sacrifice his life in such a great and
glorious undertaking, or who does not feel capable of meeting the enemy in
such a desperate fight as will follow, let him step out, and he may go hence
to the arms of his sweetheart and read of the braves who swept through
the city of Richmond. We want no man who cannot feel sure of success in
such a holy cause. We will have a desperate fight, but stand up to it when it

comes and all will be well. Ask the blessing of the Almighty and do not fear the enemy.

U. Dahlgren

Colonel, Commanding

Also found on Dahlgren's person were his orders to Capt. John F. B. Mitchell of the 2nd New York Cavalry for leading a separate detachment down the north bank of the James River, parallel to the route taken by the rest of Dahlgren's command.

Guides.—Pioneers (with oakum, turpentine, and torpedoes), signal offi-cer, quartermaster, commissary. Scouts and pickets. Men in Rebel uniform. These will remain on the north bank and move down with the force on the south bank, not getting ahead of them, and if the communication can be kept up without giving an alarm it must be done; but everything depends upon a surprise, and no one must be allowed to pass ahead of the column. Information must be gathered in regard to the crossings of the river, so that should we be repulsed on the south side we will know where to recross at the nearest point. All mills must be burned and the canal destroyed, and also everything which can be used by the Rebels must be destroyed, including the boats on the river. Should a ferry-boat be seized and can be worked, have it moved down. Keep the force on the south side posted of any important movement of the enemy, and in case of danger some of the scouts must swim the river and bring us information. As we approach the city the party must take great care that they do not get ahead of the other party on the south side, and must conceal themselves and watch our movements. We will try and secure the bridge to the city, one mile below Belle Isle, and release the prisoners at the same time. If we do not succeed they must then dash down, and we will try and carry the bridge from each side. When necessary, the men must be filed through the woods and along the river bank. The bridges once secured, and the prisoners loose and over the river, the bridges will be burned and the city destroyed. The men must keep together and well in hand, and once in the city it must be destroyed and Jeff. Davis and Cabinet killed. Pioneers will go along with combustible material. The officer must use his discretion about the time of meeting us. Horses and cattle which we do not need immediately must be shot rather than left. Everything on the canal and elsewhere of service to the Rebels must be destroyed. As General Custer may follow me, be careful not to give a false alarm.

There were also general instructions to the men of his command:

> This Signal Officer must be prepared to communicate at night by rockets, and in other things pertaining to his department.
>
> The quartermasters and commissaries must be on the lookout for their departments, and see that there are no delays on their account.
>
> The engineer officer will follow to survey the road as we pass over it, etc.
>
> The pioneers must be prepared to construct a bridge or destroy one. They must have plenty of oakum and turpentine for burning, which will be rolled in soaked balls and given to the men to burn when we get in the city. Torpedoes will only be used by the pioneers for destroying the main bridges, etc. They must be prepared to destroy railroads. Men will branch off to the right with a few pioneers, and destroy the bridges and railroads south of Richmond, and then join us at the city. They must be well prepared with torpedoes, etc. The line of Falling Creek is probably the best to work along, or as they approach the city Goode's Creek, so that no reinforcements can come up on any cars. No one must be allowed to pass ahead for fear of communicating news. Rejoin the command with all haste, and if cut off cross the river above Richmond and rejoin us. We will stop at Bellona Arsenal and totally destroy it, and anything else but hospitals; then follow on and rejoin the command at Richmond with all haste, and if cut off cross the river and rejoin us. As General Custer may follow me, be careful not to give a false alarm.

Dahlgren also prepared a rough itinerary for the expedition, which he evidently cobbled together during the time that he spent at Kilpatrick's winter camp in the days before the expedition began.

> Saturday. Leave camp at dark (Six P.M.). Cross Ely's Ford at ten P.M.
>
> Twenty miles—Cross North Anna at four A.M. Sunday—feed and water—one hour.
>
> Three miles—Frederick's Hall Station, six A.M.—destroy art'y, eight A.M.
>
> Twenty miles—Near James River, two P.M. Sunday—feed and water, 1 ½ hour.
>
> Thirty miles to Richmond—March towards Kilpatrick for one hour, and then, as soon as dark, cross the river, reaching Richmond in the morning (Monday).

One squadron remains on the north side, and one squadron to cut the rail-road bridge at Falling Creek, and join at Richmond—eighty-three miles.

Gen. K.—cross at one A.M. Sunday—ten miles. Pass river at five A.M. (resistance).

Chilesburg—fourteen miles—eight A.M.

Resistance at North Anna—three miles.

Railroad bridges at South Anna—twenty-six miles—two P.M. Destroy bridges—pass the South Anna and feed until after dark—then signal each other. After dark move down to Richmond, and be in front of the city at daybreak.

Return—in Richmond during the day—feed and water men outside.

Be over the Pamunkey at daybreak—feed and water, and then cross the Rappahannock at night (Tuesday night) when they must be on the lookout.

Spies should be sent on Friday morning early, and be ready to cut.

This extremely ambitious schedule probably could not have been met, even under optimal circumstances.

Finally, the pocket notebook found on Dahlgren's body contained some miscellaneous notes that dealt with the expedition's details.

Pleasonton will govern details.

Will have details from other commands, (four thousand).

Michigan men have started.

Colonel J. H. Devereux has torpedoes.

Hanover Junction (B. T. Johnson). Maryland Line.

Chapin's Farm—Seven miles below Richmond.

One brigade (Hunton's relieved, Wise sent to Charleston).

River can be forded half a mile above the city. No works on south side. Hospitals near them. River fordable. Canal can be crossed.

Fifty men to remain on north bank, and keep in communication if possible. To destroy mills, canal, and burn everything of value to the Rebels. Seize any large ferry boats, and note all of any important movement of the Rebels, and as we approach the city, communicate with us, and do not give the alarm before they see us in possession of Belle Isle and the bridge. If engaged there or unsuccessful, they must assist in securing the bridges until we cross. If the ferry-boat can be taken and worked, bring it down. Everything that cannot be secured or made use of must be destroyed. Great care must be taken not to be seen or any alarm given. The men must be filed along off the road or along the main bank. When we enter the city the office must use his discretion as to when to assist in crossing the bridges.

The prisoners once loosed and the bridges crossed, the city must be destroyed, burning the public buildings, etc.

Prisoners to go with party.

Spike the heavy guns outside.

Pioneers must be ready to repair, destroy, etc. Turpentine will be provided. The pioneers must be ready to destroy the Richmond bridges, after we have all crossed, and to destroy the railroad near Frederick's Hall (station, artillery, etc.).

Fifteen men to halt at Bellona Arsenal, while the column goes on, and destroy it. Have some prisoners. Then rejoin us at Richmond, leaving a portion to watch if anything follows, under a good officer.

Will be notified that Custer may come.

Main column, four hundred.

One hundred men will take the bridge after the scouts, and dash through the streets and open they way to the front, or if it is open destroy everything in the way.

While they are on the big bridges, one hundred men will take Belle Isle, after the scouts, instructing the prisoners to gut the city. The reserve (two hundred) will see this fairly done and everything over, and then follow, destroying the bridges after them, but not scattering too much, and always having a part well in hand.

Jeff. Davis and Cabinet must be killed on the spot.

The Richmond newspapers published all of these documents verbatim. They were also photographed, and Robert E. Lee provided copies of the photographs to Maj. Gen. George Gordon Meade with his April 1864 letter. The photographs of the Dahlgren Papers repose in the National Archives today.

Having set forth the full content of the Dahlgren Papers, and having seen why their contents spurred so much controversy, we may now turn to the issue of their validity.[1]

As pointed out in Chapter 12, Admiral Dahlgren vigorously disputed the authenticity of the Dahlgren Papers. He attacked their authenticity upon two main grounds: that his son always wrote out his whole name and did not use the abbreviation "U. Dahlgren" and that the last name was misspelled

"Dalhgren." As a result of his impassioned defense of his son's honor, a number of contemporary refutations emerged.

The first to read the Dahlgren Papers was Edward Halbach, who saw them shortly after his student, thirteen-year-old William Littlepage, found them on Ulric's body. Halbach believed that they contained:

> Every line and every word as afterwards copied into the Richmond news-papers. Dahlgren's name was signed to one or more of the papers, and also written on the inside of the front cover of his memorandum-book. There the date of purchase, I suppose, was added. The book had been written with a degree of haste clearly indicated by the frequent interlineations and corrections, but the orders referred to had also been re-written on a separate sheet of paper; and, as thus copied, were published to the world. Some of the papers were found loose in Dahlgren's pockets, others were between the leaves of the memorandum-book.
>
> The papers thus brought to light were reserved by myself to the continual presences of witnesses of unquestionable veracity, until about two o'clock in the afternoon of the day after their capture; at which time myself and party met Lieut. Pollard, who, up to this time, knew nothing in the world of the existence of the Dahlgren Papers. At his request, I let him read the papers; after doing which he requested me to let him carry them to Richmond. At first, I refused, for I thought that I knew what to do with them quite as well as any one else. But I was finally induced, by my friends, against my will, to surrender the papers to Lieut. Pollard, mainly in the consideration of the fact that they would reach Richmond much sooner through him than through a semi-weekly mail. The papers which were thus handed over to the Confederate Government—I state it again—were correctly copies by the Richmond newspapers.
>
> If Lieut. Pollard had made any alterations in the papers, these would have been detected by every one who read the papers before they were given to him, and afterwards read them in the newspapers. But all agree that they were correctly copied. In short, human testimony cannot establish any fact more fully than the fact that Col. Ulric Dahlgren was the author of the "Dahlgren Papers."[2]

Halbach was just one of many who saw the original documents and asserted their authenticity.

Maj. Gen. Fitzhugh Lee, who personally delivered them to Jefferson Davis, also weighed in. He observed that "what appeared in the Richmond papers of that period as the 'Dahlgren papers,' was correctly taken from the papers I carried in person to Mr. Davis; and that those papers were not added to or changed in the minutest particular, before they came into my possession, as far as I know and believe; and that, from all the facts in my possession, I have every reason to believe they were taken from the body of Colonel Ulric Dahlgren, and came to me without alteration of any kind."[3]

Confederate Secretary of State Judah P. Benjamin, who was meeting with Davis when Fitz Lee delivered the Dahlgren Papers to the Confederate White House, also vouched for their authenticity. Benjamin and Davis read the documents together that day, and Benjamin believed that "exact copies were furnished to the Richmond journals for publication. I am, therefore, able to vouch personally for the fact that the passage as to the killing of the President and Cabinet existed in the original, and the photographic copy leaves no room for doubt upon the point."[4]

Col. Richard L. T. Beale, the commander of the 9th Virginia Cavalry, who had possession of Dahlgren's pocket notebook for a time before turning it over to the Confederate government, sent it on with the following note:

> The book, amongst other memoranda, contains a rough pencil sketch of his address to his troops, differing somewhat from his pen-and-ink copy. I embrace this occasion to add, the original papers bore no marks of alteration, nor could they possibly have been changed except by the courier who brought them to me, which is in the highest degree improbable, and the publication of them in the Richmond papers were exact copies in every respect of the originals.[5]

Thus, the chain of custody appears complete and unbroken. All of the people who had actual possession of the documents vouched for the veracity of what the Richmond newspapers reported. They also demonstrate that there was little, if any at all, opportunity for anyone to tamper with or otherwise modify the documents. It appears, therefore, that the newspaper accounts were accurate and complete.

Nevertheless, numerous Northerners disputed the validity of the documents. Most focused on the misspelling of Dahlgren's last name. For years, the issue of the spelling of Dahlgren's name remained a mystery. Lt. Gen. Jubal A. Early, who had a photographic copy of the Dahlgren Papers in his possession, was intrigued by the controversy. In 1879, Early solved the mystery of the misspelling of the name. He realized that the paper upon which these documents was written was so thin that the writing on one side of the page could plainly be seen from the reverse side. If he used a mirror, Early discovered that he could read the reverse writing. He realized that the tail of the "y" in the word "destroying" on the first page came through at the right point and right angle to make it appear that they letter "l" came before the letter "h" in the signature on the reverse side.[6]

In May 1958, historian Virgil Carrington Jones engaged the services of a police handwriting expert to review the photographic copies of the Dahlgren Papers against known examples of Ulric Dahlgren's handwriting. Ira N. Gullickson, the handwriting expert retained by Jones, wrote a report. "After making an examination and comparison of the questioned writing with the standards, it is my opinion that these reproductions, which were made from reproductions of the original, show conclusively more than normally required evidence to establish the genuineness of the questioned original."

Gullickson noted that for the documents to have been forged, three things would have had to have happened. First, the forger would have had to have had access to the official stationery of the Third Cavalry Division of the Army of the Potomac. Second, the forger would have had to have possessed extensive examples of Dahlgren's handwriting available to copy. Third, the forger would have had to have been intimately familiar with—and able to reproduce—Ulric Dahlgren's handwriting. Gullickson did not believe it possible for these unlikely events to have converged, and probably for good reason.

Finally, Gullickson confirmed Early's theory regarding the misspelling of Dahlgren's name. "Referring to Exhibit No. 4, the infrared reproduction of the document, this exhibit explains and proves itself insofar as the misspelling of the name 'Dahlgren,'" Gullickson wrote. "It completely illustrates a condition which undoubtedly occurred due to the type of paper and the pen and ink used. The paper was very thin and quite absorbent and the ink very penetrating. Therefore, the tail of the 'y' in the word 'destroying' on the front side of the document penetrated the paper creating an allusion at the signature misspelling the name 'Dahlgren.'"

He addressed the issue of forgery. "There is nothing in the questioned document that can be pointed to as indicative of forgery, such as tremor or line-quality found in copying. There is no appearance of copying, patching, or repairing, therefore, I can arrive at but one conclusion, that the questioned document was written in its entirety by Ulric Dahlgren, Col. Commanding." Gullickson concluded strongly. "To reiterate, it is my opinion that the questioned document is genuine and not a skillfully or carefully prepared forgery," he declared.[7]

As for the use of the initial "U." as opposed to writing out the name "Ulric," it was an extremely common practice for officers to sign official military correspondence with their first initials and then their whole last name during the Civil War; the U. S. Navy still employs that practice today. A review of any volume of the Official Records demonstrates that such was the case beyond any possible dispute. Ully Dahlgren, who was by then fully indoctrinated as a soldier, would have followed ordinary Army protocol if he had signed the orders to his men with his initial and not his whole first name; had he done so, he would have been very much an exception and not the rule for serving Army officers in 1864. Thus, while Admiral Dahlgren may have encouraged his son to sign his entire name—which he did in personal correspondence—it would have been a real anomaly for him to do so on his official military correspondence by 1864.

However, in the interest of fairness, it bears noting that Dahlgren's proposal for a raid on Richmond in May 1863, which appears in volume 25 of the Official Records, was signed, "Ulric Dahlgren, Captain and Aide-de-Camp."[8] This supports Admiral Dahlgren's contention that Ulric only signed things with his full name. However, and as pointed out above, his doing so would be inconsistent with normal usage and protocol among serving Army officers in 1863. Once promoted to colonel, it would be a surprise if Dahlgren did not sign documents consistent with normal protocol for a senior field-grade officer.

In 1983, historian James O. Hall published an important article on the validity of the Dahlgren Papers in Civil War Times Illustrated magazine. Hall, who was a student of the conspiracy that led to the Lincoln assassination, devoted years to the study and evaluation of the Dahlgren Papers. Hall pointed out that "it is easy to see what happened" with the "transposed" letters. "To obtain a clean copy, the lithographic technician was forced to touch up bad spots," he wrote. "To complicate this, it was decided to move the last six lines, with the signature and designation of rank, to the bottom of the second page of the lithographic copy. This simplified things greatly as the whole text could then be reproduced on a single wide sheet containing two pages, side by side." However, the lithographic technician was not familiar with the name "Dahlgren", so that when he touched up the document, it made it appear that the name was actually spelled "Dalhgren."[9] That explanation makes sense, and is entirely consistent with the findings of General Early and Gullickson.

Therefore, in spite of Admiral Dahlgren's vehement efforts to protect his son's legacy and reputation, it appears that the Dahlgren Papers were, in fact, authentic documents written by Ulric Dahlgren.

Like so many other things associated with the Kilpatrick-Dahlgren Raid, the fate of the Dahlgren Papers themselves remains a mystery lost to the ages. When the Confederate leadership abandoned Richmond on April 2, 1865, they took the Confederate archives with them in an effort to protect them. After Gen. Joseph E. Johnston surrendered his army in North Carolina a few weeks later, he told the Federal authorities where to find the contents of the archives, and U. S. authorities took possession of the documents on May 16, 1865. Dr. Francis Lieber, head of a bureau in the office of the adjutant general, took custody of the documents for eventual publication and inclusion in the National Archives.

In November of that same year, Secretary Stanton ordered Dr. Lieber to turn over the Dahlgren Papers to him. Dr. Lieber responded on December 1, surrendering possession of four packages associated with the Dahlgren Papers, including Dahlgren's notebook, the address to his men, a letter to Dahlgren marked "confidential," and supporting documents gathered by the Confederate government to authenticate the documents found on Dahlgren's body. These four packages then disappeared. There is no record of them remaining anywhere. When the official records of the Civil War were being compiled, the compilers made a request for them. In 1879, that request, directed to Adjutant General Edward Townsend, came back endorsed "No record is found upon the War Department books or files of the papers herein referred to." Thus, once Edwin Stanton took possession of the Dahlgren Papers in November 1865, they vanished. There has been no record of them since, other than one set of photographic copies in the National Archives (the ones sent to Meade by Lee) and a second photographic copy that later surfaced in the Virginia Historical Society in 1975, as well as the accounts of them published in the Richmond newspapers in 1864.[10]

It is, of course, pure speculation as to what might have happened to them. Today, we know that they were authentic, and that they vanished for reasons that have never been stated or otherwise ascertained. History has suffered for their loss.

Present-Day Maps

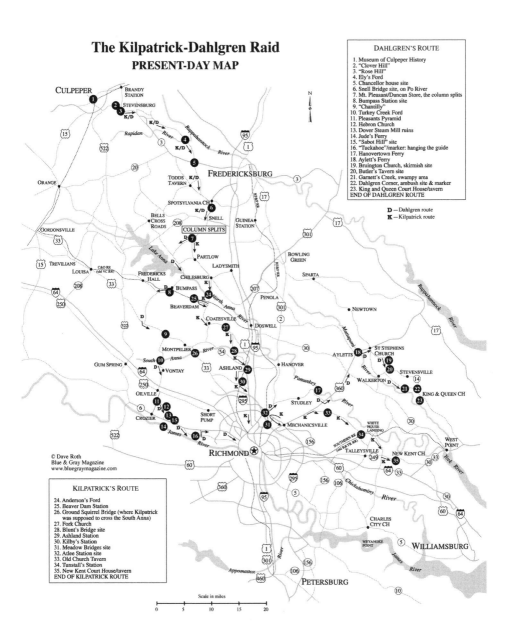

The Kilpatrick-Dahlgren Raid
PRESENT-DAY MAP

DAHLGREN'S ROUTE

1. Museum of Culpeper History
2. "Clover Hill"
3. "Rose Hill"
4. Ely's Ford
5. Chancellor house site
6. Snell Bridge site, on Po River
7. Mt. Pleasant/Duncan Store, the column splits
8. Bumpass Station site
9. "Chantilly"
10. Turkey Creek Ford
11. Pleasants Pyramid
12. Hebron Church
13. Dover Steam Mill ruins
14. Jude's Ferry
15. "Sabot Hill" site
16. "Tuckahoe"/marker: hanging the guide
17. Hanovertown Ferry
18. Aylett's Ferry
19. Bruington Church, skirmish site
20. Butler's Tavern site
21. Garnett's Creek, swampy area
22. Dahlgren Corner, ambush site & marker
23. King and Queen Court House/tavern
END OF DAHLGREN ROUTE

D – Dahlgren route
K – Kilpatrick route

© Dave Roth
Blue & Gray Magazine
www.bluegraymagazine.com

KILPATRICK'S ROUTE

24. Anderson's Ford
25. Beaver Dam Station
26. Ground Squirrel Bridge (where Kilpatrick was supposed to cross the South Anna)
27. Fork Church
28. Blunt's Bridge site
29. Ashland Station
30. Kilby's Station
31. Meadow Bridges site
32. Atlee Station site
33. Old Church Tavern
34. Tunstall's Station
35. New Kent Court House/tavern
END OF KILPATRICK ROUTE

Scale in miles
0   5   10   15   20

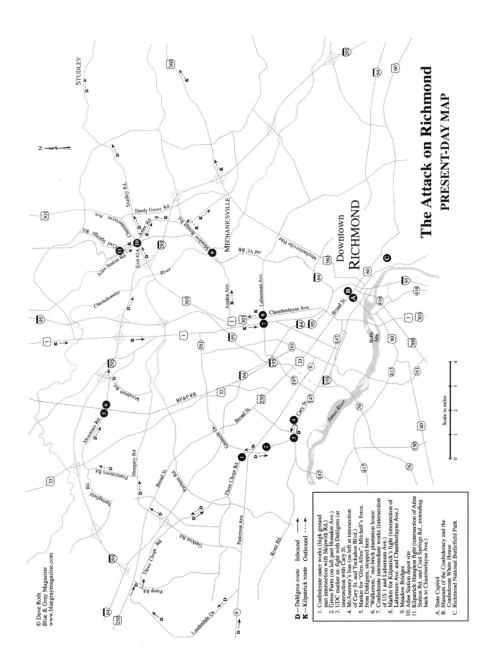

The Attack on Richmond
PRESENT-DAY MAP

STUDLEY

N

MECHANICSVILLE

Shady Grove Rd.
Studley Rd.
Cool Springs Rd.
Chamberlayne Ave.
Exit 41A
Atlee Rd.
Atlee Station Rd.
Meadow Bridge Rd.
Chickahominy River

Azalea Ave.
Laburnum Ave.
Chamberlayne Ave.
old VC RR
Mechanicsville Pike

Downtown
RICHMOND

Belle Isle

Mountain Rd.
Hungary Rd.
Francistown Rd.
Springfield Rd.
Woodman Rd.
RF&P RR
Broad St.
Glenside Dr.
Gaskins Rd.
Patterson Ave.
Three Chopt Rd.
Pump Rd.
Lauderdale Dr.
River Rd.
Cary St.
James River

© Dave Roth
Blue & Gray Magazine
www.bluegraymagazine.com

D — Dahlgren route   Inbound ———
K — Kilpatrick route   Outbound - - - - -

1. Confederate outer works (high ground past intersection with Skipwith Rd.)
2. Green Farm (on left past Honaker Ave.)
3. UDC marker re: fight with Dahlgren (at intersection with Cary St.
4. McAnerney's line (on left at intersection of Cary St. and Tuckahoe Blvd.)
5. Marker for "Glen Allen"; Mitchell's force, from Dahlgren, stopped here
6. "Walkerton," red-brick plantation house
7. Confederate intermediate works (intersection of US 1 and Laburnum Ave.)
8. Marker for Kilpatrick's fight (intersection of Laburnum Ave. and Chamberlayne Ave.)
9. Meadow Bridges
10. Atlee Station depot site
11. Kilpatrick-Hampton fight (intersection of Atlee Station Rd. and Cool Springs Rd., extending back to Chamberlayne Ave.)

A. State Capitol
B. Museum of the Confederacy and the Confederate White House
C. Richmond National Battlefield Park

Scale in miles
0   1   2   3   4

Notes

CHAPTER ONE

1 Rev. Byron Sunderland, *A Sermon in Memory of Colonel Ulric Dahlgren, Delivered in the First Presbyterian Church, Washington, D. C., Sabbath Evening, April 24, 1864* (Washington, D.C.: McGill & Witherow, 1864), 6.

2 *Ibid.*

3 Genealogy of the Dahlgren Family, Dahlgren Family Papers 1818-1934, Tennessee State Library and Archives, Nashville, Tennessee.

4 Dahlgren, *Memoir of John A. Dahlgren*, 5-6.

5 *Ibid.*, 6.

6 *Ibid.*, 6-7. When Rear Admiral John A. Dahlgren's memoir of Ulric's life was published posthumously in 1872, Sir Johan Adolph translated the work and re-published it in Swedish. Like his father and grandfather, Sir Johan Adolph was a man of letters and of great intellect.

7 *Ibid.*, 7.

8 For an early but detailed discussion of the influence of the Swedes on the eastern portion of the United States, see Jehu Curtis Clay, *Annals of the Swedes on the Delaware* (Philadelphia: J. C. Pechin, 1835).

9 As the early center for Swedish culture in North America, it makes sense that the American Swedish Historical Museum is located in Philadelphia. Its collections were an important resource for the writing of this book.

10 Rev. John Craig Roak, *An Historical Sketch of Gloria Dei Church (Old Swedes') Philadelphia: Oldest Church in Pennsylvania* (Privately published, 1947), 15.

11 Herschel Gower, *Charles Dahlgren of Natchez: The Civil War and Dynastic Decline* (Washington, D. C.: Brassey's, 2002), 5. Napoleon did not place Count Bernadotte on the Swedish throne. Rather, the Swedish parliament did that, not realizing that Napoleon and Bernadotte were in fact not friends at all.

12 "List of Papers Delivered to B. Dahlgren," folder 7, box 11, General John Cadwalader Section, Cadwalader Family Papers, Historical Society of Pennsylvania, Philadelphia ("HSP"); Petition for bridge over the Susquehanna, November 29, 1810, folder 2, box 4b, "Petitions," Society Miscellaneous Collections, HSP.

13 Dahlgren, *Memoir of John A. Dahlgren*, 7-8.

14 Robert J. Schneller, *A Quest for Glory: A Biography of Rear Admiral John A. Dahlgren* (Annapolis: Naval Institute Press, 1996), 4.

15 Affidavit of Jane Rowan, included in Revolutionary War Pension and Bounty Land Warrant Application Files, 1800-1900, M804, Reel 2901, The David Library of the American Revolution, Washington's Crossing, Pennsylvania.

16 Gower, *Charles Dahlgren*, 5.

17 The de Rohans were a family of viscounts, later dukes and princes, coming from the locality of Rohan in Brittany. The family was descended from the viscounts of Porhoët

and said to trace back to Conan Meriadoc, and also traced their lineage to the Dukes of Brittany, with whom the family intermingled again in after its inception. The de Rohans developed close ties with the French and English royal houses, and played an important role in French and European history.

18 Dahlgren, *Memoir of John A. Dahlgren*, 8.

19 *Ibid.*, 9.

20 Quoted in Schneller, *A Quest for Glory*, 5.

21 Gloria Dei Church is the oldest church in Pennsylvania, dating back to 1700. The congregation was originally founded in 1646. It remains an active congregation today, and is a National Historic Site under the protection of the National Park Service. It is part of the Independence National Historical Park in downtown Philadelphia. In 1845, it became affiliated with the Episcopal Church. It still retains the affectionate nickname "Old Swedes Church." See Roak, *An Historical Sketch*, for a brief history of the church.

22 Dahlgren, *Memoir of John A. Dahlgren*, 8.

23 *Ibid.*, 12.

24 Schneller, *A Quest for Glory*, 10.

25 *Ibid.*, 11.

26 Dahlgren, *Memoir of John A. Dahlgren*, 70-75.

27 Diary of John A. Dahlgren, entry for April 1, 1844, John A. Dahlgren Papers, Manuscripts Division, Library of Congress, Washington, D. C.

28 Dahlgren to Mary Bunker Dahlgren, February 2, 1845, Dahlgren Papers, LOC.

29 Dahlgren, *Memoir of John A. Dahlgren*, 79-80. John Dahlgren maintained regular diaries of his farming activities that paint a clear picture of just how much he enjoyed farming.

30 Ann Pollock, "Hartsville Yesterday and Today," *Bucks County Life Past and Present*, Vol. 1, No. 5 (May 1961), 26.

31 Alice Jones, "Hartsville Civil War Hero," *Panorama6 The Magazine of Bucks County*, Vol. 8, No. 1 (January 1971), 4. The old house no longer stands. It was torn down in the 1990's to make way for a strip shopping center. Its address was 85 Bristol Road, Warwick Township, Bucks County, Pennsylvania.

32 Schneller, *A Quest for Glory*, 37.

33 Dahlgren, *Memoir of John A. Dahlgren*, 170-71.

34 John A. Dahlgren, *Memoir of Ulric Dahlgren* (Philadelphia: J. B. Lippincott, 1872), 17-18.

35 John and Mary Dahlgren later named two of their sons Paul and Lawrence in honor of their uncles.

36 Schneller, *A Quest for Glory*, 44.

37 Charles Bunker Dahlgren followed his father into the Navy. He became a Master's Mate by appointment of Capt. Charles Wilkes on the *U.S.S. San Jacinto* in September 1861. Three months later, he was promoted to Third Assistant Engineer, and in December 1862, he was promoted to Acting Ensign. He was promoted to Master on May 14, 1863, and served in that role for the rest of the Civil War. Charles took part in the capture of New Orleans and in the initial attacks on Vicksburg, and then served under his father as fleet ordnance officer in the Atlantic Blockading Squadron, and also served as executive officer on the steamship *U.S.S. Gettysburg*, which participated in the assaults on Fort Fisher. Although he was offered a commission as lieutenant in the regular service, he resigned his commission on April 1, 1865, and moved west, where he spent

the rest of his life in the mining industry. When his son was born on December 27, 1870, Charles named him Ulric in memory of his dead uncle. See MOLLUS-Pennsylvania, Commandery Scrapbook Vol. 43, Insignia Record No. 1866, Civil War Museum and Library, Philadelphia and *Philadelphia Public Ledger*, January 11, 1912.

38 Dahlgren, *Memoir of Ulric Dahlgren*, 11.

39 Sunderland, *A Sermon in Memory of Colonel Ulric Dahlgren*, 6.

40 Schneller, *A Quest for Glory*, 45. Unfortunately, this letter foreshadowed further heartbreak and suffering yet to come with Ully's untimely death in March 1864.

41 *Ibid.*

42 Dahlgren, *Memoir of Ulric Dahlgren*, 12.

43 Sunderland, *A Sermon in Memory of Colonel Ulric Dahlgren*, 6.

44 Dahlgren, *Memoir of Ulric Dahlgren*, 12.

45 Dahlgren, *Memoir of John A. Dahlgren*, 132.

46 *Ibid*; Sunderland, *A Sermon in Memory of Colonel Ulric Dahlgren*, 7.

47 Dahlgren, *Memoir of Ulric Dahlgren*, 13.

CHAPTER TWO

1 Dahlgren, *Memoir of John A. Dahlgren*, 177.

2 *Ibid.*

3 *Ibid.*, 134-5.

4 *Ibid.*, 153.

5 *Ibid.*, 173.

6 Carl Abbott, *Political Terrain: Washington, D.C., from Tidewater Town to Global Metropolis* (Chapel Hill: University of North Carolina Press, 1999), 52 and 56.

7 *Ibid.*, 67.

8 Madeleine Vinton Dahlgren, *Etiquette of Social Life in Washington* (Washington, D. C.: n.p., 1873), 4.

9 Dahlgren, *Memoir of Ulric Dahlgren*, 13-14.

10 John A. Dahlgren to Epes Sargent, August 22, 1864, John A. Dahlgren Papers, Special Collections, Augustana College, Rock Island, Illinois.

11 Sunderland, *A Sermon in Memory of Colonel Ulric Dahlgren*, 7.

12 Dahlgren, *Memoir of Ulric Dahlgren*, 14-15.

13 Obviously, a detailed discussion of the far-reaching implications of the Crisis of 1850 and the compromise that resolved it goes far beyond the scope of this work. Readers interested in additional reading on this critical period of American history should see John C. Waugh, *On the Brink of Civil War: The Compromise of 1850 and How It Changed the Course of American History* (Wilmington, Del.: Scholarly Resources, 2003).

14 Dahlgren, *Memoir of Ulric Dahlgren*, 16.

15 *Ibid.*, 16-17.

16 Dahlgren to Sargent, August 22, 1864.

17 Dahlgren, *Memoir of Ulric Dahlgren*, 17.

18 *Ibid.*

19 *Ibid.*, 18.

20 *Ibid.*, 23.

21 Schneller, *A Quest for Glory*, 134.

22 John Dahlgren diary, entry for June 6, 1855, Dahlgren Papers.

23 Dahlgren, *Memoir of Ulric Dahlgren*, 18.

24 Schneller, *A Quest for Glory*, 135.

25 Ulric Dahlgren to Aunt Sallie and Uncle Abbott, November 8, 1855, John A. Dahlgren Papers, Special Collections and Research Center, Syracuse University, Syracuse, New York.

26 Sunderland, *A Sermon in Memory of Colonel Ulric Dahlgren*, 9.

27 *Circular of the Rittenhouse Academy, Corner of Third Street and Indiana Avenue, Washington City. Otis C. Wight, Proprietor and Principal* (Washington, D.C.: Towers, 1858), 13.

28 *Ibid.*, 5-8.

29 Sunderland, *A Sermon in Memory of Colonel Ulric Dahlgren*, 10.

30 *Ibid.*

31 *Circular of the Rittenhouse Academy*, 8-9.

32 Michael W. Kauffman, "David Edgar Herold: The Forgotten Conspirator," *The Surratt Society News* (November 1981), 23-24; Edward Steers, Jr., *Blood on the Moon: The Assassination of Abraham Lincoln* (Lexington: The University Press of Kentucky, 2001), 81-82.

33 Sunderland, *A Sermon in Memory of Colonel Ulric Dahlgren*, 11.

34 Dahlgren, *Memoir of Ulric Dahlgren*, 15.

35 Sunderland, *A Sermon in Memory of Colonel Ulric Dahlgren*, 11.

36 Fortunately, John Dahlgren compulsively kept all of his correspondence, and so did Ulric. Their letters survive and are available to researchers and interested readers. These letters can be found among the thousands of pages of John Dahlgren's papers that were donated to the Library of Congress after the admiral's death in 1872.

37 Dahlgren, *Memoir of Ulric Dahlgren*, 18-19.

38 John A. Dahlgren to Patty Read, June 3, 1858, John A. Dahlgren Papers, Archives, Newberry Library, Chicago, Illinois.

39 Dahlgren, *Memoir of Ulric Dahlgren*, 20.

40 For an excellent treatment of the life of Charles Dahlgren, see Herschel Gower, *Charles Dahlgren of Natchez: The Civil War and Dynastic Decline* (Washington, D.C.: Brassey's, 2002).

41 Ulric Dahlgren to his father, July 1 and November 10, 1859, Dahlgren Papers, LOC.

42 Dahlgren, *Memoir of Ulric Dahlgren*, 21.

43 Ulric Dahlgren to his father, November 22, 1859, Dahlgren Papers, LOC. On January 1, 1860, Ully reported to his father, "I am here with Charlie and the boys who spent the week with us. We hunted all this week and killed four deer, one weight 205 lbs. cleaned. Charlie killed two and I two."

44 *Ibid.*, May 19, 1859.

45 *Ibid.*, June 21, 1859.

46 *Ibid.*, August 12, 1859.

47 *Ibid.*

48 *Ibid.*, June 5, 1859.

49 Sunderland, *A Sermon in the Memory of Colonel Ulric Dahlgren*, 12.

50 Dahlgren, *Memoir of Ulric Dahlgren*, 22.

51 John A. Dahlgren to Ulric Dahlgren, February 20, 1860, Dahlgren Papers, Newberry Library.

52 Dahlgren, *Memoir of Ulric Dahlgren*, 25.

53 Ulric Dahlgren to his father, no date, 1860, Dahlgren Papers, LOC.

54 Ulric Dahlgren to Dear Frank, May 3, 1860, Simon Gratz Collection, Union Colonels ALS, Historical Society of Pennsylvania, Philadelphia, Pennsylvania.

55 Gower, *Charles Dahlgren of Natchez*, 35.

56 Ulric Dahlgren to Dear Frank, May 3, 1860.

57 The photograph is part of the Matthew Brady collection housed in the National Archives and Records Administration. NAIL Control Number NWDNS-111-B-4725, RG 111, Records of the Office of the Chief Signal Officer, 1860-1982, NARA II, College Park, Maryland.

58 John A. Dahlgren to Ulric Dahlgren, November 26, 1860, Dahlgren Papers, LOC.

59 Dahlgren, *Memoir of Ulric Dahlgren*, 26.

60 Gower, *Charles Dahlgren of Natchez*, 38.

61 *Ibid.*, 38-9.

62 Ulric Dahlgren to his father, October 2 and October 6, 1860, Dahlgren Papers, LOC.

63 Dahlgren, *Memoir of Ulric Dahlgren*, 27.

64 John A. Dahlgren to Ulric Dahlgren, December 18, 1860, Dahlgren Papers, LOC.

65 Sunderland, *A Sermon in the Memory of Colonel Ulric Dahlgren*, 14.

66 Ulric Dahlgren to his father, October 19, 1860, Dahlgren Papers, LOC.

67 *Ibid.*, November 3, 1860.

68 Dahlgren, *Memoir of Ulric Dahlgren*, 28.

69 John A. Dahlgren to Ulric Dahlgren, December 18, 1860, Dahlgren Papers, LOC.

70 *Ibid*, December 20, 1860.

71 *Ibid.*, December 24, 1860.

72 *Ibid.*

73 Sunderland, *A Sermon in the Memory of Colonel Ulric Dahlgren*, 15.

74 Dahlgren, *Memoir of Ulric Dahlgren*, 29.

CHAPTER THREE

1 *Ibid.*, January 12, 1861.

2 *Ibid.*

3 *Ibid.*, January 20, 1861.

4 *Ibid.*

5 *Ibid.*, January 26, 1861.

6 *Ibid.*, February 11, 1861.

7 Gower, *Charles Dahlgren*, 43-45.

8 Ulric Dahlgren to his father, March 12, 1861, Dahlgren Papers, LOC.

9 Dahlgren, *Memoir of Ulric Dahlgren*, 30.

10 Ulric Dahlgren to his father, February 26, 1861, Dahlgren Papers, LOC.

11 For a detailed discussion of the events that led to coming of war, see David Detzer, *Allegiance: Fort Sumter, Charleston, and the Beginning of the Civil War* (New York, Harcourt, 2001) and Maury Klein, *Days of Defiance: Sumter, Secession, and the Coming of the Civil War* (New York: Vintage Books, 1997).

12 Ulric Dahlgren to his father, March 4, 1861, Dahlgren Papers, LOC.

13 E. Milby Burton, *The Siege of Charleston 1861-1865* (Columbia: University of South Carolina Press, 1970), 42-51.

14 Schneller, *Quest for Glory*, 180.

15 Dahlgren, *Memoir of Ulric Dahlgren*, 35.

16 John Dahlgren diary, entry for June 9, 1861, Dahlgren Papers, LOC.

17 Schneller, *Quest for Glory*, 186-189.

18 John A. Dahlgren to Ulric Dahlgren, June 16, 1861, Dahlgren Papers, LOC.

19 Dahlgren, *Memoir of Ulric Dahlgren*, 39.

20 *Ibid.*, 42-3.

21 Taylor Peck, *Round Shot to Rockets: A History of the Washington Navy Yard and U. S. Naval Gun Factory* (Annapolis: United States Naval Institute Press, 1949), 127.

22 Dahlgren, *Memoir of Ulric Dahlgren*, 45-47.

23 *Ibid.*, 48-49.

24 Ulric Dahlgren to his father, September 5, 1861, Dahlgren Papers, LOC.

25 Dahlgren, *Memoir of Ulric Dahlgren*, 50. Prince Napoleon was a grandson of Emperor Napoleon's younger brother, Lucien.

26 *Ibid.*, 51.

27 *Ibid.*; Ulric Dahlgren to his father, September 19, 1861, Dahlgren Papers, LOC.

28 John F. Frazer, ed., *Journal of the Franklin Institute of the State of Pennsylvania, for the Promotion of the Mechanic Arts. Devoted to Mechanical and Physical Science, Civil Engineering, the Arts and Manufactures*, 3rd Series, Vol. 42 (Philadelphia: Published by the Franklin Institute, 1861), 283-285. Capt. James H. Ward was mortally wounded while aiming *U.S.S. Thomas Freeborn*'s bow gun in an engagement with Confederate forces at Mathias Point on the Maryland side of the Potomac River. He was the first U.S. Navy officer killed in action during the Civil War.

29 Ulric Dahlgren to his father, September 19, 1861, Dahlgren Papers, LOC.

30 Dahlgren, *Memoir of Ulric Dahlgren*, 51-52.

31 John A. Dahlgren to Ulric Dahlgren, November 2, 1861, Dahlgren Papers, LOC.

32 Sunderland, *A Sermon in Memory of Colonel Ulric Dahlgren*, 15.

33 Ulric Dahlgren to his father, November 15, 1861, Dahlgren Papers, LOC.

34 *Ibid.*, February 5, 1862. A few days later, his father responded. "Seven times a minute is doing very well, but do not attempt to accomplish that number when you commence to load in earnest," instructed John Dahlgren. "Let the rapidity of your practice be gradual then, and every movement performed with coolness and care—the coolness of the man at the lockstring being the most essential." John A. Dahlgren to Ulric Dahlgren, February 13, 1862, Dahlgren Papers, LOC.

35 *Ibid.*; John D. Brandt to Ulric Dahlgren, February 6, 1862, Dahlgren Papers, LOC. Augustus Pleasonton was the older brother of General Alfred Pleasonton, who later commanded the Army of the Potomac's Cavalry Corps. Ulric Dahlgren briefly served on Alfred Pleasonton's staff in the spring of 1863.

36 Dahlgren, *Memoir of Ulric Dahlgren*, 52.

37 John A. Dahlgren to Ulric Dahlgren, January 11, 1862, Dahlgren Papers, LOC.

38 Dahlgren, *Memoir of Ulric Dahlgren*, 54.

39 *Ibid.*

40 John A. Dahlgren to Ulric Dahlgren, March 11, 1862, Dahlgren Papers, LOC.

41 For a detailed discussion of these events and of the impact that the crisis caused by the arrival of the *Virginia* on the scene, see Schneller, *A Quest for Glory*, 190-216.

42 Dahlgren, *Memoir of John A. Dahlgren*, 364.

43 *Ibid.*, 366.
44 Sunderland, *A Sermon in Memory of Colonel Ulric Dahlgren*, 16.
45 Dahlgren, *Memoir of Ulric Dahlgren*, 55.

CHAPTER FOUR
12 *Ibid.*, 55-56.
3 Quoted in Schneller, *Quest for Glory*, 215.
4 Dahlgren, *Memoir of Ulric Dahlgren*, 56-57.
5 Robert G. Tanner, *Stonewall in the Valley: Thomas J. Stonewall Jackson's Shenandoah Valley Campaign, Spring 1862* (Mechanicsburg, Pa.: Stackpole, 1996), 264.
6 William Allen, *History of the Campaign of Gen. T. J. (Stonewall) Jackson in the Shenandoah Valley of Virginia: From November 4, 1861, to June 17, 1862* (Philadelphia: J. B. Lippincott & Co., 1880), 153.
7 James J. Gillette Papers and letters. Washington D.C.: Library of Congress. (Taken from *Voices of the Civil War: Shenandoah 1862*, Editors of Time-Life Books, Alexandria, Virginia pg. 113.
8 F. A. Parker to Gustavus V. Fox, May 25, 1862, Microfilm Group 625 Reel 18, Naval Records Collection, Records for Area 7, May-June 1862 ("Harpers Ferry Naval Records").
9 Gustavus F. Fox to John A. Dahlgren, May 25, 1862, Harpers Ferry Naval Records; Edward W. Callahan, *List of Officers of the Navy of the United States and the Marine Corps* (New York: L.R. Hamersly & Co., 1901), 148. Secretary Stanton also offered John Dahlgren the position of Chief of Artillery for the Army if the Navy Department would permit it. However, Secretary of the Navy Gideon Welles refused to release Dahlgren from any position other than as commandant of the Navy Yard, and but left the final decision to Lincoln. Lincoln favored the idea until Undersecretary of the Navy Gustavus V. Fox called upon him and persuaded the President to leave Dahlgren at the Navy Yard. The idea was then dropped. Peck, *Round-Shot to Rockets*, 143.
10 Dahlgren, *Memoir of Ulric Dahlgren*, 58-59.
11 Charles H. Daniels to Commissioner of Pensions, June 19, 1891, Charles H. Daniels Pension File, M1469, certificate #20175, fiche #19434, NARA. Daniels later claimed that the roar of the explosion caused him to go deaf in one ear.
12 F. A. Parker to Gustavus V. Fox, May 25, 1862, Harpers Ferry Naval Records.
13 Charles H. Daniels midshipman file, Archives, United States Naval Academy, Annapolis, Maryland; United States Bureau of Naval Personnel, *Register of Commissioned and Warrant Officers of the United States Navy and Marine Corps* (Washington: U. S. Government Printing Office, 1859-1867) and United States Naval Academy Alumni Association, Inc., *Register of Alumni, Graduates and Former Naval Cadets and Midshipmen* (Annapolis, Md.: United States Naval Academy Alumni Association, Inc., 2003). Although Daniels leaves our story at this point, the mystery surrounding his actions continues. Shortly after his successes at Harpers Ferry, he resigned as Acting Master on July 22, 1862 to accept an at large appointment as a second lieutenant in the United States Marine Corps. In 1863, he was stationed in California, and later performed good service as part of Admiral Dahlgren's Atlantic Blockading Squadron. In 1868, he was promoted to first lieutenant, and then disappeared from the Marine Corps records. Nothing further is known of his life or service. *Ibid.* See, also, Charles H. Daniels pension file.

14 Ezra J. Warner, *Generals in Blue* (Baton Rouge: Louisiana State University Press, 1964), 420-21.

15 O. R. vol. 12, part 1, 639.

16 *Philadelphia Press*, June 9, 1862.

17 Allen, *Stonewall Jackson's Campaign*, 154.

18 Dahlgren, *Memoir of Ulric Dahlgren*, 60.

19 C. H. Daniels to John A. Dahlgren, May 27, 1862, Harpers Ferry Naval Records.

20 William Allen, "Stonewall Jackson's Valley Campaign," included in *Annals of the War: Written by Leading Participants North & South* (Reprint, Dayton, Ohio: Morningside, 1986), 741.

21 O. R. vol. 12, part 1, 634.

22 Ulric Dahlgren's narrative of the Harpers Ferry expedition, entry for May 28, 1862, Dahlgren Papers, LOC.

23 Dahlgren, *Memoir of John A. Dahlgren*, 371.

24 *Ibid.*

25 Ulric Dahlgren's narrative of the Harpers Ferry expedition, entry for May 29, 1862.

26 Dahlgren, *Memoir of Ulric Dahlgren*, 63.

27 Dahlgren, *Memoir of John A. Dahlgren*, 371.

28 Ulric Dahlgren's narrative of the Harpers Ferry expedition, entry for May 30, 1862.

29 Sunderland, *A Sermon in Memory of Colonel Ulric Dahlgren*, 16.

30 *Philadelphia Press*, June 9, 1862.

31 Dahlgren, *Memoir of Ulric Dahlgren*, 64.

32 O. R. vol. 12, part 1, 641.

33 *Ibid.*, 640.

34 *Ibid.*, 638.

35 Ulric Dahlgren's narrative of the Harpers Ferry expedition, entry for May 31, 1862.

36 *Ibid.*

37 Ulric Dahlgren's narrative of the Harpers Ferry expedition, entry for May 31, 1862.

38 Ulric Dahlgren to his father, May 31, 1862, Dahlgren Papers, LOC.

39 John D. Imboden, "Stonewall Jackson in the Shenandoah," included in Robert U. Johnson and Clarence C. Buel, eds., *Battles and Leaders of the Civil War*, 4 vols. (New York: Century Publishing Co., 1884-1888), 289-290.

40 Allen, *Stonewall Jackson's Campaign*, 156.

41 O. R. vol. 12, part 1, 636.

42 Dahlgren to his father, May 31, 1862.

43 O. R. vol. 12, part 1, 641.

44 *New York Daily Tribune*, June 3, 1862. In fact, Saxton received a Medal of Honor in 1893 in recognition of his defense of Harpers Ferry against Jackson's army.

45 Ulric Dahlgren's narrative of the Harpers Ferry expedition, entry for June 1, 1862.

46 O. R. vol. 12, part 1, 641.

47 Dahlgren to his father, June 10, 1862, Dahlgren Papers, LOC.

48 *Ibid.*, May 31, 1862.

49 *Ibid.*

50 Dahlgren, *Memoir of Ulric Dahlgren*, 64-5.

51 Carl Schurz, *The Reminiscences of Carl Schurz*, 3 vols. (New York: The McClure Company, 1907), 3:348.

52 *Ibid.*, 349-350.

53 Warner, *Generals in Blue*, 447-48. For the only full-length biography of Franz Sigel, see Stephen D. Engle, *The Yankee Dutchman: The Life of Franz Sigel* (Fayetteville: University of Arkansas Press, 1993).

54 O. R. vol. 12, part 3, 323.

55 *Ibid.*, 369.

56 John C. Frémont was known as "The Pathfinder" for his good work in exploring and opening the American west, a duty to which he was well suited. Frémont was also the first presidential nominee of the nascent Republican Party, losing the 1856 election to James Buchanan. However, his military skills were suspect at best, and he was not well-liked within the military, which viewed him as an egotistical outsider. There is one scholarly biography of Frémont, but it contains exactly one paragraph on the spring of 1862, which is quite disappointing indeed. However, it does provide good insight into Frémont's character and has plenty of good information on Frémont's exploits in opening the west. See Tom Chaffin, *Pathfinder: John Charles Fremont and the Course of American Empire* (New York: Hill and Wang, 2002).

57 *Philadelphia Inquirer*, June 4, 1862.

58 Dahlgren to his father, June 4, 1862, Dahlgren Papers, LOC.

59 *Ibid.*

60 *Philadelphia Inquirer*, June 5, 1862.

61 Dahlgren, *Memoir of Ulric Dahlgren*, 67.

62 O. R. vol. 12, part 1, 814.

63 Dahlgren to his father, June 4, 1862.

64 For the most detailed treatment of the Battle of Port Republic yet written, see Robert K. Krick, *Conquering the Valley: Stonewall Jackson at Port Republic* (New York: Morrow, 1996).

65 Tanner, *Stonewall in the Valley*, 286-310.

66 Dahlgren to his father, June 10, 1862.

67 *Ibid.*

68 *Ibid.* The nomination, as captain and aide-de-camp, to Maj. Gen. John C. Frémont, as of May 29, 1862, was submitted to the Senate for its approval by Secretary Stanton on July 17, 1862. The Senate unanimously approved the nomination, which was one of dozens of similar ones. *Journal of the Executive Proceedings of the Senate of the United States of America*, 36th Congress, 2nd Session, July 17, 1862.

69 Dahlgren to his father, June 11, 1862, Dahlgren Papers, LOC.

70 John A. Dahlgren to Ulric Dahlgren, June 13, 1862, Dahlgren Papers, LOC.

71 Dahlgren to his father, June 15, 1862, Dahlgren Papers, LOC.

72 *Ibid.*, June 21, 1862, Harpers Ferry Naval Records.

73 John A. Dahlgren to Ulric Dahlgren, June 21, 1862, Harpers Ferry Naval Records.

74 Ulric Dahlgren to John A. Dahlgren, June 23, 1862, Dahlgren Papers, LOC.

75 Dahlgren, *Memoir of Ulric Dahlgren*, 68-9.

76 *Ibid.*, 69-70.

77 Sunderland, *A Sermon in Memory of Colonel Ulric Dahlgren*, 17.

78 Dahlgren to his father, June 23, 1862.

79 John A. Dahlgren to Ulric Dahlgren, June 24, 1862, Harpers Ferry Naval Records.

80 O. R. vol. 12, part 3, 435.

CHAPTER FIVE

12 Cozzens and Girardi, *The Military Memoirs of John Pope*, 114.

3 *Ibid.*, 127.

4 *Chicago Tribune*, June 30, 1862.

5 O. R. vol. 12, part 3, 444 and part 2, 54.

6 *Ibid.*, part 3, 473-74.

7 Engel, *The Yankee Dutchman*, 129.

8 Cozzens, *General John Pope*, 80.

9 O. R. vol. 12, part 3, 494. On July 21, Sigel reported that he had the following hodgepodge of artillery: 13 ten-pounder Parrotts, 8 six-pounder steel guns, 4 12-pounder steel guns, 4 12-pounder brass howitzers, 6 3-inch ordinance rifles, 10 6-pounder Napoleons, and six 12-pounder mountain howitzers.

10 Dahlgren diary, entry for July 3, 1862, Dahlgren Papers, LOC.

11 O. R. vol. 12, part 3, 455.

12 *Ibid.*, 469.

13 Dahlgren, *Memoir of John A. Dahlgren*, 376.

14 Dahlgren, *Memoir of Ulric Dahlgren*, 71.

15 Obviously, a detailed discussion of the Peninsula Campaign strays far beyond the scope of this book. For the best treatments of the topic yet published, see Stephen W. Sears, *To the Gates of Richmond: The Peninsula Campaign* (New York: Ticknor & Fields, 1992) for an overview of the entire campaign, and Brian K. Burton, *Extraordinary Circumstances: The Seven Days Battles* (Bloomington: Indiana University Press, 2001) for a detailed study of the Seven Days.

16 John J. Hennessy, *Return to Bull Run: The Campaign and Battle of Second Manassas* (New York: Simon & Schuster, 1993), 21-2. Hennessy's book is far and away the best treatment of this campaign yet written.

17 *Chicago Tribune*, July 23, 1862; Hennessy, *Return to Bull Run*, 24-25.

18 *New York Times*, August 2, 1862.

19 O. R. vol. 12, part 3, 527 and 536.

20 *New York Times*, August 12, 1862.

21 *Chicago Tribune*, August 12, 1862.

22 For a detailed tactical treatment of the Battle of Cedar Mountain, see Robert K. Krick, *Stonewall Jackson at Cedar Mountain* (Chapel Hill: University of North Carolina Press, 1990).

23 Ulric Dahlgren diary, entry for August 9, 1862.

24 Dahlgren, *Memoir of Ulric Dahlgren*, 74-76.

25 Hennessy, *Return to Bull Run*, 29.

26 *Chicago Tribune*, August 16, 1862.

27 O. R. vol. 12, part 3, 675.

28 William B. Styple, ed., *Writing and Fighting from the Army of Northern Virginia: A Collection of Confederate Soldier Correspondence* (Kearny, N. J.: Belle Grove Publishing, 2003), 137.

29 *New York Times*, August 18, 1862.

30 Hennessy, *Return to Bull Run*, 45-48.

31 *Chicago Tribune*, August 19, 1862.

32 *Ibid.*, August 23, 1862.

33 Hennessy, *Return to Bull Run*, 73.

34 Dahlgren to his father, August 26, 1862, Dahlgren Papers, LOC.

35 *Chicago Tribune*, August 26, 1862.

36 *Brooklyn Eagle*, September 1, 1862.

37 O. R. vol. 12, part 3, 627.

38 Hennessy, *Return to Bull Run*, 85.

39 Dahlgren to his father, August 26, 1862.

40 O. R. vol. 12, part 2, 706.

41 Styple, *Writing & Fighting from the Army of Northern Virginia*, 140.

42 Franz Sigel to John A. Dahlgren, quoted in Dahlgren, *Memoir of Ulric Dahlgren*, 78-79.

43 Hennessy, *Return to Bull Run*, 104-105.

44 O. R. vol. 12, part 3, 653.

45 Quoted in Engel, *Yankee Dutchman*, 137.

46 O. R. vol. 12, part 2, 553 and part 3, 942.

47 Jackson's infantry was regularly referred to as "foot cavalry" in recognition of its ability to make long marches at a rapid rate of speed, often covering as much ground in a day as their comrades in the cavalry.

48 Dahlgren to his father, August 26, 1862.

49 *Ibid.*

50 Ulric Dahlgren to his father, August 27, 1862, Dahlgren Papers, LOC.

51 O. R. vol. 12, part 1, 159.

52 *Ibid.*, 160.

53 The specifics of the Battle of Brawner's Farm, which was the first large-scale engagement of the Union Iron Brigade, go far beyond the scope of this book, as Sigel's command was not engaged. For those interested in a book-length treatment of the vicious fight at Brawner's Farm from the Union perspective, see Alan D. Gaff, *Brave Men's Tears: The Iron Brigade at Brawner Farm* (Dayton, Ohio: Morningside, 1985).

54 Hennessy, *Return to Bull Run*, 153-161.

55 *Ibid.*, 195.

56 O. R. vol. 12, part 2, 279-80.

57 *Ibid.*, 670.

58 *Chicago Tribune*, September 4, 1862.

59 O. R. vol. 12, part 2, 671.

60 Hennessy, *Return to Bull Run*, 214-223.

61 In fact, Pope preferred court-martial charges against Porter for insubordination, and Porter was tried, convicted and cashiered from the Army as a surrogate for his friend, George B. McClellan. It took Porter years and a Presidential order for him to get a court of inquiry that cleared his name, and an act of Congress to be reinstated to his Regular Army rank, colonel. Obviously, the specifics of the Porter court-martial stray far beyond the scope of this book. For a detailed study of this injustice, see Curt Anders, *Injustice on Trial: Second Bull Run, General Fitz John Porter's Court Martial, and the Schofield Board Investigation That Restored His Good Name* (Zionsville, Ind.: Emmis Books, 2002).

62 Hennessy, *Back to Bull Run*, 328-330.

63 Styple, *Writing and Fighting from the Army of Northern Virginia*, 139.

64 William T. Lusk, *War Letters of William Thompson Lusk: Captain, Assistant Adjutant General, J. S. Volunteers, 1861-1865* (New York: privately published, 1911), 180-81.

65 Quoted in Dahlgren, *Memoir of Ulric Dahlgren*, 82.

66 *New York Times*, September 2, 1862.

67 O. R. vol. 12, part 2, 80.

68 *Ibid.*, 305-306.

69 *Ibid.*, 603-604.

70 *Ibid.*, 748.

71 For a detailed discussion of the Battle of Chantilly, see either David A. Welker, *Tempest at Ox Hill: The Battle of Chantilly* (New York: DaCapo, 2002) or Paul Taylor, *He Hath Loosed the Fateful Lightning: The Battle of Ox Hill (Chantilly), September 1, 1862* (Shippensburg, Pa: White Mane, 2003).

72 O. R. vol. 12, part 3, 797.

73 Engel, *The Yankee Dutchman*, 146.

74 Record of Charles B. Dahlgren, No. 9492, Military Order of the Loyal Legion of the United States, Pennsylvania Commandery, May 5, 1892, Civil War Museum and Library, Philadelphia, Pennsylvania.

75 Dahlgren, *Memoir of Ulric Dahlgren*, 83.

76 *Ibid.*, 253.

77 Sunderland, *A Sermon in Memory of Ulric Dahlgren*, 19.

CHAPTER SIX

1 *Ibid.*, 84-5.

2 *Ibid.*, 84-5.

3 O. R. vol. 19, part 1, 144 and part 2, 590-1.

4 For a more detailed discussion, see Jeffry D. Wert, *The Sword of Lincoln: The Army of the Potomac* (New York: Simon & Schuster, 2005), 142-148.

5 *Chicago Tribune*, September 10, 1862.

6 *Ibid.*, October 1, 1862.

7 A corps of observation, also sometimes called a *corps d'observation*, is a force of indeterminate size and strength that is placed in an advanced position for the purpose of watching the actions of the enemy, as suggested by the name itself. It is to hold its position and not attempt to conquer additional territory, and is to retreat in the event of a full-scale attack by the enemy. A Napoleonic historian gives this definition: "*Corps D'observation* - formation detached from the main army to protect its line of march, watch or cover a minor enemy formation. Used in secondary roles." David Chandler, *The Campaigns of Napoleon* (New York: Macmillan, 1966), 1148.

8 *New York Times*, September 29, 1862.

9 Dahlgren, *Memoir of Ulric Dahlgren*, 87.

10 Styple, *Writing & Fighting from the Army of Northern Virginia*, 154.

11 Obviously, the specifics of the Maryland Campaign, and of the Battle of Antietam in particular, stray far beyond the scope of this study. For a detailed examination of the Maryland Campaign, see James V. Murfin, *The Gleam of Bayonets: The Battle of Antietam and the Maryland Campaign of 1862* (New York: T. Yoseloff, 1965) and Stephen W. Sears, *Landscape Turned Red: The Battle of Antietam* (New York: Ticknor & Fields, 1983), which are the best accounts of this critical campaign yet written.

12 Undated entry in John A. Dahlgren's scrapbook, Dahlgren Papers, LOC.

13 Dahlgren, *Memoir of Ulric Dahlgren*, 85.

14 John A. Dahlgren to Sargent, August 22, 1864.

15 O. R. vol. 19, part 2, 356.

16 Styple, *Writing & Fighting from the Army of Northern Virginia*, 154.

17 Ulric Dahlgren to his father, September 26, 1862, Dahlgren Papers, LOC.

18 Franz Sigel to Gov. Andrew G. Curtin, September 27, 1862, Abraham Lincoln Papers, Manuscripts Division, LOC; Dahlgren, *Memoir of Ulric Dahlgren*, 87-8.

19 O. R. vol. 19, part 2, 375.

20 *Ibid.*, 418-9.

21 *New York Times*, October 7, 1862.

22 O. R. vol. 19, part 2, 72.

23 *Ibid.*, 395.

24 William T. H. Brooks to his father, October 2, 1862, Brooks Papers, USAMHI.

25 For a detailed discussion of McClellan's conduct during this period, see Ethan S. Rafuse, *McClellan's War: The Failure of Moderation in the Struggle for the Union* (Bloomington: Indiana University Press, 2005), 335-359.

26 O. R. vol. 19, part 2, 380.

27 *Ibid.*, part 1, 87. For a detailed examination of McClellan's operations during the last week of October and the first week of November 1862, see Patrick J. Brennan, "Little Mac's Last Stand: Autumn 1862 in Loudoun Valley, Virginia," *Blue & Gray* vol. 17, no. 2 (December 1999): 6-20 and 48-57, for the most detailed examination of these events yet written.

28 Rafuse, *McClellan's War*, 363-64.

29 O. R. vol. 19, part 2, 504.

30 Dahlgren, *Memoir of John A. Dahlgren*, 381.

31 *New York Times*, October 15, 1862.

32 Sunderland, *A Sermon in Memory of Colonel Ulric Dahlgren*, 19.

33 Dahlgren, *Memoir of Ulric Dahlgren*, 89.

34 *Ibid.*

35 *Burlington Hawk-Eye*, November 1, 1862.

36 O. R. vol. 19, part 2, 100; *New York Times*, October 27, 1862.

37 *Baltimore American*, October 29, 1862. Conger was in a great deal of discomfort. On October 28, he wrote to his wife, "I was in a good deal of pain to day I am much easier and the Dr. thinks the serious danger is over. I think so to. Northing vital has been touched in it course which was very singular and fortunate." Conger to his wife, October 28, 1862, included in Conger's pension file, RG94, NARA.

38 *Ibid.*; O. R. vol. 19, part 2, 101. Sigel wrote, "Your services are much appreciated by me." Sigel to Conger, undated, included in Conger's pension file. Conger eventually recovered from the multiple wounds he had received on October 25, and returned to duty. By the spring of 1865, he was a lieutenant colonel in Lafayette Baker's 1st District of Columbia Cavalry, which became part of the secret service, and commanded the detachment of cavalry troopers that ran down and ultimately killed John Wilkes Booth in the wake of Abraham Lincoln's assassination. Conger's brother Seymour B. Conger was promoted to captain and commanded the squadron of the 3rd West Virginia Cavalry that served in the Battle of Gettysburg. Seymour Conger was killed in action in 1864.

39 Quoted in Dahlgren, *Memoir of Ulric Dahlgren*, 89.

40 *Chicago Tribune*, November 7, 1862.

41 *Ibid.*; Dahlgren, *Memoir of Ulric Dahlgren*, 90.

42 Francis August'n O'Reilly, *The Fredericksburg Campaign: Winter War on the Rappahannock* (Baton Rouge: Louisiana State University Press, 2003), 5.

43 Rafuse, *McClellan's War*, 372.

44 O. R. vol. 19, part 2, 550-51.

45 Stephen W. Sears, ed., *The Civil War Papers of George B. McClellan* (New York: Ticknor & Fields, 1989), 519.

46 Brennan, "Little Mac's Last Stand," 56.

47 Sears, *The Civil War Papers of George B. McClellan*, 485-86.

CHAPTER SEVEN

1 *Ibid.*, 137.

2 *Ibid.*

3 *Ibid.*, 162.

4 Abram Sharra pension and service records, RG 94, NARA. He was promoted to major in the spring of 1864 and to lieutenant colonel on May 26, 1864. He was then transferred to the 11th Indiana Cavalry, and received a promotion to colonel in May 1865. He mustered out on September 19, 1865 and died October 26, 1893. He proved himself a capable soldier.

5 O. R. vol. 19, part 2, 162.

6 Richard J. Staats, ed., *A Grassroots History of the American Civil War Vol. IV: The Life and Times of Colonel William Stedman of the 6th Ohio Cavalry* (Bowie, Md.: Heritage Books, 2003), 1-32.

7 *Western Reserve Chronicle*, December 17, 1862.

8 *Ibid.*

9 Dahlgren, *Memoir of Ulric Dahlgren*, 93.

10 Ulric Dahlgren memorandum of the Fredericksburg raid, November 11, 1862, Dahlgren Papers, LOC.

11 O. R. vol. 19, part 2, 162.

12 *Boston Evening Journal*, November 13, 1862.

13 *Daily Richmond Inquirer*, November 10, 1862.

14 John Fortier, *15th Virginia Cavalry* (Lynchburg, Va.: H. E. Howard, Inc., 1993), 5.

15 "Dahlgren's Ride Into Fredericksburg," *Southern Historical Society Papers* 3 (1877), 88-9.

16 William Stedman to Carlos McDonald, November 14, 1862, included in Staats, *Colonel William Stedman*, 127.

17 Dahlgren, *Memoir of Ulric Dahlgren*, 104.

18 O. R. vol. 19, part 2, 162; Staats, *Colonel William Stedman*, 127.

19 *Boston Journal*, November 13, 1862.

20 Staats, *Colonel William Stedman*, 127.

21 *Boston Evening Journal*, November 13, 1862.

22 As reported in the *Daily Richmond Enquirer*, November 15, 1862. J. H. Kelly, a local newspaper correspondent, had a different recollection. "The first intimation I had of the affair was a small colored boy's coming into the chamber (about 8 o'clock in the morning, or possibly 9) with the announcement, 'De Yankees is in town.' It was Sunday morning, as you recollect. Directly thereafter I heard the clatter of horses' feet, and on going to the parlor window saw the head of the invading force. The horses were in a walk, and

no dash whatever. I looked for some moments before I realized that they were indeed Federal soldiers. I saw the blue overcoats, but thought they belonged to Colonel Bell's company, he having arrived, as I understood, the evening before," he recalled in 1877. "Dahlgren's Dash Into Fredericksburg", 90.

23 Noel G. Harrison, *Fredericksburg Civil War Sites*, 2 vols. (Lynchburg, Va.: H. E. Howard, Inc. 1995), 1:130.

24 *Daily Richmond Enquirer*, November 15, 1862.

25 Horatio C. Haggard, "Cavalry Fight at Fredericksburg," *Confederate Veteran* 21 (June 1913): 295.

26 *Richmond Daily Dispatch*, November 11, 1862.

27 E. T. Hebb, "A Reconnoissance: A Lively Call with Dahlgren at Falmouth Station," *The National Tribune*, April 26, 1900.

28 O. R. vol. 19, part 2, 162.

29 *Boston Evening Journal*, November 13, 1862.

30 John B. Jones, *A Rebel War Clerk's Diary at the Confederate States Capital*, 2 vols. (Philadelphia: J. B. Lippincott & Co., 1866), 1:186-87.

31 *Richmond Daily Dispatch*, November 12, 1862.

32 O. R. vol. 19, part 2, 163.

33 G. W. Gillis, "A Narrow Escape," *National Tribune*, October 2, 1884.

34 J. M Herndon to Dear Seth, November 9, 1862, copy in files, Archives, Fredericksburg and Spotsylvania National Military Park, Fredericksburg, Virginia.

35 *Boston Evening Journal*, November 13, 1862.

36 Haggard, "Cavalry Fight at Fredericksburg," 295.

37 *Daily Richmond Enquirer*, November 12, 1862. The dead man was Pvt. Walter B. Thompson of Kentsville, Princess Anne County, Virginia.

38 Haggard, "Cavalry Fight at Fredericksburg," 295.

39 O. R. vol. 19, part 2, 163.

40 Haggard, "Cavalry Fight at Fredericksburg," 295.

41 Gillis, "A Narrow Escape."

42 Richard J. Staats, *The History of the Sixth Ohio Volunteer Cavalry 1861-1865*, 2 vols. (Westminster, Md.: Heritage Books, 2006), 1:209.

43 Hebb, "A Reconnaissance."

44 Dahlgren memorandum of November 11, 1862.

45 O. R. vol, 19, part 2, 163.

46 Presley Thornton to W. Ware, November 10, 1862, copy in files, Archives, Fredericksburg and Spotsylvania National Military Park, Fredericksburg, Virginia.

47 *Philadelphia Inquirer*, November 11, 1862.

48 Fortier, *15ᵗʰ Virginia Cavalry*, 18.

49 *Philadelphia Inquirer*, November 13, 1862.

50 *Richmond Daily Dispatch*, November 12, 1862.

51 Barbara P. Willis, ed., *The Journal of Jane Howison Beale, Fredericksburg, Virginia 1850-1862* (Fredericksburg: Historic Fredericksburg Foundation, Inc., 1979), 120.

52 James H. Ogden, "Prelude to Battle: Burnside and Fredericksburg, November, 1862." *The Morningside Notes* (1988), 7.

53 *Western Reserve Chronicle*, December 17, 1862.

54 *Boston Evening Journal*, November 13, 1862.

55 O. R. vol. 19, part 2, 163.

56 Staats, *Colonel William Stedman*, 127.

57 O. R. vol. 19, part 2, 163.

58 Staats, *Colonel William Stedman*, 127.

59 O. R. vol. 19, part 2, 567.

60 *Boston Evening Journal*, November 13, 1862.

61 O. R. vol. 19, part 2, 567.

62 *Ibid.*, 574. "There are no bridges across the Rappahannock, the Potomac and Accokeek Creeks, as stated in a former report, all these bridges having been destroyed," wrote Sigel.

63 Franz Sigel dispatch, Nov. 11, 1862, Ambrose E. Burnside Papers, NARA; Franz Sigel, dispatch, Nov. 13, 1862, Burnside Papers.

64 Willis, *The Journal of Jane Howison Beale*, 120.

65 *Charleston Daily Courier*, November 20, 1862.

66 *Richmond Whig*, November 13, 1862.

67 O. R. vol. 19, part 2, 163.

68 *Baltimore American*, November 22, 1862.

69 Haggard, "Cavalry Fight at Fredericksburg," 295.

70 "Dahlgren's Ride Into Fredericksburg," 89.

71 O. R. vol. 19, part 2, 164.

72 Ogden, "Prelude to Battle," 9.

73 *Boston Evening Journal*, November 13, 1862.

74 *New York Times*, November 16, 1862.

75 *Philadelphia Inquirer*, November 11, 1862.

76 *New York Tribune*, November 12, 1862.

77 *Daily Richmond Inquirer*, November 10, 1862.

78 *Portage County Democrat*, December 19, 1862.

79 The prisoners, unfortunately, ended up at Richmond's notorious Libby Prison. Perhaps their fate triggered Ulric Dahlgren's fascination with freeing the Union prisoners of war being held in Richmond. *Richmond Whig*, November 11 and 12, 1862. "Five more abolition soldiers, captured near Fredericksburg, were brought to Richmond yesterday. Strange to say, every one of the five held the rank of sergeant, and one of them wore sundry bandages to conceal wounds inflicted by rebel sabers," reported the *Richmond Whig* on November 12.

80 *Richmond Whig*, November 13, 1862 and Daily *Richmond Enquirer*, November 15, 1862.

81 Herndon to Dear Seth, November 9, 1862.

82 *Richmond Daily Dispatch*, November 12, 1862.

83 Sunderland, *A Sermon in Memory of Colonel Ulric Dahlgren*, 20.

84 Dahlgren, *Memoir of Ulric Dahlgren*, 112.

85 *Western Reserve Chronicle*, December 17, 1862.

86 Staats, *Colonel William Stedman*, 133.

87 Dahlgren, *Memoir of Ulric Dahlgren*, 111-12.

88 John A. Dahlgren to Ulric Dahlgren, November 12, 1862, Dahlgren Papers, LOC.

89 Dahlgren, *Memoir of John A. Dahlgren*, 332.

CHAPTER EIGHT

1 *Ibid.*, 579.
2 *Ibid.*, 579.
3 *Ibid.*, 583.
4 Quoted in Engle, *The Yankee Dutchman*, 150.
5 *Philadelphia Inquirer*, November 18, 1862.
6 *Ibid.*
7 *Ibid.*, November 22, 1862.
8 *New York Times*, November 20, 1862.
9 *Philadelphia Inquirer*, November 22, 1862.
10 *Chicago Tribune*, November 25, 1862.
11 Dahlgren, *Memoir of Ulric Dahlgren*, 118.
12 *New York Times*, November 29, 1862.
13 *Ibid.*, December 3, 1862.
14 *Ibid.*
15 *Ibid.*
16 O. R. vol. 21, 848.
17 *Ibid.*, 847.
18 Sunderland, *A Sermon in Memory of Colonel Ulric Dahlgren*, 20.
19 Dahlgren, *Memoir of Ulric Dahlgren*, 119. Burnside's chief of staff said that he "detained" Dahlgren at headquarters until he could prepare and give Sigel a well-informed progress report on the campaign. According to Parke, therefore, Ulric was not reassigned. O. R. vol. 21, 848.
20 Miscellaneous note dates January 5, 1863, included in Dahlgren Papers, LOC.
21 Dahlgren, *Memoir of Ulric Dahlgren*, 119-20.
22 Obviously, a detailed discussion of the Battle of Fredericksburg strays far beyond the scope of this book. For the best tactical treatment of this battle yet written, see O'Reilly, *The Fredericksburg Campaign*.
23 O. R. vol. 21, 848.
24 *Ibid.*, 850.
25 William H. Harrison, "Personal Experiences of a Cavalry Officer 1861-66," Military Order of the Loyal Legion of the United States, Pennsylvania Commandery, *War Papers* 1 (1895), 244.
26 *Ibid.*
27 Dahlgren, *Memoir of Ulric Dahlgren*, 121-22.
28 Sunderland, *A Sermon in Memory of Colonel Ulric Dahlgren*, 20.
29 O. R. vol. 21, 862.
30 *Ibid.*, vol. 12, part 1, 159-60.
31 *New York Times*, December 31, 1862.
32 O. R. vol. 21, 971.
33 Isaac Ressler diary, entry for January 19, 1863, *Civil War Times Illustrated* Collection, USAMHI.
34 Samuel L. Gracey, *Annals of the Sixth Pennsylvania Cavalry* (Philadelphia: E. H. Butler & Co., 1868), 127-28.
35 Hillman A. Hall, ed., *History of the Sixth New York Cavalry (Second Ira Harris Guards), Second Brigade-First Division-Cavalry Corps, Army of the Potomac 1861-1865* (Worcester

Mass.: Blanchard Press, 1908), 90.

36 O. R. vol. 21, 752 and 755.

37 George N. Bliss to Dear Gerald, January 23, 1863, George N. Bliss letters, Rhode Island Historical Society, Providence, Rhode Island.

38 Samuel J. B. V. Gilpin diary, entry for January 17, 1863, Gilpin Diary, Manuscripts Division, Library of Congress.

39 Worthington C. Ford, ed., *A Cycle of Adams Letters, 1861-1865*, 2 vols. (Boston: Houghton-Mifflin, 1920), 1:241.

40 Robert L. Winder, ed., *Jacob Beidler's Book: A Diary Kept by Jacob Beidler from November 1857 through July 1863* (Mifflintown, Pa.: Juniata County Historical Society, 1994), 141.

41 Warner, *Generals in Blue*, 233-34.

42 E. R. Hagemann, ed., *Fighting Rebels and Redskins: Experiences in Army Life of Colonel George B. Sanford, 1861-1892* (Norman: University of Oklahoma Press, 1968), 194.

43 Dahlgren, *Memoir of Ulric Dahlgren*, 126.

44 Engle, *The Yankee Dutchman*, 156-59.

45 Ulric Dahlgren to his father, February 20, 1863, Dahlgren Papers, LOC.

46 *Ibid.* and telegram of February 21, 1863.

47 *Ibid.*, February 22, 1863.

48 O. R. vol. 25, part 2, 167.

49 Dahlgren, *Memoir of Ulric Dahlgren*, 127.

50 For an excellent overview of the Chancellorsville Campaign, see Stephen W. Sears, *Chancellorsville* (New York: Houghton-Mifflin, 1996).

51 Obviously, the specifics of the Stoneman Raid go far beyond the scope of this study. For a detailed examination of this expedition, see Eric J. Wittenberg, *The Union Cavalry Comes of Age: Hartwood Church to Brandy Station 1863* (Dulles, Va.: Brassey's, 2003).

52 Ulric Dahlgren diary, entry for April 22, 1863, Dahlgren Papers, LOC.

53 Dahlgren, *Memoir of Ulric Dahlgren*, 131-32.

54 Ulric Dahlgren diary, entry for April 24, 1863.

55 *Ibid.*, entry for April 27, 1863.

56 *Ibid.*, entry for April 30, 1863.

57 *Ibid.*

58 *Ibid.*, entry for May 1, 1863.

59 *Ibid.*, entry for May 2, 1863.

60 *Ibid.*

61 Dahlgren, *Memoir of Ulric Dahlgren*, 135. Jackson was mortally wounded that evening by his own men, a loss the Confederacy could ill afford.

62 Ulric Dahlgren to his father, May 7, 1863, Dahlgren Papers, LOC.

63 Ulric Dahlgren diary, entry for May 6, 1863.

64 Welles, *Diary of Gideon Welles*, 293.

65 Ulric Dahlgren diary, entry for May 6, 1863.

66 Sunderland, *A Sermon in Memory of Colonel Ulric Dahlgren*, 21.

67 Dahlgren to his father, May 21, 1863.

68 Dahlgren referred to "several men in the provost-marshal's service" in his proposal. He was referring to the newly-formed Bureau of Military Information, which was part of the Provost Marshal General's office. Headed by Col. George Sharpe, a number of brave and gifted scouts, under command of John C. Babcock, operated far behind enemy lines,

gathering intelligence and often doing so in civilian clothing. These men provided crucial information, and Dahlgren came to know them well from his own scouting expeditions. A number of these BMI operatives played major roles in Dahlgren's military career.

69 O. R. vol. 25, part 2, 517-18.

70 Ulric Dahlgren diary, entry for May 23, 1863.

71 Dahlgren, *Memoir of Ulric Dahlgren*, 142.

72 Ulric Dahlgren diary, entries for May 29 and June 4, 1863.

CHAPTER NINE

1 Ulric Dahlgren diary, entry for June 6, 1863.

2 *Ibid.*

3 Dahlgren, *Memoir of Ulric Dahlgren*, 142.

4 Ulric Dahlgren diary, entry for June 8, 1863.

5 Dahlgren, *Memoir of Ulric Dahlgren*, 125.

6 O.R. vol. 27, part 3, 25. Dahlgren refers to Col. Alfred N. Duffie, commanding the Third Division of the Army of the Potomac's Cavalry Corps, and to Maj. Gen. Julius Stahel, commanding the cavalry division assigned to the defenses of Washington. In the reorganization of the Cavalry Corps that occurred after the fighting in the Loudoun Valley during the second half of June, Duffie was reduced to colonel of the 1st Rhode Island Cavalry, and Stahel was relieved of command. His division became the Third Division of the Cavalry Corps of the Army of the Potomac, under the command of Brig. Gen. Judson Kilpatrick.

7 The 6th Pennsylvania Cavalry was formed in Philadelphia in 1861. Its first commanding officer was Col. Richard H. Rush, grandson of one of the founding fathers of the United States. In November 1861, pursuant to a request by Maj. Gen. George B. McClellan, the regiment was armed with eight-foot-long wooden lances tipped with eleven-inch steel blades. Hence, for most of its career in the Army of the Potomac, this regiment was also known as Rush's Lancers, although the regiment turned in their lances subsequent to McClellan's Peninsula Campaign. Two companies of the 6th Pennsylvania Cavalry, Companies E and I, were nowhere near the fighting at Brandy station that day. This squadron served as headquarters escort to Hooker, as the commanding officer of the Army of the Potomac. Admiral Dahlgren described them as "a splendid body of Lancer cavalry." For a detailed history of the Lancers, see Eric J. Wittenberg, *Rush's Lancers: The Sixth Pennsylvania Cavalry in the Civil War* (Yardley, Pa.: Westholme Publishing, 2006).

8 Richard L. T. Beale, *History of the Ninth Virginia Cavalry in the War Between the States* (Richmond: B. F. Johnson Publishing, 1899), 85.

9 Brig. Gen. John Buford to Lt. Col. A. J. Alexander, June 13, 1863, Box 15, Folder A, Joseph Hooker Papers, Huntington Library, San Marino, California.

10 Fairfax Downey, *Clash of Cavalry: The Battle of Brandy Station* (New York: David McKay Co., 1959), 103.

11 Maj. Henry C. Whelan to Lt. James F. McQueston, June 11, 1863, Box 15, Folder A, Joseph Hooker Papers, Huntington Library, San Marino, California.

12 Major Henry C. Whelan to Charles C. Cadwalader, 6th Pennsylvania Cavalry, June 11, 1863, Cadwalader Family Collection, Historical Society of Pennsylvania, Philadelphia.

13 Dahlgren, *Memoir*, 147-8.

14 Sgt. Thomas W. Smith to Joseph Smith, June 15, 1863, Thomas W. Smith Papers,

Historical Society of Pennsylvania, Philadelphia.

15 Dahlgren, *Memoir of Ulric Dahlgren*, 149.

16 O.R. vol. 27, part 1, 1046.

17 Buford to Alexander, June 13, 1863, Hooker Papers.

18 *New York Times*, June 11, 1863.

19 Dahlgren, *Memoir of Ulric Dahlgren*, 150.

20 *Ibid.*, 151.

21 Dahlgren diary, entry for June 11, 1863.

22 RG 393 part 1 (US Army Continental Command, 1821-1920), Army of the Potomac, 1861-1865, entry 3976, Letters Received, 1863, box 8 (A-E), NARA.

23 John A. Dahlgren to Ulric Dahlgren, June 11, 1863, Dahlgren Papers, LOC.

24 Ulric Dahlgren to his father, June 12, 1863.

25 O.R. vol. 27, part 3, 86.

26 Dahlgren diary, entry for June 16, 1863.

27 Welles, *Diary of Gideon Welles*, 331.

28 Dahlgren, *Memoir of John A. Dahlgren*, 394.

29 Roy P. Basler, Marion Dolores Pratt, and Lloyd A. Dunlap, eds., *The Collected Works of Abraham Lincoln*, 9 vols. (Springfield, Ill.: Abraham Lincoln Association; New Brunswick, N.J.: Rutgers University Press, 1953), 6:281-82.

30 Ulric Dahlgren to Daniel Butterfield, June 17, 1863, RG 107, Records of the Office of the Secretary of War, Telegrams Collected by the Secretary of War (Unbound), M504, Roll 130, NARA. Thanks to Robert F. O'Neill, Jr. for bringing this correspondence to the attention of the author.

31 *Ibid.*; Daniel Butterfield to Alfred Pleasonton, June 17, 1863, Charles Venable Papers, Southern Historical Collections, University of North Carolina, Chapel Hill, North Carolina.

32 O. R. vol. 27, part 3, 171; *Report of the Joint Committee on the Conduct of the War at the Second Session, Thirty-Eighth Congress*, 2 vols. (Washington, D. C.: U. S. Government Printing Office, 1865-66), 1:32-33

33 John A. Dahlgren to Ulric Dahlgren, June 15, 1863, Dahlgren Papers, LOC; Ulric Dahlgren to John A. Dahlgren, June 18, 1863, Dahlgren Papers, LOC.

34 John A. Dahlgren to Ulric Dahlgren, June 22, 1863, Dahlgren Papers, LOC; Dahlgren, *Memoir of John A. Dahlgren*, 394.

35 John A. Dahlgren to Ulric Dahlgren, June 23, 1864, Dahlgren Papers, LOC.

36 The specifics of the fighting in the Loudoun Valley stray far beyond the scope of this work. For the best study of these actions, see Robert F. O'Neill, Jr., *The Cavalry Battles of Aldie, Middleburg and Upperville, Small but Important Riots, June 10-27, 1863* (Lynchburg, Va.: H. E. Howard Co., 1993).

37 Dahlgren, *Memoir of Ulric Dahlgren*, 154.

38 *Ibid.*, 152.

39 *Ibid.*, 155.

40 Joseph Hooker to Admiral John Dahlgren, July 20, 1863, Letters Sent and Received, Army of the Potomac, Book 3, pp. 487-488, NARA.

41 *Ibid.*

42 This episode has been largely lost to history. On June 29, Alexander took his small force and crossed into Pennsylvania. The column failed to find the Confederates, but

followed the sounds of combat emanating from the battle raging at Hanover on June 30, arriving to pitch into the decisive charge at Hanover. After the Federal victory that day, Alexander led his small command to the main Federal position at Gettysburg, arriving on Cemetery Hill late on the afternoon of July 1. For a time, Alexander's column was out of contact with the Army of the Potomac, causing great consternation among the high command. This prompted John Buford to write to Maj. Gen. John F. Reynolds, "Nothing has been learned of Col. Alexander's Command and I have pushed the pickets, or rather the rear guard of the Rebs 6 miles towards Cashtown." The only known narrative of this expedition is found in James H. Wilson, *The Life and Services of Brevet Brigadier General Andrew Jonathan Alexander, United States Army* (New York: privately published, 1887), 36-39.

43 Frederick C. Newhall, *Dedication of the Monument of the Sixth Pennsylvania Cavalry on the Battlefield of Gettysburg, October 14, 1888* (Philadelphia: privately published, 1889), 14-15. Newhall recorded, "I had been sent by Pleasonton with a small party towards York, far off there in the north-east, to see if any of Lee's army was thereabouts, and it was the afternoon of the second dayÖ" when Newhall and his small force arrived on the main battlefield at Gettysburg and Newhall rejoined Pleasonton's staff.

44 Sunderland, *A Sermon in Memory of Colonel Ulric Dahlgren*, 23.

45 *New York Times*, March 9, 1864.

46 Dahlgren, *Memoir of Ulric Dahlgren*, 159-160.

47 F. A. Bushey, "That Historic Dispatch: How It Was Captured by Dahlgren and His Little Band," *The National Tribune*, May 14, 1896.

48 Edwin C. Fishel, *The Secret War for the Union: The Untold Story of Military Intelligence in the Civil War* (Boston: Houghton-Mifflin, 1996), 306.

49 *Ibid.*, 421.

50 Ulric Dahlgren diary, entry for June 30, 1863.

51 W. P. Conrad and Ted Alexander, *When War Passed This Way* (Greencastle, Pennsylvania: Lilian S. Besore Memorial Library, 1982), 172.

52 Jacob Hoke, *The Great Invasion of 1863* (New York: Thomas Yoseloff, 1867), 180.

53 Bushey, "That Historic Dispatch."

54 *Ibid.*

55 Conrad and Alexander, *When War Passed This Way*, 173.

56 O.R. vol. 27, part 1, 75-7.

57 Bushey, "That Historic Dispatch."

58 Hoke, *The Great Invasion*, 181.

59 All of the remaining mail was put back into its bags, the arms and accouterments of the captured Confederates were stashed in a nearby house, and the entire party headed down the Leitersburg road, through Waynesboro, arriving at the Monterey House about midnight, where they stopped to eat. From there, they proceeded by the main road to Emmitsburg, reaching there about 4:00 a.m. Finding the town occupied by Union troops, they turned over the captured mail and their 28 prisoners, having made four additional captures during the day in addition to those taken with the mail. The raiding party was then disbanded, and the men returned to their respective regiments. Bushey, "That Historic Dispatch."

60 Dahlgren, *Memoir of Ulric Dahlgren*, 162.

61 *Ibid.*, part 2, 300; Fishel, *The Secret War*, 685, n. 33.

62 Edward P. Alexander, *Fighting for the Confederacy: The Personal Recollections of Edward Porter Alexander*, Gary W. Gallagher, ed. (Chapel Hill: University of North Carolina Press, 1989) p. 247. Porter Alexander was an appropriate person to make such an observation. Prior to the outbreak of the Civil war, the young officer had served in the U. S. Army's Signal Corps, where he was responsible for precisely the sort of security measures that he commented on in this matter.

63 William L. Royall, *Some Reminiscences* (New York: Neale Publishing Co., 1909), 23.

64 Co. Edward A. Palfrey, "Some of the Secret History of Gettysburg," *Southern Historical Society Papers*, Vol. VIII (18__), 521-526. William L. Royall, a private in the 9th Virginia Cavalry, spent years investigating the circumstances of the Greensburg expedition of July 2. He corresponded extensively with participants in the raid and battle, as well as with Ulric's stepmother and brother Charley. Royall wrote, "One of the leakiest things in the world was the Confederate War Office, and Lee had hardly asked for this force to be put at Culpeper Court House before it was known in Washington, and Meade fought the first two days' battles with the fear of an attack upon his rear haunting him. Ulric Dahlgren, son of the Admiral, was an adventurous young captain of twenty-one on Meade's staff While the battle was in progress he, with a small command, was scouting in rear of the Confederate army, and he fell in with Mr. Davis's courier in the streets of Greencastle and searched him and got his letter. On reading the letter he saw the importance of getting it to General Meade, and so he rode hard and handed it to him just as the council of war ended. The probabilities all are that Meade was going to change his position at Gettysburg, leaving the Confederates the moral effect of a great victory gained there, but that this information relieving him from all fear as to his rear, determined him to stay there and fight the third day's battle." Royall, *Some Reminiscences*, 23-24. Ironically, Royall, who was a 19-year-old scout, was badly wounded while out searching for Dahlgren's raiders in the first days of March, 1864.

65 Fishel, *Secret War*, 532. Fishel refers to Special Orders No. 191, the operational orders for the Army of Northern Virginia in Maryland before the Battle of Antietam. Some Indiana infantrymen found a copy of the order, intended for Maj. Gen. D. H. Hill, wrapped around three cigars. The intelligence contained in this order gave Maj. Gen. George B. McClellan, then commanding the Army of the Potomac, a picture of the disposition of Lee's army in the days before the Battle of Antietam, and prompted McClellan to boast, "Here is a paper with which, if I cannot whip Bobby Lee, I am willing to go home." The intelligence found by Dahlgren was of the same level of strategic importance, even if it was not as significant tactically.

66 That dispatch provides:
Head-Quarters, Army of the Potomac
July 3, 1863
General O.O. Howard
Cmdg 11th Corps
General:
With respect to the report that Beauregard has a large force at Hagerstown, I am instructed by the Commanding General to say that a dispatch was yesterday captured showing that the proposition to concentrate a large army under Beauregard for the support of Lee's army is regarded by President Davis as impracticable an intimation will be given to General [Henry] Slocum that General [David M.] Gregg is probably

wasting his ammunition.

Your obt srvt

S Williams

Adjt

[Endorsed]

Head Quarters Army of the Potomac

P103/237 July 3, 1863

S. Williams Asst Adjt Genl

Recd HQ 11 Corps July 3, 1863, RG 393, Part II (US Army Continental Command, 1821-1920), Entry 5319: 11th Army Corps Letter Received, January 1863-1864 (Unarranged) Box 1, NARA.

67 This is modern-day Thurmont, Maryland.

68 Newhall, *Dedication*, 18.

69 Ulric Dahlgren diary, entry for July 3, 1863.

70 Newhall, *Dedication*, 18-19.

71 John D. Imboden, "The Confederate Retreat from Gettysburg," included in Robert U. Johnson and Clarence C. Buel, eds. *Battles and Leaders of the Civil War*, 4 vols. (New York: Century Publishing Co. 1884-1904), 3:423.

72 Samuel L. Gracey, *Annals of the Sixth Pennsylvania Cavalry* (Philadelphia: E. H. Butler & Co. 1868), 189. Albert P. Morrow was a fine soldier. At the war's outbreak, he was a sergeant. By the war's end, he was a lieutenant colonel commanding the regiment. In the interim, his daring-do in leading this charge caught the attention of John Buford, who appointed the young lieutenant to his staff not long after the conclusion of the Gettysburg Campaign. After Buford's death in December 1863, Morrow returned to active duty in the field with the Lancers. With the war's end, he accepted a commission in the newly formed 7th U.S. Cavalry. Morrow stayed in the Regular Army until 1895, when he retired as a colonel. "Record of Albert P. Morrow," Sydney L. Wright Family Papers, Collection #2096, William Redwood Wright Section, Historical Society of Pennsylvania, Philadelphia. Morrow's fellow staff officer, Capt. Myles W. Keogh, observed of Morrow, "he was considered quite a handsome fellow and was a very gallant soldieróas we would say in the Green Isle. The Devil among women,'" Myles W. Keogh to Thomas Keogh, December 24, 1865, Keogh Papers, National Library, Dublin, Ireland.

73 Hoke, *The Great Invasion*, 182.

74 Samuel P. Bates, *History of Pennsylvania Volunteers, 1861-5*, 10 vols. (Harrisburg, Pennsylvania: State Printer, 1869-1871), 4:748.

75 Dahlgren, *Memoir of Ulric Dahlgren*, 165.

76 Conrad and Alexander, *When War Passed This Way*, 178-179.

77 Gracey, *Annals of the Sixth Pennsylvania Cavalry*, 190.

78 John Hyde Cameron memoirs, Archives, Virginia Military Institute, Lexington, Virginia.

79 Newhall, *Dedication*, 19.

80 Memorandum of Ulric Dahlgren, included in Dahlgren Papers, LOC.

81 Gracey, *Annals of the Sixth Pennsylvania Cavalry*, 190.

82 Imboden, "The Confederate Retreat," 3:425.

83 Dahlgren, *Memoir of Ulric Dahlgren*, 167.

84 *Wheeling Daily Intelligencer*, July 14, 1863.

85 Gracey, *Annals of the Sixth Pennsylvania Cavalry*, 190.

86 W. A. Popkins, "Imboden's Brigade at Gettysburg," *Confederate Veteran* 22 (1914), 552.

87 Newhall, *Dedication*, 19.

88 Stuart Wright, ed., *Memoirs of Alfred Horatio Belo: Reminiscences of a North Carolina Volunteer* (Gaithersburg, Md.: Olde Soldier Books, n.d.), 22.

89 Gracey, *Annals of the Sixth Pennsylvania Cavalry*, 190-91.

90 *Ibid.*, 190.

91 *Ibid.*, 191.

92 Dahlgren, *Memoir of Ulric Dahlgren*, 168.

93 Samuel L. Gillespie, *A History of Company A, First Ohio Cavalry, 1861-1865: A Memorial Volume Compiled from Personal Records and Living Witnesses* (Washington, Ohio: Ohio State Register, l898), 161.

94 W. W. Jacobs, "Custer's Charge: Little Hagerstown the Scene of Bloody Strife in 1863," *The National Tribune*, August 27, 1896.

95 Dahlgren, *A Memoir of Ulric Dahlgren*, 169.

96 Bates, *History of Pennsylvania Volunteers*, 4:1044.

97 Samuel St. Clair, "The Fight at Hagerstown," included in *History of the Eighteenth regiment of Cavalry Pennsylvania Volunteers 1862-1865* (New York: Regimental Publication Committee, 1909), 94-5. W. W. Goldsborough, the historian of the Maryland Confederate forces during the Civil War, claimed that the shot that cost Dahlgren his leg was fired by Capt. Frank Bond, the commander of the Co. A of the 1st Maryland Cavalry. W. W. Goldsborough, *The Maryland Line in the Confederate Army, 1861-1865* (Baltimore: Guggenheimer, Weil & Co., 1900), 182. There is no way to substantiate this claim. Bond, who was also badly wounded in the melee in the streets of Hagerstown, made no such claim in his post-war account of the role of Company A in the fight at Hagerstown. Frank A. Bond, "Company A, First Maryland Cavalry." *Confederate Veteran* VI (1898), 80.

98 W. W. Goldsborough, *The Maryland Line in the Confederate Army. 1861-1865* (Baltimore: Guggenheimer, Weil & Co., 1900), 182.

99 Sunderland, *A Sermon in Memory of Colonel Ulric Dahlgren*, 23.

100 Dahlgren, *Memoir of Ulric Dahlgren*, 169-70.

101 Luther Trowbridge to J. Allen Bigelow, undated, copy in files, Gettysburg National Military Park, Gettysburg, Pennsylvania.

102 Ulric Dahlgren diary, entry for July 6, 1863.

103 O.R. vol. 27, part I, 995.

104 Ulric Dahlgren diary, entry for July 7, 1863.

105 *Ibid.*, entry for July 8, 1863.

106 Charles E. Cadwalader to his mother, July 10, 1863, copy in files, Archives, Gettysburg National Military Park, Gettysburg, Pennsylvania.

107 Edwin M. Stanton to Lorenzo Thomas, July 4, 1863, RG94, Records of the Adjutant General's Office, Military command Correspondence Relating to "Official Records"/ Miscellaneous Commands, Letters, Telegrams, and Reports, May 1863-Jan. 1864, Entry 730, Box 163, NARA.

108 Samuel P. Heintzelman diary, entry for July 4, 1863, Heintzelman Papers, LOC.

109 For an interesting and balanced study of the question of whether Meade did all he could have in pursuing Lee, see A. Wilson Greene, "From Gettysburg to Falling Waters," included in Gary W. Gallagher, ed. *The Third Day at Gettysburg and Beyond* (Chapel

Hill, University of North Carolina, 1994), 161-202.

110 Edwin P. Coddington, *The Gettysburg Campaign: A Study in Command* (New York: Charles Scribner's Sons, 1968), 572.

CHAPTER TEN

1 Sunderland, *A Sermon in Memory of Colonel Ulric Dahlgren*, 24.

2 Dahlgren, *Memoir of Ulric Dahlgren*, 175.

3 Charles B. Dahlgren to William L. Royall, June 30, 1895, Royall Papers, Virginia Historical Society, Richmond, Virginia.

4 Dahlgren, *Memoir of Ulric Dahlgren*, 174-76.

5 Martha Read to William L. Royall, June 25, Royall Papers, Virginia Historical Society, Richmond, Virginia.

6 Edwin M. Stanton to Ulric Dahlgren, July 24, 1863, Dahlgren Papers, LOC.

7 Charles B. Dahlgren to Royall, June 30, 1895.

8 Read to Royall, June 25, 1895.

9 Sunderland, *A Sermon in Memory of Colonel Ulric Dahlgren*, 24.

10 Dahlgren, *Memoir of Ulric Dahlgren*, 177-78.

11 Conrad and Alexander, *When War Passed This Way*, 181. Unfortunately, this building no longer exists. Apparently, when the walls were opened, there was no sign of the leg bone remaining. "Some suggested that the leg-funeral was staged as a camouflage, the the 'coffin' actually held important state documents," recounted one newspaper in 1964. "Others guessed that the missing leg had been reunited with it owner in the Philadelphia cemetery." *Gettysburg Times*, June 22, 1964.

12 Michael Burlingame, ed., *Lincoln Observed: Civil War Dispatches of Noah Brooks* (Baltimore: Johns Hopkins University Press, 1998), 61. Interestingly, Brooks got a number of important facts wrong. In praising Ulric's valor in leading a cavalry charge, he claimed that the November 1862 charge occurred in Fairfax and not Fredericksburg. He likewise claimed that Dahlgren had captured the dispatches to General Lee in Williamsport and not in Greencastle.

13 Sunderland, *A Sermon in Memory of Colonel Ulric Dahlgren*, 27.

14 Dahlgren, *Memoir of Ulric Dahlgren*, 178.

15 Obviously, the specifics of the campaign to reduce the defenses of Charleston strays far beyond the scope of this study. For those interested in further reading on this issue, the best treatment of the campaign is Stephen R. Wise, *Gate of Hell: Campaign for Charleston Harbor, 1863* (Columbia: University of South Carolina Press, 1994).

16 John A. Dahlgren to Patty Dahlgren, July 17, 1863, John A. Dahlgren Papers, Newberry Library.

17 Dahlgren, *Memoir of John A. Dahlgren*, 404.

18 John A. Dahlgren to Ulric Dahlgren, July 20, 1863, Dahlgren Papers, LOC.

19 Sunderland, *A Sermon in Memory of Colonel Ulric Dahlgren*, 27.

20 Ulric Dahlgren to Patty Dahlgren, date unknown, as quoted in Virgil Carrington Jones, *Eight Hours Before Richmond* (New York: Henry Holt & Co., 1957), 32.

21 Gower, *Charles Dahlgren of Natchez*, 90.

22 Dahlgren, *Memoir of John A. Dahlgren*, 406.

23 John A. Dahlgren to Ulric Dahlgren, August 19, 1863, Dahlgren Papers, LOC.

24 Dahlgren, *Memoir of Ulric Dahlgren*, 183.

25 A carte-de-visite of Ulric Dahlgren in the author's collection has a Philadelphia back mark, which is the source for this statement.

26 Dahlgren, *Memoir of Ulric Dahlgren*, 183-4; Sunderland, *A Sermon in Memory of Colonel Ulric Dahlgren*, 28.

27 Michael Burlingame and John R. Turner Ettlinger, eds., *Inside Lincoln's White House: The Complete Civil War Diary of John Hay* (Carbondale: Southern Illinois University Press, 1997),99.

28 Ulric Dahlgren to his father, October 28, 1863, Dahlgren Papers, LOC.

29 Ulric Dahlgren to Lt. Edward Conroy, November 6, 1863, Simon Gratz Collection, Colonels, Historical Society of Pennsylvania, Philadelphia.

30 Ulric Dahlgren to Dear Doctor, December 10, 1863, Dreer Collection of Union Officers' ALS, Historical Society of Pennsylvania, Philadelphia.

31 Burlingame and Ettlinger, *Inside Lincoln's White House*, 110-111.

32 Ulric Dahlgren diary, entry for November 20, 1863.

33 *Ibid.*, entry for November 22, 1863.

34 Dahlgren, *Memoir of Ulric Dahlgren*, 185-86.

35 Dahlgren, *Memoir of John A. Dahlgren*, 427.

36 Wise, *Gate of Hell*, 164.

37 *Ibid.*

38 For a more detailed discussion of Admiral Dahlgren's frustrating efforts to take Fort Sumter, see Burton, *The Siege of Charleston*, 183-210.

39 Burlingame and Ettlinger, *Inside Lincoln's White House*, 96.

40 For the most detailed treatment of the Union shelling of Charleston, see W. Chris Phelps, *The Bombardment of Charleston 1863-1865* (Gretna, La.: Pelican Publishing Co., 1999).

41 Dahlgren, *Memoir of Ulric Dahlgren*, 188-89.

42 Ulric Dahlgren diary, entry for November __, 1863, Dahlgren Papers, LOC.

43 James W. Hagy, *To Take Charleston: The Civil War on Folly Island* (Charleston, W.V.: Pictorial Histories Publishing Co., 1993), 47 and 63.

44 Ulric Dahlgren diary, entry for November 25, 1863.

45 Dahlgren, *Memoir of Ulric Dahlgren*, 189-90.

46 Quoted in Sunderland, *A Sermon in Memory of Colonel Ulric Dahlgren*, 28

47 *Ibid.*, 29.

48 Dahlgren, *Memoir of Ulric Dahlgren*, 190.

49 Ulric Dahlgren diary, entries for November 28 and December 1, 1863.

50 Dahlgren, *Memoir of Ulric Dahlgren*, 190-91.

51 Dahlgren diary, entry for December 5, 1863.

52 Warner, *Generals in Blue*, 421.

53 Ulric Dahlgren diary, entry for December 8, 1863.

54 Ulric Dahlgren to Dear Doctor, December 10, 1863.

55 *Ibid.* In fact, Gillmore and John Dahlgren never did repair their relationship. If anything, it grew worse. "To Gillmore and his command, the navy's failure to run the obstructions [in Charleston Harbor] capped a bittersweet campaign. For two months soldiers had toiled and died on Morris Island. They captured their objectives and smashed Fort Sumter into rubble, but their accomplishments were negated when the navy refused to carry out the final strike," commented historian Stephen Wise. "On the other hand,

Dahlgren and his sailors believed that the army was still responsible for capturing Sumter, which would then allow the navy to clear the channel. Because of these disputes, the bitterness and mistrust that had become evident in the final weeks of the siege grew into a professional and personal feud between Gillmore and Dahlgren that would not end until Dahlgren's death in 1870. For all the work and cost in material and lives, there had been few results; the army and navy blamed each other for falling short of victory." Wise, *Gate of Hell*, 211.

56 Dahlgren, *Memoir of Ulric Dahlgren*, 191-92.

57 Ulric Dahlgren diary, entry for December 11, 1863.

58 Dahlgren, *Memoir of John A. Dahlgren*, 431.

59 Ulric Dahlgren diary, entry for December 12, 1863.

60 Ulric Dahlgren to Henry A. Wise, December 13, 1863, Henry A. Wise Papers, New York Historical Society, New York, New York.

61 *Janesville Daily Gazette*, January 6, 1864.

62 Dahlgren, *Memoir of Ulric Dahlgren*, 196-97.

63 Ulric Dahlgren diary, entry for December 28, 1863.

64 Dahlgren, *Memoir of Ulric Dahlgren*, 198-99.

65 Ulric Dahlgren diary, entry for December 30, 1863.

66 *Ibid.*, entry for December 31, 1863.

67 *Ibid.*, entry for January 1, 1864.

68 Dahlgren, *Memoir of Ulric Dahlgren*, 201.

69 Dahlgren, *Memoir of John A. Dahlgren*, 435.

70 Ulric Dahlgren to Edwin M. Stanton, January 10, 1864, Dahlgren Papers, LOC.

71 Ulric Dahlgren diary, entry for January 12, 1864.

72 *Ibid.*, entry for January 16, 1864.

73 Dahlgren, *Memoir of Ulric Dahlgren*, 201.

74 *Ibid.*, 202-3.

75 Dahlgren, *Memoir of John A. Dahlgren*, 437.

76 Ulric Dahlgren diary, entry for January 24, 1864.

77 *Ibid.*, entry for January 26, 1864.

78 *Harper's Weekly*, February 13, 1864.

79 Edward Winslow Martin, *The Life and Public Services of Schuyler Colfax Together With His Most Important Speeches* (San Francisco: H. H. Bancroft & Co., 1868), 475. Colfax served as vice president in the Grant Administration.

80 Dahlgren, *Memoir of Ulric Dahlgren*, 205.

81 Ulric Dahlgren to his father, January 31, 1864, Dahlgren Papers, LOC.

82 Duane Schultz, *The Dahlgren Affair: Terror and Conspiracy in the Civil War* (New York: W. W. Norton, 1998), 99.

83 William O. Stoddard, *Inside the White House in War Times* (New York: Charles L. Webster & Co., 1890), 224-226.

84 David W. Lowe, ed., *Meade's Army: The Private Notebooks of Lt. Col. Theodore Lyman* (Kent, Ohio: Kent State University Press, 2007), 107.

85 Sunderland, *A Sermon in Memory of Colonel Ulric Dahlgren*, 32-3. I have spent several years searching for this article, which was evidently published in a newspaper. The problem is that insufficient information was provided for me to locate it, and I have been unable to locate a copy in spite of having searched any number of war-time newspapers,

including every Philadelphia and Washington, D.C. newspaper from January 1-April 30, 1864, which encompasses the date of the memorial sermon preached by Rev. Sunderland in April 1864. I wish I could have included the text of this article as an appendix to this book, and deeply regret that I am unable to do so.

86 *Ibid.*, 32.

CHAPTER ELEVEN

1   Samuel J. Martin, *"Kill-Cavalry:" Sherman's Merchant of Terroró The Life of Union General Hugh Judson Kilpatrick* (Cranbury, N.J.: Associated University Presses, 1996), 15-16.

2   James Harrison Wilson, *Under the Old Flag: Recollections of Military Operations in the War for the Union, the Spanish War, the Boxer Rebellion, Etc.*, 2 vols. (New York: D. Appleton, 1912): 1:370-71.

3   Martin, *Kill-Cavalry*, 17-20. A member of the 9th Pennsylvania Cavalry described Kilpatrick's battle flag. "It is pure red, perfectly red, with three white stars denoting the number of brigades in our division. Above the flag float two white streamers about three feet in length, one of them bearing the inscription in letters of goldóëKilpatrick's Cavalry', the other 'Alice.'" This veteran noted, "The rebels hate the flag infernally. They look upon it with horror; and well they may. For wherever it waves, the cavalry make their mark." Diary of William W. Pritchard, entry for June 2, 1865, Civil War Miscellaneous Collection, United States Army Military History Institute, Carlisle, Pennsylvania.

4   G. Wayne King, "General Judson Kilpatrick", *New Jersey History* vol. XCI, no. 1 (Spring 1973), 35-38.

5   For a detailed discussion of Elon Farnsworth's charge and death, see Eric J. Wittenberg, *Gettysburg's Forgotten Cavalry Actions* (Gettysburg, Pa.: Thomas Publications, 1998).

6   Martin, *Kill-Cavalry*, 127-28.

7   O. R. vol 25, part 2, 448.

8   *Philadelphia Evening Bulletin*, May 9, 1863. That same day, the *Philadelphia Inquirer* declared, "Richmond was entirely without a garrison and a handful of infantry could have occupied it. Oh! What an opportunity has thus gone by."

9   Don Allison, ed., *Hell on Belle Isle: Diary of a Civil War POW* (Bryan, Ohio: Faded Banner Publications, 1997), 124.

10   Luigi Palma di Cesnola, *Ten Months in Libby Prison* (New York: n. p., 1865), 4.

11   Willard W. Glazier, *The Capture, the Prison Pen, and the Escape: An Account of Prison Life in the South 1863-1866* (Albany: J. Munsell, 1866), 58-59.

12   Thomas M. Boaz, ed., *Libby Prison & Beyond: A Union Staff Officer in the East, 1862-1865* (Shippensburg, Pa.: Burd Street Press, 1999), 103.

13   *Ibid.*, 103-104. They dug an underground passage from the dining hall on the first floor of Libby Prison by cutting a hole through a brick chimney with knives, descending through the chimney with a smuggled ladder. They cut a hole in the wall of the eastern basement, and then dug a fifty-foot tunnel under the guard posts to an adjoining lot, where a board fence screened the tunnel's exit. It took them 51 days to complete their tunnel.

14   Handwritten extract by George Sharpe, Scouts, Guides, Spies, and Detectives File, Records of the Provost Marshal General's Office, RG 110, Entry 31, NARA; See, also, William B. Feis, *Grant's Secret Service: The Intelligence War from Belmont to Appomattox* (Lincoln: University of Nebraska Press, 2002), 239.

15 Isaac J. Wistar, *The Autobiography of Isaac Jones Wistar* (Philadelphia: Wistar Institute of Anatomy and Biology, 1914), 426-27.

16 O. R. vol. 33, 143-148 and 172; Wistar *Autobiography*, 428-30.

17 Wistar, *Autobiography*, 430. Wistar also wrote, "Boyle escaped the hemp he so richly deserved and disappeared for many years, but was at last recognized and identified in the dead body of one of the victims of a great mine explosion in Colorado, January 24, 1884." *Ibid.*

18 *Ibid.*, 431.

19 During February 1864, Pleasonton testified before the Joint Committee on the Conduct of the War, and strongly blamed Meade for failing to bring Lee's defeated army to battle in the wake of the Union victory at Gettysburg. This alienated Meade, who spent the fall and winter of 1863-64 defending Pleasonton from his many critics, and keeping the beleaguered Cavalry Corps commander in place. Pleasonton was definitely on the outs with the Army of the Potomac's high command after giving that testimony, which may help to explain why Pleasonton was cut out of the process.

20 O. R. vol. 33, 172-3.

21 *Ibid.*

22 *Ibid.*, 171.

23 Lowe, *Meade's Army*, 106.

24 O. R. vol. 33, 170.

25 Wert, *The Sword of Lincoln*, 325.

26 Jefferson Davis, *The Rise and Fall of the Confederate Government*, 2 vols. (New York: D. Appleton & Co., 1881), 2:504-505.

27 George Meade, *The Life and Letters of George Gordon Meade Major-General United States Army*, 2 vols. (New York: Charles Scribner's Sons, 1915), 2:168.

28 The specifics of the Kilpatrick-Dahlgren Raid stray far beyond the scope of this book. The best and most detailed account of the raid is Virgil Carrington Jones, *Eight Hours Before Richmond* (New York: Henry Holt and Co., 1957). Unfortunately, Jones' book is dated, and did not take advantage of the many primary sources that have surfaced in the years since its publication. For the best modern treatment of these events, see Bruce Venter, "The Kilpatrick-Dahlgren Raid on Richmond, February 28-March 4, 1864," *Blue & Gray* vol. 20, no. 3 (2003): 6-22, 44-51.

29 Dahlgren, *Memoir of Ulric Dahlgren*, 209.

30 Jones, *Eight Hours Before Richmond*, 7.

31 Lowe, *Meade's Army*, 104.

32 Sunderland, *A Sermon in Memory of Colonel Ulric Dahlgren*, 33.

33 J. Landegan, "He was There and Proceeds to Tell How Richmond was Not Entered," *The National Tribune*, May 31, 1894.

34 Quoted in Venter, "The Kilpatrick-Dahlgren Raid," 10.

35 Lowe, *Meade's Army*, 104.

36 Samuel L. Gillespie, *A History of Company A, First Ohio Cavalry, 1861-1865: A Memorial Volume Compiled from Personal Records and Living Witnesses* (Washington, Ohio: Ohio State Register, l898), 192-93.

37 RG 94, U. S. Army Generals' Reports of Civil War Service, 1864-1887. Henry E. Davies, Jr. Report, NARA.

38 George R. Agassiz, ed., *Meade's Headquarters, 1863-1865: Letters of Colonel Theodore*

Lyman (Boston: Atlantic Monthly Press, 1922), 77-8.

39 Venter, "The Kilpatrick-Dahlgren Raid," 9.

40 Lowe, *Meade's Army*, 105.

41 Dahlgren, *Memoir of Ulric Dahlgren*, 210.

42 O. R. vol. 33, 183.

43 Dahlgren, *Memoir of Ulric Dahlgren*, 208-9.

44 Sunderland, *A Sermon in Memory of Colonel Ulric Dahlgren*, 33.

45 Reuben Bartley, "The Dahlgren Expedition," unpublished manuscript, Virginia Historical Society, Richmond, Virginia, 3.

46 The chief proponent of this theory is Prof. David E. Long of East Carolina University, a Lincoln scholar. Professor Long is writing a book on the Kilpatrick-Dahlgren Raid that will lay out this theory in detail. However, there is no evidence to suggest that Lincoln had any advance knowledge of these events. Long laid out his theory in a concise magazine article. See David E. Long, "Lincoln, Davis, and the Dahlgren Raid." *North & South*, Vol. 9, No. 5 (October 2006): 70-83.

47 O. R. vol. 33, 194.

48 Dahlgren to his father, February 26, 1864, Dahlgren Papers, LOC.

49 Quoted in Jones, *Eight Hours Before Richmond*, 37.

50 2 different messages, George H. Sharpe to P. H. McCord, February 27, 1863, Microcopy 473, Roll 270, p. 308, NARA.

51 George H. Sharpe to Ulric Dahlgren, February 28, 1864, Microcopy 504, Roll 303, NARA.

52 O. R. vol. 33, 173.

53 *Ibid.*, 174.

54 *Ibid.*, 183.

55 Joseph Hooker formed the BMI in the spring of 1863, as part of the Provost Marshal General's department. The BMI played a critical role in tracking the activities of the enemy. Feis, *Grant's Secret Service*, 305, n. 38. David W. Gaddy, a former intelligence officer who has studied the Lincoln assassination at great length, has an interesting theory on the reasons why so many BMI men accompanied the column. In a letter to the author, Gaddy wrote:

> By e-mail I also wrote of the composition of the Kilpatrick-Dahlgren columns, seeing evidence of "task-organization" that seemed so modern to me. For example, the assignment of men from the BMI, headed by Capt. McEntee, one of the (if not *the*) top men of Sharpe's organization; the assignment of two signal officers (which should have entailed a small team of accompanying signal specialists each); engineers, pioneers, commissaries, quartermasters, etc., plus "specialized equipment" for raiders, such as oakum, turpentine, and torpedoes/minesóplaced under control of signal officers. I do appreciate your desire not to be drawn into a detailed examination of the raid itself. But, for example, Prof. William B. Feis identifies "at least" eight BMI "employees" as accompanying the raiders Capt McEntee plus two with Kilpatrick and five with Dahlgren. The latter include Hogan (Lt., 1ˢᵗ Ind Cav) and Swisher, whom you refer to as Dahlgren's guides [Chapter 11, pp. 28, which I'll ref here as 11-28, and 35, more or less], but their relationship with BMI may reveal another dimension to the origin and composition of the raid.

What I'm pressing is the level of "who knew what," who sketched the concept, who authorized it, who allowed (or directed) Dahlgren's involvement, etc., which are treated in 11-4, 5 and elsewhere. In a commentary ("Reflections on *Come Retribution*") published in the Winter 1989 issue (Vol. III, No. 4) of *The International Journal of Intelligence and Counter-Intelligence*, 567-573, I stressed our discovery of the covert executive-level authorization and funding of secret service activities in the CSA and suggested that it perhaps followed a familiar USA model, namely, that Congress appropriated (starting with Geo. Washington) a "privy purse" to be disbursed at the direction of the President, by his executive agent, the Secretary of State, to the mission agent (say, Secretary of War, for further relay down the line). This provided "executive deniability" for the President and offered two or more cabinet level officials who could "take the fall" if something went wrong. After the publication of *CR*, James O. Hall directed my attention to proof that the US did follow that model, namely, a Lincoln authorization to Seward to advance "secret service" funds to Meigs for a mission to Pensacola. (This continued until the creation of CIA in 1947 and the deniability aspect disappeared when Eisenhower "'fessed up" to U2 overflights of the Soviet Union.) Sorry for the long-winded digression. My point is that too much behind the story of the raid (talk about foreshadowing the Son Tay Raid in Viet Nam!) smacks of White House secrecy and drew me later to the George/Wistar argument, perhaps stemming from Lincoln's interview with senior escapees from Richmond. I find it difficult to stop (or start) with Stanton. Wily Mr. Lincoln and his SecWar were as adept at covering their tracks as were Davis and Benjamin. Ditto Butler. (I confess that the psychological complexity of Stanton gives me fits.) There seem to be traces of prior PYA thinking (e.g., Kilpatrick's acceptance and possible setting-up of Dahlgren as fall guy or sponsored hero), ex post facto cover-up (e.g., the disappearance of the Dahlgren papers originals), and promulgation of the heroic patriot "take." (That there was genuine concern for the plight of brave men in prison I do not doubt, and I cannot read Adm Dahlgren's grief-stricken writing unmoved.)—David W. Gaddy to the author, August 3, 2006.

56 Sharpe to Dahlgren, February 28, 1864.

57 James J. Lowden to Daniel S. Lamont, March 27, 1895, included in George C. Platt Medal of Honor file, NARA.

58 George W. Beale, *A Lieutenant of Cavalry in Lee's Army* (Boston: Houghton-Mifflin, 1918), 135. Hogan accompanied Dahlgren on the Fredericksburg Raid in November 1862, and was probably known to him. Jones, *Eight Hours Before Richmond*, 156, n. 5.

59 H. A. D. Merritt, "Dahlgren's Raid," included in Peter Cozzens, ed., *Battles and Leaders of the Civil War*, Vol. 6 (Urbana, Ill.: University of Illinois Press, 2004), 383.

60 John S. Belmont, and R. Lockwood Tower, eds., *Lee's Adjutant: The Wartime Letters of Colonel Walter Herron Taylor, 1862-1865* (Columbia: University of South Carolina Press, 1995), 130.

61 O. R. vol. 33, 189.

62 *Ibid.*, 183-84.

63 *Grand Rapids Daily Democrat*, February 6, 1887.

64 A. B. Carney, "In Tight Places: Adventures of One of Our Scouts on the Kilpatrick Raid," *National Tribune*, March 29, 1894.

65 Edward C. Garrigan, "One of the 500: Col. Ulric Dahlgren's Command, and What Became of It," *National Tribune*, October 25, 1894.

66 Dahlgren, *Memoir of Ulric Dahlgren*, 212.

67 Tower and Belmont, *Lee's Adjutant*, 129.

68 Samuel Harris, *Personal Reminiscences of Samuel Harris* (Chicago: The Rogerson Press, 1897), 72.

69 O. R. vol. 33, 194.

70 *Richmond Times Dispatch*, June 10, 1906.

71 Merritt, "Dahlgren's Raid," 384; Bartley, "The Dahlgren Expedition," 5.

72 *Richmond Examiner*, March 7, 1864.

73 Dave Roth, with Bruce M. Venter, "The General's Tour: The Kilpatrick-Dahlgren Raid," *Blue and Gray* vol. 20, no. 3 (1993), 56.

74 O. R. vol. 33, 1200.

75 Bartley, "The Dahlgren Expedition," 6.

76 Dahlgren, *Memoir of Ulric Dahlgren*, 212.

77 Harris, *Personal Reminiscences*, 71.

78 O. R. vol. 33, 194.

79 Roth and Venter, "The Genera's Tour," 58.

80 Bartley, "The Dahlgren Expedition," 6.

81 Dahlgren, *Memoir of Ulric Dahlgren*, 213.

82 Bartley, "The Dahlgren Expedition," 5.

83 *Ibid.*, 7.

84 O. R. vol. 33, 221. John C. Babcock of the Army of the Potomac's Bureau of Military Information provided the guide. Babcock wrote, "At the last moment I have found the man you want; well acquainted with the James River from Richmond up. I send him to you mounted on my own private horse. You will have to furnish him a horse. Question him five minutes, and you will find him the very man you want."

85 *Ibid.*, 195.

86 *Detroit Free Press*, March 11, 1882.

87 William Preston Cabell, "How a Woman Helped to Save Richmond," *Confederate Veteran* 31 (1923), 177.

88 *Ibid.*, 178.

89 "What is the Truth of Dahlgren's Raid?" *Tyler's Quarterly Historical and Genealogical Magazine* 28 (October 1946), 69.

90 Ellen Wise Mayo, "A Wartime Aurora Borealis," typescript in collection, Virginia Historical Society, Richmond, Virginia. According to General Wise's daughter Ellen, a Federal horse soldier missed the General by moments. Wise dashed away, using his knowledge of the local road network to reach safety in Richmond. Ellen claimed that her father gave the Confederate War Department its first notice of the raid, not Mrs. Seddon.

91 Sallie A. Brock Preston, *Richmond During the War: Four Years of Personal Observation By a Richmond Lady* (New York: G. W. Carleton & Co., 1867), 277.

92 O. R. vol. 33, 195. One Richmond resident went so far as to suggest that Dahlgren "employed a negro to guide him to a ford in the river, and for this service paid him what the black supposed to be a five-dollar note, but which in fact proved to be a barber's advertisement, gotten up in the ingenious fashion common at the North." Preston,

Richmond During the War, 277. "This man was a faithful creature who had protected and nursed for 9 days, one of our offices escaped from Libby, (and who was sick) and afterwards brought him safe through our lines passing in the midst of the whole Rebel army," wrote Meade's staffer, Lt. Col. Theodore Lyman, of Martin Robinson. Lowe, *Meade's Army*, 107.

93 C. T. Jeffers, "Those Splendid Boots: How One of Dahlgren's Boys Came to Trade Them Off for a Pair Made of Bull Hide," *The National Tribune*, December 14, 1911.

94 Landegan, "He was There."

95 Addison Baker Thompson, "A Brief History of Tuckahoe," included in *Tuckahoe Plantation* (Richmond, Va.: Tuckahoe Plantation Enterprises, Ltd., 1997), 15. There is no corroboration for this story, which is why it is repeated with a caveat.

96 The church in question is the Ridge Baptist Church.

97 *Grand Rapids Daily Democrat*, February 6, 1887.

98 Venter, "The Kilpatrick-Dahlgren Raid", 20.

99 *Ibid.*, 16-19, 22, and 44. Obviously, a detailed discussion of Kilpatrick's failed assault on the defenses of Richmond strays far beyond the scope of this work. The author also recommends not only Venter's article, but also Jones, *Eight Hours from Richmond*, 61-70.

100 O. R. vol. 33, 189.

101 Wood was captured and narrowly escaped being hanged. He was instead tossed into first Libby Prison and then Belle Isle, where he nearly died of malnutrition. He eventually escaped and made his way back to the Army of the Potomac, rejoining the army during the Overland Campaign. On June 6, during the Battle of Cold Harbor, Wood undertook an arduous mission to the Shenandoah Valley to get information about the whereabouts of Maj. Gen. David Hunter's army. He returned safely, and was nominated for a Medal of Honor in 1897. Lowden to Lamont, March 27, 1895.

102 Merritt, "Dahlgren's Raid," 387; Willard J. Brown, *The Signal Corps, U. S. A. in the War of the Rebellion* (Boston: U. S. Veteran Signal Corps Association, 1896), 360.

103 O. R. vol. 33, 195.

104 John B. Jones, *A Rebel War Clerk's Diary at the Confederate States Capital*, 2 vols. (Philadelphia: J. B. Lippincott, 1866), 2:165.

105 Preston, *Richmond During the War*, 283.

106 "A Native Virginian," "A Union Man in Richmond: Personal Recollections of the Great Rebellion by a Man on the Inside." *National Tribune*, September 14, 1899.

107 Joseph R. Haw, "The Army Battalion at Green's Farm," *Confederate Veteran* 16 (1908), 153.

108 Edward P. Tobie, *History of the First Maine Cavalry, 1861-1865* (Boston: Press of Emery & Hughes, 1887), 237-38.

109 Merritt, "Dahlgren's Raid," 387.

110 Col. John McAnerny, "Dahlgren's Raid on Richmond," *Confederate Veteran* 29 (1921), 20-21 and Jones, *Eight Hours Before Richmond*, 156, n. 5. McAnerny received a promotion to colonel as a consequence of his performance during the fighting against Dahlgren's raiders, the thanks of the Confederate government, and the moniker "Savior of Richmond" from no less than Jefferson Davis himself.

111 Miles Carey, "How Richmond was Defended," *Confederate Veteran* 15 (1907), 558-59.

112 Jones, *A Rebel War Clerk's Diary*, 2:163.

113 Venter, "The Kilpatrick-Dahlgren Raid," 22.

114 Davis, *The Rise and Fall of the Confederate Government*, 2:506.

115 Merritt, "Dahlgren's Raid," 387.

116 O. R. vol. 33, 195-6.

117 Brown, *The Signal Corps, U. S. A.*, 380.

118 Merritt, "Dahlgren's Raid," 387.

119 After failing to make it through the defenses of Richmond, Kilpatrick pulled back to Atlee Station on the Richmond, Fredericksburg & Potomac Railroad and bivouacked there. A force of 300 North Carolina cavalrymen from Hampton's division marched nearly 40 miles through a snowstorm and pounced on Kilpatrick's unguarded camp. This small force of Tar Heel horsemen drove off Kilpatrick's command and sent it scurrying down the Peninsula to the safety of the Union forces holding Williamsburg. Hampton later praised the North Carolinians lavishly for their feat. See Wharton J. Green, *Recollections and Reflections: An Auto of Half a Century and More* (Raleigh, N.C.: Edwards and Broughton Printing Co., 1906), 273-274.

120 Dahlgren, *Memoir of Ulric Dahlgren*, 215.

121 *Ibid.*, 215-6.

122 *Grand Rapid Daily Democrat*, February 6, 1887; *Detroit Advertiser & Tribune*, March 16, 1864.

123 Venter, "The Kilpatrick-Dahlgren Raid," 45.

124 *Ibid.*

125 O. R. vol. 33, 197.

126 Dahlgren, *Memoir of Ulric Dahlgren*, 216-7.

127 William Gilmore Beymer, *On Hazardous Service: Scouts and Spies of the North and South* (New York: Harper & Bros., 1912), 90.

128 Most of the Army of the Potomac used this same crossing when it moved on Richmond at the end of May 1864.

129 Dahlgren, *Memoir of Ulric Dahlgren*, 218.

130 Richard L. T. Beale, *History of the Ninth Virginia Cavalry in the War Between the States* (Richmond: B. F. Johnson Publishing, 1899), 109.

131 Dahlgren, *Memoir of Ulric Dahlgren*, 219.

132 *Ibid.*, 219-20.

133 Rev. Alfred Bagby, *King and Queen County, Virginia* (New York: The Neale Publishing Co., 1908), 134.

134 Jeffers, "Those Splendid Boots."

135 Merritt, "Dahlgren's Raid," 388.

136 Dahlgren, *Memoir of Ulric Dahlgren*, 220-21.

137 Bartley, "The Dahlgren Expedition," 13.

138 *McKean Miner*, May 10, 1864.

139 Venter, "The Kilpatrick-Dahlgren Raid," 47.

140 Dahlgren, *Memoir of Ulric Dahlgren*, 221.

141 *Richmond Examiner*, March 7, 1864.

142 Edward A. Pollard, *The Lost Cause* (New York: E. B. Treat, 1867), 504.

143 O. R. vol. 33, 205 and 208. Jeb Stuart specifically credited Pollard with designing and executing the ambush, and praised his performance and that of his men that night. O. R. vol. 33, 209. Robert E. Lee endorsed Stuart's note, and Confederate Secretary of War

James A. Seddon called it "A gallant exploit, and one which exhibits what a few resolute men may do to punish the enemy on their marauding raids."

144 Henry C. Pendleton, "The Death of Colonel Dahlgren," *William and Mary College Quarterly Historical Magazine* vol. 12, no. 1 (January 1932), 2.

145 William White, "Death of Dahlgren," *National Tribune*, August 14, 1884.

146 Merritt, "Dahlgren's Raid", 389. Virtually every traditional account of the raid, including that of Virgil Carrington Jones, indicates that Louis N. Beaudrye, the regimental chaplain of the 5th New York, rode at Dahlgren's side and spoke those words. However, Beaudrye's war-time diary, which was published in 1996 makes it clear that Beaudrye, as chaplain, did not accompany the expedition and that he remained at Cavalry Corps headquarters in Culpeper County. See Richard E. Beaudrye, ed., *War Journal of Louis N. Boudrye, Fifth New York Cavalry* (Jefferson, N.C.: McFarland, 1996), 96-98. However, Beaudrye authored the regimental history of the 5th New York Cavalry, and it contains a first-person account of the raid. That account is not attributed, and it also does not indicate that a third party wrote it. In 2004, an account by Lieutenant Merritt that originally appeared in *The Philadelphia Weekly Times* was re-published. A review of this account indicates plainly that it is the same one referenced in Beaudrye's regimental history. Therefore, I have corrected this easily-made error and have properly identified Merritt as the officer riding at Dahlgren's side, not Chaplain Beaudrye.

147 Dahlgren, *Memoir of Ulric Dahlgren*, 222. The commander of the Confederate ambush, Captain Fox of the 5th Virginia Cavalry, reported, "Our fire was reserved until the head of their column rested within a few yards, when they opened fire, which was instantly returned. Colonel Dahlgren fell dead, pierced with five balls." Dahlgren was killed, and 92 of his men were captured the next morning, along with 38 blacks who were accompanying them. O. R. vol. 33, 205. The March 7, 1864 edition of the *Richmond Dispatch* claimed, "five balls struck Dahlgren—two in the head, two in the body, and one in the leg. He immediately fell from his horse and expired."

CHAPTER TWELVE

1 Louis N. Boudrye, *Historic Records of the Fifth New York Cavalry, First Ira Harris Guard: Its Organization, Marches, Raids, Scouts, Engagements and General Services, During the Rebellion of 1861-1865* (Albany, N. Y.: J. Munsell, 1868), 109.

2 *Richmond Examiner*, March 7, 1864.

3 *Ibid*. Ninety-one new prisoners were marched to Richmond the next day. Their ranks included Major Cooke, Lieutenant Merritt of the 5th New York Cavalry, and Lieutenant Bartley, the signal officer assigned to accompany the expedition.

4 White, "Death of Dahlgren."

5 Someone else took Ully's sword, although that person's identity remains unknown. The sword was returned to the family anonymously in 1876. The Admiral re-married in late 1865, after the Confederate surrender. He wed Madeleine Vinton, a renowned novelist of Catholic extraction, which infuriated his Protestant family. Admiral Dahlgren died in 1870. Six years after his death, a Catholic priest returned the sword to Mrs. Dahlgren, saying, "This is returned to you through the confessional. No questions can be asked." And none were. *The Daily News*, May 26, 1886.

6 Pollard, *The Lost Cause*, 505.

7 O. R. vol. 33, 208.

8 *Ibid.*, 217.

9 Letter of Fitzhugh Lee, included in *Southern Historical Society Papers* 13 (1887), 553.

10 "What is the Truth of Dahlgren's Raid," 83.

11 *McKean Miner*, May 10, 1864.

12 B. H. Walker, M.D., "The First Man to Reach Dahlgren After He Was Killed." *Richmond Times-Dispatch*, April 11, 1909.

13 *Richmond Whig*, March 8, 1864.

14 *Richmond Times-Dispatch*, November 17, 1901.

15 *Richmond Examiner*, March 3, 1864 and *Richmond Daily Dispatch*, March 8, 1864.

16 Davis, *The Rise and Fall of the Confederate Government*, 2:507.

17 Benjamin F. Butler, *Private and Official Correspondence of Gen. Benjamin F. Butler During the Period of the Civil War*, 5 vols. (Privately published, 1917), 4:484.

18 O. R. vol. 33, 219-20.

19 *Ibid.*, 220-21.

20 *Richmond Examiner*, March 5, 1864.

21 *Richmond Whig*, March 7, 1864.

22 *Richmond Inquirer*, March 5, 1864.

23 *Richmond Whig*, March 5, 1864.

24 *Richmond Daily Dispatch*, March 5, 1864.

25 *Richmond Examiner*, March 5, 1864.

26 O. R. vol. 33, 218.

27 *Ibid.*, 222-3.

28 Mary Bandy Daughtry, *Gray Cavalier: The Life and Wars of General W.H.F. "Rooney" Lee* (Cambridge, Mass.: Da Capo Press, 2002), 149-51.

29 O. R. vol. 33, 223.

30 *Ibid.*, 178.

31 *Ibid.*, 180.

32 *Ibid.*

33 Lowe, *Meade's Army*, 124.

34 Meade, *Life and Letters*, 2:190-91.

35 Tower and Belmont, *Lee's Adjutant*, 153.

36 Mary Boykin Chesnut, *A Diary from Dixie*, Isabella D. Martin and Myrta Lockett Avary, eds. (New York: D. Appleton and Co., 1905), 394.

37 Varina Davis, *Jefferson Davis: Ex-President of the Confederate States of America. A Memoir by His Wife*, 2 vols. (New York: Belford Co., 1890), 2:470-72.

38 Welles, *Diary of Gideon Welles*, 1:538.

39 Meade, *Life and Letters*, 2:170.

40 Burlingame and Ettlinger, *Inside Lincoln's White House*, 179.

41 Allan Nevins, ed., *A Diary of Battle: The Personal Journals of Colonel Charles S. Wainwright, 1861-1865* (New York: Harcourt, Brace & World, 1962), 334.

42 *Philadelphia Inquirer*, March 9, 1864.

43 *Sacramento Daily Union*, April 9, 1864.

44 *New York Times*, March 9, 1864.

45 *Harper's Weekly*, March 26, 1864.

46 *Saturday Evening Post*, April 2, 1864.

47 Dahlgren, *Memoir of John A. Dahlgren*, 442.

48 Butler, *Letters*, 4:488.

49 *Ibid.*, 4:489.

50 *Ibid.*, 4:493; Dahlgren, *Memoir of John A. Dahlgren*, 444.

51 *Ibid.*, 444-45.

52 John A. Dahlgren to Martha Read, March 10, 1865, John A. Dahlgren Papers, Newberry Library, Chicago, Illinois.

53 Dahlgren, *Memoir of John A. Dahlgren*, 445.

54 Butler, *Letters*, 4:504. Admiral Dahlgren responded that same day. He wrote:

> I am deeply indebted for your kind sympathy, and submit to your better judgment in preferring the regular Flag of Truce. There is hardly any sacrifice that I would not incur to obtain the remains of my beloved son; but what can I say to the Rebel authorities that might not interfere with my purpose,—for my heart swells with indignation at the accounts given by the Richmond press, and their approval of the inhuman treatment which his dead body received. My own official position also forbids the least concession that might be construed to lie in the path of duty. For these reasons I feel desirous that the request should come from you, stating if you choose that I have come here in the hopes of obtaining the body of my son, and await the decision. Be assured, my friend, that the blood of this young soldier has not been shed in vain,—and his example will nerve many a hard in struggles as desperate as that in which he fell.

55 Until Ulysses S. Grant ended the cartel in the spring of 1864, the Union and Confederacy had operated an exchange cartel whereby prisoners of war of like rank were exchanged for each other. For a detailed explanation of the terms of the cartel, see Parker, *Richmond's Civil War Prisons*, 16.

56 O. R. series 2, vol. 6, 1034-35.

57 Dahlgren, *Memoir of John A. Dahlgren*, 446.

58 Butler, *Letters*, 4:519.

59 O. R. vol. 33, 242.

60 *Ibid.*, 245.

61 Dahlgren, *Memoir of John A. Dahlgren*, 446.

62 *Ibid.*, 447.

63 Butler, *Letters*, 4:547.

64 John A. Dahlgren diary, entry for April 5, 1864, Dahlgren Papers, LOC.

65 John A. Dahlgren to Martha Read, March 10, 1864, John A. Dahlgren Papers, Newberry Library, Chicago, Illinois.

66 Welles, *Diary of Gideon Welles*, 2:7.

67 John A. Dahlgren diary, entry for April 18, 1864, Dahlgren Papers, LOC.

68 Gower, *Charles Dahlgren*, 96.

69 O. R. series 2, vol. 6, 1082.

70 For an excellent biography of Crazy Bet Van Lew, see Elizabeth R. Varon, *Southern Lady, Yankee Spy: The True Story of Elizabeth Van Lew, a Union Agent in the Heart of the Confederacy* (New York: Oxford University Press, 2003).

71 Elizabeth L. Van Lew to Ulysses S. Grant, October 2, 1869, included in Elizabeth L. Van Lew, *A Yankee Spy in Richmond: The Civil War Diary of "Crazy Bet" Van Lew*, Davis D. Ryan, ed. (Mechanicsburg, Pa.: Stackpole Books, 1996), 121.

72 *Ibid.*, 69.

73 *Ibid.*, 70.

74 *Ibid.*, 71-2.

75 *Ibid.*, 72.

76 Dahlgren, *Memoir of John A. Dahlgren*, 449.

77 *Richmond Examiner*, April 14, 1864.

78 Dahlgren, *Memoir of John A. Dahlgren*, 450.

79 O. R. vol. 33, 181.

80 *Ibid.*

81 Dahlgren, *Memoir of John A. Dahlgren*, 451.

82 Sunderland, *A Sermon in Memory of Colonel Ulric Dahlgren*, 5 and 48.

83 *Washington Post*, November 23, 1891.

84 Members of the Dahlgren family apparently remain deeply committed to clearing Ulric's name to this day. Denise Dahlgren is the great-great-great granddaughter of Ulric's brother Charley. "My ancestors staunchly refused to believe that Ulric was part of any kind of conspiracy and sought to 'vindicate' him," she wrote in October 2006. "I can recall seeing a copy of the 'Dahlgren Papers' as a child and being chastised for daring to ask if there was any truth to the claims." Denise Dahlgren to the author, October 4, 2006.

85 Wiley Sword, ed., "Admiral John A. Dahlgren Defends His Son the Day After Ulric's Public Memorial Service," *Blue & Gray* vol. 20, no. 3 (2003): 53.

86 John A. Dahlgren to Martha Read, May 6, 1867, John A. Dahlgren Papers, Newberry Library, Chicago, Illinois.

87 Dahlgren, *Memoir of Ulric Dahlgren*, 233 (emphasis in original).

88 *New York Times*, July 28, 1864.

89 Quoted in Dahlgren, *Memoir of Ulric Dahlgren*, 235 (emphasis in original).

90 John A. Dahlgren to Martha Read, April 18, 1865, John A. Dahlgren Papers, Newberry Library, Chicago, Illinois.

91 Brooks D. Simpson and Jean V. Berlin, *Sherman's Civil War: Selected Correspondence of William T. Sherman, 1860-1865* (Chapel Hill: University of North Carolina Press, 1999), 841.

92 *New York Herald*, April 13, 1865.

93 O. R. vol. 46, part 3, 712.

94 *Army and Navy Journal*, April 15, 1865.

95 Dahlgren, *Memoir of Ulric Dahlgren*, 275.

96 Quoted in Meriwether Stuart, "Colonel Ulric Dahlgren and Richmond's Union Underground, 1864," *Virginia Magazine of History and Biography* vol. 72 (1964), 169.

97 Schultz, *The Dahlgren Affair*, 259.

98 Dahlgren, *Memoir of Ulric Dahlgren*, 277.

99 *Ibid.*, 278. Tragedy also haunted Ulric's brother, Paul. Like Ulric, tall, fair, handsome, and charismatic, Paul was a member of the West Point class of 1868. He served in the artillery during his short Regular Army career and resigned his commission in December 1870, not long after his father's death, to pursue a more lucrative career as a civil engineer. He joined a railroad firm in New York called Wilson and Wilson, which included Civil War cavalry general Maj. Gen. James H. Wilson. Paul worked to the point of exhaustion and began developing major health problems, commonly attributed to a heart condition, during the second half of 1871. He was married in May 1873, and was then appointed U. S. Consul General to Rome at the age of 27, becoming the youngest diplomat in the Foreign Service. Not long after, his behavior became erratic and alarming to those

around him. In February 1875, he was arrested after an altercation in which he threatened a fellow citizen with a revolver. By January 1876, he was demonstrating clear signs of mental instability and he began drinking heavily. On March 13, his physician found him suffering from delirium tremens and talking of suicide. Ten days later a servant found him lying dead in a hallway of the consulate after consuming 12-15 times the amount of digitalis prescribed for him by his doctor, and, on one occasion, 24 times the prescribed dosage. Dead at 30, Paul Dahlgren's life also ended tragically young. For more detail on Paul Dahlgren's life and death, see Brian C. Pohanka, ed., *A Summer on the Plains with Custer's 7ᵗʰ Cavalry: The 1870 Diary of Annie Gibson Roberts* (Lynchburg, Va.: Schroeder Publications, 2004), 111-112.

100 *Washington Post*, November 23, 1891.
101 Dahlgren, *Memoir of Ulric Dahlgren*, 283.
102 *Ibid.*, 285.
103 Diary of John A. Dahlgren, entry for November 1, 1865, Dahlgren Papers, LOC.
104 *Philadelphia Inquirer*, November 2, 1865.
105 *Ibid.*
106 *Ibid.*
107 Diary of John A. Dahlgren, entry for November 1, 1865, Dahlgren Papers, LOC.
108 *Philadelphia Inquirer*, November 2, 1865.

CHAPTER THIRTEEN

1. Charley named his first son John Adolph, in honor of his father. After recovering from malaria, Charley became fleet ordnance officer on the iron-clad squadron commanded by his father in front of Charleston and in the North Atlantic blockading squadron, 1864. He then became senior watch officer of the *U.S.S. Onondaga*, which protected the right flank of Grant's army at Petersburg; and was executive officer of the U.S. steamer *Gettysburg*, 7 guns, in the attack and capture of Fort Fisher in 1865. Charley received honorable mention in orders and reports, and for his services was promoted first lieutenant and captain during the progress of the war. Upon tendering his resignation in 1865 he was asked by the secretary of the navy to reconsider and accept service in the regular Navy. Charley declined and instead engaged in mining and mechanical engineering in the far west and Mexico. He was married in 1867 to Augusta Smith, great-great granddaughter of the Hon. Henry Wisner, delegate to the Continental Congress from Orange County, N.Y., and a Revolutionary patriot. After living in the far west for 25 years, he returned to the east, residing at Nantucket, Mass., and at Trenton, N.J., alternately. In 1898, he commanded a battalion of the New Jersey naval reserves and furnished the officers and crews for two ships in the Spanish war, the monitor *U.S.S. Montauk* and then the *U.S.S. Resolute*. He was elected a fellow of the American Geographical Society and a member of the Long Island Historical Society, the Grand Army of the Republic, the Military Order of the Loyal Legion of the United States, the Naval Order and the Masonic order. He published: *Historic Mines of Mexico* (1883); *The Dahlgren Gun and Its Services during the late Civil War* (1889); and numerous historical, biographical and technical papers. He died in Trenton in 1911. His second son, named Ulric in honor of the fallen hero, became a major player in the field of academic biology studies. Prof. Ulric Dahlgren spent a long and very successful career as a leading scholar of biology at Princeton University, including winning a Nobel Prize for his work.

2   Martin, *The Life and Public Services of Schuyler Colfax*, 475.

3   Michael Burlingame, ed., *With Lincoln in the White House: Letters, Memoranda, and Other Writings of John G. Nicolay, 1860-1865* (Carbondale, Ill.: Southern Illinois University Press, 2000), 129.

4   Franz Sigel, unpublished manuscript about the Second Bull Run Campaign, Container 6, Folder 3, Franz Sigel Papers, Western Reserve Historical Society, Cleveland, Ohio.

5   O. R. series 3, vol. 4, 173.

6   Dahlgren to Sargent, August 22, 1864.

7   Fitzhugh Lee, *General Lee* (New York: D. Appleton & Co., 1913), 324.

8   E. A. Paul, "A Review of the Expedition," included in Frank Moore, ed., *The Rebellion Record*, 12 vols. (New York: D. Van Nostrand, 1865), 8:593.

9   See, e.g., Gower, *Charles Dahlgren of Natchez*, 38, wherein Gower relates a story about a friend of Charles G. Dahlgren's who "remembered him as an arrogant young man with patronizing ways toward the people in the little mountain community."

10   Quoted in J. William Jones, "The Kilpatrick-Dahlgren Raid Against Richmond." *Southern Historical Society Papers* 13 (1888), 555.

11   *Richmond Examiner*, November 23, 1863.

12   Parker, *Richmond's Civil War Prisons*, 63.

13   *Ibid.*, 64.

14   *Ibid.*, 65-66.

15   For more on the failure of Stoneman's effort, see David Evans, *Sherman's Horsemen: Union Cavalry Operations in the Atlanta Campaign* (Bloomington: University of Indiana Press, 1996), 291-340.

16   Victor Vifquain, who was awarded a Medal of Honor in 1865, wrote the one surviving account of the aborted 1862 plot. The book is based on a manuscript by Vifquain that languished mostly unseen in the Nebraska State Historical Society for years. Historians Jeffrey H. Smith and Phillip Thomas Tucker edited Vifquain's manuscript and published it as a book in 1998. See Victor Vifquain, *The 1862 Plot to Kidnap Jefferson Davis*, Jeffrey H. Smith and Phillip Thomas Tucker, eds. (Mechanicsburg, Pa.: Stackpole Books, 1998).

17   See Schultz, *The Dahlgren Affair*.

18   William A. Tidwell, James O. Hall, and David Winfred Gaddy, *Come Retribution: The Confederate Secret Service and the Assassination of Lincoln* (Jackson: University Press of Mississippi, 1988), 19 and 241-251. Interestingly, James O. Hall, who co-authored this book, wrote an article that demonstrated almost beyond dispute that the so-called Dahlgren Papers were, in fact, authentic. This article will be discussed at length in the appendix to this book.

19   Kauffman, "David Edgar Herold," 24.

20   William T. Sherman, *Memoirs of W. T. Sherman* (New York: The Library of America, 1990), 812.

21   *Ibid.*, 814.

22   O. R. series 3, vol. 3, 162-63. Interestingly enough, Lieber had one son fighting for the Union and another fighting for the Confederacy.

23   For an interesting explication of this theory, see Joseph George, Jr., "'Black Flag Warfare': Lincoln and the Raids Against Richmond and Jefferson Davis," *The Pennsylvania Magazine of History and Biography*, Vol. CXV, No. 3 (July 1991), 291-318.

24 William W. Patteson typescript memoirs, Maryland Historical Society, Baltimore, Maryland, 25-26.

25 In Latin, Occam's Razor is the *lex parsimoniae* (law of succinctness): *entia non sunt multiplicanda praeter necessitatem*, which translates to: *entities should not be multiplied beyond necessity.*

26 For more on McEntee and the crucial role that he played in the operations of the Bureau of Military Intelligence, see Fishel, *The Secret War for the Union*, 293-294 and following pages.

27 Marsena R. Patrick, *Inside Lincoln's Army: The Diary of Marsena Rudolph Patrick, Provost Marshal General, Army of the Potomac*, ed. David S. Sparks (New York: Yoseloff, 1964), 347-48.

28 *Inter-Ocean*, June 17, 1875.

29 Quoted in Schultz, *The Dahlgren Affair*, 248.

30 Mosby to Major Stiles, January 13, 1871, included in Adele H. Mitchell, ed., *The Letters of John S. Mosby* (Richmond, Va.: Stuart-Mosby Historical Society, 1986), 45.

31 Wiley Sword, ed., "Lt. Col. Judson Kilpatrick Complains to President Lincoln of the Harsh Injustice of Col. Lafayette C. Baker, Who Threw 'Kill-Cavalry' Into Prison," *Blue & Gray* vol. 23, no. 4 (2006): 37-40.

APPENDIX

1 Historian Stephen W. Sears wrote an extensive and detailed article that determined that the Dahlgren Papers were authentic. It is quite persuasive, and the author commends it you as the definitive word on the subject. See Stephen W. Sears, "The Dahlgren Papers Revisited," *Columbiad* Vol. 3, No. 2 (Summer 1999): 63-87. I will simply amplify on Sears' conclusions with newly-discovered evidence and by focusing on the timeline that demonstrates that the documents could not have been forged by the Confederates.

2 Pollard, *The Lost Cause*, 505-6.

3 Quoted in Jones, "The Kilpatrick-Dahlgren Raid Against Richmond," 555.

4 James D. Richardson, ed., *A Compilation of the Messages and Papers of the Confederacy, Including the Diplomatic Correspondence, 1861-1865*, 2 vols. (Nashville: United States Publishing Co., 1905), 2:639.

5 O.R. vol. 33, 224.

6 Jubal A. Early to John William Jones, February 24, 1879, included in Jones, "The Kilpatrick-Dahlgren Raid Against Richmond," 559.

7 Ira N. Gullickson to Virgil Carrington Jones, May 20, 1958, copy in possession of Robert Huddleston, Denver, Colorado. I am grateful to Mr. Huddleston for providing me with a copy of this important letter and for granting me permission to quote from it in this book.

8 O. R. vol. 25, part 2, 517.

9 James O. Hall, "The Dahlgren Papers: Fact or Fabrication?", *Civil War Times Illustrated*, Vol. XXII, No. 7 (November 1983), 37-38.

10 *Ibid.*, 38-39. For Riggs' analysis of the authenticity of the Dahlgren Papers, and for his take on finding the photographic copies of the Papers, see David F. Riggs, "The Dahlgren Papers Reconsidered." *The Lincoln Herald* (Summer 1981): 658-667.

Bibliography

PRIMARY SOURCES

NEWSPAPERS

Army and Navy Journal
Baltimore American
Boston Evening Journal
Boston Globe
Brooklyn Eagle
Burlington Weekly Hawk-Eye (Burlington, Iowa)
Charleston Daily Courier
Charleston Mercury
Chicago Tribune
Cincinnati Daily Commercial
Detroit Free Press
Gettysburg Times
Grand Rapids Daily Democrat
Harper's Weekly
Inter-Ocean (Chicago, Illinois)
Janesville Daily Gazette
Milwaukee Daily Sentinel
National Tribune
New Haven Journal and Courier
New York Herald
New York Times
New York Tribune
New York World
Philadelphia Evening Bulletin
Philadelphia Inquirer
Philadelphia Press
Philadelphia Public Ledger
Philadelphia Weekly Times
Portage County Democrat
Richmond Daily Dispatch

Richmond Enquirer
Richmond Examiner
Richmond Sentinel
Richmond Times-Dispatch
Richmond Whig
Sacramento Daily Union
Saturday Evening Post
The Daily News (Frederick, Maryland)
The McKean Miner (Smithport, Pennsylvania)
The Star and Sentinel (Gettysburg, Pennsylvania)
Washington Evening Star
Washington Post
Waynesboro Village Record
Western Reserve Chronicle
Wheeling Daily Intelligencer

MANUSCRIPT MATERIALS

Special Collections, Augustana College, Rock Island, Illinois:
  John A. Dahlgren Papers

Richard Carlile Collection, Dayton, Ohio:
  Hamilton S. Ballentine Letters

Civil War Museum and Library, Philadelphia, Pennsylvania:
  Record of Charles B. Dahlgren, No. 9492, Military Order of the Loyal Legion of
  the United States, Pennsylvania Commandery, May 5, 1892
  MOLLUS-Pennsylvania Commandery Scrapbooks

The David Library of the American Revolution, Washington's Crossing, Pennsylvania:
  Revolutionary War Pension and Bounty Land Warrant Applications, 1800-1900,
  M804, Reel 2091

Archives, Fredericksburg & Spotsylvania National Military Park, Fredericksburg, Virginia:
  J. M. Herndon letter of November 9, 1862
  Henry W. Moore letter of March 6, 1864
  Franz Sigel Military Telegraph Dispatches, November 1862
  Presley Thornton letter of November 10, 1862.

Archives, Georgetown University, Washington, D. C.:
  Madeleine Vinton Dahlgren Papers

Archives, Gettysburg National Military Park, Gettysburg, Pennsylvania:
 Battle of Hagerstown file
 Charles E. Cadwalader letter of July 10, 1863
 Luther Trowbridge undated letter to J. Allen Bigelow

Archives, Historical Society of Pennsylvania, Philadelphia, Pennsylvania:
 General John Cadwalader Section, Cadwalader Family Papers
 Dreer Collection, Union Officers ALS
 Simon Gratz Civil War Collection, Union Colonels, ALS
 Society Miscellaneous Collections

Robert Huddleston Collection, Denver, Colorado:
 Ira N. Gullickson letter to Virgil Carrington Jones of May 20, 1958

Huntington Library, San Marino, California:
 Joseph Hooker Papers

Manuscripts Division, Library of Congress, Washington, D. C.:
 John A. Dahlgren Papers
 John A. Dahlgren Diaries
 John A. Dahlgren Letters
 Ulric Dahlgren Diaries
 Ulric Dahlgren Letters
 Ulric Dahlgren Scrapbooks
 Samuel J. B. V. Gilpin Diary
 Samuel P. Heintzelman Papers
 John G. Nicolay Papers

Archives, Maryland Historical Society, Baltimore, Maryland:
 William W. Patteson typescript memoirs

National Archives and Record Administration, Washington, D. C.:
 Ambrose E. Burnside Papers
 Charles H. Daniels Pension File, M1469, certificate #20175, fiche #19434
 Microcopy 473, Roll 270
 Microcopy 504, Roll 303
 Microfilm Group 625 Reel 18, Naval Records Collection, Records for Area 7,
 May-June 1862.
 RG 93, Combined Service Records
 RG 94, Records of the Adjutant General's Office
 RG 94, U. S. Army Generals' Reports of Civil War Service 1864-1887

RG 94, Entry 731, General's Papers, November 1862 Folder
RG 107, Records of the Office of the Secretary of War, Telegrams Collected by the
Secretary of War (Unbound), M504, Roll 130
RG 110, Entry 31, Scouts, Guides, Spies, and Detective File, Records of the
Provost Marshal General's Office
RG 111, Records of the Office of the Chief Signal Officer, 1860-1892
RG 393, Entry 3976, Army of the Potomac, Letters Received 1863
RG 393, Part II (US Army Continental Command, 1821-1920), Entry 5319:
11th Army Corps Letters Received, January 1863-1864 (Unarranged),
Box 1
George C. Platt Medal of Honor file

Archives, New York Historical Society, New York, New York:
Henry Augustus Wise Papers

Archives, Newberry Library, Chicago, Illinois:
John A. Dahlgren Papers

Rhode Island Historical Society, Providence, Rhode Island:
George N. Bliss letters

Swedish Historical Museum and Library, Philadelphia, Pennsylvania:
Dahlgren Family Papers

Tennessee State Archives, Nashville, Tennessee:
Dahlgren Family Papers

United States Army Military History Institute, Carlisle, Pennsylvania:
William T. H. Brooks Papers
Civil War Miscellaneous Collection
William W. Pritchard Diary
Civil War Times Illustrated Collection

Archives, United States Naval Academy, Annapolis, Maryland:
Charles H. Daniels Midshipman Records

*Southern Historical Collections, Wilson Library, University of North Carolina, Chapel
Hill, North Carolina:*
Charles Venable Papers

Archives, Alderman Library, University of Virginia, Charlottesville, Virginia:
  William Silliman Hillyer Papers

Archives, Virginia Historical Society, Richmond, Virginia:
  Reuben Bartley Manuscript, "The Dahlgren Expedition"
  Chappelear Family Papers
  W. P. Shelton, "The Truth About Dahlgren's Raid"
  Ulric Dahlgren Papers (photographic copies)
  Robert E. English Memoirs
  Ellen Wise Mayo, "A Wartime Aurora Borealis"
  Uriah Parmalee Correspondence
  John Singleton Mosby Papers
  H. Douglass Pitts, "Landmarks of Dahlgren's Raid Along Three Chopt Road"
  William L. Royall Papers

Archives, Virginia Military Institute, Lexington, Virginia:
  John Hyde Cameron Memoirs
  Andrew J. McCoy Letters

Archives, Western Reserve Historical Society, Cleveland, Ohio:
  Franz Sigel Papers

Eric J. Wittenberg Collection, Columbus, Ohio:
  Miscellaneous correspondence
  Frederick Morris Letter of February 11, 1887.

PUBLISHED SOURCES

"A Native Virginian." "A Union Man in Richmond: Personal Recollections of the Great
  Rebellion by a Man on the Inside." *National Tribune*, September 14, 1899.
Agassiz, George R., ed. *Meade's Headquarters, 1863-1865: Letters of Colonel Theodore
  Lyman*. Boston: Atlantic Monthly Press, 1922.
Alexander, Edward P. *Fighting for the Confederacy: The Personal Recollections of Edward
  Porter Alexander*. Gary W. Gallagher, ed. Chapel Hill: University of North Carolina
  Press, 1989.
Allen, William. *History of the Campaign of Gen. T. J. (Stonewall) Jackson in the
  Shenandoah Valley of Virginia: From November 4, 1861, to June 17, 1862*. Philadelphia:
  J. B. Lippincott & Co., 1880.
———. "Stonewall Jackson's Valley Campaign," included in *Annals of the War: Written
  by Leading Participants North & South*. Reprint, Dayton, Ohio: Morningside, 1986:
  724-749.

Allison, Don, ed. *Hell on Belle Isle: Diary of a Civil War POW*. Bryan, Ohio: Faded Banner Publications, 1997.

Bagby, Rev. Alfred. *King and Queen County, Virginia*. New York: Neale Publishing Co., 1908.

Basler, Roy P., Marion Dolores Pratt, and Lloyd A. Dunlap, eds. *The Collected Works of Abraham Lincoln*. 9 vols. Springfield, Ill.: Abraham Lincoln Association; New Brunswick, N.J.: Rutgers University Press, 1953.

Beaudrye, Louis N. *Historic Records of the Fifth New York Cavalry, First Ira Harris Guard: Its Organization, Marches, Raids, Scouts, Engagements and General Services, During the Rebellion of 1861-1865*. Albany, N. Y.: J. Munsell, 1868.

Beaudrye, Richard E., ed. *War Journal of Louis N. Beaudrye, Fifth New York Cavalry*. Jefferson, N.C.: McFarland, 1996.

Beale, George W. *A Lieutenant of Cavalry in Lee's Army*. Boston: Houghton-Mifflin, 1918.

Beale, Richard L. T. *History of the Ninth Virginia Cavalry in the War Between the States*. Richmond: B. F. Johnson Publishing, 1899.

———. "Part Taken by the Ninth Virginia Cavalry in Repelling the Dahlgren Raid." *Southern Historical Society Papers* 3 (1877): 219-21.

Belmont, John S. and R. Lockwood Tower, eds. *Lee's Adjutant: The Wartime Letters of Colonel Walter Herron Taylor, 1862-1865*. Columbia: University of South Carolina Press, 1995.

Bettes, W. H. "A Daring Reconnaissance." *National Tribune*, March 12, 1896.

Boaz, Thomas M., ed. *Libby Prison & Beyond: A Union Staff Officer in the East, 1862-1865*. Shippensburg, Pa.: Burd Street Press, 1999.

Bond, Frank A. "Company A, First Maryland Cavalry." *Confederate Veteran* VI (1898): 78-80.

Borden, William C. "Swinging 'Round the Circle: The Raid Thru 'Ol' Virginny,' to Richmond and Back." *National Tribune*, March 8, 1923.

Brown, J. Willard. *The Signal Corps, U. S. A. in the War of the Rebellion*. Boston: U. S. Veteran Signal Corps Association, 1896.

Buckingham, John E., Sr. *Reminiscences and Souvenirs of the Assassination of Abraham Lincoln*. Washington, D.C.: Press of Rufus H. Darby, 1884.

Burlingame, Michael, ed. *At Lincoln's Side: John Hay's Civil War Correspondence and Selected Writings*. Carbondale: Southern Illinois University Press, 2000.

———. *Lincoln's Journalist: John Hay's Anonymous Writings for the Press, 1860-1864*. Carbondale: Southern Illinois University Press, 1998.

———. *Lincoln Observed: Civil War Dispatches of Noah Brooks*. Baltimore: Johns Hopkins University Press, 1998.

———. *With Lincoln in the White House: Letters, Memoranda, and Other Writings of John G. Nicolay, 1860-1865*. Carbondale: Southern Illinois University Press, 2000.

Burlingame, Michael and John R. Turner Ettlinger, eds. *Inside Lincoln's White House:*

The Complete Civil War Diary of John Hay. Carbondale: Southern Illinois University Press, 1997.

Bushey, F. A. "That Historic Dispatch: How It Was Captured by Dahlgren and His Little Band." *The National Tribune*, May 14, 1896.

Butler, Benjamin F. *Private and Official Correspondence of Gen. Benjamin F. Butler During the Period of the Civil War*. 5 vols. Privately published, 1917.

Cabell, William Preston. "How a Woman Helped to Save Richmond." *Confederate Veteran* 31 (1923): 177-78.

Carey, Miles. "How Richmond was Defended." *Confederate Veteran* 15 (1907): 557-559.

Carney, A. B. "In Tight Places: Adventures of One of Our Scouts in the Kilpatrick Raid." *National Tribune*, March 29 and April 5, 1894.

Cesnola, Luigi Palma di. *Ten Months in Libby Prison*. New York: n. p., 1865.

Chase, Philip S. "Service with Battery F, First Rhode Island Light Artillery." *Military Order of the Loyal Legion of the United States—Rhode Island War Papers* 6 (Providence: Published by the Society, 1889): 87-135.

Chesnut, Mary Boykin. *A Diary from Dixie*. Isabella D. Martin and Myrta Lockett Avary, eds. New York: D. Appleton and Co., 1905.

Circular of the Rittenhouse Academy, Corner of Third Street and Indiana Avenue, Washington City. Otis C. Wright, Proprietor and Principal. Washington, D.C.: Towers, 1858.

Clark, Stephen A. "Kilpatrick's Raid: The Second Trip to Richmond in March, 1864." *National Tribune*, September 20, 1888.

Clay, Jehu Curtis. *Annals of the Swedes on the Delaware*. Philadelphia: J. C. Pechin, 1835.

Considine, Patrick H. "Was With Col. Dahlgren." *National Tribune*, March 25, 1896.

Cozzens, Peter and Robert I. Girardi, eds. *The Military Memoirs of John Pope*. Chapel Hill: University of North Carolina Press, 1998.

Crouch, Richard G. "The Dahlgren Raid." *Southern Historical Society Papers* 34 (1906): 178-190.

Dahlgren, John A. *Memoir of Ulric Dahlgren by His Father*. Philadelphia: J. B. Lippincott, 1872.

———. *Shells and Shell Guns*. Philadelphia: King & Baird, 1856.

Dahlgren, Madeleine Vinton. "Col. Ulric Dahlgren. A Boy Hero Who Rendered Most Important Service." *National Tribune*, February 6, 1896.

———. *Etiquette of Social Life in Washington*. Washington, D. C.: n.p., 1873.

———. *Memoir of John A. Dahlgren, Rear-Admiral United States Navy*. Boston: James R. Osgood and Co., 1882.

"Dahlgren's Ride Into Fredericksburg." *Southern Historical Society Papers* 3 (1877): 87-90.

Davis, Jefferson. *The Rise and Fall of the Confederate Government*. 2 vols. New York: D. Appleton and Co., 1881.

Davis, Sidney Morris. *Common Soldier, Uncommon War: Life as a Cavalryman in the Civil War*. Charles F. Cooney, ed. Bethesda, Maryland, SMD Group, 1994.

Davis, Varina. *Jefferson Davis: Ex-President of the Confederate States of America. A Memoir by His Wife*. 2 vols. New York: Belford Co., 1890.

Dow, Neal. *The Reminiscences of Neal Dow: Recollections of Eighty Years*. Portland, Me.: The Evening Express Publishing Co., 1898.

Foley, B. F. "Prisoners Taken in Dahlgren's Raid." *Confederate Veteran* 16 (1908): 280.s

Ford, Worthington C., ed. *A Cycle of Adams Letters, 1861-1865*. 2 vols. Boston, Houghton-Mifflin, 1920.

Frazer, John F., ed. *Journal of the Franklin Institute of the State of Pennsylvania for the Promotion of the Mechanic Arts. Devoted to Mechanical and Physical Science, Civil Engineering, the Arts and Manufactures*. 3rd Series, Vol. 42. Philadelphia: Franklin Institute, 1861.

Gardner, Alexander. *Gardner's Photographic Sketch Book of the War*. 2 vols. Washington, D.C.: Philip & Solomons, 1866.

Garrigan, Edward C. "One of the 500: Col. Ulric Dahlgren's Command, and What Became of It." *National Tribune*, October 25, 1894.

Gilles, G. W. "A Narrow Escape." *National Tribune*, November 6, 1884.

Gillespie, Samuel L. *A History of Company A, First Ohio Cavalry, 1861-1865: A Memorial Volume Compiled from Personal Records and Living Witnesses*. Washington, Ohio: Ohio State Register, l898.

Glazier, Willard W. *The Capture, the Prison Pen, and the Escape*. Hartford, Conn.: H. E. Goodwin, 1868.

Goldsborough, W. W. *The Maryland Line in the Confederate Army, 1861-1865*. Baltimore: Guggenheimer, Weil & Co., 1900.

Goode, Mrs. Lizzie Redwood. "Memories of Long Ago." *Confederate Veteran* 36 (1928): 88-89.

Gracey, Samuel L. *Annals of the Sixth Pennsylvania Cavalry*. Philadelphia: E. H. Butler & Co. 1868.

Green, Wharton J. *Recollections and Reflections: An Auto of Half a Century and More*. Raleigh, N.C.: Edwards and Broughton Printing Co., 1906.

Greene, Charles S. *Thrilling Stories of the Great Rebellion*. Philadelphia: The Keystone Publishing Co., 1889.

Hagemann, E. R., ed. *Fighting Rebels and Redskins: Experiences in Army Life of Colonel George B. Sanford, 1861-1892*. Norman: University of Oklahoma Press, 1968.

Haggard, Horatio C. "Cavalry Fight at Fredericksburg." *Confederate Veteran* 21 (1913): 295.

Hall, Hillman A., ed. *History of the Sixth New York Cavalry (Second Ira Harris Guards), Second Brigade-First Division-Cavalry Corps, Army of the Potomac 1861-1865*. Worcester Mass.: Blanchard Press, 1908.

Harris, Samuel. *A Story of the War of the Rebellion: Why I Was Not Hung.* Chicago: Chicago Globe Print, 1890.

———. *Personal Reminiscences of Samuel Harris.* Chicago: The Rogerson Press, 1897.

Harrison, William H. "Personal Experiences of a Cavalry Officer 1861-66." *War Papers, Pennsylvania Commandery, Military Order of the Loyal Legion of the United States,* vol. 1 (1895): 225-254.

Haw, Joseph R. "That Fight at Green's Farm Near Richmond." *Confederate Veteran* 17 (1909): 452.

———. "The Armory Battalion at Green's Farm." *Confederate Veteran* 16 (1908): 153-55.

Hebb, E. T. "A Reconnaissance." *National Tribune,* April 29, 1900.

Hoke, Jacob. *The Great Invasion of 1863.* New York: Thomas Yoseloff, 1867.

Horton, R. G. *A Youth's History of the Great Civil War in the United States, From 1861 to 1865.* New York: Van Evrie, Horton & Co., 1868.

Ide, Horace K. *History of the First Vermont Cavalry Volunteers in the War of the Great Rebellion.* Edited by Elliott W. Hoffman. Baltimore: Butternut & Blue, 2000.

Imboden, John D. "Stonewall Jackson in the Shenandoah," included in Robert U. Johnson and Clarence C. Buel, eds. *Battles and Leaders of the Civil War.* 4 vols. New York: Century Publishing Co. 1884-1904. 2:282-297.

———. "The Confederate Retreat from Gettysburg," included in Robert U. Johnson and Clarence C. Buel, eds. *Battles and Leaders of the Civil War.* 4 vols. New York: Century Publishing Co. 1884-1904. 3:420-429.

Jacobs, W. W. "Custer's Charge: Little Hagerstown the Scene of Bloody Strife in 1863." *The National Tribune,* August 27, 1896.

James, Dr. G. Watson. "Dahlgren's Raid: Fiftieth Anniversary of the Defense of Richmond." *Southern Historical Society Papers* 39 (1914): 63-72.

Jeffers, C. T. "Those Splendid Boots: How One of Dahlgren's Boys Came to Trade Them Off for a Pair Made of Bull Hide." *National Tribune,* December 14, 1911.

Jones, John B. *A Rebel War Clerk's Diary at the Confederate States Capital.* 2 vols. Philadelphia: J. B. Lippincott & Co., 1866.

Jones, J. William. "The Kilpatrick-Dahlgren Raid Against Richmond." *Southern Historical Society Papers* 13 (1888): 515-526.

Jones, Marius. "Dahlgren's Raid." *Richmond Times-Dispatch,* May 5, 1912.

Journal of the Executive Proceedings of the Senate of the United States of America, 36th Congress, 2nd Session, July 17, 1862.

Kidd, James H. *Personal Recollections of a Cavalryman in Custer's Michigan Brigade.* Ionia, Mich.: Sentinel Printing Co., 1908.

Landegan, J. W. "He was There and Proceeds to Tell How Richmond was Not Entered." *National Tribune,* May 31, 1894.

Lee, Fitzhugh. *General Lee.* New York: D. Appleton & Co., 1913.

Lincoln, Abraham. *The Collected Works of Abraham Lincoln.* Roy P. Basler, ed. 8 vols. and index. New Brunswick, N. J.: Rutgers University Press, 1953-1955.

Lowe, David W., ed. *Meade's Army: The Private Notebooks of Lt. Col. Theodore Lyman.* Kent, Ohio: Kent State University Press, 2007.

Lusk, William. *War Letters of William Thompson Lusk: Captain, Assistant Adjutant General, J. S. Volunteers, 1861-1865.* New York: privately published, 1911.

Martin, Edward Winslow. *The Life and Public Services of Schuyler Colfax Together With His Most Important Speeches.* San Francisco: H. H. Bancroft & Co., 1868.

McAnerny, Col. John. "Dahlgren's Raid on Richmond." *Confederate Veteran* 29 (1921): 20-21.

Meade, George G. *The Life and Letters of George Gordon Meade, Major-General United States Army.* 2 vols. New York: Charles Scribner's Sons, 1913.

Merritt, H. A. D. "Dahlgren's Raid." *Battles and Leaders of the Civil War.* Ed. Peter Cozzens. Vol. 6. Urbana, Ill.: University of Illinois Press, 2004: 382-392.

Mitchell, Adele H., ed. *The Letters of John S. Mosby.* Richmond, Va.: Stuart-Mosby Historical Society, 1986.

Mitgang, Herbert, ed. *Washington, D.C., in Lincoln's Time.* Athens: University of Georgia Press, 1989.

Moore, Frank, ed. *The Rebellion Record: A Record of American Events.* 12 vols. New York: Arno Press, 1977.

Moran, Frank E. "War Romance." *National Tribune,* March 24, 1893.

Nevins, Allan, ed. *A Diary of Battle: The Personal Journals of Colonel Charles S. Wainwright, 1861-1865.* New York: Harcourt, Brace & World, 1962.

Newhall, Frederick C. *Dedication of the Monument of the Sixth Pennsylvania Cavalry on the Battlefield of Gettysburg, October 14, 1888.* Philadelphia: privately published, 1889.

Palfrey, Col. Edward A. "Some of the Secret History of Gettysburg," *Southern Historical Society Papers* 8 (18___): 521-526.

"Passed the Boundary: Rev. Dr. Byron Sunderland Celebrates His Seventy-Second Birthday." *Washington Post,* November 23, 1891.

Patrick Marsena R. *Inside Lincoln's Army: The Diary of Marsena Rudolph Patrick, Provost Marshal General, Army of the Potomac.* Ed. David S. Sparks. New York: Yoseloff, 1964.

Paul, E. A. "A Review of the Expedition", in Frank Moore, ed. *The Rebellion Record: A Diary of American Events.* 12 vols. New York: D. Van Nostrand, 1865. 8:593-94.

Pendleton, Henry C. "The Death of Colonel Dahlgren." *William and Mary College Quarterly Historical Magazine* vol. 12, no. 1 (January 1932): 1-3.

Penfield, James. *The 1863-1864 Civil War Diary of Captain James Penfield, 5th New York Volunteer Cavalry, Company H.* Crown Point, N. Y.: Penfield Foundation, 1999.

Pohanka, Brian C., ed. *A Summer on the Plains with Custer's 7th Cavalry: The 1870 Diary of Annie Gibson Roberts.* Lynchburg, Va.: Schroeder Publications, 2004.

Pollard, Edward A. *The Lost Cause*. New York: E. B. Treat, 1867.

Pond, George E. "Kilpatrick's and Dahlgren's Raid to Richmond," included in Robert U. Johnson and Clarence C. Buel, eds. *Battles and Leaders of the Civil War*. 4 vols. New York: Century Publishing Co. 1884-1904. 4:95-96.

Popkins, W. A. "Imboden's Brigade at Gettysburg." *Confederate Veteran* 22 (1914): 552-554.

Powell, Hans. "Ulric Dahlgren: Was His Corpse Mutilated and Insulted—Call for More Information." *National Tribune*, August 21, 1884.

Preston, Sallie A. Brock. *Richmond During the War: Four Years of Personal Observation By a Richmond Lady*. New York: G. W. Carleton & Co., 1867.

Report of the Joint Committee on the Conduct of the War at the Second Session, Thirty-Eighth Congress. 2 vols. Washington, D. C.: U. S. Government Printing Office, 1865-66.

Richardson, James D., ed. *A Compilation of the Messages and Papers of the Confederacy, Including the Diplomatic Correspondence, 1861-1865*. 2 vols. Nashville: United States Publishing Co., 1905.

Robertson, John, comp. *Michigan in the War*. Lansing: W. S. George & Co., 1882.

Royall, William L. *Some Reminiscences*. New York: Neale Publishing Co., 1909.

Schmucker, Samuel M. *A History of the Civil War in the United States: With a Preliminary View of Its Causes and Biographical Sketches of its Heroes*. Philadelphia: J. W. Bradley, 1863.

Schurz, Carl. *The Reminiscences of Carl Schurz*. 3 vols. New York: The McClure Company, 1907.

Sears, Stephen W., ed. *The Civil War Papers of George B. McClellan*. New York: Ticknor & Fields, 1989.

Sherman, William T. *Memoirs of W. T. Sherman*. New York: The Library of America, 1990.

Simpson, Brooks D. and Jean V. Berlin. *Sherman's Civil War: Selected Correspondence of William T. Sherman, 1860-1865*. Chapel Hill: University of North Carolina Press, 1999.

St. Clair, Samuel. "The Fight at Hagerstown," included in *History of the Eighteenth Regiment of Cavalry Pennsylvania Volunteers 1862-1865*. New York: Regimental Publication Committee, 1909: 94-95.

Staats, Richard J., ed. *A Grassroots History of the American Civil War, Vol. IV: The Life and Times of Colonel William Stedman of the 6th Ohio Cavalry*. Bowie, Md.: Heritage Books, Inc., 2003.

Stoddard, William O. *Inside the White House During War Times*. New York: Charles L. Webster & Co., 1890.

Styple, William B., ed. *Writing & Fighting from the Army of Northern Virginia: A Collection of Confederate Soldier Correspondence*. Kearny, N.J.: Belle Grove Publishing, 2003.

Sulivane, Col. Clement. "Miles Cary's Report Criticised." *Confederate Veteran* 16 (1908): 398.

Sunderland, Rev. Byron. *A Sermon in Memory of Colonel Ulric Dahlgren, Delivered in the First Presbyterian Church, Washington, D. C., Sabbath Evening, April 24, 1864.* Washington, D.C.: McGill & Witherow, 1864.

Sword, Wiley, ed. "Admiral John A. Dahlgren Defends His Son the Day After Ulric's Public Memorial Service." *Blue & Gray* vol. 20, no. 3 (2003): 52-53.

———. "Lt. Col. Judson Kilpatrick Complains to President Lincoln of the Harsh Injustice of Col. Lafayette C. Baker, Who Threw 'Kill-Cavalry' Into Prison." *Blue & Gray* vol. 23, no. 4 (2006): 37-40.

"The Court-Martial Caught by Dahlgren." *Richmond Times-Dispatch*, June 10, 1906.

"The Savior of Richmond." *Confederate Veteran* 36 (1928): 197.

The War of the Rebellion: A Compilation of the Official Records of the Union and Confederate Armies, 128 volumes in 3 series. Washington, D.C.: United States Government Printing Office, 1889.

Tobie, Edward P. *History of the First Maine Cavalry, 1861-1865.* Boston: Press of Emery & Hughes, 1887.

United States Bureau of Naval Personnel. *Register of Commissioned and Warrant Officers of the United States Navy and Marine Corps.* Washington: U. S. Government Printing Office, 1859-1867.

Van Lew, Elizabeth L. *A Yankee Spy in Richmond: The Civil War Diary of "Crazy Bet" Van Lew.* Ed., Davis D. Ryan. Mechanicsburg, Pa.: Stackpole Books, 1996.

Vifquain, Victor. *The 1862 Plot to Kidnap Jefferson Davis.* Eds. Jeffrey H. Smith and Phillip Thomas Tucker. Mechanicsburg, Pa.: Stackpole Books, 1998.

Walker, B. H., M.D. "The First Man to Reach Dahlgren After He Was Killed." *Richmond Times-Dispatch*, April 11, 1909.

Walker, Thad. J. "A Romantic Incident of the War, Ending in the Death of Colonel Ulric Dahlgren." *Blue and Gray* vol. 3, no. 6 (1894): 330-332.

"War Time Story of Dahlgren's Raid." *Southern Historical Society Papers* 37 (1909): 198-202.

Welles, Gideon. *Diary of Gideon Welles, Secretary of the Navy Under Lincoln and Johnson.* 3 vols. Boston: Houghton-Mifflin, 1911.

White, William. "Death of Dahlgren." *National Tribune*, August 14, 1884.

Willis, Barbara P., ed. *The Journal of Jane Howison Beale, Fredericksburg, Virginia 1850-1862.* Fredericksburg: Historic Fredericksburg Foundation, Inc., 1979.

Wilson, James H. *The Life and Services of Brevet Brigadier General Andrew Jonathan Alexander, United States Army.* New York: privately published, 1887.

———. *Under the Old Flag: Recollections of Military Operations in the War for the Union, the Spanish War, the Boxer Rebellion, Etc.* 2 vols. New York: D. Appleton, 1912.

Winder, Robert L., ed. *Jacob Beidler's Book: A Diary Kept by Jacob Beidler from November 1857 through July 1863.* Mifflintown, Pa.: Juniata County Historical Society, 1994.

Wistar, Isaac J. *The Autobiography of Isaac Jones Wistar*. Philadelphia: Wistar Institute of Anatomy and Biology, 1914.

Wittenberg, Eric J., ed. *"We Have It Damn Hard Out Here": The Civil War Letters of Sergeant Thomas W. Smith, 6th Pennsylvania Cavalry*. Kent, Ohio: Kent State University Press, 1999.

Wright, Stuart, ed. *Memoirs of Alfred Horatio Belo: Reminiscences of a North Carolina Volunteer*. Gaithersburg, Md.: Olde Soldier Books, n.d.

SECONDARY SOURCES

ARTICLES

Adams, W. T. "Guns for the Navy: Rear Admiral John A. Dahlgren Altered the Art of Sea Warfare With His Invention of the Boat Howitzer and Large-Caliber Shipboard Cannon." *Ordnance* XLV (January-February 1961): 508-510.

Beymer, William Gilmore. "Miss Van Lew." *Harper's Monthly Magazine* (June 1911): 86-99.

Brennan, Patrick J. "Little Mac's Last Stand: Autumn 1862 in Loudoun Valley, Virginia." *Blue & Gray* vol. 17, no. 2 (December 1999): 6-20 and 48-57.

"Cornerstone Houses Hero's Leg." *Washington Post*, November 11, 1923.

Dunston, Bruce. "Letter to the Editor." *Richmond Times-Dispatch*, July 25, 1955.

Gaddy, David Winfred. "Reflections on *Come Retribution*." *The International Journal of Intelligence and Counter-Intelligence*, Vol. III, No. 4 (Winter 1989): 567-573.

George, Joseph, Jr. "'Black Flag Warfare': Lincoln and the Raids Against Richmond and Jefferson Davis." *The Pennsylvania Magazine of History and Biography*. Vol. 115, No. 3 (July 1991): 291-318.

Guelzo, Allan C. "Gloria Dei: Old Swedes Church." *Early American Life*. Vol. VIII, No. 3 (June 1977): 18-20.

Hall, James O. "The Dahlgren Papers: Fact or Fabrication?" *Civil War Times Illustrated* vol. 22, no. 7 (1983): 30-39.

Jones, Alice. "Hartsville Civil War Hero." *Panorama—The Magazine of Bucks County*, Vol. 8, No. 1 (January 1971): 4-5.

Kauffman, Michael W. "David Edgar Herold: The Forgotten Conspirator." *The Surratt Society News* (November 1981): 23-28.

King, G. Wayne. "General Judson Kilpatrick." *New Jersey History* vol. XCI, no. 1 (Spring 1973): 35-38.

Long, David E. "Lincoln, Davis, and the Dahlgren Raid." *North & South*, Vol. 9, No. 5 (October 2006): 70-83.

McPherson, James M. "A Failed Richmond Raid and Its Consequences." *Columbiad: A Quarterly Review of the War Between the States* 2, no. 4 (Winter 1999): 130.

Ogden, James H. "Prelude to Battle: Burnside and Fredericksburg, November, 1862." *The Morningside Notes* (1988): 1-11.

Pollock, Ann. "Hartsville: Yesteryear and Today." *Bucks County Life Past and Present*, Vol. 1, No. 5 (May 1961): 26-28.

Prokopowicz, Gerald J. "Word of Honor: The Parole System in the Civil War." *North & South* vol. 6, no. 4 (May 2003): 24-33.

Riggs, David F. "The Dahlgren Papers Reconsidered." *The Lincoln Herald* (Summer 1981): 658-667.

Roth, Dave, with Bruce M. Venter. "The General's Tour: The Kilpatrick-Dahlgren Raid." *Blue & Gray* vol. 20, no. 3 (2003): 54-64.

Sears, Stephen W. "Raid on Richmond." *MHQ: The Quarterly Journal of Military History* 11, no. 1 (Autumn 1998): 88-96.

———. "The Dahlgren Papers Revisited." *Columbiad* Vol. 3, No. 2 (Summer 1999): 63-87.

Stewart, Lucy S. "Colonel Ulric Dahlgren." *New York Historical Society Quarterly Newsletter* 29-30(1945-1946): 30-35.

Stuart, Meriwether. "Colonel Ulric Dahlgren and Richmond's Union Underground, April 1864." *Virginia Magazine of History and Biography* 72, no. 2 (Apr. 1964): 152-204.

Thompson, Addison Baker. "A Brief History of Tuckahoe." In *Tuckahoe Plantation*. Richmond, Va.: Tuckahoe Plantation Enterprise, Ltd., 1997: 7-18.

Venter, Bruce M. "The Kilpatrick-Dahlgren Raid on Richmond, February 28-March 4, 1864." *Blue & Gray* vol. 20, no. 3 (2003): 6-22, 44-51.

"What is the Truth of Dahlgren's Raid?" *Tyler's Quarterly Historical and Genealogical Magazine* 28 (October 1946): 65-90.

Wittenberg, Eric J. "Ulric Dahlgren in the Gettysburg Campaign." *Gettysburg: Historical Articles of Lasting Interest*, No. 22 (January 2000): 96-111.

BOOKS:

Abbott, Carl. *Political Terrain: Washington, D.C., from Tidewater Town to Global Metropolis*. Chapel Hill: University of North Carolina Press, 1999.

Anders, Curt. *Injustice on Trial: Second Bull Run, General Fitz John Porter's Court Martial, and the Schofield Board Investigation That Restored His Good Name*. Zionsville, Ind.: Emmis Books, 2002.

Bates, Samuel P. *History of Pennsylvania Volunteers, 1861-5*. 10 vols. Harrisburg, Pa.: B. Singerly, State Printer, 1869-1871.

Beatie, Russel H. *The Army of the Potomac: Birth of Command, November 1860-September 1861*. New York: DaCapo Press, 2002.

———. *The Army of The Potomac: McClellan Takes Command, September 1861-February 1862*. New York: DaCapo Press, 2004.

Benson, Adolph B. and Naboth Hedin. *Americans from Sweden*. Philadelphia: J. B. Lippincott Co., 1950.

Beymer, William Gilmore. *On Hazardous Service: Scouts and Spies of the North and South*. New York: Harper & Bros., 1912.

Brown, Kent Masterson. *Retreat from Gettysburg: Lee, Logistics, and the Pennsylvania Campaign*. Chapel Hill: University of North Carolina Press, 2005.

Bruce, Robert V. *Lincoln and the Tools of War*. Indianapolis: Bobbs-Merrill, 1956.

Burton, Brian K. *Extraordinary Circumstances: The Seven Days Battles*. Bloomington: Indiana University Press, 2001.

Burton, E. Milby. *The Siege of Charleston 1861-1865*. Columbia: University of South Carolina Press, 1970.

Callahan, Edward W. *List of Officers of the Navy of the United States and the Marine Corps*. New York: L.R. Hamersly & Co., 1901.

Chaffin, Tom. *Pathfinder: John Charles Fremont and the Course of American Empire*. New York: Hill and Wang, 2002.

Chandler, David. *The Campaigns of Napoleon*. New York: Macmillan, 1966.

Clay, Jehu Curtis. *Annals of the Swedes on the Delaware*. Philadelphia: J.C. Pechin, 1835.

Coddington, Edwin P. *The Gettysburg Campaign: A Study in Command*. New York: Charles Scribner's Sons, 1968.

Conrad, W. P. and Ted Alexander. *When War Passed This Way*. Greencastle, Pennsylvania: Lilian S. Besore Memorial Library, 1982.

Cozzens, Peter. *General John Pope: A Life for the Nation*. Champaign: University of Illinois Press, 2000.

Daughtry, Mary Bandy. *Gray Cavalier: The Life and Wars of General W.H.F. "Rooney" Lee*. Cambridge, Mass.: Da Capo Press, 2002.

Detzer, David. *Allegiance: Fort Sumter, Charleston, and the Beginning of the Civil War*. New York: Harcourt, 2001.

Downey, Fairfax. *Clash of Cavalry: The Battle of Brandy Station*. New York: David McKay Co., 1959.

Driver, Robert J., Jr. *5th Virginia Cavalry*. Lynchburg, Va.: H. E. Howard, Inc., 1997.

Dyer, Frederick H. *A Compendium of the War of the Rebellion, Compiled and Arranged from Official Records of the Federal and Confederate Armies, Reports of the Adjutant Generals of the Several States, the Army Registers, and Other Reliable Documents and Sources*. 3 vols. Des Moines, Iowa: The Dyer Publishing Co., 1908.

Engle, Stephen D. *The Yankee Dutchman: The Life of Franz Sigel*. Fayetteville: University of Arkansas Press, 1993.

Feis, William B. *Grant's Secret Service: The Intelligence War from Belmont to Appomattox*. Lincoln: University of Nebraska Press, 2002.

Fishel, Edwin C. *The Secret War for the Union: The Untold Story of Military Intelligence in the Civil War*. Boston: Houghton-Mifflin Co., 1996.

Fortier, John. *15th Virginia Cavalry*. Lynchburg, Va.: H. E. Howard Co., 1993.

Furgurson, Ernest B. *Chancellorsville 1863: The Souls of the Brave*. New York: Random House, 1995.

Gaff, Alan D. *Brave Men's Tears: The Iron Brigade at Brawner Farm*. Dayton, Ohio: Morningside, 1985.

Goodwin, Doris Kearns. *Team of Rivals: The Political Genius of Abraham Lincoln*. New York: Simon & Schuster, 2005.

Gower, Herschel. *Charles Dahlgren of Natchez: The Civil War and Dynastic Decline*. Washington, D. C.: Brassey's, 2002.

Grimsley, Mark. *The Hard Hand of War: Union Military Policy Toward Southern Civilians, 1861-1865*. New York: Cambridge University Press, 1995.

Hagy, James W. *To Take Charleston: The Civil War on Folly Island*. Charleston, W.V.: Pictorial Historiecs Publishing Co., 1993.

Harrison, Noel G. *Fredericksburg Civil War Sites*. 2 vols. Lynchburg, Va.: H.E. Howard, Inc. 1995.

Heitman, Francis E. *Historical Register and Dictionary of the U. S. Army*. 2 vols. Washington, D. C.: U. S. Government Printing Office, 1903.

Hennessy, John J. *Return to Bull Run: The Campaign and Battle of Second Manassas*. New York: Simon & Schuster, 1992.

———. *Second Manassas Battlefield Map Survey*. Lynchburg, Va.: H. E. Howard Co., 1991.

Hokanson, Nels. *Swedish Immigrants in Lincoln's Time*. New York: Harper & Brothers, 1942.

Hunt, Roger D. and Jack R. Brown. *Brevet Brigadier Generals in Blue*. Gaithersburg, Md.: Olde Soldier Books, 1997.

Jones, Virgil Carrington. *Eight Hours Before Richmond*. New York: Holt, 1957.

Kastrup, Allan. *The Swedish Heritage in America: The Swedish Element in America and American-Swedish Relations in Their Historical Perspective*. Minneapolis: Swedish Council of America, 1975.

Klein, Maury. *Days of Defiance: Sumter, Secession, and the Coming of the Civil War*. New York: Vintage Books, 1997.

Krick, Robert K. *Conquering the Valley: Stonewall Jackson at Port Republic*. New York: Morrow, 1996.

———. *Stonewall Jackson at Cedar Mountain*. Chapel Hill: University of North Carolina Press, 1990.

Marolda, Edward J. *The Washington Navy Yard: An Illustrated History*. Washington, D. C.: Naval Historical Center, 1999.

Martin, Samuel J. *"Kill-Cavalry:" Sherman's Merchant of Terror—The Life of Union General Hugh Judson Kilpatrick*. Cranbury, N.J.: Associated University Presses, 1996.

Murfin, James V. *The Gleam of Bayonets: The Battle of Antietam and the Maryland Campaign of 1862*. New York: T. Yoseloff, 1965.

Niven, John. *Gideon Welles: Lincoln's Secretary of the Navy*. New York: Oxford University Press, 1973.

O'Neill, Robert F., Jr. *The Cavalry Battles of Aldie, Middleburg and Upperville, Small but Important Riots, June 10-27, 1863*. Lynchburg, Va.: H. E. Howard Co., 1993.

O'Reilly, Francis Augustín. *The Fredericksburg Campaign: Winter War on the Rappahannock*. Baton Rouge: Louisiana State University Press, 2003.

Parker, Sandra V. *Richmond's Civil War Prisons*. Lynchburg, Va.: H. E. Howard Co., 1990.

Peck, Taylor. *Round-Shot to Rockets: A History of the Washington Navy Yard and U. S. Naval Gun Factory*. Annapolis: United States Naval Institute, 1949.

Peterson, Clarence Stewart. *Admiral John A. Dahlgren*. New York: The Hobson Book Press, 1945.

Phelps, W. Chris. *The Bombardment of Charleston 1863-1865*. Gretna, La.: Pelican Publishing Co., 1999.

Roak, Rev. John Craig. *An Historical Sketch of Gloria Dei Church (Old Swedes') Philadelphia: Oldest Church in Pennsylvania*. Privately published, 1947.

Schneller, Robert J., Jr. *A Quest for Glory: A Biography of Rear Admiral John A. Dahlgren*. Annapolis: Naval Institute Press, 1996.

Schultz, Duane. *The Dahlgren Affair: Terror and Conspiracy in the Civil War*. New York: W. W. Norton, 1998.

Sears, Stephen W. *Chancellorsville*. New York: Houghton & Mifflin, 1996.

———. *Controversies & Commanders: Dispatches from the Army of the Potomac*. Boston: Houghton Mifflin, 1999.

———. *Landscape Turned Red: The Battle of Antietam*. New York: Ticknor & Fields, 1983.

———. *To the Gates of Richmond: The Peninsula Campaign*. New York: Ticknor & Fields, 1992.

Speer, Lonnie R. *Portals to Hell: Military Prisons of the Civil War*. Mechanicsburg, Pa.: Stackpole Books, 1997.

Staats, Richard J. *The History of the Sixth Ohio Volunteer Cavalry 1861-1865*. 2 vols. Westminster, Md.: Heritage Books, 2006.

Steers, Edward, Jr. *Blood on the Moon: The Assassination of Abraham Lincoln*. Lexington: The University Press of Kentucky, 2001.

Sullivan, David M. *The United States Marine Corps in the Civil War—The Second Year*. Shippensburg, Pa.: White Mane, 1997.

Tanner, Robert G. *Stonewall in the Valley: Thomas J. "Stonewall" Jackson's Shenandoah Valley Campaign Spring 1862*. Mechanicsburg, Pa.: Stackpole, 1996.

Taylor, Paul. *He Hath Loosed the Fateful Lightning: The Battle of Ox Hill (Chantilly), September 1, 1862*. Shippensburg, Pa.: White Mane, 2003.

Tidwell, William A., James O. Hall, and David Winfred Gaddy. *Come Retribution: The Confederate Secret Service and the Assassination of Lincoln*. Jackson: University Press of Mississippi, 1988.

United States Naval Academy Alumni Association, Inc. *Register of Alumni, Graduates and Former Naval Cadets and Midshipmen*. Annapolis, Md.: United States Naval Academy Alumni Association, Inc., 2003.

Varon, Elizabeth R. *Southern Lady, Yankee Spy: The True Story of Elizabeth Van Lew, a Union Agent in the Heart of the Confederacy*. New York: Oxford University Press, 2003.

Warner, Ezra J. *Generals in Blue: Lives of the Union Commanders*. Baton Rouge: Louisiana State University Press, 1964.

——————————. *Generals in Gray: Lives of the Confederate Commanders*. Baton Rouge: Louisiana State University Press, 1959.

Waugh, John C. *On the Brink of Civil War: The Compromise of 1850 and How It Changed the Course of American History*. Wilmington, Del.: Scholarly Resources, 2003.

Weigley, Russell F. *Philadelphia: A 300-Year History*. New York: W. W. Norton, 1982.

Welker, David A. *Tempest at Ox Hill: The Battle of Chantilly*. New York: DaCapo, 2002.

Wert, Jeffry D. *The Sword of Lincoln: The Army of the Potomac*. New York: Simon & Schuster, 2005.

Wise, Barton H. *The Life of Henry A. Wise of Virginia 1806-1876*. New York: The MacMillan Co., 1899.

Wise, Stephen R. *Gate of Hell: Campaign for Charleston Harbor, 1863*. Columbia: University of South Carolina Press, 1994.

Wittenberg, Eric J. *Gettysburg's Forgotten Cavalry Actions*. Gettysburg, Pa.: Thomas Publications, 1998.

———. *The Union Cavalry Comes of Age: Hartwood Church to Brandy Station, 1863*. Dulles, Va.: Brassey's, 2003.

———. *Rush's Lancers: The Sixth Pennsylvania Cavalry in the Civil War*. Yardley, Pa.: Westholme Publishing, 2006.

Wittenberg, Eric J., J. David Petruzzi, and Michael F. Nugent. *One Continuous Fight: The Retreat from Gettysburg and the Pursuit of Lee's Army of Northern Virginia, July 4-13, 1863*. New York: Savas-Beatie, 2008.

Index

235, 236, 246, 254, 257, 262, 263, 270,
275, 276, 278-281, 286, 290, 291, 298,
299, 302, 304-310

Lindsay, William C. 141

Littlepage, William 3, 194, 231, 243

Lohmann, F. W. E. 209, 210, 215, 216

Longstreet, James 66, 67, 71-75, 116, 121,
129, 139

Lyman, Theodore 170, 277, 280, 283,
297, 302

Lyon, Nathaniel 54, 218

M

Manassas, Va. 38, 71, 72, 73, 78, 81, 82,
86, 128, 260, 308

Marye's Heights 109, 116, 117

Mattaponi River 168, 189, 190

McAnerny, John H. 185, 186, 283, 302

McClellan, George B. 39, 40, 42, 45,
55, 60-68, 71, 77-85, 87-89, 104, 112,
162, 184, 261, 263, 264, 269, 272, 303,
307

McDowell, Irwin 39, 45, 51, 60, 62, 63,
67, 70, 72, 73, 74, 80, 110

McEntee, John 132, 173, 174, 234, 235,
280, 291

Meade, George G. 116, 130, 133, 134,
135, 143, 144, 167, 168, 169, 170, 182,
200-204, 217, 222, 231, 234, 235, 242,
247, 272, 274, 277, 279, 280, 283, 286,
297, 302

Mechanicsville Pike 166

Merrimack, U.S.S. 25, 42

Merritt, Henry 135, 136, 170, 174, 175,
187, 193, 194, 281-285, 302

Merritt, Wesley 135, 136, 170, 174, 175,
187, 193, 194, 281-285, 302

Middleburg, Va. 106, 107, 129, 270,
309

Mitchell, John F. B. 179, 181, 182, 184,
186, 187, 188, 208, 239, 291, 302

Monitor, U.S.S. 42, 43

Morris Island 147, 151, 153, 276

Morris, Robert, Jr. 122-125, 147, 151, 153,
155, 171, 276, 297, 300

Morrow, Albert P. 136-138, 259, 273,
308

Mosby, John S. 85, 129, 233, 235, 291,
297, 302

Munson's Hill 39

N

Natchez, Miss. 26-29, 148, 251, 254,
255, 275, 290, 308

Navy Department 58, 79, 126, 129, 257

Norfolk, Va. 42

Norrköping, Sweden 7

O

Orange & Alexandria Railroad 62, 80,
84, 86, 87, 171

Orrick, Robert 211, 212

P

Parker, Foxhall A. 38, 39, 41, 257, 287,
290, 309

Patrick, Marsena 234, 263, 291, 299,
302, 305

Patteson, William W. 233, 291, 295

Paul Dahlgren 16, 289

Philadelphia, Penn. xiv, 8-11, 13, 15, 21,
26, 31, 34, 40-42, 55, 97, 101, 105, 122,
147-155, 157, 158, 163, 181, 204, 205,
206, 214, 215, 217, 218, 235, 251, 252,
253, 255-259, 262, 265-271, 273, 275,